Kraken Latin 1
Teacher Edition

MORE LATIN FROM CANON PRESS

Latin Primer: Book 1, Martha Wilson
Latin Primer 1: Student Edition
Latin Primer 1: Teacher's Edition
Latin Primer 1: Flashcard Set
Latin Primer 1: Audiō Guide CD

Latin Primer: Book 2, Martha Wilson
Latin Primer 2: Student Edition
Latin Primer 2: Teacher's Edition
Latin Primer 2: Flashcard Set
Latin Primer 2: Audiō Guide CD

Latin Primer: Book 3, Martha Wilson
Latin Primer 3: Student Edition
Latin Primer 3: Teacher's Edition
Latin Primer 3: Flashcard Set
Latin Primer 3: Audiō Guide CD

KRAKEN LATIN for the Logic Years: Book 1, Natali H. Monnette
KRAKEN LATIN 1: Student Edition
KRAKEN LATIN 1: Teacher Edition

KRAKEN LATIN for the Logic Years, Book 2, Natali H. Monnette
KRAKEN LATIN 2: Student Edition
KRAKEN LATIN 2: Teacher Edition

KRAKEN LATIN for the Logic Years, Book 3, Natali H. Monnette
KRAKEN LATIN 3: Student Edition (forthcoming)
KRAKEN LATIN 3: Teacher Edition (forthcoming)

Orbis Pictus 1: The Natural World, Timothy Griffith

Published by Canon Press
P.O. Box 8729, Moscow, Idaho 83843
800.488.2034 | www.canonpress.com

Natali H. Monnette, *Kraken Latin for the Logic Years 1: Teacher Edition*
Second edition. Copyright © 2015, 2019 by Natali H. Monnette. First edition 2015.

Cover design by Rachel Rosales (orangepealdesign.com). Cover illustration by Forrest Dickison. Interior design by Phaedrus Media and Valerie Anne Bost. Typesetting by Laura Storm and Valerie Anne Bost.

Printed in the United States of America.

All rights reserved. The owner of this book is permitted to download and duplicate the quizzes and tests available at canonpress.com/kraken-latin-1-teacher. Otherwise, no part of this publication may be reproduced, stored in a retrieval system, or transmitted in any form by any means, electronic, mechanical, photocopy, recording, or otherwise, without prior permission of the author, except as provided by USA copyright law.

Library of Congress Cataloging-in-Publication Data

Monnette, Natali H.
Kraken Latin for the logic years, book 1 / Natali H. Monnette—Teacher's edition.
    pages. cm.—(Kraken Latin for the Logic Years ; 1)
ISBN 978-1-947644-49-6
1. Latin language—Textbooks. I. Title. II. Series: Kraken Latin; 1.
PA2087.5.M58 2012
478.2'421—dc23
                2012001760

19 20 21 22 23 24 25 26 27 28 29   10 9 8 7 6 5 4 3 2 1

Kraken Latin
for the Logic Years

BOOK 1

TEACHER EDITION

by NATALI H. MONNETTE

canonpress
Moscow, Idaho

Contents

Introduction vi
Pronunciation Guide vii
How to Use This Book ix
Latin Grammar Basics xiii
Recommended Schedules xxv

Unit 1: Lessons 1–8   1

Lesson 1: First Conjugation Verbs & Present Active Indicative 3
Lesson 2: First Declension Nouns / Introduction to Case Usage—
    Nominative, Dative & Accusative 14
Lesson 3: Verbs: *Sum* / Nouns: More Case Usage—Genitive & Ablative /
    Prepositions 28
Lesson 4: Second Declension Masculine 39
Lesson 5: Second Declension Neuter 49
Lesson 6: Verbs: First Conjugation, Imperfect & Future Active Indicative /
    Principal Parts 59
Lesson 7: Adjectives 73
Lesson 8: Review & Test 85

Unit 2: Lessons 9–16   99

Lesson 9: Second Conjugation: Present, Imperfect & Future Active
    Indicative / Substantive Adjectives 101
Lesson 10: Verbs: *Sum*, Imperfect & Future 115
Lesson 11: Verbs: *Possum*—Present, Imperfect & Future / Complementary
    Infinitives; ImperativesNouns: Case Usage—Vocative Case 125
Lesson 12: Nouns: Third Declension Masculine/Feminine 137
Lesson 13: Nouns: Third Declension Neuter 148
Lesson 14: Verbs: Perfect Active Indicative 159
Lesson 15: Pluperfect & Future Perfect Active Indicative 173
Lesson 16: Review & Test 184

Unit 3: Lessons 17–24 — 201

Lesson 17: Personal Pronouns 203
Lesson 18: Third Declension i-stems 217
Lesson 19: Third Declension Adjectives 227
Lesson 20: Verbs: Present, Imperfect & Future Passive Indicative 241
Lesson 21: Numerals / Review of Present Passive System 255
Lesson 22: Perfect, Pluperfect & Future Perfect Passive Indicative 267
Lesson 23: More Numerals: Ordinals 280
Lesson 24: Review & Test 290

Unit 4: Lessons 25–32 — 309

Lesson 25: Fourth Declension Nouns 311
Lesson 26: Verbs: Third Conjugation Active & Imperative 323
Lesson 27: Verbs: Third Conjugation Passive 335
Lesson 28: Nouns: Fifth Declension / Time Constructions 348
Lesson 29: Verbs: Fourth Conjugation, Active, Passive & Imperative /
   Irregular Verb *eō* 359
Lesson 30: Demonstratives 375
Lesson 31: Verbs: Third *-io* Conjugation, Active & Passive / Irregular Verbs
   faciō & *fīō* 390
Lesson 32: Review & Test 406

Appendices — 425

Chant Charts 426
English-Latin Glossary 438
Latin-English Glossary 450
Grammatical Concepts Index 459
Sources & Helps 461
Verb Formation Chart 463

Introduction

Avē, imperator, moriturī tē salutant!
"Hail, emperor, they who are about to die salute you!"

Discipulī Discipulaeque,

Perhaps you are familiar with the Latin phrase quoted above. Suetonius, a Roman historian, recorded that captives and criminals uttered these words to Emperor Claudius just before they were forced to fight to the death in a mock naval battle.* And perhaps you, just as other Latin students before you, feel that these words appropriately describe your mental state as you approach this year of Latin! Some of you have never studied Latin before, and may be approaching this book with some trepidation. Some of you have already spent several years learning this language, and have the battle scars to prove it. Take courage. Although the study of Latin may seem daunting at times, you will survive and be all the better for it. I won't pretend that Latin is easy for everyone, because—as with any other language—you will need to study hard in order to master it.

This primer is the first in a series that will guide you through some major basics of Latin grammar. The goal is not merely to revel in these grammatical delights (although you are certainly welcome do so), but to equip you to translate and then read "real" Latin.

And so welcome to Kraken Latin. Whether Latin feels like a battle or a journey, may you prosper in your endeavors!

Avēte atque valēte,
Natali H. Monnette,
Magistra Discipulaque

---

* Suetonius, *Dē Vitā Caesārum, Dīvus Claudius* 21.6.

Pronunciation Guide

When approaching Latin for the first time, many teachers are concerned that they pronounce the words correctly. Due to the many schools of thought on Latin pronunciation (classical, ecclesiastic, Italian, English, and any hybrid thereof), I would advise teachers not to worry, but to simply choose a pronunciation and stick with it. Spoken Latin has been dead so long that no one can be sure what a "proper" pronunciation would sound like, and there is no point in straining at gnats (or macrons). In this book, classical pronunciation is used.

Vowels

Vowels in Latin have only two pronunciations, long and short. When speaking, long vowels are held twice as long as short vowels. Long vowels are marked with a "macron" or line over the vowel (e.g., ā). Vowels without a macron are short vowels.

When spelling a word, including the macron is important, as it can clarify the meaning of the word (e.g., *liber* is a noun meaning "book," and *līber* is an adjective meaning "free").

	LONG VOWELS		SHORT VOWELS
ā	like a in father: frāter, suprā	a	like a in idea: canis, mare
ē	like e in obey: trēs, rēgīna	e	like e in bet: et, terra
ī	like i in machine: mīles, vīta	i	like i in this: hic, silva
ō	like o in holy: sōl, glōria	o	like o in domain: bonus, scopulus
ū	like oo in rude: flūmen, lūdus	u	like u in put: sum, sub
ȳ	like i in chip: grȳps, cȳgnus		

Diphthongs

A combination of two vowel sounds collapsed together into one syllable is a diphthong:

- ae like ai in aisle: caelum, saepe
- au like ou in house: laudō, nauta
- ei like ei in reign: deinde
- eu like eu in eulogy: Deus
- oe like oi in oil: moenia, poena
- ui like ew in chewy: huius, huic

Consonants

Latin consonants are pronounced like English consonants, with the following exceptions:

c	like c in come	never soft like city, cinema, or peace
g	like g in go	never soft like gem, geology, or gentle
v	like w in wow	never like Vikings, victor, or vacation
s	like s in sissy	never like easel, weasel, or peas
ch	like ch in chorus	never like church, chapel, or children
r	is trilled	like a dog snarling or a machine gun
i	like y in yes	when used before a vowel at the beginning of a word or between two vowels within a word (otherwise it's usually a vowel)

HOW TO USE THIS BOOK

Welcome to *Kraken Latin for the Logic Years 1*

Does the world really need another Latin book? In the last decade or so, the study of Latin has grown in popularity, and there are actually quite a few curricula floating about. Since you are reading this introduction, I assume that you have done some research into which book(s) you want to use and why. Each textbook has its own goals and method, and there are many good ones out there. There is even a resurgence of spoken Latin, which is fantastic—the only drawback is that you need to have a teacher who can speak it! However, for students and teachers desiring to learn Latin from a classical Christian perspective, resources can get a little thin. My hope is that this text will help fill that gap. I have written it for teachers, for homeschool moms, for students teaching themselves—whether they have had a good deal of Latin experience or very little.

This book can either function as a continuation of a grammar-stage series or stand on its own. It has been designed with students in the logic or pert stage of the Trivium in mind. In her essay "The Lost Tools of Learning," Dorothy Sayers connects various age groups with the Trivium (grammar, logic, and rhetoric) model of education. Younger students (elementary) are in the Poll-parrot stage of life, where they easily memorize and absorb factual information—in other words, they are suited to learn the *grammar* of each subject. Students in junior high enter the Pert stage, where they like to discuss, argue, and figure things out. Thus it is wise to teach them the *logic* of each subject—how that subject fits together. Older students (high school) are in the Poetic stage, where they need to learn how to express themselves and the material they have learned in the Poll-parrot and Pert stages. Therefore they study the *rhetoric* of each subject.

The classical approach to learning can easily be applied to learning Latin. Students in the Poll-Parrot stage focus on memorizing the basics of the language—vocabulary, chants, etc. In *Kraken Latin 1* (and the upcoming *Kraken Latin 2* and *Kraken Latin 3*), Pert students will of course need to memorize some things, but the emphasis is on putting those basic elements together and figuring out the language. This will prepare students to enter into the Poetic or rhetoric stage of their Latin study, where they can work on translating Latin into polished English and appreciating the beauty and form of the original language.

Of course, not every student picking up this book will have had the benefit of previous Latin study. That is why I have also designed the book to stand on its own. It begins with an emphasis on the logic of Latin, but after a unit or so all of your students—whether they have had previous Latin experience or not—will be on a fairly level playing field.

In addition to gearing this book toward the logic stage of learning, I also endeavored to emphasize the importance of story. Many Latin texts emulate the works of Caesar or Cicero or some other author from the Golden Age of Latin, but frankly, most junior high students will find such works boring. I have always been much more interested in stories (whether original or from the Bible), mythologies, epic poems, and fairy tales. Students—especially of the junior high age group—enjoy tales told in traditional norms ("Once upon a time there were three sons . . .") with bizarre or random elements (thus my usage of camels, goats, etc.). Your job as the teacher is to make the Latin language come alive for your students; if they do not love it as you do (brace yourself—only about 10 percent or less of your students will really get into it), they should at least learn to appreciate it.

General Overview

This book covers all five conjugations of verbs in the indicative mood (active and passive), all five noun declensions, first/second and third declension adjectives, personal pronouns, and basic demonstratives. It is divided into four units, each with eight lessons. The eighth lesson of each unit is a review, ending with a unit test.

Lesson Overview

Word List

Every lesson (except for the final lesson of each unit), students will memorize 20–25 words. Most of these are review words from Canon Press's *Latin Primer* Series, so students who have used those books may only need to review. Derivatives from these words and memorization tips are given in the Teaching Notes.

Derivatives

A derivative is not an "original" word, but a word that can be traced as coming directly from another word. (The word "derivative" itself has roots meaning "to flow downstream from" a source.) In the following example, the Latin word *māter* means "mother" in English. One of the English derivatives of *māter* is "maternal," meaning "motherly."

Latin	English	Derivative
frāter	brother	fraternal

The basic guidelines for determining if an English word is a derivative of a certain Latin word are:

1. In part or in whole, they have **similar spellings.**
2. They have **some of the same meaning.**

These are not foolproof tests—some words appear to be unlikely descendants, but in fact are, while others present themselves as heirs and are not. Discerning likely derivatives requires practice throughout the year. Some students take to it quickly; others need practice in applying the two little tests above. Working with derivatives is a good path to the growth of English vocabulary. It is also helpful for memorizing Latin vocabulary when the meaning of an English derivative is already known, and it is preferable to memorization based on fiction such as "I praise loudly" to help one remember the meaning of *laudō*. You may also find more derivatives in the Latin entries of a Latin dictionary, or refer to an English dictionary (such as *The Oxford English Dictionary*) that gives the history of the English word.

Working with derivatives should be part of the student's regular routine. After introducing the lesson's Word List, you may want to lead students in brainstorming possible derivatives. Included in the Teaching Notes for each lesson are lists of derivatives for the current Word List. The lists are not exhaustive, but include words which will be most useful. There will be more derivatives given than you will want to use; these are for your reference rather than the students' use. Some words will not have any listed derivatives.

In the student text, on the page following each lesson's Word List, is a section where students can list the derivatives you discuss together each lesson.

Memorization

Each unit, students are required to memorize a couple of lines per lesson from a famous piece of Latin. In Unit 1, the memorization is the *Pater Noster* (Lord's Prayer), Unit 2 is the *Magnificat* (Mary's song from Luke 1), Unit 3 is the *Symbolum Nicaenum* (Nicene Creed), and Unit 4 is *Psalmus XXIII* (Psalm 23). These memorization projects are cumulative (i.e., students are responsible for lines 1–2 the first lesson, lines 1–4 the second lesson, etc.). I have found this method to be the most effective!

Grammar

Most lessons, students will be introduced to new grammatical concepts, and will need to learn a chant or two. Chants are a nifty way to help keep straight the many forms of Latin parts of speech.

Worksheet

Each lesson, students will begin by working on the words and chants they need to memorize. Every worksheet has a vocabulary, a grammar (chants), and a memorization section. Then the students will move on to apply these things first in some English to Latin sentences (it is always more difficult to make one's brain work that way), followed by a Latin to English translation (usually a short story or myth). In two worksheets out of each Unit, I have also included an optional for-fun exercise, such as a crossword puzzle, word search, matching, etc. These are designed to (hopefully) cheer up any students who are getting bogged down. However, it is also *your* job as the teacher to be on the lookout for students' eyes glazing over.

If you feel like you're losing the interest of the class, then stop the lesson and play a game of some kind—Around the World with their vocabulary, Hangman, etc. Or, tell them a story (if you've ever been to see any Roman ruins, perfect! Tell them about it!).

Quiz

Students will take a quiz each lesson. The study of any language, but especially Latin, requires constant review and accountability. Printable PDFs of the quizzes are available at canonpress.com/KL1teacher.

Unit Test

At the end of each unit, students will spend the final lesson doing review exercises and then will take the unit test. The tests have the same format as the quizzes but are a bit longer. Printable PDFs of the unit tests are available at canonpress.com/kraken-latin-1-teacher.

LATIN GRAMMAR BASICS

This overview of Latin grammar is designed for the teachers and educators working through this book, especially those who are fairly new to the study or teaching of Latin. Depending on the age and abilities of your students, you may or may not wish to give them this broad overview before beginning to teach the specifics. I have found that older students (high school and college) generally appreciate getting the big picture first, as it gives them something to refer to throughout the year and enables them to fill in the broad sketch with the details they learn each lesson. However, junior high students may find all of this information bewildering, so beware.

As you undertake the teaching of Latin, do not hesitate to draw comparisons between Latin and English grammar. This will not only reinforce what the students have (hopefully) learned about their native tongue, but students will also begin to appreciate both languages more and more. Whenever they happen to groan about the difficulty of some Latin concept (and they will!), simply point out how odd English is, and that, actually, Latin is in many ways easier to learn because the grammar generally follows a more orderly and predictable system than English. Take the verb of being, for example: I *am*, you *are*, he *is*—how weird is that? Or imagine learning English as a second language and trying to figure out the past tense of verbs—when you should add *-ed* (as in *jump, jumped*) or use a new stem altogether (*bring, brought*).... Or, imagine mastering when to use the definite (*the*) versus the indefinite (*a, an*) article.

Latin, unlike English, is a heavily inflected language. This means that the endings (usually) of the words change to show their grammatical function in the sentence. English, on the other hand, most often depends on word order to show function: *Oswald killed the dragon* is quite different from *The dragon killed Oswald*. In Latin, the endings of the words tell you which is the subject and which is the object: *Oswaldus dracōnem necāvit*, *Dracōnem Oswaldus necāvit*, and *Necāvit Oswaldus dracōnem* all mean "Oswald killed the dragon."

Although word order does not usually indicate grammatical function in Latin, it does matter in terms of habit and style. The Romans were fond of putting verbs at the end, but they also would switch things up to emphasize certain words or for poetic picturesqueness. We actually can do this in English as well (especially in poetry): *Brave he was, and true*. This sentence emphasizes the word *brave*, and also sounds more grand and poetic than simply *He was brave and true*.

Although English is not as heavily inflected as Latin, it does retain some inflection from Old English, which you can see in pronouns, for example: **He** saw **me**, and **I** saw **him** (*He* and *I* are subject pronouns; *me* and *him* object pronouns). In Latin, verbs, nouns, adjectives, and pronouns are inflected. The next few sections will give a broad overview of how these parts of speech function in Latin.

VERBS: Part 1

Latin verbs have five attributes or characteristics: person, number, tense, voice, and mood.

1. ***Person:*** The one who is performing the action (i.e., the subject)

    a. First Person: *I, we*

    b. Second Person: *you, you all*

    c. Third Person: *he, she, it, they*

2. ***Number:*** How many are performing the action

    a. Singular: One person (I, you, he, she, it)

    b. Plural: More than one (we, you all, they)

    These two attributes form a handy chart which will become all too familiar to you and your students:

	SINGULAR	PLURAL
1ST	I	we
2ND	you	you all
3RD	he/she/it	they

3. ***Tense:*** When the action is performed (technically, tense includes aspect as well as time—that is, whether the action is continuous or completed)

    a. Present: Action happening now

    > Oswald **is killing** the dragon. (continuous present)
    >
    > Oswald **kills** the dragon. (simple present)
    >
    > Oswald **does kill** the dragon. (emphatic present; also used for negatives and questions:
    >
    > Oswald **does** not **kill** the dragon; **Does** Oswald **kill** the dragon?) Notice that English has at least three ways of expressing one Latin verb. English also may use helping verbs where Latin will only have one word. Don't let that throw you.

    b. Imperfect: Continuous, repeated, or habitual action in the past

    > Oswald **was killing** dragons. Oswald **used to kill** dragons. In his prime, Oswald **would kill** dragons on the weekends. When he was a young knight, Oswald **killed** dragons. Again, you can use numerous English idioms to express the Latin imperfect. When in doubt, "was X-ing" will usually work.

c. Future: Action that will take place, well, in the future

Oswald **will kill** the dragon. Oswald **is going to kill** the dragon. Oswald **is about to kill** the dragon.

d. Perfect: Completed action in the past

Oswald has killed the dragon!

Oswald killed the dragon yesterday. (Note that the English killed can be used to translate either the Latin imperfect or perfect. In the example under the imperfect section, notice how the context tells you that this was a continuous habit of Oswald's. In the perfect tense example, the action is simple and completed in the past.)

Oswald did kill the dragon. (Again, this emphatic form can also be used in negatives and questions: Oswald **did** not **kill** the dragon; **Did** Oswald **kill** the dragon?)

e. Pluperfect: Completed action past the past; that is, a past action completed before another event in the past.

Before he returned to the castle, Oswald **had** already **killed** the dragon.

f. Future Perfect: Completed action prior to some point in the future

Oswald **will have killed** the dragon by suppertime.

4. **Voice:** The direction of the action; whether the subject is giving or receiving the action

   a. Active: Subject performs the action

   Oswald **kills** the dragon.

   b. Passive: Subject receives the action

   The dragon **is killed** by Oswald.

   Note: The passive voice can occur in all six tenses. The examples given above under Tense are all in the active voice, but notice how each can be made passive:

   Present: The dragon **is being killed** by Oswald. (continuous present)

   The dragon **is killed** by Oswald. (simple present; emphatic doesn't work for the passive)

   Imperfect: Dragons **were being killed** by Oswald. Dragons **used to be killed** by Oswald. Dragons **would be killed** on the weekends by Oswald in his prime. Dragons **were killed** by Oswald when he was a young knight.

   Future: The dragon **will be killed** by Oswald. The dragon **is going to be killed** by Oswald. The dragon **is about to be killed** by Oswald.

   Perfect: The dragon **has been killed** by Oswald! The dragon **was killed** by Oswald yesterday. (Again, the emphatic perfect only occurs in the active.)

   Pluperfect: Before Oswald returned to the castle, the dragon **had** already **been killed** by him.

   Future Perfect: The dragon **will have been killed** by Oswald before suppertime.

   c. Deponents: There are a large number of Latin verbs that are passive in form but active in meaning; these are called deponent verbs. A few deponent verbs will crop up in translations in this book, but the concept will not officially be taught until the next volume.

5. *Mood:* The quality or type of the action performed

   a. Indicative: States or describes the action

   All of the examples given above under Tense and Voice are in the indicative mood. The Latin indicative roughly corresponds to what you may have learned in English grammar classes as "declaratives" and "interrogatives." (In Latin, you would ask a question about real action using the indicative and probably some sort of interrogative word or indicator.)

   b. Imperative: States a command

   > Oswald, **kill** that dragon!

   c. Infinitive: The basic form of the verb in Latin—the "to" form; so called because it is not bound by person and number and therefore is "infinite"

   > Oswald ought **to kill** the dragon.
   >
   > That dragon ought **to have been killed** ages ago.

   Note that Latin infinitives can have tense and voice as well; more on that later.

   d. Subjunctive: Portrays hypothetical, potential, or indirect action

   > If Oswald **were** king, he **would kill** the dragons terrorizing our borders.
   >
   > Did you know that Oswald **killed** the dragon yesterday?
   >
   > Oswald strode into the cave **to kill** the dragon.

   Note that in the last two examples, we would use an English indicative and infinitive respectively to translate a Latin subjunctive. Welcome to the joyous world of translation! We will not cover subjunctives until *Kraken Latin 3*.

   e. Participle: A verbal adjective

   Strictly speaking, the participle is not considered to be a separate Latin mood (so all of you grammar snobs out there can relax). I like to smuggle it in as its own mood, however, because it plays such an important role in the Latin language and is a key concept for students to master. Plus, it makes the moods total five in number, which is nice and tidy.

   > Oswald, **killing** the dragon, proved his bravery to all.
   >
   > The dragon **having been killed**, Oswald proceeded to rescue the princess.

   Again, note that Latin participles have tense and voice too. We will not cover participles until *Kraken Latin 2*.

I should mention here that in Latin, all the moods do not appear in every tense and voice. The table below should clarify what combinations actually occur in Latin.

	PRESENT	IMPERFECT	FUTURE	PERFECT	PLUPERFECT	FUTURE PERFECT
INDICATIVE	Active & Passive	Active & Passive	Active & Passive	Active & Passive	Active & Passive	Active & Passive
IMPERATIVE	Active & Passive		Active & Passive*			
INFINITIVE	Active & Passive		Active & Passive	Active & Passive		
SUBJUNCTIVE	Active & Passive	Active & Passive		Active & Passive	Active & Passive	
PARTICIPLE	Active only		Active & Passive	Passive only		

*Future imperatives are less common than present imperatives and need not be taught at this level of Latin. (Basically, a future imperative is more emphatic, much like when a mother says, "You will clean your room, young man!" She is not prophesying, but commanding in emphatic tones.) If a future imperative happens to appear in any of the translations, it will be glossed.

This book will guide students through the entire indicative mood (all tenses in active and passive), imperatives, and introduce them to infinitives. Infinitives, subjunctives, and participles will be covered in the second book.

VERBS: Part 2

Conjugations: Verbs are "born" into certain families called conjugations. Verbs in each conjugation share a common present stem vowel. There are strictly speaking four (but again, I like to call it five) conjugations in Latin:

First Conjugation—stem vowel ā: *necō, necāre,* I kill

Second Conjugation—stem vowel ē: *videō, vidēre,* I see

Third Conjugation—stem vowel e: *ducō, ducere,* I lead

Third -iō (i-stem) Conjugation—stem vowel e: *capiō, capere,* I capture

Fourth Conjugation—stem vowel ī: *audiō, audīre,* I hear

Principal Parts: Most Latin dictionaries will list the principal parts of a verb under each verb entry. A regular Latin verb usually has four principal parts. These forms are important to learn because the different verb stems are derived from them to form the various tenses, moods, and voices of each verb. For example, if you were to look up the verb *necō*, you would probably see the following:

necō, necāre, necāvī, necātum, I kill

1. *necō*: The first principal part given is the first person singular present active indicative form of the verb. If you recall the discussion above of the five attributes of a verb, you will remember that **first person** means I or we, and **singular** narrows that down to I. **Present active indicative** tells us that this verb is happening in the here and now, the subject is performing the action, and that the action described by the verb is actually occurring. Thus, all those five attributes combine to give us the translation I kill. Simple, really! The first principal part helps us determine the conjugation of the verb (more on this later) and shows us if the present stem vowel was contracted into (in other words, was swallowed up by) the final *-ō* (again, this will be explained more fully later).

2. *necāre*: The second principal part (some dictionaries actually skip *necō* and start with *necāre* as the first principal part) is the present active infinitive form of the verb. Remember that infinitives are not bound by person and number, and therefore only have three attributes: tense, voice, and mood. The present active infinitive is simply translated "to kill." This principal part is very important because from it is derived the present stem of the verb. We find the present stem by taking off the *-re*, giving us *necā-*. From this stem we can form the entire present system (which includes the present, imperfect, and future tenses of the verb in the appropriate moods and voices).

3. *necāvī*: The third principal part is the first person singular perfect active indicative of the verb, meaning "I killed" or "I have killed." From this principal part we derive the perfect active stem by removing the final *-ī*: *necāv-*. With the perfect active stem we can form the perfect active system (which includes the perfect, pluperfect, and future perfect tenses of the verb in the active voice in the appropriate moods).

4. *necātum*: The fourth principal part listed is the neuter singular nominative perfect passive participle. We have not yet discussed nouns and adjectives, where **neuter** and **nominative** will be defined and discussed. For now, suffice it to say that this form can be translated "having been killed," or simply "killed" (as in The dragon **killed** by Oswald was three hundred years old). This principal part is used to form the perfect passive system (the perfect, pluperfect, and future perfect tenses of the verb in the passive voice in the appropriate moods). As a final side note, some dictionaries may list *necātus* rather than *necātum*. This is just the masculine rather than the neuter form of the participle, and it can be used to form perfect passive verbs in the same way.

Below is another handy table to illustrate which principal part is used for which tense, voice, and mood.

	FIRST	SECOND	THIRD	FOURTH
	necō	necāre	necāvī	necātum
DEFINITION/ FUNCTION	1st Sg. Present Active Indicative—I kill Helps identify conjugations and shows if present stem vowel has contracted	Present Active Infinitive—to kill; Present Stem: necā-	1st Sg. Perfect Active Indicative—I killed, have killed Perfect Active Stem: necāv-	Neuter Sg. Nom. Perfect Passive Participle— killed, having been killed Forms Perfect Passives, so in that sense may be considered Perfect Passive "stem"
INDICATIVE		Present Active Present Passive Imperfect Active Imperfect Passive Future Active Future Passive	Perfect Active Pluperfect Active Future Perfect Active	Perfect Passive Pluperfect Passive Future Perfect Passive
IMPERATIVE		Present Active Present Passive Future Active Future Passive		
INFINITIVE		Present Active Present Passive	Perfect Active	Perfect Passive Future Active Future Passive
SUBJUNCTIVE		Present Active Present Passive Imperfect Active Imperfect Passive	Perfect Active Pluperfect Active	Perfect Passive Pluperfect Passive
PARTICIPLE		Present Active Future Passive		Perfect Passive Future Active

Although this chart may be more handy in *Kraken Latin 2*, you may want to have your students use the blank version (found on the very last page of the student workbook) to fill in throughout the year as they learn the various verb forms.

The basics of verb formation will be covered in the first lesson, Lesson 1.

NOUNS: Part 1

As in English, a Latin noun is a person, place, thing, or idea. Latin nouns have three attributes or characteristics:

1. ***Gender: Masculine, Feminine, and Neuter:*** Linguistic gender is not to be confused with biological gender, although there can be overlap between the two. For example, *vir*, meaning "man," is linguistically masculine as well as referring to a male. *Fēmina* ("woman") is a feminine Latin noun and refers to a female. However, many Latin nouns that we would think of as having no gender have linguistic gender in Latin. *Stella* ("star") is feminine, *mors* ("death") is masculine, and *saxum* ("rock") is neuter. If you have studied Spanish, French, German, or most other modern languages, you have already encountered this phenomenon. Modern English nouns do not have as highly a developed system of linguistic gender, although there are a few examples. Modes of transportation (cars, ships,

etc.) are most often feminine. At a full service gas station (rare except in Oregon and New Jersey), you might say "fill 'er up" without thinking, automatically referring to your car as "her." If you walk around a marina and look at the names of boats, in addition to loads of really bad puns you would also find numerous women's names. Sailors also use "she" when talking about their ships or boats. However, English speakers are not always consistent in this area, as we can also use the pronoun "it," as in "It's a great car" instead of "She's a great car."

In Latin, students will need to learn the gender of each noun, and some are more intuitive than others. Generally, nouns referring to biologically male and female entities are linguistically masculine and feminine respectively. There are also other trends that you can point out to your students. Abstract nouns, for instance, are almost always feminine (this is true in other languages as well): justice, virtue, liberty, power, etc., are all feminine in Latin. Students can perhaps remember this by thinking of the Statue of Liberty, which is a woman, or the common statue of Justice, which also portrays that abstract concept as a woman blindfolded and holding a pair of scales. Students (especially the male ones), when learning the word *virtūs*, are often disturbed or confused when they discover that although this word means "virtue, manliness," it is feminine. They simply need to remember that since "manliness" is an abstract concept, it of course is linguistically feminine. When the gender of a noun is not necessarily intuitive, it must simply be memorized.

2. *Number:* As with verbs, a noun can be either singular or plural.

   a. Singular: One person, place, thing, or idea

   b. Plural: More than one person, place, thing, or idea

3. *Case:* The cases of a Latin noun are simply the various inflected forms, each performing their own functions.

   As already mentioned above, Latin is an inflected language. The inflection of Latin verbs has been discussed above, with all the possible combinations of person, number, tense, voice, and mood. In Latin, the nouns also take different endings to show different functions in a sentence. (Noun inflection also occurs in other languages such as German or Ancient Greek.) English nouns have lost most of their inflection from Anglo-Saxon days, but one familiar form to us is when we add -s to change a noun from singular to plural, as in one dragon, one hundred dragons. Some of our pronouns (first and third person) also retain case inflection, as touched on before:

   I, we, he, she, it, they: subject pronouns

   my/mine, our(s), his, her(s), its, their(s): possessive pronouns

   me, us, him, her, them: object pronouns

Once upon a time, English speakers would distinguish the case of second person pronouns as well:

	SINGULAR	PLURAL
SUBJECT	thou	ye
POSSESSIVE	thy, thine	your(s)
OBJECT	thee	you

Nowadays we would associate these pronouns with the King James Bible, old hymns, or Shakespeare, but "thou" or "ye" once simply clarified whether the singular or plural pronoun was being used. It's a shame we don't use them normally anymore; that clarification could be quite helpful sometimes!

I have alluded to subject case, possessive case, and object case in English. Latin actually has five cases*:

Nominative: Indicates the subject of the sentence, or the predicate (with a linking verb)

Oswald killed the dragon. That brave knight is *Oswald*.

Genitive: Indicates possession and a few other things

Oswald's sword is sharp and glittering.

Dative: Indicates indirect object

The rescued princess gave *Oswald* a kiss (or, gave a kiss to *Oswald*).

Accusative: Indicates direct object; also can be used for object of certain prepositions

The dragon espied *Oswald* from afar.

Ablative: Can indicate a number of things, including object of the preposition (uses of the ablative will be taught throughout these books)

The trusty hound came with *Oswald*.

NOUNS: Part 2

Declensions: There are five families or declensions of Latin nouns. Just as each verb is "born" into a particular conjugation, so also a Latin noun is born into its own declension. Each declension has its own set of endings which will be covered in this book. Examples of each declension follow:

First Declension: fēmina, -ae (f) woman

Second Declension: equus, -ī (m) horse

Third Declension: draco, dracōnis (m) dragon

Fourth Declension: fructus, -ūs (m) fruit

Fifth Declension: diēs, -ēī (m) day

---

* Technically, there are seven cases once you include the Vocative (direct address, as in "*O king,* live forever") and Locative ("I got this scarf *in Paris*"). However, these cases are easily learned as they appear. The Vocative is introduced in Lesson 11, and the Locative will be discussed in *Kraken Latin 2*.

Dictionary Listing: Most Latin dictionaries will list nouns in a manner similar to that above. The first part given is the nominative case of the noun; the second word or part of a word is the genitive. With these two cases you can determine two things: which declension the noun belongs to, and what the stem of the noun is. Nouns beginning *-a, -ae* are in the first declension; those starting out *-us, -ī* (or *-r, -ī*, as will be explained later) are second declension; and so on. The stem of the noun is determined by looking at the genitive case and removing the genitive singular ending. In the examples above, the stems of the nouns are as follows:

fēmin-

equ-

dracōn-

fruct-

di-

The next bit of information given in a dictionary listing is an (m), (f), or (n), which stands for masculine, feminine, or neuter, and of course tells you the gender of the noun.

Brief Notes on the Other Parts of Speech

Pronouns

As in English, in Latin a pronoun is a word that takes the place of a noun.

Personal: A personal pronoun refers back to (or takes the place of) a noun. *I, you, he, she, it, we,* and *they* are all personal pronouns. Many Latin personal pronouns will look familiar to anyone who has studied a modern Romance language: *ego (I), tū (you), is (he), ea (she), id (it), nōs (we), vōs (you plural),* and *eī (they).*

Demonstrative: A demonstrative pronoun points to someone or something, such as *this* or *that* in English. Latin has several demonstrative pronouns which you will come to know and love.

Relative: A relative pronoun points back to a noun (called its antecedent), as in this sentence: *Oswald,* **who** *killed the dragon, will marry the princess.* The relative pronoun will not be taught until *Kraken Latin 2*.

Reflexive: A reflexive pronoun points back to the subject. In the sentence *He hurt him, him* is a personal pronoun obviously referring to someone other than the subject. In *He hurt himself, himself* is a reflexive pronoun referring back to the subject. In English this can sometimes get confusing, but Latin is so much clearer. For example, in the sentence *He said that he killed the dragon,* it is unclear whether the speaker is the dragon-slayer or whether he is referring to another person. In Latin, however, the meaning would be quite clear since the reflexive pronoun (*se*) is a different word than the personal pronoun that would be used in this example (*eum*).

Interrogative: An interrogative pronoun is used to ask a question. In English, we readily think of *Who?* and *What?* as in ***Who** did it?* and ***What** did she say?* Latin also has interrogative pronouns, which can be used not only in direct questions (such as those English examples), but also in indirect ones: *I know **who** did it* or *He didn't hear **what** she said.*

Adjectives

An adjective modifies (in other words, describes) a noun. In English, we show that an adjective goes with a noun by word order: *The **brave** knight approached the **fiery** dragon.* In Latin, although word order can be helpful in determining which noun the adjective is modifying, the true test is if the adjective matches the noun in gender, number, and case. Those three things should sound familiar, because yes, they are the three attributes of a noun. If the noun is masculine, singular, and genitive (e.g., *virī*, "of the man, the man's"), then the adjective must also be masculine, singular, and genitive: *virī fortis*, "of the brave man, the brave man's." Notice that in this example the endings of the two words are not identical (that's because they are from different declensions), but that does not matter—they match in gender, number, and case. This concept will be reviewed more thoroughly as adjectives are introduced.

One other thing to note with adjectives is that sometimes they can stand on their own and act as nouns. We can use substantive adjectives in English as well, when we say *Blessed are the merciful*—meaning of course "the merciful people."

Adverbs

As in English, a Latin adverb can modify a verb, adjective, or other adverb. You will be pleased to learn that Latin adverbs are indeclinable—that is, they only have one form and that's it.

Prepositions

A preposition introduces a prepositional phrase (original term, isn't it?) with a noun, pronoun, or substantive adjective (called the object of the preposition). A prepositional phrase describes a noun or verb by conveying some sort of spatial or temporal relationship: *He looked fearlessly **into** the dragon's eyes. The dragon flew **over** the castle. The duel was **at** high noon.*

In Latin, the preposition itself is indeclinable. The preposition, however, will take an object either in the accusative or ablative case. When students learn a preposition in their vocabulary list, they should also learn which case it takes. *Ad,* meaning "to, towards" is followed by the accusative case, so if I wanted to say "toward the dragon," I would need to put "dragon" in the accusative: *ad dracōnem.* Other prepositions, such as *cum,* "with," take the ablative: "with the dragon" becomes *cum dracōne.* A few prepositions take *both* accusative and ablative, usually with a slight difference of meaning between the two. The Latin preposition *in* means "into, against" when followed by the accusative, but "in, on" with the ablative.

Although each preposition should be learned individually, there are patterns: prepositions taking accusative often indicate motion toward, whereas prepositions taking ablative can indicate rest or separation. However, these patterns are only loosely applicable, so the only sure way to identify the case of the object of any given preposition is to memorize it.

Conjunctions

A conjunction joins words, phrases, or sentences together. Latin conjunctions are indeclinable.

Interjections

An interjection is a word expressing emotion and is grammatically unconnected to the sentence. Some English examples would be *Alas! Hey! Ouch!* and, of course, swear words. Latin interjections are also indeclinable.

Recommended Schedules

As a teacher, you should remember that the most important thing for the student is not how fast they go, but how well they learn the material. To help you, however, if you are trying to pace yourself to finish this text in a year, here is a recommended schedule. If you prefer to go slower, there is a two-year schedule starting on the next page. And of course adjust either schedule as needed.

One-Year Schedule

WEEK	MONDAY	TUESDAY	WEDNESDAY	THURSDAY	FRIDAY
1	Introduction/ Latin Grammar Overview	Memorize Vocab / Read Grammar	Lesson 1 Worksheet	Finish Worksheet / Study for Quiz	Lesson 1 Quiz
2	Memorize Lesson 2 Vocab / Chant	Read Lesson 2 Grammar	Lesson 2 Worksheet	Finish Worksheet / Study for Quiz	Lesson 2 Quiz
3	Memorize Lesson 3 Vocab / Chant	Read Lesson 3 Grammar	Lesson 3 Worksheet	Finish Worksheet / Study for Quiz	Lesson 3 Quiz
4	Memorize Lesson 4 Vocab / Chant	Read Lesson 4 Grammar	Lesson 4 Worksheet	Finish Worksheet / Study for Quiz	Lesson 4 Quiz
5	Memorize Lesson 5 Vocab / Chant	Read Lesson 5 Grammar	Lesson 5 Worksheet	Finish Worksheet / Study for Quiz	Lesson 5 Quiz
6	Memorize Lesson 6 Vocab / Chant	Read Lesson 6 Grammar	Lesson 6 Worksheet	Finish Worksheet / Study for Quiz	Lesson 6 Quiz
7	Memorize Lesson 7 Vocab / Chant	Read Lesson 7 Grammar	Lesson 7 Worksheet	Finish Worksheet / Study for Quiz	Lesson 7 Quiz
8	Lesson 8 Worksheet	Finish Worksheet	Study for Unit Test 1	Study for Unit Test 1	Unit Test 1
9	Memorize Lesson 9 Vocab / Chant	Read Lesson 9 Grammar	Lesson 9 Worksheet	Finish Worksheet / Study for Quiz	Lesson 9 Quiz
10	Memorize Lesson 10 Vocab / Chant	Read Lesson 10 Grammar	Lesson 10 Worksheet	Finish Worksheet / Study for Quiz	Lesson 10 Quiz
11	Memorize Lesson 11 Vocab / Chant	Read Lesson 11 Grammar	Lesson 11 Worksheet	Finish Worksheet / Study for Quiz	Lesson 11 Quiz
12	Memorize Lesson 12 Vocab / Chant	Read Lesson 12 Grammar	Lesson 12 Worksheet	Finish Worksheet / Study for Quiz	Lesson 12 Quiz
13	Memorize Lesson 13 Vocab / Chant	Read Lesson 13 Grammar	Lesson 13 Worksheet	Finish Worksheet / Study for Quiz	Lesson 13 Quiz
14	Memorize Lesson 14 Vocab / Chant	Read Lesson 14 Grammar	Lesson 14 Worksheet	Finish Worksheet / Study for Quiz	Lesson 14 Quiz
15	Memorize Lesson 15 Vocab / Chant	Read Lesson 15 Grammar	Lesson 15 Worksheet	Finish Worksheet / Study for Quiz	Lesson 15 Quiz
16	Lesson 16 Worsheet	Finish Worksheet	Study for Unit Test 2	Study for Unit Test 2	Unit Test 2
17	Memorize Lesson 17 Vocab / Chant	Read Lesson 17 Grammar	Lesson 17 Worksheet	Finish Worksheet / Study for Quiz	Lesson 17 Quiz

18	Memorize Lesson 18 Vocab / Chant	Read Lesson 18 Grammar	Lesson 18 Worksheet	Finish Worksheet / Study for Quiz	Lesson 18 Quiz
19	Memorize Lesson 19 Vocab / Chant	Read Lesson 19 Grammar	Lesson 19 Worksheet	Finish Worksheet / Study for Quiz	Lesson 19 Quiz
20	Memorize Lesson 20 Vocab / Chant	Read Lesson 20 Grammar	Lesson 20 Worksheet	Finish Worksheet / Study for Quiz	Lesson 20 Quiz
21	Memorize Lesson 21 Vocab / Chant	Read Lesson 21 Grammar	Lesson 21 Worksheet	Finish Worksheet / Study for Quiz	Lesson 21 Quiz
22	Memorize Lesson 22 Vocab / Chant	Read Lesson 22 Grammar	Lesson 22 Worksheet	Finish Worksheet / Study for Quiz	Lesson 22 Quiz
23	Memorize Lesson 23 Vocab / Chant	Read Lesson 23 Grammar	Lesson 23 Worksheet	Finish Worksheet / Study for Quiz	Lesson 23 Quiz
24	Lesson 24 Worksheet	Finish Worksheet	Study for Unit Test 3	Study for Unit Test 3	Unit Test 3
25	Memorize Lesson 25 Vocab / Chant	Read Lesson 25 Grammar	Lesson 25 Worksheet	Finish Worksheet / Study for Quiz	Lesson 25 Quiz
26	Memorize Lesson 26 Vocab / Chant	Read Lesson 26 Grammar	Lesson 26 Worksheet	Finish Worksheet / Study for Quiz	Lesson 26 Quiz
27	Memorize Lesson 27 Vocab / Chant	Read Lesson 27 Grammar	Lesson 27 Worksheet	Finish Worksheet / Study for Quiz	Lesson 27 Quiz
28	Memorize Lesson 28 Vocab / Chant	Read Lesson 28 Grammar	Lesson 28 Worksheet	Finish Worksheet / Study for Quiz	Lesson 28 Quiz
29	Memorize Lesson 29 Vocab / Chant	Read Lesson 29 Grammar	Lesson 29 Worksheet	Finish Worksheet / Study for Quiz	Lesson 29 Quiz
30	Memorize Lesson 30 Vocab / Chant	Read Lesson 30 Grammar	Lesson 30 Worksheet	Finish Worksheet / Study for Quiz	Lesson 30 Quiz
31	Memorize Lesson 31 Vocab / Chant	Read Lesson 31 Grammar	Lesson 31 Worksheet	Finish Worksheet / Study for Quiz	Lesson 31 Quiz
32	Lesson 32 Worksheet	Finish Worksheet	Study for Unit Test 4	Study for Unit Test 4	Unit Test 4

Two-Year Schedule

Be sure that you are constantly reviewing as they you through this schedule; for instance, you should memorize vocabulary and work on their Latin memorization on Monday of odd-numbered weeks, but you should also be reviewing them throughout the week.

Also, note that there is a "Fun Activity" recommended for a lot of Fridays; use your imagination to think of ways to have fun while practicing Latin.

Year 1

WEEK	MONDAY	TUESDAY	WEDNESDAY	THURSDAY	FRIDAY
1	Introduction / Lesson Overview	Overview: Nouns	Overview: Verbs, etc.	Lesson 1 Word List / Memorization	Lesson 1 Grammar
2	Worksheet 1 A-C	Worksheet A-C Cont'd.	Study for Quiz / Review	Study for Quiz / Review	Lesson 1 Quiz
3	Lesson 2 Word List / Memorization	Lesson 2 Grammar	Lesson 2 Grammar Cont'd.	Worksheet A-C	Worksheet A-C / Activity

RECOMMENDED SCHEDULES

4	Worksheet D	Worksheet E	Worksheet Cont'd. / Review	Quiz Review	Lesson 2 Quiz
5	Lesson 3 Word List / Memorization	Read Lesson 3 Grammar	Lesson 3 Grammar Cont'd.	Worksheet A-C	Worksheet A-C / Crossword
6	Worksheet D	Worksheet E	Worksheet Cont'd. / Review	Quiz Review	Lesson 3 Quiz
7	Lesson 4 Word List / Memorization	Read Lesson 4 Grammar	Worksheet A-C	Worksheet A-C Cont'd.	Vocab Review / Fun Activity
8	Worksheet D	Worksheet E	Worksheet Cont'd. / Review	Quiz Review	Lesson 4 Quiz
9	Lesson 5 Word List / Memorization	Read Lesson 5 Grammar	Worksheet A-C	Worksheet A-C Cont'd.	Vocab Review / Fun Activity
10	Worksheet D	Worksheet E	Worksheet Cont'd. / Review	Quiz Review	Lesson 5 Quiz
11	Lesson 6 Word List / Memorization	Read Lesson 6 Grammar	Lesson 6 Grammar Cont'd.	Worksheet A-C	Worksheet A-C Cont'd.
12	Worksheet D	Worksheet E-F	Worksheet Cont'd. / Review	Quiz Review	Lesson 6 Quiz
13	Lesson 7 Word List / Memorization	Read Lesson 7 Grammar	Lesson 7 Grammar Cont'd.	Worksheet A-C	Worksheet A-C Cont'd.
14	Worksheet D	Worksheet E	Worksheet Cont'd. / Review	Quiz Review	Lesson 7 Quiz
15	Review Vocabulary	Review Vocabulary	Review Chants / Pater Noster	Worksheet A-C	Worksheet A-C Cont'd.
16	Worksheet 8 D Cont'd.	Worksheet 8 E Cont'd.	Study for Unit 1 Test	Study for Unit 1 Test	Unit Test 1
17	Lesson 9 Word List / Memorization	Read Lesson 9 Grammar	Lesson 9 Grammar Cont'd.	Worksheet A-C	Worksheet A-C Cont'd.
18	Worksheet D	Worksheet E	Worksheet Cont'd. / Review	Quiz Review	Lesson 9 Quiz
19	Lesson 10 Word List / Memorization	Read Lesson 10 Grammar	Worksheet A-C	Worksheet A-C Cont'd.	Vocab Review / Fun Activity
20	Worksheet D	Worksheet E	Worksheet Cont'd. / Review	Quiz Review	Lesson 10 Quiz
21	Lesson 11 Word List / Memorization	Read Lesson 11 Grammar	Lesson 11 Grammar Cont'd.	Lesson 11 Grammar Cont'd.	Worksheet A-C
22	Worksheet A-C Cont'd.	Worksheet D- F	Worksheet D-F Cont'd. / Review	Quiz Review	Lesson 11 Quiz
23	Lesson 12 Word List / Memorization	Read Lesson 12 Grammar	Worksheet A-C	Worksheet A-C Cont'd.	Vocab Review / Fun Activity
24	Worksheet D	Worksheet E	Worksheet Cont'd. / Review	Quiz Review	Lesson 12 Quiz
25	Lesson 13 Word List / Memorization	Read Lesson 13 Grammar	Worksheet A-C	Worksheet A-C Cont'd.	Vocab Review / Fun Activity
26	Worksheet D	Worksheet E	Worksheet Cont'd. / Review	Quiz Review	Lesson 13 Quiz
27	Lesson 14 Word List / Memorization	Read Lesson 14 Grammar	Lesson 14 Grammar Cont'd.	Worksheet A-C	Worksheet A-C Cont'd.

28	Worksheet D	Worksheet E-F	Worksheet Cont'd. / Review	Quiz Review	Lesson 14 Quiz
29	Lesson 15 Word List / Memorization	Read Lesson 15 Grammar	Worksheet A-C	Worksheet A-C Cont'd.	Vocab Review / Fun Activity
30	Worksheet D	Worksheet E	Worksheet Cont'd. / Review	Quiz Review	Lesson 2 Quiz
31	Review Vocabulary	Review Vocabulary	Review Chants / Pater Noster	Worksheet A-C	Worksheet A-C Cont'd.
32	Worksheet 8 D Cont'd.	Worksheet 8 D Cont'd.	Study for Unit 2 Test	Study for Unit 2 Test	Unit Test 2

Year 2

WEEK	MONDAY	TUESDAY	WEDNESDAY	THURSDAY	FRIDAY
1	List 17 Word List / Memorization	Lesson 1 Grammar	Lesson 1 Grammar Cont'd.	Worksheet A-C	Worksheet A-C Cont'd.
2	Worksheet D	Worksheet E	Worksheet Cont'd. / Review	Quiz Review	Lesson 7 Quiz
3	Lesson 18 Word List / Memorization	Lesson 2 Grammar	Worksheet A-C	Worksheet A-C Cont'd.	Vocab Review / Fun Activity
4	Worksheet D	Worksheet E	Worksheet Cont'd. / Review	Quiz Review	Lesson 18 Quiz
5	Lesson 19 Word List / Memorization	Read Lesson 3 Grammar	Worksheet A-C	Worksheet A-C Cont'd.	Vocab Review / Fun Activity
6	Worksheet D	Worksheet E-F	Worksheet E-F Cont'd. / Review	Quiz Review	Lesson 19 Quiz
7	Lesson 20 Word List / Memorization	Read Lesson 4 Grammar	Worksheet A-C	Worksheet A-C Cont'd.	Vocab Review / Fun Activity
8	Worksheet D	Worksheet E	Worksheet Cont'd. / Review	Quiz Review	Lesson 20 Quiz
9	Lesson 21 Word List / Memorization	Read Lesson 5 Grammar	Worksheet A-C	Worksheet A-C Cont'd.	Vocab Review / Fun Activity
10	Worksheet D	Worksheet E	Worksheet Cont'd. / Review	Quiz Review	Lesson 21 Quiz
11	Lesson 22 Word List / Memorization	Read Lesson 6 Grammar	Worksheet A-C	Worksheet A-C Cont'd.	Vocab Review / Fun Activity
12	Worksheet D	Worksheet E-F	Worksheet Cont'd. / Review	Quiz Review	Lesson 22 Quiz
13	Lesson 23 Word List / Memorization	Read Lesson 7 Grammar	Worksheet A-C	Worksheet A-C Cont'd.	Vocab Review / Fun Activity
14	Worksheet D	Worksheet E	Worksheet Cont'd. / Review	Quiz Review	Lesson 23 Quiz
15	Review Vocabulary	Review Vocabulary	Review Chants / Pater Noster	Worksheet A-C	Worksheet A-C Cont'd.
16	Worksheet 24 D Cont'd.	Worksheet D Cont'd.	Study for Unit 3 Test	Study for Unit 3 Test	Unit Test 3
17	Lesson 25 Word List / Memorization	Read Lesson 25 Grammar	Worksheet A-C	Worksheet A-C	Vocab Review / Fun Activity

RECOMMENDED SCHEDULES

18	Worksheet D	Worksheet E	Worksheet E Cont'd. / Review	Quiz Review	Lesson 25 Quiz
19	Lesson 26 Word List / Memorization	Read Lesson 26 Grammar	Lesson 26 Grammar Cont'd.	Worksheet A-C	Worksheet A-C Cont'd.
20	Worksheet D	Worksheet E	Worksheet Cont'd. / Review	Quiz Review	Lesson 26 Quiz
21	Lesson 27 Word List / Memorization	Read Lesson 27 Grammar	Worksheet A-C	Worksheet A-C Cont'd.	Vocab Review / Fun Activity
22	Worksheet D-E	Worksheet E-F	Worksheet E-F Cont'd. / Review	Quiz Review	Lesson 27 Quiz
23	Lesson 28 Word List / Memorization	Read Lesson 28 Grammar	Lesson 28 Grammar	Worksheet A-C	Worksheet A-C Cont'd.
24	Worksheet D	Worksheet E	Worksheet E Cont'd. / Review	Quiz Review	Lesson 28 Quiz
25	Lesson 29 Word List / Memorization	Read Lesson 29 Grammar	Lesson 29 Grammar Cont'd.	Worksheet A-C	Worksheet A-C Cont'd.
26	Worksheet D	Worksheet E	Worksheet E Cont'd. / Review	Quiz Review	Lesson 29 Quiz
27	Lesson 30 Word List / Memorization	Read Lesson 30 Grammar	Lesson 30 Grammar Cont'd.	Worksheet A-C	Worksheet A-C Cont'd.
28	Worksheet D	Worksheet E-F	Worksheet E-F Cont'd. / Review	Quiz Review	Lesson 30 Quiz
29	Lesson 31 Word List / Memorization	Read Lesson 31 Grammar	Lesson 31 Grammar Cont'd.	Lesson 31 Grammar Cont'd.	Worksheet A-C
30	Worksheet A-C Cont'd.	Worksheet D-E	Worksheet D-E Cont'd. / Review	Quiz Review	Lesson 31 Quiz
31	Review Vocabulary	Review Vocabulary	Review Chants / Pater Noster	Worksheet A-C	Worksheet A-C Cont'd.
32	Worksheet 32 D Cont'd.	Worksheet 32 D Cont'd.	Study for Unit 4 Test	Study for Unit 4 Test	Unit Test 4

Unit One

UNIT 1 GOALS

Lessons 1–8

By the end of Unit 1, students should be able to . . .

- Understand the five attributes of a verb: person, number, tense, voice, and mood
- Chant from memory the endings for the present, imperfect, and future active indicative verbs
- Identify and conjugate a first conjugation verb in the present, imperfect, and future active indicative
- Understand the three attributes of a noun: gender, number, and case
- Chant from memory the endings of first and second declension nouns
- Decline any first or second declension noun
- Decline first and second declension adjectives and know how to use them
- Translate basic sentences
- Know all vocabulary from Unit 1
- Write out from memory the *Pater Noster* (Lord's Prayer) in Latin

LESSON 1 (Student Edition p. 3)

First Conjugation Verbs & Present Active Indicative

1. Word List

Introduce the students to their first Word List and to Latin pronunciation in general if this is their first year of Latin (for more, refer to the "Pronunciation Guide" on page VII). Nearly all of these words will be review vocabulary if you've used any of the *Latin Primer* series, but if you haven't, that's not a problem. You may want to briefly explain the principal parts of verbs (see Verbs: Part 2, pages XIV–XV) since you will be requiring the students to memorize them, and they will want to know what each is for.

A few notes on individual words from this lesson:

5. *dō, dare, dedī, datum*, I give—Note that unlike nearly all first conjugation verbs, the infinitive of *dō* has a short vowel *–are* ending rather than the typical *–āre* of other first conjugation verbs. In addition, the fourth principal part also has a short *–atum* (instead of the usual *–ātum*).

11. *stō, stāre, stetī, statum*, I stand—*Stō* also has a short *–atum* in its fourth principal part.

19. *et*, and, even, also; *et . . . et*, both . . . and—Notice that *et . . . et* can mean "both . . . and." An example: *Et stant . . . et cantant*, "They both stand and sing." Depending on the context, this could also be translated, "And they stand and sing" or "They also stand and sing."

2. Derivatives/Memorization Helps

Ask the students to come up with English derivatives for this lesson's Word List. I recommend having an *American Heritage Dictionary* (or similar dictionary that lists each word's etymology) handy so that you can double-check derivations if need be. English has such a varied and complicated history that there are many words which may look alike but which are not related at all. If a Latin vocabulary word is more difficult to remember (prepositions, adverbs, and conjunctions can be the trickiest), try to come up with a story or mental picture to help the students remember the word. I'll share examples from my own experience as they come up.

The following derivatives are not comprehensive; feel free to add to them. For some of the words which had no readily available derivatives, I have included memory helps.

1. ambulō, I walk: ambulance, perambulator (became "pram"), ambulatory
2. amō, I love: amateur, amorous
3. cantō, I sing: cantata, chanson, chant
4. clāmō, I shout: exclamation
5. dō, I give: datum, data, date
6. laudō, I praise: laud, laudable
7. līberō, I set free: liberate; from related parts of speech—liberty, liberal
8. necō, I kill: internecine; this root is related (cognate) to the Greek root *necro-*
9. pugnō, I fight: pugnacious
10. spectō, I watch: spectacle, spectator; compounds like inspect, expect, respect
11. stō, I stand: stance, status, state
12. vocō, I call: vocation, vocal, vocabulary; compounds like invoke, evoke, provoke
13. vulnerō, I wound: vulnerable, invulnerable
14. bene, well: the prefix bene-, as in benefactor, beneficence, benevolent, benediction, benefit
15. male, badly: the prefix male-, as in malefactor, maleficence, malevolent
16. nōn, not: (this should be an easy one) no, not, non-
17. nunc, now: quidnunc (meaning "a busybody," from quid nunc? "What now?")
18. aut, or: memory help—"Get aut or else . . . !"
19. et, and: et cetera (etc.)
20. sed, but: memory help—"But you sed I could go."

3. Memorization—*Pater Noster*

Each unit, your students will memorize one chunk of famous Latin. In Unit 1 they will learn one line per lesson of the Lord's Prayer, and of course will be reviewing the previous lines each lesson. Every lesson you should go over the meaning of the new line and point out any interesting derivatives from the unfamiliar vocabulary.

Memorizing more advanced Latin is quite helpful, since later on when the students learn relative clauses (for example), you can point them back to the *Pater Noster*: "Remember how quī *es in caelis* means 'who is in heaven'?" The entire text is below for your reference.

Pater noster, quī es in caelīs,
> *Our Father, who is in heaven,*

Sanctificētur nōmen tuum. Adveniat regnum tuum.
> *May/let Your name be made holy. May/let Your kingdom come.*

Fīat voluntās tua, sīcut in caelō et in terrā.
> *May/let Your will be done, as in heaven also on earth.*

Pānem nostrum quotīdiānum dā nōbīs hodiē,
Give us today our daily bread,
et dīmitte nōbīs dēbita nostra
And forgive us our debts
sīcut et nōs dīmittimus dēbitōribus nostrīs.
Just as we also forgive our debtors,
Et nē nōs indūcās in tentātiōnem, sed līberā nōs ā malō. Āmēn.
And do not lead us into temptation, but deliver us from evil [or "the Evil One"]. Amen.

Note: This text is the "traditional" liturgical version, used in choral versions and in the Roman Catholic Latin Mass. It differs slightly from the Vulgate passages of Matthew 6:9-13 and Luke 11:2-4. Some traditional versions also contain slight spelling variations: *coelīs* and *coelō* instead of *caelīs* and *caelō,* and *cotīdiānum* instead of *quotīdiānum.* The doxology "For Thine is the kingdom and the power and the glory forever and ever" is absent in the traditional Latin text.

The interlinear English translation given above is very literal (to help you see the connection between the Latin text and its English translation), and will sound a bit different from the traditional one that you and your class might have already memorized. As far as the Latin goes, feel free to search online for people saying or singing the Latin text aloud if you are uncomfortable with the pronunciation (a quick search led me to a chanted version, for instance). Speaking of pronunciation, if you really want to mix it up, you may want to have the students memorize the *Pater Noster* using ecclesiastical pronunciation—basically, read the Latin like it's Italian. Anytime Latin is sung, ecclesiastical pronunciation is used. Thus in the first line, *caelis*, which is pronounced KAY-leese in classical pronunciation, would be CHEY-leese in ecclesiastical. (The "c" is a "ch" and the diphthong "ae" is a long "a" sound rather than a long "i" sound.)

4. Grammar

Present Active Indicative

This lesson you will introduce students to the present active indicative verb endings. Students may ask if this chant "means" anything. These are simply verb endings that won't appear on their own in a Latin text—they must be attached to a verb stem to "mean" something. However, you can mention that each ending does indicate a certain person and number (see chart below). Students should memorize this chant since they will be using it all year. To say this new chant, start at the top of the left column and say all the singular endings, then go to the top of the right column and run down the plural endings. Chant through the whole thing several times as a class; if you like you can then erase most of the endings and call on students to fill them in orally.

	SINGULAR	PLURAL
1ST	-ō	-mus
2ND	-s	-tis
3RD	-t	-nt

If you need to review verb basics, refer to pages XI-XVI. This lesson you will introduce students to First Conjugation verbs. Explain that Latin verbs, like people, are "born" into certain families and therefore share similar features. First Conjugation verbs share the stem vowel *ā*. Our example verb for this lesson is *necō, necāre, necāvī, necātum*. To find the stem vowel, go to the second principal part *necāre* (the present active infinitive, remember) and remove the *-re*. That leaves you with *necā-*, the present active and passive stem which will be used over and over again in upcoming lessons.

To this stem you simply add the present active indicative verb endings:

	SINGULAR	PLURAL
1ST	necō	necāmus
2ND	necās	necātis
3RD	necat	necant

Now that we have this verb neatly conjugated in the present active indicative, what does it mean? All your students need to do is apply some simple logic.

Necō is in the first person singular box, and we know that first person is either *I* or *we*, but the singular form can only be *I*.

These endings are for the indicative mood, so we know that this verb must be telling us some factual happening.

It is in the present tense and active voice, so we know that it is happening now and that the subject (*I*) is performing the action. Since this verb means "to kill," we can deduce that *necō* means "I kill" (or, "I am killing," "I do kill"—see pages XI-XVI on verb basics for details).

Moving down, *necās* is second person singular, present active indicative. Thus, it means "you kill." The complete Latin chart with English meanings would look like this:

	LATIN SINGULAR	ENGLISH SINGULAR
1ST	necō	I kill
2ND	necās	you kill
3RD	necat	he/she/it kills

	LATIN PLURAL	ENGLISH PLURAL
1ST	necāmus	we kill
2ND	necātis	you all kill
3RD	necant	they kill

Some of you may be wondering why the first person singular form is *necō* and not *necāō*. Quite simply, the *ā* and *ō* have contracted—or, you can think of it as the *ō* has swallowed up the *ā* (try saying *āō* over and over and you will see how easily this happens).

5. Worksheet

One of the verbs to conjugate is *dō*, which is an irregular first conjugation verb. Don't sweat the macrons on this one, and you may need to help your students work through it, because a short stem can be confusing.

On the sentences, remind the students that the present tense can be translated in several ways. For example, the first Latin to English sentence is *Cantant aut clamant*. This can be translated either "They sing or they shout," "They are singing or they are shouting," "They do sing or they do shout," or any combination thereof. Also point out to the students that in English we can leave out the second "they"—"They sing or shout," "They are singing or shouting," or "They do sing or shout." The goal is to have an English translation that is both accurate and sounds like good English!

Follow the directions given and complete the worksheet.

Section E, 10: *"Nōn bene," clāmō, "cantātis!"*: Your students may ask (and you may be wondering) why the *clāmō* is in the midst of the quote. The Romans often did this, perhaps because they did not use quotation marks and so this particular method showed that they were quoting somebody. Your students should translate it so that it sounds natural in English: *"You do not sing well!" I shout* sounds much better than *"Not well," I shout, "do you sing!"*

6. Quiz

When you are assigning points and grading quizzes, I recommend that you allot only half a point to each principal part and a whole point to the meaning of the verb.

You will also need to learn how to grade your students' translations, which can be tough. You will have to make many judgment calls on whether the student's word choice is close enough or not. The main thing is to approach grading with a flexible mindset and not to expect students to always have a translation that matches the answer key word for word. I will try to give several possible correct translations for each sentence, but students can get fairly creative—so be prepared.

I also recommend the policy of "double jeopardy"—that is, if a student misses a word in the vocabulary list and makes the same mistake in a sentence later on, only take off a mark once.

I also confess that on tests, I have allowed students to come up and ask me for the meaning or principal part of a word, and I have given it to them in red ink, taking off the point(s) then and there. This can really help some students get past their mental block and at least get partial credit on a translation or chart.

Administer Quiz 1 when the students are ready.

Lesson 1 Worksheet

A. Vocabulary

Translate the following words from Latin to English or English to Latin as appropriate. For the verbs, also fill in the missing principal parts.

1. now: **nunc**
2. clāmō, **clamāre**, **clamāvī**, clamātum: **I shout**
3. I call, summon, invite: **vocō**, **vocāre**, **vocāvī**, **vocātum**
4. stō, stāre, **stetī**, **statum**: I stand
5. aut: **or**
6. necō, **necāre**, necāvī, **necātum**: **I kill, slay**
7. I walk: **ambulō**, **ambulāre**, **ambulāvī**, **ambulātum**
8. laudō, **laudāre**, laudāvī, laudātum: **I praise**
9. but: **sed**
10. **vulnerō**, vulnerāre, vulnerāvī, **vulnerātum**: **I wound**
11. līberō, līberāre, līberāvī, līberātum: **I set free**
12. not: **nōn**
13. I fight: **pugnō**, **pugnāre**, **pugnāvī**, **pugnātum**
14. male: **badly, ill, wrongly**
15. cantō, **cantāre**, **cantāvī**, **cantātum**: **I sing, play (music), predict**
16. spectō, spectāre, spectāvī, spectātum: **I look at, watch**
17. amō, **amāre**, amāvī, **amātum**: **I love**
18. well: **bene**
19. dō, dare, **dedī**, **datum**: **I give**
20. et: **and, even, also**

B. Grammar

Find the stem of the following verbs.

1. amō: **amā-**
2. stō: **stā-**
3. clāmō: **clāmā-**
4. ambulō: **ambulā-**
5. spectō: **spectā-**
6. līberō: **līberā-**

7. Write out the present active indicative verb endings.

	SINGULAR	PLURAL
1ST	-ō	-mus
2ND	-s	-tis
3RD	-t	-nt

Conjugate the following verbs in the Present Active Indicative with their English meanings.

8. *cantō*

	LATIN SINGULAR	ENGLISH SINGULAR	LATIN PLURAL	ENGLISH PLURAL
1ST	cantō	I sing	cantāmus	we sing
2ND	cantās	you sing	cantātis	you all sing
3RD	cantat	he/she/it sings	cantant	they sing

9. *vulnerō*

	LATIN SINGULAR	ENGLISH SINGULAR	LATIN PLURAL	ENGLISH PLURAL
1ST	vulnerō	I wound	vulnerāmus	we wound
2ND	vulnerās	you wound	vulnerātis	you all wound
3RD	vulnerat	he/she/it wounds	vulnerant	they wound

10. *dō*

	LATIN SINGULAR	ENGLISH SINGULAR	LATIN PLURAL	ENGLISH PLURAL
1ST	dō	I give	damus	we give
2ND	dās	you give	datis	you all give
3RD	dat	he/she/it gives	dant	they give

C. Memorization

Write out the first line of the Lord's Prayer in Latin.

<u>Pater noster, quī es in caelīs,</u>

D. English to Latin Translation

1. Now you (pl.) are loving, but I am fighting.

   Nunc amātis, sed pugnō.

2. We do not sing.

   Nōn cantāmus.

3. She gives well.

   Bene dat.

4. They stand and now they are walking.

   Stant et nunc ambulant.

5. He sings badly, but you all sing well.

   Male cantat, sed bene cantātis.

6. He fights, he wounds, and he slays.

   Pugnat, vulnerat, et necat.

7. I shout and sing, but you (sg.) do not love.

   Clamō et cantō, sed nōn amās.

8. You (sg.) are fighting and now you (sg.) set free.

   Pugnās et nunc līberās.

9. We watch and praise.

   Spectāmus et laudāmus.

10. I fight, but I do not kill wrongly.

    Pugnō, sed male nōn necō.

E. Latin to English Translation

1. Cantant aut clāmant.

   They are singing or [they are] shouting [*or* They sing or shout].

2. Male pugnās, sed stō et bene pugnō.

   You (sg.) fight badly, but I stand and fight well.

3. Līberāmus, sed necātis.

   We set free, but you (pl.) kill.

4. Nōn amās; vulnerās.

   You do not love; you wound.

5. Male pugnant et nōn līberant.

   They fight badly and are not setting free [do not set free].

6. Stat, sed ambulant.

   He/she/it is standing, but they are walking.

7. Bene amāmus et bene cantāmus.

   We love well and [we] sing well.

8. Vocātis et clāmātis, sed stat et spectat.

   You (pl.) call and shout, but he stands and watches.

9. Laudant et nunc dant.

   They praise and now they are giving [*or* they give].

10. "Nōn bene," clāmō, "cantātis!"

    "You (pl.) do not sing well!" I shout.

Lesson 1 Quiz (40 points)

A. Vocabulary (10 points)

Translate the following words from Latin to English or English to Latin as appropriate. For the verbs, also fill in the missing principal parts as well.

1. bene: **well**
2. amō, **amāre**, **amāvī**, **amātum**: **I love**
3. or: **aut**
4. līberō, **līberāre**, **līberāvī**, **līberātum**: **I set free**
5. vulnerō, **vulnerāre**, **vulnerāvī**, **vulnerātum**: **I wound**
6. clāmō, **clāmāre**, **clāmāvī**, **clāmātum**: **I shout**
7. nunc: **now**
8. badly: **male**
9. ambulō, **amāre**, **amāvī**, **amātum**: **I walk**
10. spectō, **spectāre**, **spectāvī**, **spectātum**: **I watch, look at**

B. Grammar (15 points)

Conjugate *pugnō* in the present active indicative and give the English translations for each form.

	LATIN SINGULAR	ENGLISH SINGULAR	LATIN PLURAL	ENGLISH PLURAL
1ST	pugnō	I fight	pugnāmus	we fight
2ND	pugnās	you fight	pugnātis	you (pl.) fight
3RD	pugnat	he/she/it fights	pugnant	they fight

C. Translation (11 points)

Translate each sentence.

1. They are standing and singing. **Stant et cantant.**

2. Nōn dant, sed amāmus. **They are not giving, but we are loving [*or* They do not give, but we love].**

3. Vocat et nunc laudat. **He/she/it calls [*or* is calling] and now praises [is praising].**

D. Memorization (4 points)

Write out the first line of the Lord's Prayer in Latin.

<u>Pater noster, quī es in caelīs,</u>

Lesson 2 (Student Edition p. 10)

First Declension Nouns / Introduction to Case Usage—Nominative, Dative & Accusative

1. Word List

As your students acquire more vocabulary, keep in mind that generally speaking, nouns, adjectives, and verbs are easier to learn and remember because they often have obvious or semi-obvious English derivatives. They are also easier to guess in context. For example, if you were translating a passage from the Gospels about Jesus healing a *caecum*, who could then see, and you didn't know the word *caecum*, you could easily guess it means "blind man" (and you would be correct). However, the short little adverbs and conjunctions and prepositions are more difficult to guess and often do not have English derivatives. Therefore, encourage your students to work harder at memorizing those. In this book, I also tend to emphasize them more heavily in the vocabulary section of quizzes and tests, just to keep the students accountable.

Most first conjugation verbs are highly regular with principal parts ending in *-ō, -āre, -āvī, -ātum*. Therefore, from now on, all regular first conjugation verbs will be listed with a (1) after the first principal part by way of abbreviation. Any irregular ones will be given with all of their principal parts.

4. *dīvitiae, -ārum* (f) riches, wealth—This word only appears in the plural, which makes sense, because "riches" and "wealth" are inherently plural. There will be more of these only-plural nouns popping up here and there throughout this book.

2. Derivatives/Memorization Helps

1. *aqua*, water: aquarium, aquatic, aquamarine
2. *bēstia*, beast: beast, bestial, bestiality
3. *corōna*, crown: coronation
4. *dīvitiae*, riches, wealth
5. *fābula*, story, legend, tale: fable, fabulous [note how the meaning of this word has changed from the original!]
6. *fēmina*, woman: feminine, feminist
7. *īra*, anger: irate, ire
8. *lūna*, moon: lunar, lunatic, lunacy

9. *pīrāta*, pirate: piratical
10. *poēta*, poet: poetic
11. *rēgia*, palace
12. *rēgīna*, queen: Regina
13. *turba*, crowd, mob, throng: disturb, perturb
14. *villa*, farmhouse, country house: villa, villain
15. *cremō*, I burn, consume by fire: cremate, cremation
16. *narrō*, I tell relate, recount: narrate, narration, narrator
17. *superō*, I conquer, defeat: insuperable
18. *cūr*, why: Memory help—"Why are you such a *cur*?"
19. *hodiē*, today: Several traditional Christmas songs have the lyrics *Hodie Christus natus est* ("Today Christ is born").
20. *itaque*, and so, therefore

3. Memorization—*Pater Noster*

In the second line, the two verbs *sanctificētur* and *adveniat* are subjunctives and literally mean "Let/may it be hallowed" and "Let/may it come." Have the students make any observations they can about these new words: "sanctify" comes from *sanctificētur*, and literally means "make holy" (the English *hallow* means "holy," as in All Hallows' Eve, which is the Eve of All Saints' [holy ones] Day); *nōmen* gives us words like "nomenclature," "nominate," and of course "nominative"; *adveniat* is from *ad* ("to, toward") plus *veniō* ("I come"), and we get "advent" and "adventure" from it, not to mention tons of words from *veniō*; *regnum* is related to this lesson's vocabulary word *rēgīna*.

Also, notice that your students will have to review the first line as they learn the second line. (When I was teaching, I learned that requiring one and only one line per lesson was not as effective as the cumulative method!)

4. Grammar

First Declension Noun Endings

Now that students are getting acquainted with verbs, they of course need some nouns to work with. This lesson you will be introducing them to the first of five noun declensions. (If you need to review Latin nouns, see pages XVI-XIX in Latin Grammar Basics.)

Explain the three attributes of nouns—gender, number, and case. You will spend the most time explaining case. Although you should define each case, focus on this lesson's cases: nominative, dative, and accusative.

A noun in the nominative case will be the subject of the sentence (or a predicate nominative, but that won't be covered till next lesson): **Oswald** *sees the dragon*.

Accusative case denotes direct object (*The dragon sees* **Oswald**).

Dative indicates the indirect object (*The princess gave* **Oswald** *a kiss*; or, *The princess gave a kiss* **to Oswald**).

The chart below provides a summary reference point. You may need to remind the students that, just like the verb endings, these noun endings don't "mean" anything in isolation. They need to be attached to a noun stem first. By themselves they simply indicate a specific case in the singular or plural.

As with the verb chant, to say this new chant, start at the top of the left column and say all the singular endings, then go to the top of the right column and run down the plural endings. Chant through the whole thing several times as a class; if you like you can then erase most of the endings and call on students to fill them in orally.

	LATIN SINGULAR	ENGLISH SINGULAR		LATIN PLURAL	ENGLISH PLURAL
NOMINATIVE	-a	a/the *noun* [subject]		-ae	the *nouns* [subject]
GENITIVE	-ae	of the *noun*, the *noun's*		-ārum	of the *nouns*, the *nouns'*
DATIVE	-ae	to/for the *noun*		-īs	to/for the *nouns*
ACCUSATIVE	-am	a/the *noun* [object]		-ās	the *nouns* [object]
ABLATIVE	-ā	by/with/from the *noun*		-īs	by/with/from the *nouns*

After the students have become familiar with the first declension chant, they need to know how to use it. Remind them that verbs are born into certain conjugations; nouns are also born into specific families called declensions. Thus, one *conjugates* verbs but *declines* nouns.

Now go back to this lesson's word list (which preferably you will have already gone over). Explain the listing—that the first form given is the nominative case, the second is the genitive, then the gender of the noun is given in parentheses, then the meaning. If it is helpful to your students, they can think of the first declension as a family with mostly girls and a few boys. (But don't let them confuse biological and linguistic gender; see pages XVI-XVII.)

In general, first declension vocational nouns—that is, nouns referring to a particular job—are masculine. Thus, the following words are all masculine: *agricola* (farmer), *aurīga* (charioteer), *incola* (colonist, settler), *nauta* (sailor), *poēta* (poet), and *propheta* (prophet). Some of these (such as *aurīga* and *incola*) can be either masculine or feminine, depending on the sex of their referent. It is extremely important that the students learn the gender of the nouns in their vocabulary lists, since they will need that bit of information when adjectives come on the scene in Lesson 7.

The dictionary listing of the noun is helpful because it starts students along the proper chant and gives the gender and definition of the word, and it also enables them to find the base of the noun. To find the base, you need to look at the genitive, not the nominative, of the noun. Thus, with the noun *corōna, -ae*, we see that nothing unusual happens and the stem is *corōn-*. Although the base of most first and second declension nouns is fairly easy to determine, get your students in the habit of going to the genitive for the base, since they will absolutely need to do so when they learn the third declension. Pick about five words from the Word List and have different students find the base. Then show them how to attach the first declension endings to the base of a noun:

rēgīna, -ae (f) *queen*; stem: *rēgīn-*

	LATIN SINGULAR	ENGLISH SINGULAR	LATIN PLURAL	ENGLISH PLURAL
NOM.	rēgīna	a/the queen [subject]	rēgīnae	the queens [subject]
GEN.	rēgīnae	of the queen, the queen's	rēgīnārum	of the queens, the queens'
DAT.	rēgīnae	to/for the queen	rēgīnīs	to/for the queens
ACC.	rēgīnam	the queen [direct object]	rēgīnās	the queens [direct object]
ABL.	rēgīnā	by/with/from the queen	rēgīnīs	by/with/from the queens

Decline a few more nouns with the students to practice (two examples from the vocabulary are given below). Now they are ready to see how these nouns work in a sentence.

	LATIN SINGULAR	LATIN PLURAL	LATIN SINGULAR	LATIN PLURAL
NOM.	pīrāta	pīrātae	lūna	lūnae
GEN.	pīrātae	pīrātārum	lūnae	lūnārum
DAT.	pīrātae	pīrātīs	lūnae	lūnīs
ACC.	pīrātam	pīrātās	lūnam	lūnās
ABL.	pīrātā	pīrātīs	lūnā	lūnīs

Nominative and Accusative Cases

Let's begin with the nominative and accusative in action, and then move on to the dative. Here is a very simple sentence to start with: **Rēgīna pīrātam amat.**

Encourage your students to read through the entire sentence first, of course paying attention to the individual words, but also getting a feel for the overall structure and meaning (this skill will be more useful later on as the sentences get longer). As you may remember (page XI), word order in Latin usually does not determine grammatical function (as in English); however, word endings do. Thus, this sentence could be rearranged a number of ways and still mean the same thing: *Pīrātam rēgīna amat. Amat rēgīna pīrātam.*

However, to avoid possible confusion later, you should point out to your students that there are patterns of word order in Latin. Very often, the Romans would put the subject first and the verb at the end. However, because Latin is a highly inflected language, they could rearrange things for emphasis, for the sake of poetic meter, etc. (Analyze a few English hymns or poems to see how in English we can also rearrange normal word order for the sake of poetry—although not as flexibly as in Latin.)

Back to our sentence. Have a student point out the verb: *amat.*

Call on another student to analyze the verb: which person? number? tense? voice? mood? This analysis is called *parsing;* your students will become quite adept at this activity. Right now it's fairly easy to parse verbs, since students have only learned the present active indicative. Thus, *amat* should be parsed third person singular, present active indicative. When translated, it means "he/she/it loves."

Now that we have nouns in play, we should look for a noun in the nominative case that could be the subject. The subject must also be singular, because the verb is singular, and in Latin (as in English), the verb and subject must agree in number. There might not be a noun in the nominative case. If not, you can stick with "he/she/it" as the subject. But, as it happens, in this sentence *rēgīna* is nominative. Thus, "queen" *replaces* that third person singular pronoun "she" and becomes our subject: "The queen loves."

Now have another student identify what case *pīrātam* is in: accusative, which means it is our direct object. (Accusative case can also be used for the object of a preposition; more on that next lesson.) Whom does the queen love? "The queen loves the pirate." If we had been translating one of the rearranged examples, we might put a little emphasis in our tone as we translated: *Pīrātam rēgīna amat:* "The queen loves *the pirate*" (possible implications: we can't believe she loves a pirate, or this particular one; or, the queen loves him as opposed to someone else). *Amat rēgīna pīrātam:* "The queen *loves* the pirate" (possible implication: we thought she hated him, but apparently she loves him). And again, none of these implications might be correct; all depends upon the context.

A brief comment on definite and indefinite articles: classical Latin does not have any words for *a, an,* or *the.* Breathe a sigh of relief if you were expecting the *le, la, il,* or *el* of previously studied modern Romance languages! Therefore, when translating Latin into English we can use either a definite or indefinite article (or no article), depending on the context and on what sounds best. To me at least, in this isolated sentence "*The* queen loves" sounds better than "*A* queen loves." It might work if we had more to go on, as in "Once upon a time, there was *a* queen who loved *a* pirate." However, with "The queen loves *a* pirate" versus "The queen loves *the* pirate," either article sounds fine and it would depend on our story—if said pirate had been introduced already, for example, I would use "the." However, if some lady-in-waiting were whispering the latest gossip that the queen loves "a" pirate (identity yet unknown).

After a few more examples of the nominative and accusative in action, we will move on to the dative.

Example 1: **Lūnam spectātis.** Read through the sentence and identify the verb: *spectātis.* Now parse and translate it: second person plural, present active indicative, "you all look at."

Look over the rest of the sentence for a nominative plural noun (the subject would have to be plural since the verb is plural). Since there isn't a nominative plural noun, we will leave "you all" as our subject and seek out a direct object. Lo and behold, *lūnam* is in the accusative, so our sentence means "You all look at the moon." (Or, "you all are looking [or "do look"] at the moon.") You may wonder how a nominative would have worked with this sentence. If we had had *Pīrātae lūnam spectātis,* our sentence would have meant "You pirates are looking at the moon."

Example 2: **Fēminae dīvitiās dant.** Again, read through the sentence, noting items of interest. Our verb, *dant,* is third person plural, present active indicative, meaning "they give." Now we look for a plural nominative, and we have *fēminae.* (Of course, *fēminae* could be genitive singular or dative singular as well, but we will worry about those trifles later. Keep your students focused on the nominative for now.) Thus, in answer to the question, "Who gives?" we can swap "women" for "they," and have "The women give." What do they give? Why, we look for an accusative (singular or plural), and find *dīvitiās*. Answer: "The women give riches."

Dative Case

Now we will add the dative to the mix. While the accusative case indicates a direct object, the dative case is used for the indirect object. In the example immediately above, the "riches" are the direct object because they are directly receiving the action of the verb "give." Now if the women were giving the wealth *to* somebody, then that somebody would be the indirect recipient of the action and thus the indirect object: **Fēminae pīrātīs dīvitiās dant,** "The women give riches to the pirates." In English we can also say "The women give the pirates riches" (*pīrātīs* is dative plural).

I hinted in the previous paragraph that *fēminae* could potentially be in the dative case, since that *-ae* ending does appear three times in the first declension chant. If we took it as dative singular, then our example sentence of *Fēminae dīvitiās dant* would read: "They give riches to the woman." This also makes perfect sense. So which is it? "The women give riches" or "They give riches to the woman"? Well, as a teacher you should accept either translation as correct *unless there is a context indicating otherwise.*

I have already mentioned context a few times, and will continue to do so since it is extremely important in translation. When students are first learning Latin and translating isolated little sentences that focus on a specific grammatical concept, these sentences are not contextualized. Thus, you may get a few different translations which could be correct. This is not a problem, and indeed, you should point these out to your students so that they will be training themselves to anticipate all possibilities. However, when they start translating the short stories and move on to "real" Latin texts, the context of a particular passage will eliminate some of the potential translations.

For example, say that our sentence appeared in the following story: "Once upon a time five women lived by the sea. They caught fish and sold them, and also wove rich robes that they sold to the castle for much gold. In this way they became wealthy. These women loved five pirates who sailed the world in their ship. The pirates had been gone for a whole year, but the women remembered them and waited for them. Finally, the ship appeared over the horizon—they had returned! The women were eager to give the pirates gifts." And then we have our sentence *Fēminae dīvitiās dant.* Clearly, in this context, the correct translation will be "The women give riches"—the women were the subject of the sentence immediately prior, and they have been waiting for the pirates so they could give them money. If one of your students translated the sentence "They give riches to the woman," you should mark it as incorrect, because although technically *fēminae* could be dative singular, the context has eliminated that possibility.

Here are a few more examples of the dative case in action:

Poēta turbae fābulās narrat. "The poet tells the crowd stories" (or "tells stories to the crowd"). *Narrat* is third person singular, present active indicative. We look for a singular nominative to be our subject and find *poēta*. Who is telling? "The poet." What is the poet telling? Our accusative is *fābulās*—stories. To whom is the poet telling stories?—*turbae*, to the crowd.

Rēgīnae corōnam dās. "You give the queen a crown" (or "You give a crown to the queen"). The verb *dās* is second person singular, present active indicative, "you give." There is no nominative singular noun to be our subject, so we keep "you" as the subject and move on to our direct object. What do you give? The accusative is *corōnam*—"a crown." To whom do you give the crown? *Rēgīnae* in isolation could be nominative plural, genitive singular, or dative singular. However, since our verb is singular that eliminates *rēgīnae* as a nominative plural. Although the genitive might work (more on that in the next lesson), we will go with the dative since it makes the most sense: "to the queen."

No Definite or Indefinite Articles!

Classical Latin does not have any words for *a, an,* or *the*. Therefore, when translating Latin into English we can use either a definite or indefinite article (or no article at all), depending on the context and on what sounds best. To me at least, in this isolated sentence "The queen loves" sounds better than "A queen loves." It might work if we had more to go on, as in "Once upon a time, there was a queen who loved a pirate." However, with "The queen loves **a** pirate" versus "The queen loves **the** pirate," either article sounds fine and the best choice would depend on the overall story in which this particular sentence appeared.

Review

Make sure you are reviewing your verb endings as you do this lesson!

UNIT ONE \\ LESSON 2

5. Translation

This lesson your students get to translate a simple story as well as some isolated sentences. These stories will teach them how to translate in context, since obviously they will one day be translating whole passages and will not be doing practice sentences forever. Now that your students have more grammar to work with, there will be more opportunities for various interpretations of the Latin. Make sure to discuss these with the class—they will be learning how to balance a literal, accurate translation with one that sounds good in English. My Latin professor in college always said, "Good Latin makes good English, and good English makes good Latin." Sometimes literalness has to be sacrificed for a more idiomatic rendering.

You can help your students develop these skills in a number of ways. You might first require them to render the text absolutely literally. Then point out how stiff and awkward it sounds in English, and how if they turned that paragraph in to their English teacher, they would not do so well. Have them experiment with different "flavors" to their translation: translate the story to sound like a romantic medieval ballad, translate it as if you were telling it to your best friend in whatever is the current slang of the day, etc.

Example translations follow below, but first, one other translational note: Since the students have only learned the present tense, this story utilizes the present. However, it can sound a bit awkward. Fortunately for us, there is such a thing as the *historical present*—telling a story that happened in the past in the present tense to convey immediacy and interest to the audience. No doubt you have told stories in this way yourself: "So, last week I flew to California. *I'm* on the plane, and this weird guy with a paper bag *sits* next to me. During the whole flight, the paper bag *is twitching* and *rustling,* and *I'm wondering* what on earth *is* in that thing?!" Notice how the speaker switches from the past tense in the first sentence to the present, using both tenses to tell a story about *past* events.

And now for two possible interpretative translations to our story from this lesson's translation. The first is the more literal version given in the answer key, the second is a romantic ballad style, and the last is a modern slangy version (of course I'm not that up on current slang and it will probably be outdated as soon as I finish typing it). N.B.: In the Teacher Edition translations I have included possessive adjectives in brackets, as in "The queen loves [her] crowns. . ." Students will not learn these possessives until Lesson 11, but they do make the story sound better—thus, the brackets. In "real" Latin, sometimes possessive adjectives are implied but left out, so again, use context to determine if the addition is permissable.

Literal: A poet tells a tale to the crowd, and sings: "A pirate loves a queen, but the queen does not love the pirate. The queen loves [her] crowns and palace and riches. The pirate looks at the moon, and sings tales to the queen, but the woman does not love. Today the queen is walking, and a beast burns up the palace! He burns up the palace and the crowns and the riches, and wounds the queen. But the pirate stands, fights the beast, and slays the beast. He frees the queen and gives the queen [his] riches. Now therefore the queen loves the pirate, and the pirate sings tales to the queen and to the moon."

Ballad: A bard tells his tale unto the throng, and sings: "A pirate is in love with a queen, but she does not love him. She loves her tiaras and palace and treasuries. The pirate gazes upon the moon, and sings lovesongs to the queen, but she loves him not. Today the royal lady is walking along, and a dragon engulfs the palace in flames. His breath burns the palace and tiaras and treasuries, and he even wounds the queen. But the heroic pirate takes his stand, fights the beast, and slays it. He sets the queen at liberty and bestows upon her his gold. Now therefore the queen dotes upon the pirate, and he sings unto her and unto the silvery moon sweet songs of love."

Slang: This guy is telling a bunch of people a story and said: "A pirate guy had a huge crush on the queen, but she totally did not like him. She was more in love with her bling and mansion and cash. The pirate is totally moonstruck and writes songs for her, but she shuts him down. One day she's out walking and this monster burns up her palace. He toasted everything—her house, her jewels, all her cash, and he even singed her a bit. But the pirate guy comes along and fights the thing and takes it out. Now of course the queen digs him and he writes his love songs for her and the moon."

One final note: in my experience, students in the logic years have a very hard time straying from the absolute literal and wooden translation. They want to be exactly right, color precisely in the lines, and so on, and it really bothers them that there is ambiguity in language. But you might have a class which prefers to translate along broader lines, and in that case you might want them to translate more literally, or just ask them enough specific questions about their translation to ensure that they understand what is going on and they aren't just guessing at what it means. If your class is overly rigid about translations, push them the other way (otherwise they will run into trouble when the grammar gets more complicated).

6. Quiz

Administer Quiz 2 when the students are ready.

Lesson 2 Worksheet

A. Vocabulary

Translate the following words from Latin to English or English to Latin as appropriate. For the verbs, also fill in the missing principal parts. (There are a few review words mixed in.)

1. dīvitiae: **riches, wealth**
2. today: **hodiē**
3. bēstia: **beast**
4. fēmina: **woman**
5. crowd: **turba**
6. nunc: **now**
7. īra: **anger**
8. water: **aqua**
9. narrō, **narrāre**, **narrāvī**, narrātum: **I tell, relate, recount**
10. I stand: **stō**, **stāre**, **stetī**, **statum**
11. poēta: **poet**
12. itaque: **and so, therefore**
13. palace: **rēgia**
14. cūr: **why**
15. sed: **but**
16. pirate: **pīrāta**
17. rēgīna: **queen**
18. fābula: **story, legend, tale**
19. farmhouse: **villa**
20. well: **bene**
21. clāmō, **clāmāre**, **clāmāvī**, clāmātum: **I shout**
22. lūna: **moon**
23. I burn: **cremō**, **cremāre**, **cremāvī**, **cremātum**
24. corōna: **crown**
25. superō, **superāre**, superāvī, **superātum**: **I conquer, defeat**

B. Grammar

1. Decline *aqua*.

	LATIN SINGULAR	LATIN PLURAL
NOMINATIVE	aqua	aquae
GENITIVE	aquae	aquārum
DATIVE	aquae	aquīs
ACCUSATIVE	aquam	aquās
ABLATIVE	aquā	aquīs

2. Decline *fābula*.

	LATIN SINGULAR	LATIN PLURAL
NOMINATIVE	fābula	fābulae
GENITIVE	fābulae	fābulārum
DATIVE	fābulae	fābulīs
ACCUSATIVE	fābulam	fābulās
ABLATIVE	fābulā	fābulīs

3. Decline *dīvitiae*.

	LATIN SINGULAR	LATIN PLURAL
NOMINATIVE	—	dīvitiae
GENITIVE	—	dīvitiārum
DATIVE	—	dīvitiīs
ACCUSATIVE	—	dīvitiās
ABLATIVE	—	dīvitiīs

C. Memorization

Fill in the blanks (but be prepared to recall both lines entirely from memory for the quiz).

Pater noster, quī es in caelīs,

Sanctificētur **nōmen tuum. Adveniat** _____ regnum **tuum** _____.

D. English to Latin Translation

Translate these sentences from English into Latin.

1. The poet looks at the moon and tells the woman a tale.

   Poēta lūnam spectat et fēminae fābulam narrat.

2. The beasts are burning the villa and the palace.

   Bēstiae villam et rēgiam cremant.

3. The pirates shout, but you (sg.) do not give the pirates wealth.

   Pīrātae clāmant, sed pīrātīs dīvitiās nōn dās.

4. I love water, but the queen loves crowns.

   Aquam amō, sed rēgīna corōnās amat.

5. Why are you (pl.) looking at the moon?

   Cūr lūnam spectātis?

6. We are now singing stories to the pirates.

   Fābulās pīrātīs nunc cantāmus.

7. The crowds fight the beast well, but the beast is wounding the crowds.

   Turbae bēstiam bene pugnant, sed bēstia turbās vulnerat.

8. The pirates kill the beast, and so the women love the pirates.

   Pīrātae bēstiam necant, itaque fēminae pīrātās amant.

9. The queen summons the women and gives the women wealth.

   Rēgīna fēminās vocat et fēminīs dīvitiās dat.

10. We pirates sing well but love badly.

    Pīrātae bene cantāmus sed male amāmus.

E. Latin to English Translation

1   Poēta turbae fābulam narrat, et cantat: "Pīrāta rēgīnam amat, sed rēgīna pīrātam nōn amat. Rēgīna corōnās et rēgiam et dīvitiās amat. Pīrāta lūnam spectat, et rēgīnae fābulās cantat, sed fēmina nōn amat. Hodiē rēgīna ambulat, et bēstia rēgiam cremat! Rēgiam et corōnās et dīvitiās cremat, et rēgīnam vulnerat. Sed pīrāta stat, bēstiam pugnat, et bēstiam necat. Rēgīnam līberat et rēgīnae dīvitiās dat. Nunc
5   itaque rēgīna pīrātam amat, et pīrāta rēgīnae et lūnae fābulās cantat."

A poet tells a tale to the crowd, and sings: "A pirate loves a queen, but the queen does not love the pirate. The queen loves [her] crowns and palace and riches. The pirate looks at the moon, and sings tales to the queen, but the woman does not love. Today the queen is walking, and a beast burns up the palace! He burns up the palace and the crowns and the riches, and wounds the queen. But the pirate stands, fights the beast, and slays the beast. He frees the queen and gives the queen [his] riches. Now therefore the queen loves the pirate, and the pirate sings tales to the queen and to the moon."

Lesson 2 Quiz (48 points)

A. Vocabulary (10 points)

Translate the following words from Latin to English.

1. rēgia: **palace**
2. fābula: **story, legend, fable**
3. hodiē: **today**
4. cremō: **I burn, consume by fire**
5. dīvitiae: **riches, wealth**
6. nunc: **now**
7. lūna: **moon**
8. corōna: **crown**
9. aut: **or**
10. cūr: **why**

B. Grammar (15 points)

Decline *villa*.

	LATIN SINGULAR	LATIN PLURAL
NOMINATIVE	villa	villae
GENITIVE	villae	villārum
DATIVE	villae	villīs
ACCUSATIVE	villam	villās
ABLATIVE	villā	villīs

C. Translation (13 points)

Translate each sentence.

1. You pirates love anger, but we poets love women.

   Pīrātae īram amātis, sed poētae fēminās amāmus.

2. Itaque rēgīnīs corōnās dant.

   Therefore they give crowns to the queens [*or* they give the queens crowns].

3. Fēmina villam et aquam et lūnam spectat.

   The woman looks at the farmhouse and the water and the moon.

D. Memorization (10 points)

Write out the first two lines of the Lord's Prayer in Latin.

Pater noster, quī es in caelīs,

Sanctificētur nōmen tuum. Adveniat regnum tuum.

Lesson 3 (Student Edition p. 18)

Verbs: *Sum* / Nouns: More Case Usage—Genitive & Ablative / Prepositions

1. Word List

Highlight #1 *agricola* and #6 *nauta* as masculine nouns of the first declension. Words #16–20 are prepositions, and the case they take (the case in parentheses) should be learned along with the meaning.

15. *sum, esse, fuī, futūrum*: I am—See the Grammatical Concepts section for more of an explanation of *sum*. You can explain to your students that although it's irregular, it's also very important.

16. *ā, ab* and 17. *ē, ex*—*Ā* and *ē* appear before words beginning with a consonant; *ab* and *ex* appear before words beginning with either a vowel or a consonant.

2. Derivatives/Memorization Helps

1. *agricola*, farmer
2. *harēna*, sand, beach: arena
3. *hasta*, spear
4. *īnsula*, island: insular, insulate, peninsula (from *paene*, "almost" + *īnsula*)
5. *nauta*, sailor: nautical
6. *patria*, native land: expatriate (but "patriot" is from a related Greek word)
7. *pecūnia*, money: impecunious, pecuniary
8. *puella*, girl
9. *sagitta*, arrow: Sagittarius (the archer, a constellation and sign of the Zodiac)
10. *sīca*, dagger
11. *silva*, forest: sylvan, Pennsylvania, silviculture
12. *spēlunca*, cave: spelunking, spelunker
13. *exspectō*, I wait for, expect: expect, expectation
14. *habitō*, I live, dwell, inhabit: inhabit, habitation
15. *sum*, I am: essence (from the infinitive)

16. *ā, ab*, from, away from: look for the *ab-* prefix on many words; e.g., absent, ablative, abduct
17. *ad*, to, toward, at, near: look for the *ad-* prefix on many words; e.g., addition, admire
18. *ē, ex*, out of, from: look for the *ex-* prefix on many words; e.g., excerpt, exceed
19. *in*, into, against, in, on: in; look for the *in-* prefix on many words; e.g., inset, insert
20. *per*, through: look for the *per-* prefix on many words; e.g., perform, percent

3. Memorization—*Pater Noster*

The new line for this lesson is *Fīat voluntās tua, sīcut in caelō et in terrā*. *Fīat* is another hortatory or jussive subjunctive, meaning "Let it/there be," and it is also used in English to refer to a decree or command, as in "divine fiat" or "royal fiat." (It is not related to the name of the car company, which is an acronym.) *Voluntās* is of course connected to "voluntary" and "volunteer," and *caelō* to "celestial." *Terra* gives us several English words and commonly used Latin phrases: terra firma, terra incognita, terrarium, etc.

Note that in the standard English version of the Lord's Prayer, we say "Thy will be done, on earth as it is in heaven" whereas that order is reversed in Latin.

4. Grammar

Verb of Being: *sum*

Sum, the Latin verb of being, is irregular, which means it doesn't follow the usual or expected verb formation rules. This shouldn't actually be surprising, since it is irregular in many languages. Take English, for example: *I **am**, you **are**, he **is***—imagine learning that as a non-native speaker of our language!

However, point out to your students that the endings of the verbs still follow our basic pattern of *-ō, -s, -t, -mus, -tis, -nt*. True, the first person singular ends in *-m*, not *-ō*, but as they learn more and more (active) verb endings, they will see that the first person singular usually ends in *-m* or *-ō*, second person singular in *-s*, third singular in *-t*, first plural in *-mus*, second plural in *-tis*, and third plural in *-nt*. If your students are familiar with Spanish or French or another Romance language, compare those verbs of being with the *sum* chant.

	LATIN SINGULAR	ENGLISH SINGULAR
1ST	su**m**	I am
2ND	e**s**	you are
3RD	es**t**	he/she/it is

	LATIN PLURAL	ENGLISH PLURAL
1ST	su**mus**	we are
2ND	es**tis**	you (pl.) are
3RD	su**nt**	they are

After the students have become familiar with this chant, they need to know how to use it. Remind them that verbs are born into certain conjugations just as nouns are also born into specific families called declensions. (One *conjugates* verbs but *declines* nouns.)

As your students (hopefully) have learned in their English grammar classes, the verb of being is a linking verb; that is, it functions like an "equals" sign. *I am a woman* is saying that *I = a woman*. Thus it is grammatically proper to say "This is she" or "It is I" rather than "This is her" or "It's me." In Latin, this means that the words (whether nouns, adjectives, or pronouns) linked to the subject by *sum* will be in the **nominative** case. This is called the **predicate nominative**. *I am a woman* should be *Fēmina sum*, not *Fēminam sum*. *The women are queens* will be *Fēminae rēgīnae sunt*, where the two words not only agree in case (both being nominative), but are both plural as well.

Another handy and common usage of *sum* is that in the third person singular or plural, it can mean "There is" or "There are" (rather than "it is" or "they are"). This is especially the case when *est* or *sunt* appear at the beginning of a sentence: *Est rēgīna!* "There is the queen!"

Genitive Case

At this point your students may worriedly ask how they are supposed to tell the difference between the genitive and dative singular (or nominative plural, for that matter!), since both end in *-ae*. You will answer "Context!" Show them that in the sentence above, the dative simply does not work, because *spectō* is not a verb that would normally have an indirect object. If we had *Corōnam rēgīnae dō,* it requires a tad more thought. This sentence could mean either "I give the queen's crown" [not mentioning to whom I am giving it] or "I give the queen a crown" [taking the queen as a dative rather than a genitive]. Now, taking both of these sentences in isolation, I believe that the latter sounds better; however, there could conceivably be a context in which the former would be the only possible answer.

Whenever two or more equally valid translations are possible, I will endeavor to mention them all—and you as the teacher should accept as correct all such valid translations! Students' differing translations can actually serve as a great platform to discuss the nuance of language and to develop an appreciation for the art of accurate and skillful translation.

Ablative Case and Prepositions

The ablative case has many functions, so it is convenient to refer to it as the **"junk drawer"** case. (I always liked calling it the MacGyver case because it can do practically anything, but chances are your students will not be familiar with that former TV series, sadly.)

In this lesson, we will focus on two uses: ***ablative of means/instrument*** and as an ***object of a preposition***. When you want to indicate the means or instrument by which an action was done, you simply put that word in the ablative: *Pīrāta bēstiam sicā necat,* "The pirate kills the beast with [*or* by/by means of] a dagger." In English we have to use a preposition such as "with" or "by" to indicate means/instrument, but in Latin all we need is a word in the ablative.

The ablative can also be the object of a preposition, and so, incidentally can the accusative. Whenever students learn a Latin preposition, they also need to know what case that preposition "takes" (in other words, the case of the noun it governs or is followed by). The preposition *ex*, for example, means "out of, from" and takes the ablative. This means that the object of the preposition *ex* will be in the ablative case: *ex spēluncā,* "out of the cave."

Some prepositions take the accusative, as with *ad*, meaning "to, toward": *ad spēluncam,* "toward the cave." Although your students should learn these prepositions and cases as they come, there are general trends. Prepositions with the accusative often indicate *motion toward,* whereas those with ablative show *rest* or *separation*. (This generalization is *very* general.)

Some prepositions can take either case and have slightly different meanings depending on the case taken: *in* with a noun in the accusative case means "into, against"; *in* plus a noun in the ablative case means "in, on." Thus *In silvam ambulāmus* would mean "We walk into the forest" (showing motion toward), but *In silvā habitāmus* means "We live in the forest" (showing rest).

5. Worksheet

Follow the directions given to complete the worksheet.

E. Crossword Puzzle: The crossword puzzle clues have to do with vocabulary and noun and verb endings, so it should be another helpful (and fun!) review for the quiz.

6. Quiz

Administer Quiz 3 when the students are ready.

Lesson 3 Worksheet

A. Vocabulary

Translate the following words from Latin to English or English to Latin as appropriate. For the verbs, also fill in the missing principal parts. For each preposition, include which case(s) it takes.

1. island: **īnsula**
2. sīca: **dagger**
3. sum, **esse**, **fuī**, futūrum: **I am**
4. native land: **patria**
5. rēgia: **palace**
6. agricola: **farmer**
7. per: (+ **acc.**) **through**
8. pecūnia: **money**
9. arrow: **sagitta**
10. itaque: **and so, therefore**
11. nauta: **sailor**
12. silva: **forest**
13. ex: (+ **abl.**) **out of, from**
14. male: **badly, ill, wrongly**
15. riches: **dīvitiae**
16. spēlunca: **cave**
17. ā, ab: (+ **abl.**) **from, away from**
18. exspectō, **exspectāre**, **exspectāvī**, exspectātum: **I wait for, expect**
19. hasta: **spear**
20. I dwell: **habitō**, **habitāre**, **habitāvī**, **habitātum**
21. **cantō**, cantāre, **cantāvī**, **cantātum**: **I sing, play (music), predict**
22. to, toward: **ad** (+ **acc.**)
23. puella: **girl**
24. in: (+ **acc.**) **into, against** (+ **abl.**) **in, on**
25. harēna: **sand, beach**

B. Grammar

1. Conjugate and translate *sum* in the present active indicative.

	LATIN SINGULAR	ENGLISH SINGULAR		LATIN PLURAL	ENGLISH PLURAL
1ST	sum	I am		sumus	we are
2ND	es	you are		estis	you (pl.) are
3RD	est	he/she/it is		sunt	they are

2. Conjugate and translate *amō* in the present active indicative.

	LATIN SINGULAR	ENGLISH SINGULAR		LATIN PLURAL	ENGLISH PLURAL
1ST	amō	I love		amāmus	we love
2ND	amās	you love		amātis	you (pl.) love
3RD	amat	he, she, it loves		amant	they love

3. Decline *sagitta*.

	LATIN SINGULAR	LATIN PLURAL
NOMINATIVE	sagitta	sagittae
GENITIVE	sagittae	sagittārum
DATIVE	sagittae	sagittīs
ACCUSATIVE	sagittam	sagittās
ABLATIVE	sagittā	sagittīs

C. Memorization

Fill in the blanks (but of course be prepared to recall all three lines entirely from memory for the quiz).

<u>Pater</u> _____ noster, <u>**quī es**</u> _____ in <u>**caelīs**</u>, _____

<u>**Sanctificētur nōmen**</u> _____ tuum. <u>**Adveniat**</u> _____ regnum <u>**tuum**</u> _____.

<u>**Fīat**</u> _____ voluntās <u>**tua, sīcut**</u> _____ in <u>**caelō et in**</u> _____ terrā.

D. English to Latin Translation

1. The beasts are walking from the water to the forest.

   Bēstiae ab/ex aquā ad silvam ambulant.

2. You are sailors and fight the beast with spears and arrows.

   Nautae estis et bēstiam hastīs et sagittīs pugnātis.

3. He loves the pirate's girl and walks through the forest to the farmhouse.

   Puellam pīrātae amat et per silvam ad villam ambulat.

4. We are not pirates; we are girls and live on a beach on an island.

   Pīrātae nōn sumus; sumus puellae et in harēnā in īnsulā habitāmus.

5. The queen summons the farmer away from the native land to the palace.

   Rēgīna agricolam ā/ab patriā ad rēgiam vocat.

6. I am the queen's farmer and I give riches and money to the girls.

   Agricola rēgīnae sum et puellīs dīvitiās et pecūniam dō.

7. The poet is telling the crowd tales in the cave today.

   Poēta turbae fābulās in spēluncā hodiē narrat.

8. The pirates kill the farmer's beasts with daggers and so the farmer does not love the pirates.

   Pīrātae bēstiās agricolae sīcīs necant itaque agricola pīrātās nōn amat.

9. The women are praising the queen's crown today.

   Fēminae corōnam rēgīnae hodiē laudant.

10. The pirates love the women in the native land and so do not burn the women's farmhouses.

    Pīrātae fēminās in patriā amant itaque villās fēminārum nōn cremant.

E. Latin to English Translation

1. Nauta et pīrāta sum, et in īnsulā in aquā habitō. Sunt spēluncae in īnsulā, et bēstiae in spēluncīs habitant. Itaque in spēluncās ambulō et bēstiās sīcīs aut hastīs aut sagittīs necō. Et agricolās pugnō, et villās cremō. Fēmināsque et puellās līberō, sed agricolās vulnerō aut necō. Fēminam amō; fēmina rēgīna est. In rēgiā in silvā habitat, sed in īnsulā habitō. Rēgīnae pecūniam dō, sed et pecūniam et dīvitiās amō. Bene pugnō,
5. bene superō, bene amō, et bene cantō. Poēta et pīrāta sum, et insulam in aquā amō.

I am a sailor and a pirate, and I live on an island in the water. There are caves on the island, and beasts live in caves. Therefore I walk into the caves and kill the beasts with daggers or [with] spears or [with] arrows. I also fight farmers, and burn [their] farmhouses. I set free the women and girls, but I wound or kill the farmers. I love a woman; [this] woman is the queen. She lives in [her] palace in the forest, but I live on [my] island. I give [some] money to the queen, but I also love money and wealth [*or*, "but I love both money and wealth"]. I fight well, conquer well, love well, and sing well. I am a poet and a pirate, and I love [my] island in the water.

F. Crossword Puzzle

Fill in the correct forms of the Latin words, and as appropriate translate the italicized English words into Latin. (Don't use macrons for the Latin words in the puzzle.)

ACROSS

1. *not*
2. ablative singular of *island*
4. *you* (pl.) *are*
5. second person singular present active indicative of *līberō*
8. first person plural present active indicative of the verb meaning *I call*
10. *out of*
13. dative plural of *story*
16. accusative singular of *crown*
17. *today*
18. *cremō* in the first person plural present active indicative
20. *or*
23. genitive plural of the word meaning *pirate*
25. *and so*
26. *the farmers'*
28. *toward*
29. *stō* in the third person plural
31. *sailor* in the nominative singular
32. *bēstia* in the accusative plural
34. *we give*
36. second person singular of *ambulō*
39. *by/with/from the girl*
41. the word for *cave* in the accusative singular
43. *arrow*, if it were the subject of a sentence
45. genitive singular of *poēta*

DOWN

1. 1st principal part of the verb meaning *I kill*
2. *on*
3. accusative plural of *native land*
4. *I wait for*
6. *īnsula* in the accusative singular
7. *you* (pl.) *conquer*
8. 4th principal part of *vulnerō*
9. *why*
11. *well*
12. *now*
14. *we love*
15. accusative plural of *īra*
16. *clāmō* in the first person plural present active indicative
19. *of the palaces*
21. *by/with/from the water*
22. *but*
23. *money* in the nominative singular
24. *they love*
27. *for the queens*
30. ablative singular of the word meaning *spear*
33. *you* (pl.) *are walking*
34. nominative plural of the word for *wealth*
35. *forests* (nominative)
37. *badly*
38. *we are*
40. *she does praise*
42. *through*
44. *away from*

UNIT ONE \\ LESSON 3

Lesson 3 Quiz (41 points)

A. Vocabulary (10 points)

Translate the following words from Latin to English or English to Latin. Give case(s) for prepositions.

1. per: **(+ acc.) through**
2. farmer: **agricola**
3. patria: **native land**
4. sīca: **dagger**
5. sand, beach: **harēna**
6. cave: **spēlunca**
7. exspectō: **I wait for, expect**
8. īra: **anger**
9. girl: **puella**
10. ab: **(+ abl.) from, away from**

B. Grammar (6 points)

Give the Latin for the following verbs.

1. We are: **sumus**
2. You (pl.) are loving: **amātis**
3. You (sg.) are: **es**
4. I stand: **stō**
5. They are: **sunt**
6. She is: **est**

C. Translation (11 points)

Translate each sentence into English.

1. He walks from the palace into the forest.

   Ab/ex rēgiā in silvam ambulat.

2. Rēgīna agricolīs villās dat.

   The queen gives the farmers farmhouses [*or* gives farmhouses to the farmers].

3. Puellae pīrātārum estis.

   You (pl.) are girls of the pirates [*or* the pirates' girls].

D. Memorization (14 points)

Write out the first three lines of the Lord's Prayer in Latin.

Pater noster, quī es in caelīs,

Sanctificētur nōmen tuum. Adveniat regnum tuum.

Fīat voluntās tua, sīcut in caelō et in terrā.

LESSON 4 (Student Edition p. 28)

Second Declension Masculine

1. Word List

As you go through the words for this lesson, take note of *alnus*, "ship, alder(wood)," which is our lone feminine second declension noun in this list of masculines. Also note that *germānus* and *servus* are second declension masculine nouns, referring to males, while their female counterparts *germāna* and *serva* are feminine first declension nouns (referring to females, of course).

2. Derivatives/Memorization Helps

1. *ager*, field: agriculture, agrarian
2. *alnus*, ship, alder(wood)
3. *camēlus*, camel
4. *caper*, billy goat: Capricorn
5. *Christus*, Christ
6. *cibus*, food
7. *Deus*, God: deify, deist
8. *deus*, god: see *Deus*
9. *dominus*, lord, master: dominate, dominion
10. *equus*, horse: equine
11. *fīlius*, son: filial
12. *germānus/germāna*, brother/sister: German, germane
13. *gladius*, sword: gladiator, gladiola
14. *ōceanus*, ocean: ocean, oceanic
15. *servus/serva*, slave, servant: servant, server, service, servile
16. *terra*, earth, land: terrain, terrarium, terrestrial
17. *vir*, man: virile, virtue
18. *nāvigō*, I sail: navigate, navigation
19. *oppugnō*, I attack
20. *portō*, I carry: porter, portable (but not port)
21. *dē* (+ abl.), from, down from, concerning: look for the *dē-* prefix on many words like descend, decline

3. Memorization—*Pater Noster*

The new line for this lesson is *Pānem nostrum quotīdiānum dā nōbīs hodiē*.

Our new line has the nice long word *quotīdiānum*, which gives us the English word *quotidian*, meaning "daily" or "mundane." The word for "bread," *pānem*, gives us "companion"—someone you break bread with.

4. Grammar

Second Declension Masculine Noun Endings

	LATIN SINGULAR	ENGLISH SINGULAR
NOMINATIVE	-us / -r	a/the *noun* [subject]
GENITIVE	-ī	of the *noun*, the *noun*'s
DATIVE	-ō	to/for the *noun*
ACCUSATIVE	-um	a/the *noun* [direct object]
ABLATIVE	-ō	by/with/from the *noun*

	LATIN PLURAL	ENGLISH PLURAL
	-ī	the *nouns* [subject]
	-ōrum	of the *nouns*, the *nouns*'
	-īs	to/for the *nouns*
	-ōs	the *nouns* [direct object]
	-īs	by/with/from the *nouns*

This lesson your students will learn the second of the five noun declensions. The chant above is frequently referred to as the second declension masculine, because most of the nouns are masculine in gender. The endings of this declension vary slightly with neuter nouns, and thus the second declension neuter chant will be taught as its own chant next lesson. Just as your students can think of the first declension as a family with mostly girls and a few boys, so they can think of the second declension as nearly all sons and a few daughters. Certain cities, countries, plants, trees, and a few other random nouns in the second declension are feminine. I have included one of these in the vocabulary: *alnus*, meaning "alder(wood)," and by extension, "ship," since alderwood was regularly used in ship-building for its rot-resistant qualities. We will be using *alnus* for "ship" until the more common third declension word *nāvis* is introduced (Lesson 18).

Have your students chant through the second declension endings a few times, review the first declension endings, and then ask them to point out any striking similarities or differences. First off, we can see that there are two options for a nominative singular ending. A second declension noun can end in either *-us* or *-r* in the nominative, but one word won't have both options. Thus *puer* is always *puer* and not *pueus*; *equus* always ends in *-us* in the nominative and does not appear as *equer*. In the plural, the genitive, dative, and ablative are similar or identical to those of the first declension.

The fabulous thing is that the second declension functions exactly like the first declension. A nominative always acts like a nominative, no matter what declension. To extend our family metaphor, all of us humans perform the same functions (walking, eating, sleeping), even though we belong to distinct families and look different from one another. You may want to review each of the five case usages with your students.

One very important concept to teach this lesson: **a noun is *born* into a declension and *stays* there** (there are a few exceptions, of course, but we need not go into those now). Thus, *agricola,* though masculine, cannot divest himself of his first declension identity and become *agricolus*. No—he is born into the first declension and will always take first declension endings.

Nouns in the second declension will also have the same sort of dictionary listing as first declensions: nominative singular, genitive singular, gender, and definition. The genitive singular is of course where we can find the stem of the noun. This wasn't too hard for our first declension nouns, but we do need to pay more attention with the second declension. Let's start by declining *equus*. The genitive is listed as simply *-ī*, so we conclude that the stem is a nice obvious *equ-*. We can then decline our noun thus:

	LATIN SINGULAR	LATIN PLURAL
NOMINATIVE	equus	equī
GENITIVE	equī	equōrum
DATIVE	equō	equīs
ACCUSATIVE	equum	equōs
ABLATIVE	equō	equīs

However, when we move from horses to billy goats, it gets more interesting. The noun *caper* has *-prī* as the genitive. This tells us that the whole genitive is *caprī,* which means that our stem is *capr-*, not *caper-*. The *-e-* has been dropped. The declension of *caper* will then look like this:

	LATIN SINGULAR	LATIN PLURAL
NOMINATIVE	caper	caprī
GENITIVE	caprī	caprōrum
DATIVE	caprō	caprīs
ACCUSATIVE	caprum	caprōs
ABLATIVE	caprō	caprīs

Here are two more examples, one of a noun ending in *-us* and one in *-r:*

	LATIN SINGULAR	LATIN PLURAL
NOMINATIVE	dominus	dominī
GENITIVE	dominī	dominōrum
DATIVE	dominō	dominīs
ACCUSATIVE	dominum	dominōs
ABLATIVE	dominō	dominīs

	LATIN SINGULAR	LATIN PLURAL
NOMINATIVE	ager	agrī
GENITIVE	agrī	agrōrum
DATIVE	agrō	agrīs
ACCUSATIVE	agrum	agrōs
ABLATIVE	agrō	agrīs

At this point you may have to give the "context" lecture again, because students will point out that the genitive singular is the same as the nominative plural, and they can't distinguish between the datives and ablatives. They will soon learn how to translate them appropriately in context.

5. Worksheet

Follow the directions given to complete the worksheet.

In Exercise B.3–12, make sure that students can distinguish between the verb of being and English helping verbs. For example, the answer for #5 "we are attacking" should not be *sumus oppugnāmus*. This would make no sense in Latin (and the translation would be "we are are attacking"—silly in English, too). The "are" in "we are attacking" is a helping verb only for "attacking," and is included in *oppugnāmus*.

6. Translation

Most of the Latin to English translations from here on out will contain words that the students have not yet learned. Part of this is because it is nearly impossible to write a story with the few words that they actually do know, but part of it is pedagogical. When your students are one day translating "real" Latin texts, original and not paraphrased, they will most likely encounter many words they haven't seen before and will need to look them up. Your students need to learn now how to deal with unfamiliar vocabulary so that they can work with it later on in their Latinic careers.

7. Quiz

Administer Quiz 4 when the students are ready.

Lesson 4 Worksheet

A. Vocabulary

Translate the following words from Latin to English or English to Latin as appropriate. For the verbs, also fill in the missing principal parts. For each preposition, include which case(s) it takes.

1. Deus: **God**
2. portō, **portāre**, **portāvī**, **portātum**: **I carry**
3. spear: **hasta**
4. lūna: **moon**
5. Christ: **Christus**
6. fīlius: **son**
7. dē: (+ **abl.**) **from, down from, concerning**
8. ōceanus: **ocean**
9. food: **cibus**
10. terra: **earth, land**
11. sister: **germāna**
12. brother: **germānus**
13. ager: **field**
14. sword: **gladius**
15. caper: **billy goat**
16. alnus: **ship, alder (wood)**
17. I sail: **nāvigō**, **nāvigāre**, **nāvigāvī**, **nāvigātum**
18. **līberō**, līberāre, **līberāvī**, **līberātum**: I set free
19. dominus: **lord, master**
20. servus: **slave, servant**
21. camel: **camēlus**
22. man: **vir**
23. per: (+ **acc.**) **through**
24. **oppugnō**, **oppugnāre**, **oppugnāvī**, oppugnātum: **I attack**
25. horse: **equus**

B. Grammar

1. Decline *vir*.

	LATIN SINGULAR	LATIN PLURAL
NOMINATIVE	vir	virī
GENITIVE	virī	virōrum
DATIVE	virō	virīs
ACCUSATIVE	virum	virōs
ABLATIVE	virō	virīs

2. Decline *terra*.

	LATIN SINGULAR	LATIN PLURAL
NOMINATIVE	terra	terrae
GENITIVE	terrae	terrārum
DATIVE	terrae	terrīs
ACCUSATIVE	terram	terrās
ABLATIVE	terrā	terrīs

Translate these verbs into Latin.

3. they sail **navigant**
4. it is **est**
5. we are attacking **oppugnāmus**
6. we are **sumus**
7. you (sg.) carry **portās**
8. she shouts **clāmat**
9. I walk **ambulō**
10. you (pl.) are telling **narrātis**
11. I am **sum**
12. you all dwell **habitātis**

C. Memorization

Fill in the blanks, and as usual, be prepared to recall the entire thing from memory for the quiz.

Pater noster, quī _____ es **in caelīs** _____,

Sanctificētur nōmen _____ tuum. **Adveniat** _____ regnum **tuum** _____.

Fīat **voluntās** _____ tua, **sīcut** _____ in **caelō et in** _____ terrā.

Pānem _____ nostrum **quotīdiānum** _____ dā **nōbīs hodiē** _____,

UNIT ONE \\ LESSON 4

D. English to Latin Translation

1. Christ is the Son of God, and Lord of the earth.

   Christus Fīlius Deī [est], et Dominus terrae est.

2. The pirate's brother dwells in the forest and gives food to the beasts.

   Germānus pīrātae in silvā habitat et bēstiīs cibum dat.

3. We love the Lord God, but the pirates love gods.

   Dominum Deum amāmus, sed pīrātae deōs amant.

4. The camel carries the queen's sister to the palace.

   Camēlus germānam rēgīnae ad rēgiam portat.

5. Christ tells stories to the crowds and is now giving the men and women food.

   Christus turbīs fābulās narrat et virīs et fēminīs cibum nunc dat.

6. The billy goat walks out of the field and attacks the farmer's son.

   Caper ex agrō ambulat et fīlium agricolae oppugnat.

7. You are pirates; therefore you sail on the ocean and carry men's wealth to the island.

   Pīrātae estis; itaque in ōceanō navigātis et dīvitiās virōrum ad insulam portātis.

8. The poet sings tales to the crowd about women, the queen, and camels.

   Poēta turbae fābulās dē fēminīs, rēgīnā, et camēlīs cantat.

9. The slave wrongly attacks the master with a sword, but the master conquers the slave with food.

   Servus dominum gladiō male oppugnat, sed dominus servum cibō superat.

10. Today the horse carries the servant, the camel carries the food, and the goat does not carry.

    Hodiē equus servum portat, camēlus cibum portat, et caper nōn portat.

E. Latin to English Translation

1 **Tragoedia[1] Bestiārum**

Camēlus, caper, et equus in īnsulā in ōceanō habitant. Est cibus in īnsulā, et equus caprō cibum dat, caper camēlō cibum dat, et camēlus equō cibum dat. Equus in agrō, caper in silvā, et camēlus in spēluncā habitat. Hodiē pīrātae ad insulam nāvigant, et pecūniam et dīvitiās in spēluncam portant. Sed camēlus
5 spēluncae caprō aut equō nihil[2] dē pecūniā et dīvitiīs narrat. Pīrātae ab īnsulā nāvigant, et camēlus dīvitiās amat et equō cibum nōn dat. Equus agrī et caper silvae ad spēluncam ambulant et dīvitiās camēlī spectant. Īra equī et caprī camēlum spēluncae cremat, et camēlum gladiīs oppugnant et necant. Dīvitiās ex spēluncā portant, sed caper ad silvam portat et equus ad agrum portat. Itaque caper silvae equum agrī oppugnat, et equus caprum pugnat. Equus caprum necat, et caper equum necat. Puella et
10 germānus bēstiās spectant, et dīvitiās ad villam portant. Fīnis.[3]

Glossary
1. *tragoedia*: tragedy
2. *nihil*: nothing [indeclinable noun]
3. *fīnis*: the end

A Tragedy of Beasts

A camel, a goat, and a horse are living on an island in the ocean. There is food on the island, and the horse gives food to the goat, the goat gives food to the camel, and the camel gives food to the horse. The horse dwells in a field, the goat in the forest, and the camel in a cave. Today, pirates sail to the island and carry money and riches into the cave. But the camel of cave tells nothing about the money and riches to the goat or the horse. The pirates sail away from the island, and the camel loves the wealth, and does not give food to the horse. The horse of the field and the goat of the forest walk to the cave and look at the camel's wealth. The anger of the horse and goat burns the camel of the cave, and they attack the camel with swords and kill [him]. They carry the wealth from the cave, but the goat carries [it] to the forest and the horse to the field. Therefore the goat of the forest attacks the horse of the field, and the horse fights the goat. The horse kills the goat and the goat kills the horse. A girl and [her] brother watch the beasts, and carry the wealth to [their] farmhouse. The end.

Lesson 4 Quiz (51 points)

A. Vocabulary (15 points)

Translate the following words and fill in the blanks. Give case(s) for prepositions.

1. today: **hodiē**
2. ad: (+ **acc.**) **to, toward**
3. badly: **male**
4. dē: (+ **abl.**) **from, down from, concerning**
5. into: **in** (+ **acc.**)
6. nunc: **now**
7. ex: (+ **abl.**) **out of, from**
8. sed: **but**
9. itaque: **and so, therefore**
10. through: **per (+ acc.)**
11. cūr: **why**
12. ā: (+ **abl.**) **from, away from**
13. bene: **well**
14. aut: **or**
15. in: **in** (+ **abl.**)

B. Grammar (15 points)

Decline *goat* in Latin.

	LATIN SINGULAR	LATIN PLURAL
NOMINATIVE	caper	caprī
GENITIVE	caprī	caprōrum
DATIVE	caprō	caprīs
ACCUSATIVE	caprum	caprōs
ABLATIVE	caprō	caprīs

C. Translation (14 points)

Translate each sentence into English.

1. The poet is the man's brother.

   Poēta germānus virī est.

2. Why does the farmer give food to the horse and not to the son?

   Cūr agricola equō sed nōn fīliō cibum dat?

D. Memorization (18 points)

Write out the first four lines of the Lord's Prayer in Latin.

Pater noster, quī es in caelīs,

Sanctificētur nōmen tuum. Adveniat regnum tuum.

Fīat voluntās tua, sīcut in caelō et in terrā.

Pānem nostrum quotīdiānum dā nōbīs hodiē,

LESSON 5 (Student Edition p. 36)

Second Declension Neuter

1. Word List

Now that the students will be working with two declensions (and three chants), you may want to ask them which declension each noun belongs to as you run through the word list. Ask them how they know (the answer is to look at the nominative *and* genitive, which basically starts you off on the correct chant). This lesson, of course, nearly all of them are second declension neuter, but it never hurts to spot-check.

2. Derivatives/Memorization Helps

1. *argentum*, silver, money: Ag (symbol for "silver" on the Periodic Table), Argentina
2. *aurum*, gold: Au (symbol for "gold" on the Periodic Table)
3. *auxilium*, help, aid: auxiliary
4. *caelum*, sky, heaven: celestial, ceiling
5. *castellum*, castle: castle
6. *crustulum*, cookie, small cake: crust (from the related word *crustum*)
7. *discipulus/discipula*, student [male/female], disciple, apprentice: disciple, discipline
8. *dōnum*, gift: donation
9. *ēvangelium*, good news, gospel: evangelism, evangelist
10. *fātum*, fate: fate, fatal, fatality
11. *gaudium*, joy, happiness: gaudy
12. *oppidum*, town
13. *perīculum*, danger: peril, perilous
14. *puer*, boy: puerile
15. *regnum*, kingdom: reign, regnal, regnant
16. *verbum*, word: verb, verbal, proverb
17. *vīnum*, wine: vine, vinegar, vintage, vinyl
18. *ibī*, there, at that place, then: memory help—some of my students came up with "I be there, you be where?" to remember *ibī* and *ubi*, "where" (Lesson 12).

19. *numquam*, never

20. *semper*, always: memory help—*semper fidelis,* "always faithful," is the motto of the Marine Corps.

3. Memorization—*Pater Noster*

The new line for this lesson is *et dīmitte nōbīs dēbita nostra:* "And forgive us our debts."

The word for "forgive" is from *dīmittō,* which comes from *dis + mittō,* literally "to send away, let go"—a wonderful metaphor for forgiveness! *Nōbīs* is the pronoun "us" (it's in the dative, in case you were wondering), and *nostra* is the possessive adjective "our." *Dēbitum* is a second declension neuter noun, and thus *dēbita* is the accusative plural. We get our word "*debit*" and related words from it.

4. Grammar

Second Declension Neuter Noun Endings:

The second declension neuter is happily just a simple variation of the second declension learned last lesson. Compare the two chants on the board and have the class point out the differences: nominative singular *-um* (not *-us/-r*), and nominative and accusative plurals ending in *-a* (not *-ī* and *-ōs,* respectively).

	LATIN SINGULAR	ENGLISH SINGULAR
NOMINATIVE	-um	a/the *noun* [subject]
GENITIVE	-ī	of the *noun,* the *noun's*
DATIVE	-ō	to/for the *noun*
ACCUSATIVE	-um	the *noun* [direct object]
ABLATIVE	-ō	by/with/from the *noun*

LATIN PLURAL	ENGLISH PLURAL
-a	the *nouns* [subject]
-ōrum	of the *nouns,* the *nouns'*
-īs	to/for the *nouns*
-a	the *nouns* [direct object]
-īs	by/with/from the *nouns*

I believe I may safely say that all second declension neuter nouns are neuter, although one can almost never say *never* or *always* when discussing language!

There are two rules of thumb for neuter nouns of any declension:

1. The nominative and accusative singular will be the same, and the nominative and accusative plural will be the same.

2. The plural nominative and accusative will end in *-a.* (There may well be exceptions to these, but that is why I am calling them rules of thumb and not the Law of the Medes and Persians.)

These rules work for third and fourth declension neuter nouns as well as second declension neuters.

Nouns in the second declension neuter decline and function like the other nouns we have studied. You must go to the genitive to find the stem before declining the noun. Several of these nouns have a stem ending in -i, which sometimes gives us a double -iī (as we have seen with the second masculine), which is not a problem. Here are a couple of examples, one with the double -iī action and one without.

	LATIN SINGULAR	LATIN PLURAL
NOMINATIVE	caelum	caela
GENITIVE	caelī	caelōrum
DATIVE	caelō	caelīs
ACCUSATIVE	caelum	caela
ABLATIVE	caelō	caelīs

	LATIN SINGULAR	LATIN PLURAL
NOMINATIVE	gaudium	gaudia
GENITIVE	gaudiī	gaudiōrum
DATIVE	gaudiō	gaudiīs
ACCUSATIVE	gaudium	gaudia
ABLATIVE	gaudiō	gaudiīs

Remind your students that nouns are born into their own particular declensions. Therefore, *gaudia* should *never* be taken as a nominative singular, because it is not a first declension noun and never will be. It was born second declension, and it was born neuter. (Therefore *gaudia* is either nominative or accusative plural.) This is one of the reasons why it is important to learn each noun's declension in addition to the meaning.

5. Worksheet

Follow the directions given to complete the worksheet.

6. Quiz

Administer Quiz 5 when the students are ready.

Lesson 5 Worksheet

A. Vocabulary

Translate the following words from Latin to English or English to Latin as appropriate. For each preposition, include the which case(s) it takes.

1. castellum: **castle**
2. food: **cibus**
3. always: **semper**
4. vīnum: **wine**
5. discipula: **student (female), disciple**
6. dē: (+ **abl.**) **from, down from, concerning**
7. joy: **gaudium**
8. ēvangelium: **good news, gospel**
9. fātum: **fate**
10. native land: **patria**
11. argentum: **silver, money**
12. there: **ibī**
13. crustulum: **cookie, small cake**
14. caelum: **sky, heaven**
15. aurum: **gold**
16. nunc: **now**
17. town: **oppidum**
18. verbum: **word**
19. aqua: **water**
20. perīculum: **danger**
21. gift: **dōnum**
22. numquam: **never**
23. boy: **puer**
24. auxilium: **help, aid**
25. kingdom: **regnum**

B. Grammar

Decline *dōnum*.

	LATIN SINGULAR	LATIN PLURAL
NOMINATIVE	dōnum	dōna
GENITIVE	dōnī	dōnōrum
DATIVE	dōnō	dōnīs
ACCUSATIVE	dōnum	dōna
ABLATIVE	dōnō	dōnīs

Identify the gender (Masc., Fem., or Neut.), number (Sg. or Pl.), and case (Nom., Gen., Dat., Acc., or Abl.) of each of the following nouns. Then translate them. If there is more than one option, give all possible answers. The first one is done for you as an example.

	NOUN	GENDER, NUMBER, CASE	TRANSLATION
1.	equōrum	Masc. Pl. Gen.	of the horses, the horses'
2.	oppidō	Neut. Sg. Dat. Neut. Sg. Abl.	to/for the town by/with/from the town
3.	fāta	Neut. Pl. Nom. Neut. Pl. Acc.	the fates (subject) the fates (direct object)
4.	fēminā	Fem. Sg. Abl.	by/with/from the woman
5.	auxilium	Neut. Sg. Nom. Neut. Sg. Acc.	help, aid (subject) help, aid (direct object)
6.	regnī	Neut. Sg. Gen.	of the kingdom, the kingdom's
7.	discipulās	Fem. Pl. Acc.	the [female] students (direct object)
8.	puerī	Masc. Sg. Gen. Masc. Pl. Nom.	of the boy, the boy's the boys (subject)

9.	vinōrum	Neut. Pl. Gen.	of the wines, the wines'
10.	terrae	Fem. Sg. Gen. Fem. Sg. Dat. Fem. Pl. Nom.	of the earth, the earth's to/for the earth/land the lands (subject)

Identify person, number, and tense of the following verbs and then translate them.

	VERB	PERSON	NUMBER	TENSE	TRANSLATION
11.	portāmus	1st	Pl.	Present	we carry
12.	sunt	3rd	Pl.	Present	they are
13.	nāvigō	1st	Sg.	Present	I sail
14.	necās	2nd	Sg.	Present	you kill
15.	oppugnant	3rd	Pl.	Present	they attack
16.	habitātis	2nd	Pl.	Present	you all live/dwell/inhabit
17.	estis	2nd	Pl.	Present	you all are
18.	laudāmus	1st	Pl.	Present	we praise
19.	clāmās	2nd	Sg.	Present	you shout
20.	est	3rd	Sg.	Present	he/she/it is

C. Memorization

Say the first five lines of the *Pater Noster* aloud a few times, then fill in the blanks from memory.

<u>Pater noster, quī es in caelīs,</u>

<u>Sanctificētur nōmen tuum. Adveniat regnum tuum.</u>

<u>Fīat voluntās tua, sīcut in caelō et in terrā.</u>

Pānem <u>**nostrum quotīdiānum**</u> dā <u>**nōbīs**</u> hodiē,

et <u>**dīmitte**</u> nōbīs <u>**dēbita**</u> nostra

D. English to Latin Translation

Translate each sentence from English to Latin.

1. God gives the kingdoms to Christ the Son of God.
   Deus Christō Fīliō Deī regna dat.

2. The pirates carry gold and silver and cookies away from the men.
   Pīrātae aurum et argentum et crustula ā/ab virīs portant.

3. Christ tells the words of the gospel to the crowds and the disciples.
   Christus turbīs et discipulīs verba ēvangeliī narrat.

4. We are queens and live in palaces, but you farmers never live in castles.
   Rēgīnae sumus et in rēgiīs habitāmus, sed agricolae in castellīs numquam habitātis.

5. The servants carry food and wines and cookies to the master's castle.
   Servī cibum et vina et crustula ad castellum dominī portant.

6. Christ is the Word of God and is Lord on earth and in heaven.
   Christus Verbum Deī est et Dominus in terrā et [in] caelō [est].

7. The sailors give gifts and help to the women, and there is joy in the town.
   Nautae fēminīs dōna et auxilium dant, et est gaudium in oppidō.

8. The boys always tell stories about the moon to the sister's camel.
   Puerī camēlō germānae fābulās dē lūnā semper narrant.

9. They praise and love gold and wealth, but you are servants of Christ.
   Aurum et dīvitiās laudant et amant, sed servī Christī estis.

10. You are the farmer's son and are now looking at the horses and goats in the field.
    Fīlius agricolae es et equōs et caprōs in agrō nunc spectās.

E. Latin to English Translation

1 Hodiē germānī et germānae in harēnā ad ōceanum ambulant. Crustula portant et gaudium amant. Sed alnus in ōceanō est, et pīrātae ad harēnam navigant. Germānae perīculum spectant et clāmant. Ōceanō crustula dant et ad oppidum festīnant.[1] Puerī perīculum semper amant et nōn festīnant. Pīrātās spectant. Pīrātae puerōs spectant. Pīrātae puerōs gladiīs oppugnant; puerī pīrātās verbīs pugnant. Pīrātae superant,
5 et puerī pīrātīs crustula dant. Interim,[2] germānae puerōrum ab oppidō festīnant et vīnum portant. Pīrātīs vīnum dant, et pīrātās vīnō superant. Germānī et germānae aurum et argentum ex alnō ad oppidum portant. Itaque nunc germānī auxilium germānārum amant et perīculum nōn amant.

Glossary
1. *festīnō* (1): I hurry, hasten
2. *interim*: meanwhile

Today brothers and sisters are walking on the beach toward the ocean. They are carrying cookies and love happiness. But there is a ship on the ocean, and pirates sail toward the beach. The sisters look at the danger and shout. They give [their] cookies to the ocean and hasten to the town. The boys always love danger and do not hasten. They look at the pirates. The pirates look at the boys. The pirates attack the boys with swords; the boys fight the pirates with words. The pirates conquer, and the boys give [their] cookies to the pirates. Meanwhile, the boys' sisters hasten from the town and are carrying wine. They give wine to the pirates and defeat the pirates with wine. The brothers and sisters carry gold and silver out of the ship to the town. Therefore now the brothers love [their] sisters' help and do not love danger.

Lesson 5 Quiz (61 points)

A. Vocabulary (10 points)

Translate the following words.

1. ēvangelium **good news, gospel**
2. dōnum **gift**
3. regnum **kingdom**
4. billy goat **caper**
5. sagitta **arrow**

6. numquam **never**
7. heaven **caelum**
8. gaudium **joy, happiness**
9. oppidum **town**
10. argentum **silver, money**

B. Grammar (20 points)

Decline *verbum* and *discipula*.

	LATIN SINGULAR	LATIN PLURAL
NOMINATIVE	verbum	verba
GENITIVE	verbī	verbōrum
DATIVE	verbō	verbīs
ACCUSATIVE	verbum	verba
ABLATIVE	verbō	verbīs

	LATIN SINGULAR	LATIN PLURAL
	discipula	discipulae
	discipulae	discipulārum
	discipulae	discipulīs
	discipulam	discipulās
	discipulā	discipulīs

C. Translation (11 points)

Translate each sentence.

1. Perīcula in villā discipulōrum semper sunt.

   There are always dangers in the students' farmhouse. [*or*, Dangers are always . . .]

2. Poēta puerīs fābulās dē fātō cantat.

   The poet sings tales to the boys about fate.

3. I am the master, you are the servant, and the horses are beasts.

   Dominus sum, servus/serva es, et equī bēstiae sunt.

D. Memorization (20 points)

Write out the first five lines of the Lord's Prayer in Latin.

Pater noster, quī es in caelīs,

Sanctificētur nōmen tuum. Adveniat regnum tuum.

Fīat voluntās tua, sīcut in caelō et in terrā.

Pānem nostrum quotīdiānum dā nōbīs hodiē,

et dīmitte nōbīs dēbita nostra

LESSON 6 (Student Edition p. 43)

Verbs: First Conjugation, Imperfect & Future Active Indicative / Principal Parts

1. Word List

Pay attention to the notes after words #1 *dea* and #2 *filia*. These two nouns are the feminine, first declension versions of *deus* and *filius*. Their special dative and ablative plural forms (*-ābus*) help to distinguish them from their second declension masculine counterparts. Otherwise, in the dative and ablative plural we would have *filiīs* and *filiīs*, *deīs* and *deīs*, and although context could be helpful in determining whether the masculine or feminine is meant, these unique forms make it much easier: *filiīs* (sons) versus *filiābus* (daughters); *deīs* (gods) versus *deābus* (goddesses).

2. Derivatives/Memorization Helps

1. *dea*, goddess: see *deus* (Lesson 4)
2. *fīlia*, daughter: see *fīlius* (Lesson 4)
3. *magister*, teacher (male): magistrate, magisterial, Mr. (mister), and see *magistra*
4. *magistra*, teacher (female): Mrs. (mistress)
5. *mundus*, world, universe: mundane
6. *nihil*, nothing, not at all: nihilist, annihilate
7. *saeculum*, generation; spirit of the age/times: secular, secularize
8. *cōgitō*, I think: cogitate
9. *creō*, I create: create, creation
10. *mandūcō*, I chew, eat: mandible
11. *occupō*, I seize: occupy, occupation
12. *ōrō*, I pray, speak: oration, orator, oracle
13. *pōtō*, I drink, drink heavily: potable
14. *regnō*, I rule, govern, reign: see *regnum* (Lesson 5)
15. *rogō*, I ask: interrogate, supererogatory
16. *servō*, I save: conserve, preserve (don't confuse with *servus*)

17. *ululō*, I howl, scream: ululate

18. *crās*, tomorrow: procrastinate

19. *herī*, yesterday: memory help—"I saw *Herī* yesterday" or "He was *herī* yesterday but shaved today."

20. *ōlim*, once upon a time, formerly, then

21. *saepe*, often: memory help—students may be tempted to confuse *saepe* with *semper*. Remind them of the Marine Corps motto, *semper fidelis*, and point out how silly it would be to have your motto be *saepe fidelis*, "Often faithful"!

3. Memorization—*Pater Noster*

The new line for this lesson is *sīcut et nōs dīmittimus dēbitōribus nostrīs*: "just as we also forgive our debtors."

This lesson's line is fairly similar to last lesson's, so make sure the students are keeping them straight.

4. Grammar

After several lessons of focusing on nouns, it's high time to add to our verb knowledge. Besides, stories told solely in the present can get wearisome. This lesson, students will learn two more tenses: the imperfect and the future.

Imperfect Active Indicative Verb Endings

	SINGULAR	PLURAL
1ST	-bam	-bāmus
2ND	-bās	-bātis
3RD	-bat	-bant

The present, imperfect, and future are the three tenses in the present system; that is, they are all formed off of the present stem. See if your students remember how to find the present stem: go to the infinitive (second principal part) and take off the *-re*. To this stem you add the present endings for the present tense, imperfect endings for the imperfect, and the future endings for the future.

Start with the imperfect. Go through the chant a few times orally and point out that even though this is a new chant, the standard endings are present: *-m, -s, -t, -mus, -tis, -nt*. (Also, if you are not yet fully confident in your pronunciation, the *-bam* is pronounced more like English "bomb" and not like the sound effect "bam!") Let's go back to the sample verb we used in Lesson 1: *necō, necāre, necāvī, necātum*. Have the class identify the verb's present stem and then conjugate it in the imperfect.

If you went over all the tenses briefly on the first day of class, see if anyone remembers the definition of the imperfect tense. While the present tense describes action occurring in the here and now, the imperfect shows continuous or incomplete action in the past. It can be translated in a number of ways: *necābam* could mean "I was killing," "I killed," "I used to kill," "I kept on killing," "I would kill," and so forth—any variation that depicts this sort of action. This is why it is named *imperfect*—in grammar, a perfect action is a completed one. Here is *necō* conjugated in full in the imperfect active indicative: *necābam, necābās, necābat, necābāmus, necābātis, necābant*.

LATIN SINGULAR	ENGLISH SINGULAR	LATIN PLURAL	ENGLISH PLURAL
necābam	I was killing	necābāmus	we were killing
necābās	you were killing	necābātis	you (pl.) were killing
necābat	he/she/it was killing	necābant	they were killing

The time is also ripe to introduce the hero of our text: *Oswaldus* (this name is second declension masculine). It is helpful to use the same or similar words to introduce new concepts—this way the students are only faced with the new concept and not new vocabulary or scenarios at the same time. I would also like to introduce dragons, but am unable to until the third declension comes along. In the meantime, we will have to use the generic "beasts." The sentence *Oswaldus bēstiās necābat* can be translated a number of ways. Perhaps the simplest is "Oswald was killing beasts." This conveys continuous action and allows us to wonder if perhaps he is still on that job.

Context will once again be helpful to us. If we are translating a story about the childhood of Oswald and this sentence appears, we could also translate **necābat** in the following ways:

"[When he was a child,] Oswald *would kill* dragons." Notice this use of the flexible English word "would." In this context, the "would" perfectly expresses the imperfect. In other contexts it can express a polite request ("Would you please pass the salt?") or a hypothetical ("I wouldn't do that if I were you!").

"[When he was a child,] Oswald *used to kill* dragons." This translation could read two ways: either Oswald used to kill dragons and doesn't anymore, or simply he had a habit of killing them in the past and still could be doing that today. The rest of the story would provide us with a context.

[When he was a child,] Oswald killed dragons. The English "killed" is ambiguous. It can express the continual, habitual action of the imperfect (an added adverb such as *often* would make this more clear). In another context, *killed* can translate a perfect or completed action: "When Oswald was six years old he killed his first dragon." That sentence is describing a one-time, completed event and would be rendered better by the Latin perfect.

Here are two more example verbs conjugated in the imperfect. As with the *necō* chant above, I have only given one English translation; encourage your students to come up with other possible translations and example sentences so that they can get used to the variety of translations. (Logic-stage students sometimes have a tough time with accepting multiple options and gray areas of translation.)

pugnō, -āre, -āvī, -ātum

	LATIN SINGULAR	ENGLISH SINGULAR	LATIN PLURAL	ENGLISH PLURAL
1ST	pugnābam	I was fighting	pugnābāmus	we were fighting
2ND	pugnābās	you were fighting	pugnābātis	you (pl.) were fighting
3RD	pugnābat	he/she/it was fighting	pugnābant	they were fighting

habitō, -āre, -āvī, -ātum

	LATIN SINGULAR	ENGLISH SINGULAR	LATIN PLURAL	ENGLISH PLURAL
1ST	habitābam	I was living	habitābāmus	we were living
2ND	habitābās	you were living	habitābātis	you (pl.) were living
3RD	habitābat	he/she/it was living	habitābant	they were living

Future Active Indicative Verb Endings

The future tense shows time in the future, obviously. In English we have several ways to express the future: *Oswald will kill the dragon. Oswald is about to kill the dragon. Oswald is going to kill the dragon. Oswald will be killing the dragon.* Any of these translations will work, provided of course that they work in their context. For our purposes, however, the first option is the simplest and will be the most commonly used in this book.

To conjugate a verb in the Future Active, simply add these new endings to the present stem:

	SINGULAR	PLURAL
1ST	-bō	-bimus
2ND	-bis	-bitis
3RD	-bit	-bunt

Here are our three example verbs from above conjugated in the future active indicative:

	LATIN SINGULAR	ENGLISH SINGULAR	LATIN PLURAL	ENGLISH PLURAL
1ST	necābō	I will kill	necābimus	we will kill
2ND	necābis	you will kill	necābitis	you (pl.) will kill
3RD	necābit	he/she/it will kill	necābunt	they will kill

	LATIN SINGULAR	ENGLISH SINGULAR
1ST	pugnābō	I will fight
2ND	pugnābis	you will fight
3RD	pugnābit	he/she/it will fight

	LATIN PLURAL	ENGLISH PLURAL
	pugnābimus	we will fight
	pugnābitis	you (pl.) will fight
	pugnābunt	they will fight

	LATIN SINGULAR	ENGLISH SINGULAR
1ST	habitābō	I will live
2ND	habitābis	you will live
3RD	habitābit	he/she/it will live

	LATIN PLURAL	ENGLISH PLURAL
	habitābimus	we will live
	habitābitis	you (pl.) will live
	habitābunt	they will live

Although it might go without saying, imperfect and future active verbs function just like present tense verbs: their subjects are in the nominative, they take accusative direct objects, etc.

Verb Synopses

Now you can also teach your students how to do synopses. A verb synopsis is one of the Latin teacher's favorite tools because it requires students to know all the verb endings and go through them all mentally to pull the correct forms out (and you only have to grade a handful of forms and not a full verb conjugation!). It's also one of the students' least favorite activities because they have to know all the verb endings and go through them all mentally to pull the correct forms out.

A **synopsis** is just that—*a summary of a verb*. Basically, you ask your students for a summary of a verb in a specific person and number for all the tenses, voices, and moods they have learned up to this point. At this point, you could ask your students for *necō* in the first person singular in present, imperfect, and future active. They would then list: *necō, necābam,* and *necābō*. You can also ask them to translate the forms. Here are a few example synopses:

Necō: second person plural

	LATIN	ENGLISH
PRESENT ACT.	necātis	you (pl.) kill
IMPERFECT ACT.	necābātis	you (pl.) were killing
FUTURE ACT.	necābitis	you (pl.) will kill

Pugnō: first person plural

	LATIN	ENGLISH
PRESENT ACT.	pugnāmus	we fight
IMPERFECT ACT.	pugnābāmus	we were fighting
FUTURE ACT.	pugnābimus	we will fight

Habitō: third person singular

	LATIN	ENGLISH
PRESENT ACT.	habitat	he/she/it lives
IMPERFECT ACT.	habitābat	he/she/it was living
FUTURE ACT.	habitābit	he/she/it will live

Verb synopses are an excellent exercise for students in the logic stage in particular, because it requires them to think in a new way about the verb forms they have memorized. They can see these forms together in a new context and make new mental connections. And you can warn them right now that practically every quiz and test from here on out will have a synopsis on it. That way they have no excuse for complaining or for being unprepared!

4. Memorization—*Pater Noster*

The new line for this week is *sīcut et nōs dīmittimus dēbitōribus nostrīs*: "just as we also forgive our debtors."

This week's line is fairly similar to last week's, so make sure the students are keeping them straight.

5. Worksheet

Follow the directions given to complete the worksheet.

E. *Litterae Mixtae*: This extra assignment will be a fun way to see how good your students are at recognizing the vocabulary and endings they've just learned. Remind them that macrons can be a good way to determine which vowels go where!

6. Quiz

Administer Quiz 6 when the students are ready.

Lesson 6 Worksheet

A. Vocabulary

Translate the following words from Latin to English or English to Latin as appropriate. For the verbs, also fill in the missing principal parts. For each preposition, include which case(s) it takes.

1. magister: **teacher (male)**
2. semper: **always**
3. saepe: **often**
4. I howl: **ululō**, **ululāre**, **ululāvī**, **ululātum**
5. fābula: **story, legend, tale**
6. through: (+ **acc.**) **per**
7. nihil: **nothing**; (adv.) **not at all**
8. cōgitō, **cōgitāre**, **cōgitāvī**, cōgitātum: **I think**
9. mandūcō, **mandūcāre**, **mandūcāvī**, **mandūcātum**: **I chew, eat**
10. once upon a time: **ōlim**
11. I seize: **occupō**, **occupāre**, **occupāvī**, **occupātum**
12. male: **badly, ill, wrongly**
13. daughter: **fīlia**
14. ōrō, **ōrāre**, **ōrāvī**, **ōrātum**: **I pray, speak**
15. herī: **yesterday**
16. pōtō, **pōtāre**, pōtāvī, **pōtātum** *or* pōtum: **I drink, drink heavily**
17. creō, creāre, **creāvī**, **creātum**: **I create**
18. regnō, **regnāre**, **regnāvī**, regnātum: **I rule, govern, reign**
19. goddess: **dea**
20. servō, **servāre**, **servāvī**, **servātum**: **I save**
21. servus: **slave, servant**
22. rogō, rogāre, **rogāvī**, rogātum: **I ask**
23. tomorrow: **crās**
24. saeculum: **generation; spirit of the age/times**
25. world: **mundus**

B. Grammar

1. Conjugate and translate *sum* in the present active indicative.

	LATIN SINGULAR	ENGLISH SINGULAR
1ST	sum	I am
2ND	es	you are
3RD	est	he/she/it is

	LATIN PLURAL	ENGLISH PLURAL
	sumus	we are
	estis	you (pl.) are
	sunt	they are

2. Conjugate and translate *ōrō* in the imperfect active indicative.

	LATIN SINGULAR	ENGLISH SINGULAR
1ST	ōrābam	I was praying
2ND	ōrābās	you were praying
3RD	ōrābat	he/she/it was praying

	LATIN PLURAL	ENGLISH PLURAL
	ōrābāmus	we were praying
	ōrābātis	you (pl.) were praying
	ōrābant	they were praying

3. Conjugate and translate *mandūcō* in the future active indicative.

	LATIN SINGULAR	ENGLISH SINGULAR
1ST	mandūcābō	I will eat
2ND	mandūcābis	you will eat
3RD	mandūcābit	he/she/it will eat

	LATIN PLURAL	ENGLISH PLURAL
	mandūcābimus	we will eat
	mandūcābitis	you (pl.) will eat
	mandūcābunt	they will eat

4. Give a synopsis of *servō* in the second person singular.

	LATIN	ENGLISH
PRESENT ACT.	servās	you save
IMPERFECT ACT.	servābās	you were saving
FUTURE ACT.	servābis	you will save

5. Give a synopsis of *rogō* in the third person plural.

	LATIN	ENGLISH
PRESENT ACT.	rogant	they ask
IMPERFECT ACT.	rogābant	they were asking
FUTURE ACT.	rogābunt	they will ask

C. Memorization

Say the first six lines of the *Pater Noster* aloud a few times, then fill in the blanks from memory.

Pater noster, quī es in caelīs,

Sanctificētur nōmen tuum. Adveniat regnum tuum.

Fīat voluntās tua, sīcut in caelō et in terrā.

Pānem **nostrum quotīdiānum** dā **nōbīs** hodiē,

et **dīmitte** nōbīs **dēbita nostra**

sīcut et nōs **dīmittimus** dēbitoribus **nostrīs**.

D. English to Latin Translation

Translate each sentence from English to Latin.

1. The pirates were often eating food and drinking wine and seizing gold.

    Pīrātae cibum [saepe] mandūcābant et vīnum [saepe] pōtābant et aurum saepe occupābant.

2. Tomorrow you students will summon the teacher and ask about fate and the gospel.

    Discipulī/discipulae magistrum/magistram crās vocābitis et dē fātō et ēvangeliō rogābitis.

3. The daughter was praying to God then for help and He will give the daughter joy.

    Fīlia Deum auxilium ōlim ōrābat et fīliae gaudium dabit.

4. Yesterday I was thinking about the world and the ocean and the moon.

    Dē mundō et ōceanō et lūnā herī cōgitābam.

5. We are the queen's servants and will give cookies to the sons and daughters.

   <u>Servī rēgīnae sumus et fīliīs et fīliābus crustula dabimus.</u>

6. A beast was killing the farmers' horses and goats in the fields yesterday, and so the farmers will wait for the beast tomorrow and will attack [it] with swords.

   <u>Bēstia equōs et caprōs agricolārum in agrīs herī necābat, itaque agricolae bēstiam crās exspectābunt et gladiīs oppugnābunt.</u>

7. The sailors and pirates were drinking heavily in the town and fighting with daggers.

   <u>Nautae et pīrātae in oppidō pōtābant et sīcīs pugnābant.</u>

8. Tomorrow the brothers will carry food and cookies into the cave and they will eat in the cave.

   <u>Germānī cibum et crustula in spēluncam crās portābunt et in spēluncā mandūcābunt.</u>

9. The women were singing tales to the boys and girls and so the beasts were howling.

   <u>Fēminae puerīs et puellīs fābulās cantābant itaque bēstiae ululābant.</u>

10. God was creating the world and the ocean and is giving [them] to the man and the woman.

    <u>Deus mundum et ōceanum creābat et virō et fēminae dat.</u>

E. Latin to English Translation

1   Ōlim erat[1] rēgīna, et oppida terrae regnābat. In castellō habitābat et crustula mandūcābat et vīnum semper ibī pōtābat. Erat pīrāta, et rēgīnam amābat sed pīrātam nōn amābat. Agricolam amābat, sed rēgīnam nōn amābat. Fēmīnās numquam amābat, sed agrōs et villam amābat. Herī pīrāta ab alnō in harēnā ad castellum ambulābat, et rēgīnae, "Tē[2] amō," narrābat. "Tibī[3] aurum et corōnās dabō. Mē[4]
5   amābis?" rogābat. Rēgīna pīrātae, "Numquam," narrābat, "tē amābō. Nihil mihi[5] dabis. Agricolam semper amābō." Itaque pīrāta rēgīnam occupābat et ad alnum portābat. Rēgīna ululābat et clamābat. Erat nauta in harēnā, et pīrātam gladiō et īrā oppugnābat. Nauta pīrātam superābat et rēgīnam servābat. Nunc rēgīna nautam amat. Et rēgīnam et crustula et vīnum amat, itaque in castellō habitābunt et feliciter in aeternum[6] mandūcābunt.

Glossary
1. *erat*: third person singular imperfect of *sum*: he/she/it was, there was
2. *tē*: you (accusative form of *tū*, second person singular pronoun)
3. *tibī*: dative form of *tū*
4. *mē*: accusative form of *ego*, first person singular pronoun: I, me
5. *mihi*: dative form of *ego*
6. *feliciter in aeternum*: happily ever after

Once upon a time there was a queen, and she was ruling the towns of the land. She lived in a castle and always ate cookies and drank wine there. There was a pirate and he loved the queen, but she was not loving the pirate. She was loving a farmer, but he did not love the queen. He was never loving women, but loved [his] fields and farmhouse. Yesterday the pirate walked from his ship on the beach to the castle, and told the queen: "I love you. I will give you gold and crowns. Will you love me?" he was asking. The queen told the pirate, "I will never love you. You will give me nothing. I will always love the farmer." The pirate therefore seized the queen and carried [her] to [his] ship. The queen screamed and shouted. There was a sailor on the beach, and he attacked the pirate with a sword and anger. The sailor overcame the pirate and saved the queen. Now the queen loves the sailor. He also loves the queen and cookies and wine, and so they will live in [her] castle and eat happily ever after.

F. For Fun: *Litterae Mixtae*

Unscramble the letters to form a Latin verb, then translate it into English.

	UNSCRAMBLE	LATIN VERB	ENGLISH TRANSLATION
1.	istulbiālu	**ululābitis**	you (pl.) will howl
2.	macōūnd	**mandūcō**	I eat
3.	āstorgibā	**rogābātis**	you (pl.) were asking
4.	ōbrāsumā	**ōrābamus**	we were praying
5.	stābipo	**potābis**	you will drink
6.	tācōbagit	**cōgitābat**	he was thinking
7.	catucop	**occupat**	he seizes
8.	trāvesanb	**servābant**	they were saving
9.	nārseg	**regnās**	you rule
10.	unbrācet	**creābunt**	they will create

Lesson 6 Quiz (58 points)

A. Vocabulary (10 points)

Translate the following words.

1. mundus: **world, universe**
2. I create: **creō**
3. ōrō: **I pray, speak**
4. rēgia: **palace**
5. regnō: **I rule, govern, reign**
6. rēgīna: **queen**
7. regnum: **kingdom**
8. equus: **horse**
9. rogō: **I ask**
10. sagitta: **arrow**

B. Grammar (15 points)

1. Decline *saeculum*.

	LATIN SINGULAR	LATIN PLURAL
NOM.	saeculum	saecula
GEN.	saeculī	saeculōrum
DAT.	saeculō	saeculīs
ACC.	saeculum	saecula
ABL.	saeculō	saeculīs

2. Give a synopsis of *pōtō* in the first person plural.

	LATIN	ENGLISH
PRESENT ACT.	pōtāmus	we drink
IMPERFECT ACT.	pōtābāmus	we were drinking
FUTURE ACT.	pōtābimus	we will drink

C. Translation (11 points)

Translate each sentence.

1. The teacher was giving nothing to the pirates and sailors.

    <u>Magister/Magistra pīrātīs et nautīs nihil dabat.</u>

2. Sunt deae in caelō et terram saepe spectābunt.

    <u>There are goddesses in heaven [*or,* goddesses are in heaven] and they often will watch the earth.</u>

3. Crustula mandūcābat et fīliābus fābulās nunc narrābit.

    <u>He/She was eating cookies and will now tell stories to the daughters [*or,* tell the daughters stories].</u>

D. Memorization (22 points)

Write out the first six lines of the Lord's Prayer in Latin.

<u>Pater noster, quī es in caelīs,</u>

<u>Sanctificētur nōmen tuum. Adveniat regnum tuum.</u>

<u>Fīat voluntās tua, sīcut in caelō et in terrā.</u>

<u>Pānem nostrum quotīdiānum dā nōbīs hodiē,</u>

<u>et dīmitte nōbīs dēbita nostra</u>

<u>sīcut et nōs dīmittimus dēbitōribus nostrīs.</u>

UNIT ONE \\ LESSON 7

Lesson 7 (Student Edition p. 53)

Adjectives

1. Word List

The word list this lesson only has adjectives in it! Most have familiar English derivatives, so learning them should not be too difficult. Note that *paucī* only declines in the plural (which makes sense, because *few* is more than one by definition).

2. Derivatives/Memorization Helps

1. *antīquus*, ancient: antique, antiquity
2. *avārus*, greedy: avarice
3. *beātus*, happy, blessed: beatify, Beatitudes, Beatrice
4. *bonus*, good: bonafide, bonus
5. *caldus*, warm, hot, fiery: cauldron, caldera
6. *ferus*, fierce, wild: feral
7. *fīdus*, faithful, trustworthy: see *fīdēs* [Lesson 28]
8. *foedus*, horrible, ugly
9. *iūstus*, just, right, fair, impartial, righteous: just, justice
10. *laetus*, happy, joyful, glad: the name Letitia (perhaps from related noun laetitia)
11. *longinquus*, distant, far away
12. *magnus*, large, big, great: magnitude, magnify
13. *malus*, bad, evil: malice: mal(e)- as a prefix on words like malevolent, malefactor
14. *mīrus*, strange, wonderful: admire, miraculous
15. *miser*, unhappy, wretched, miserable: misery, miserable
16. *multus*, much, many: multitude
17. *parvus*, little, small, unimportant: parvovirus
18. *paucī*, few: paucity
19. *pulcher*, beautiful, handsome: pulchritude
20. *stultus*, foolish: stultify

3. Memorization—*Pater Noster*

The new line for this lesson is *Et nē nōs indūcās in tentātiōnem, sed līberā nōs ā malō. Āmēn.* "And do not lead us into temptation, but deliver us from evil. Amen."

Notice that the conclusion of the Latin *Pater Noster* does not include the doxology we are used to saying in English: "For Thine is the kingdom and the power and the glory forever and ever. Amen."

4. Grammar

First and Second Declension Adjectives

Happily, the Romans were linguistic recycling fiends. Thus, even though your students technically have a new chant to learn this lesson, point out that they have already learned all of these endings. The masculine column follows the second declension masculine, the feminine column the first declension, and the neuter the second declension neuter. In this text, I will not ask the students to write out the adjective endings in a separate chart, but rather they will have to decline an adjective alongside a noun.

Begin by discussing what an adjective is and does: it modifies a noun or pronoun. In Latin, this means that the adjective will match the noun in all three of its attributes: gender, number, and case. That is, if you have a feminine singular ablative noun, you will need to put the adjective in the feminine, singular, and ablative as well. *Very important note:* **An adjective matches the noun it modifies in gender, number, and case—***not necessarily* **in declension.** Drill this into your students' heads! As an example, see the declension of "good sailor" below.

Notice that the Word List/dictionary listing of adjectives differs from that of nouns. An adjective is listed as masculine nominative, followed by feminine nominative, and then neuter nominative. You still find the stem by going to the second form—with nouns the second form is the genitive; with adjectives it is the feminine nominative. (It's easy to remember to go to the second form for the stem because it works for verbs as well as nouns and adjectives!)

Here are a few examples to clarify. First off, let's decline "good servant." Always start with the noun, since that is the word that the adjective must match. *Servus* is masculine; therefore, we select the masculine form of the adjective *bonus, -a, -um*.

The stem of *bonus* is simply *bon-*. Thus, our phrase "good servant" will be declined as follows:

	LATIN SINGULAR	LATIN PLURAL
NOM.	servus bonus	servī bonī
GEN.	servī bonī	servōrum bonōrum
DAT.	servō bonō	servīs bonīs
ACC.	servum bonum	servōs bonōs
ABL.	servō bonō	servīs bonīs

Many adjectives, unless the author wishes to emphasize them, will follow the noun they modify. However, having the adjective precede the noun is common enough that you should not mark students down for using that order. Notice how within each phrase the adjective matches its noun in gender, number, and case. With the phrase *servus bonus* they also happen to match in declension, but that is only coincidence.

Now we will decline "good sailor." Our noun, *nauta,* is masculine; therefore, we choose *bonus* again. The phrase will decline as follows:

	LATIN SINGULAR	LATIN PLURAL
NOM.	nauta bonus	nautae bonī
GEN.	nautae bonī	nautārum bonōrum
DAT.	nautae bonō	nautīs bonīs
ACC.	nautam bonum	nautās bonōs
ABL.	nautā bonō	nautīs bonīs

Each of these phrases match in gender, number, and case, but obviously they do not look alike—they do not match in declension. But remember our *very important note* above—*they do not need to match in declension.* Declension is irrelevant (in this context)!

Students will inevitably make one of two classic errors when faced with a phrase such as this. The first is that they will use the feminine adjective *bona,* and decline *nauta bona, nautae bonae,* and so on. This is what I call "putting girl clothes on a boy" (or vice versa, depending on the circumstances). Adjectives are the clothes, and although in our day and age it is difficult to tell sometimes which are guy clothes and which are girl clothes, hopefully your students will get the point. They have just made the poor sailor into a cross-dresser by clothing him in a feminine adjective.

The other error is to rip *nauta* out of the family into which he was born (the first declension) and attempt to reinstate him as a second declension noun: *nautus bonus, nautī bonī,* etc. However, *nauta* was born first declension and will always be first declension. He cannot be made into a second declension noun on the whim of a student. In order to help your students get over the mental block that prevents them from the correct phrase *nauta bonus,* make sure they decline the whole phrase, both words together, down the columns. They absolutely should *not* decline *nauta* all the way down, and then go back and fill in the forms for *bonus.* Have them write *nauta bonus,* then *nautae bonī,* then *nautae bonō,* and so on. Their logic-stage brains will profit from the exercise!

One more minor note before we leave the masculine noun-adjective combos and move on to the feminine and neuter: just as second declension masculine nouns can end in *-us* or *-r* in the nominative, so can some of these adjectives. Point out to the class *miser* and *pulcher* in the vocabulary list and have them find the stems. For *miser,* since the second form is *misera,* that means the stem is *miser-*. However, for *pulcher* the stem is *pulchr-* (dropping that *-e-*), because we must go to the second form, which is the feminine nominative *pulchra.* Thus, "handsome sailor" would decline *nauta pulcher, nautae pulchrī, nautae pulchrō,* etc.

Let's stick with our adjective "good" as we decline a feminine and then a neuter noun. "Good daughter" is declined as follows (since *filia* is feminine, we select the feminine adjective):

	LATIN SINGULAR	LATIN PLURAL
NOM.	filia bona	filiae bonae
GEN.	filiae bonae	filiārum bonārum
DAT.	filiae bonae	filiīs bonīs
ACC.	filiam bonam	filiās bonās
ABL.	filiā bonā	filiīs bonīs

These two happen to match in declension, but remember, that is not the important thing. They must match in gender, number, and case.

Although most second declension nouns are masculine, we have been using a feminine one: *alnus,* ship, alder (wood). Since it is feminine, we must again use the feminine adjective *bona.* We must *not* use *bonus,* because they would not match: we would be putting boy clothes on the girl. We also must *not* try to take *alnus* out of the second declension and try to make it into a first declension noun *alna,* because it was born second declension and so shall remain. The correct declension of "good ship" is as follows:

	LATIN SINGULAR	LATIN PLURAL
NOM.	alnus bona	alnī bonae
GEN.	alnī bonae	alnōrum bonārum
DAT.	alnō bonae	alnīs bonīs
ACC.	alnum bonam	alnōs bonās
ABL.	alnō bonā	alnīs bonīs

Finally, we will decline "good kingdom." Since *regnum* is neuter, we must use the neuter form of the adjective *bonus, -a, -um*:

	LATIN SINGULAR	LATIN PLURAL
NOM.	regnum bonum	regna bona
GEN.	regnī bonī	regnōrum bonōrum
DAT.	regnō bonō	regnīs bonīs
ACC.	regnum bonum	regna bona
ABL.	regnō bonō	regnīs bonīs

Here *regnum* and *bonum* do match in declension (and, to my knowledge, this will happen with all second declension neuter nouns and second declension neuter adjectives)—but of course the important thing is that they match in gender, number, and case.

Predicate Adjectives

When adjectives are used with the verb *sum,* they will also match the noun or pronoun they modify in gender, number, and case. We have already touched on this with nouns. When you say, "The queen is a woman," *queen* and *woman* are linked by the verb *is*, and are therefore both in the nominative. Similarly, if we have "The queen is good," we are saying that the *queen=good*, and therefore *good* needs to match in gender, number, and case: *Rēgīna bona est* (not *bonam*).

A final note on translating adjectives: Since the Romans did not use commas, they often employed *et* when using multiple adjectives to describe one noun. Thus *puer bonus et fīdus* literally means "the good and faithful boy," but you could also omit the *et* in your translation: "the good, faithful boy."

Adjective Agreement

When you have a plural subject of mixed gender, things get a little interesting. If it is a group of males and females, then the adjective will be masculine plural. I call this the "generic masculine"—similar to older and now politically incorrect English usage where we could refer to men and women as "mankind." (Think of the slang usage of "guys" to refer to males and females—"How are you guys doing?")

Here is an example sentence of how this would play out in Latin: "The men and women are good." *Virī et fēminae bonī sunt*. If you have a group of females and inanimate objects (if for some reason you wanted to say "The women and the towns are beautiful"), then the adjective will agree with the animate noun, the women: *Fēminae et oppida pulchrae sunt*.

5. Worksheet

Follow the directions given to complete the worksheet.

6. Quiz

Administer Quiz 7 when the students are ready.

Lesson 7 Worksheet

A. Vocabulary

Translate the following words from Latin to English or English to Latin as appropriate. For each preposition, include which case(s) it takes.

1. bonus, bona, bonum: **good**
2. handsome: **pulcher, pulchra, pulchrum**
3. ferus, fera, ferum: **fierce, wild**
4. danger: **perīculum**
5. multus, multa, multum: **much, many**
6. beātus, beāta, beātum: **happy, blessed**
7. antīquus, antīqua, antīquum: **ancient**
8. ugly: foedus, foeda, **foedum**
9. or: **aut**
10. malus, mala, malum: **bad, evil**
11. often: **saepe**
12. iūstus, iūsta, iūstum: **just, right, fair, impartial, righteous**
13. happy: **laetus, laeta, laetum**
14. miser, misera, miserum: **unhappy, wretched, miserable**
15. mīrus, mīra, mīrum: **strange, wonderful**
16. distant: **longinquus, longinqua, longinquum**
17. out of: **ex (+ abl.)**
18. faithful: **fīdus, fīda, fīdum**
19. magnus, magna, magnum: **large, big, great**
20. small: **parvus, parva, parvum**
21. caldus, calda, caldum: **warm, hot, fiery**
22. yesterday: **herī**
23. few: **paucī, paucae, pauca**
24. avārus, avāra, avārum: **greedy**
25. foolish: **stultus, stulta, stultum**

B. Grammar

1. Decline *happy farmer.*

	LATIN SINGULAR	LATIN PLURAL
NOM.	agricola laetus	agricolae laetī
GEN.	agricolae laetī	agricolārum laetōrum
DAT.	agricolae laetō	agricolīs laetīs
ACC.	agricolam laetum	agricolās laetōs
ABL.	agricolā laetō	agricolīs laetīs

2. Decline *beautiful sister.*

	LATIN SINGULAR	LATIN PLURAL
NOM.	germāna pulchra	germānae pulchrae
GEN.	germānae pulchrae	germānārum pulchrārum
DAT.	germānae pulchrae	germānīs pulchrīs
ACC.	germānam pulchram	germānās pulchrās
ABL.	germānā pulchrā	germānīs pulchrīs

3. Decline *fiery danger.*

	LATIN SINGULAR	LATIN PLURAL
NOM.	perīculum caldum	perīcula calda
GEN.	perīculī caldī	perīculōrum caldōrum
DAT.	perīculō caldō	perīculīs caldīs
ACC.	perīculum caldum	perīcula calda
ABL.	perīculō caldō	perīculīs caldīs

C. Memorization

Fill in the blanks from memory. (You should know most of this by now, so only a few hints!)

<u>Pater noster, quī es in caelīs,</u>

<u>Sanctificētur nōmen tuum. Adveniat regnum tuum.</u>

<u>Fīat voluntās tua, sīcut in caelō et in terrā.</u>

<u>Pānem nostrum quotīdiānum dā nōbīs hodiē,</u>

<u>et dīmitte nōbīs dēbita nostra</u>

sīcut <u>et nōs</u> dīmittimus <u>dēbitoribus nostrīs</u>.

Et <u>nē</u> nōs <u>indūcās</u> in <u>tentātiōnem, sed</u> līberā <u>nōs</u> ā <u>malō. Āmēn</u>.

D. English to Latin Translation

Translate each sentence from English to Latin.

1. The queen's castle is ancient and beautiful, and many men and women live in the castle.
   <u>Castellum rēgīnae antīquum et pulchrum est, et multī virī et fēminae in castellō habitant.</u>

2. A farmer and son were living in a distant land in an ugly farmhouse.
   <u>Agricola et fīlius in terrā/patriā longinquā in villā foedā habitābant.</u>

3. The male and female students are good, and so the just teacher will now give cookies to the boys and girls.
   <u>Discipulī et discipulae bonī sunt, itaque magister iūstus [*or* magistra iūsta] puerīs et puellīs crustula nunc dabit.</u>

4. We are beautiful women, but you are ugly pirates.
   <u>Fēminae pulchrae sumus, sed pīrātae foedī estis.</u>

5. You (sg.) were thinking then about the wretched sailor's small goat.
   <u>Dē caprō parvō nautae miserī ibī/ōlim cōgitābās.</u>

6. The horrible beasts are fierce, and a few men will attack the beasts with spears and arrows.
   <u>Bēstiae foedae sunt ferae, et paucī virī bēstiās hastīs et sagittīs oppugnābunt.</u>

7. The foolish sisters were carrying food through the ancient forest, and now they are not happy.

   Germānae stultae cibum per silvam antīquam portābant, et nunc laetae nōn sunt.

8. I am the master of many servants, and will give nothing to the greedy and wicked servants.

   Dominus multōrum servōrum sum, et servīs avarīs et malīs nihil dabō.

9. The small brother was fighting the big pirate well with bad words and an ancient sword.

   Germānus parvus pīrātam magnum verbīs malīs et gladiō antīquō bene pugnābat.

10. Christ's disciples are blessed and will always praise the good words of God.

    Discipulī Christī sunt beātī et verba bona Deī semper laudābunt.

E. Latin to English Translation

1   Ōlim multī virī et fēminae, puerī et puellae, in īnsulā longinquā in mediō[1] ōceanō habitābant. Poetae fābulās dē camēlō antīquō et malō semper narrābant et cantābant. In fābulīs, camēlus in spēluncā foedā in mediā īnsulā habitābat, et parvōs puerōs et puellās mandūcābat. Itaque, puerī et puellae in silvam in mediā īnsulā numquam ambulābant. Nauta stultus oppidō magna verba ōrābat: "Nōn est
5   camēlus in spēluncā in mediā īnsulā! Ambulābō in silvam et mē[2] exspectābitis. Mihi[3] multum aurum dabitis!" Itaque equus nautae stultī nautam in mediam īnsulam portābat. Nauta spēluncam foedam spectābat. Nauta stultus et equus camēlum antīquum et malum spectābant! Ē spēluncā ambulābat. Nauta stultus ululābat. Equus iūstus camēlō nautam avārum et stultum dabat, et ā silvā ad oppidum ambulābat. Nunc multī poētae fīliīs et fīliābus oppidī fābulās dē nautā stultō, equō iūstō, et camēlō
10 malō narrābant.

Glossary
1. *medius, -a, -um*: middle (of), midst (of)
2. *mē*: accusative form of *ego*, first person singular pronoun: I, me
3. *mihi*: dative form of *ego*

Once upon a time, many men and women, boys and girls, were living on a distant island in the midst of the ocean. Poets were always telling and singing tales about an ancient and wicked camel. In the stories, the camel lived in a horrible cave in the middle of the island, and ate little boys and girls. Therefore, the boys and girls never walked into the forest in the middle of the island. A foolish sailor spoke great words to the town: "There is not a camel [or There is no camel] in a cave in the middle of the island! I will walk into the forest and you will wait for me. You will give me much gold!" Therefore the foolish sailor's horse carried the sailor into the midst of the island. The sailor looked at a horrible cave. The foolish sailor and the horse saw the ancient and wicked camel! It was walking out of the cave. The foolish sailor screamed. The just horse gave the greedy and foolish sailor to the camel, and walked from the forest to the town. Now many poets tell tales to the sons and daughters of the town about the foolish sailor, the just horse, and the wicked camel.

Lesson 7 Quiz (65 points)

A. Vocabulary (10 points)

Translate the following words.

1. ferus: **fierce, wild**
2. necō: **I kill, slay**
3. blessed: **beātus**
4. mīrus: **strange, wonderful**
5. paucī: **few**
6. iūstus: **just, right, fair, impartial, righteous**
7. pulcher: **beautiful, handsome**
8. laetus: **happy, joyful, glad**
9. avārus: **greedy**
10. world: **mundus**

B. Grammar (15 points)

1. Decline *wicked town*.

	LATIN SINGULAR	LATIN PLURAL
NOM.	oppidum malum	oppida mala
GEN.	oppidī malī	oppidōrum malōrum
DAT.	oppidō malō	oppidīs malīs
ACC.	oppidum malum	oppida mala
ABL.	oppidō malō	oppidīs malīs

2. Give a synopsis of *cōgitō* in the third person singular.

	LATIN	ENGLISH
PRESENT ACT.	cōgitat	he/she/it thinks
IMPERFECT ACT.	cōgitābat	he/she/it was thinking
FUTURE ACT.	cōgitābit	he/she/it will think

C. Translation (15 points)

Translate each sentence.

1. The master will give much food and wine to the faithful servants.

   Dominus servīs fīdīs multum cibum et vīnum dabit.

2. Deī et deae pulchrī sunt, sed malī sunt et multōs virōs bonōs male necant.

   The gods and goddesses are beautiful, but they are evil and wickedly kill many good men.

D. Memorization (25 points)

Write out the entire Lord's Prayer in Latin.

Pater noster, quī es in caelīs,

Sanctificētur nōmen tuum. Adveniat regnum tuum.

Fīat voluntās tua, sīcut in caelō et in terrā.

Pānem nostrum quotīdiānum dā nōbīs hodiē,

et dīmitte nōbīs dēbita nostra

sīcut et nōs dīmittimus dēbitōribus nostrīs.

Et nē nōs indūcās in tentātiōnem, sed līberā nōs ā malō. Āmēn.

LESSON 8 (Student Edition p. 63)

Review & Test

1. Word List

There is no new Word List this lesson. You may want to play a few review games this lesson, not only to help the students review their words and chants, but also to lighten the mood before the big test.

2. Derivatives/Memorization Helps

There won't be any derivatives on the Unit 1 Test. However, you may want to review derivatives if you feel it will assist your students in remembering their vocabulary.

3. Memorization—*Pater Noster*

There is no new memorization this lesson. Review the entirety of the *Pater Noster*.

4. Grammar

There is no new chant this lesson. Review the verb chants for *sum* and the endings for the present, imperfect, and future active indicative. Review the noun chants for the first declension, second declension, and second declension neuter.

5. Worksheet

I've tried to give more than enough review exercises, so feel free to skip a few if your time is limited. To get through a lot of noun or verb chants more efficiently, choose several students to write out their chants on the board simultaneously. (Hopefully you have a room with more than one chalkboard or whiteboard!) Or have one student write the singular and one the plural. While they are busily writing, ask the rest of the class vocab questions or have them chant through all of their verb and noun endings. Then you can correct the students' work on the board and take every mistake as an opportunity to instruct the class. If one student does it, another one will probably make that same error too.

You can also make transparencies of the worksheet and fill them in using an overhead projector while the students tell you what to write.

Exercise D6. "The ancient man loves silver and the moon, but you boys love gold and crowns." *Vir antīquus argentum et lūnam amat, sed puerī aurum et corōnās amātis.*

Technically, *antīquus* normally doesn't refer to an "old man", but rather to ancient people of long ago (ancestors, for instance). However, two other common words for "old," *vetus* and *senex,* are in the third declension and must wait their turn to be introduced.

The Latin to English story is a very brief overview of the *Aeneid;* the *iūstus vir* is Aeneas and the *rēgīna* is Dido.

6. Quiz

There is no quiz this lesson.

7. Test

Administer Unit 1 Test when the students are ready.

Lesson 8 Worksheet

A. Vocabulary

Translate the following words from Latin to English or English to Latin as appropriate. For each preposition, include which case(s) it takes.

1. gift: **dōnum**
2. sailor: **nauta**
3. spectō: **I look at**
4. verbum: **word**
5. agricola: **farmer**
6. I drink: **pōtō**
7. perīculum: **danger**
8. sīca: **dagger**
9. daughter: **fīlia**
10. fābula: **story**
11. numquam: **never**
12. caper: **billy goat**
13. villa: **farmhouse**
14. castellum: **castle**
15. gladius: **sword**
16. ēvangelium: **good news**
17. dō: **I give**
18. goddess: **dea**
19. ager: **field**
20. fīda: **faithful**
21. aqua: **water**
22. mala: **bad, evil**
23. puella: **girl**
24. wonderful: **mīrus**
25. through: (+ **acc.**) **per**
26. I praise: **laudō**
27. dē: (+ **abl.**) **(down) from, concerning**
28. longinquus: **distant**
29. I wound: **vulnerō**
30. nothing: **nihil**
31. gold: **aurum**
32. lūna: **moon**
33. equus: **horse**
34. bonus: **good**
35. alnus: **ship, alder**
36. fēmina: **woman**
37. why: **cūr**
38. ē: (+ **abl.**) **out of, from**
39. righteous: **iūstus**
40. I love: **amō**
41. crown: **corōna**
42. Christ: **Christus**
43. magistra: **teacher**
44. vocō: **I call**
45. portō: **I carry**
46. aut: **or**
47. generation: **saeculum**
48. necō: **I kill, slay**
49. son: **fīlius**
50. hodiē: **today**

51. camēlus: **camel**
52. mandūcō: **I chew, eat**
53. pirate: **pīrāta**
54. I howl: **ululō**
55. male: **badly**
56. cave: **spēlunca**
57. yesterday: **herī**
58. queen: **rēgīna**
59. cōgitō: **I think**
60. discipula: **student**
61. servus: **slave, servant**
62. caelum: **sky, heaven**
63. cantō: **I sing**
64. man: **vir**
65. rogō: **I ask**
66. stō: **I stand**
67. ā (+ **abl.**) (away) from
68. crustulum: **cookie**
69. servō: **I save**
70. also: **et**
71. auxilium: **help, aid**
72. town: **oppidum**
73. turba: **crowd, mob**
74. ōlim: **once upon a time**
75. germānus: **brother**
76. antīqua: **ancient**
77. līberō: **I set free**
78. regnō: **I rule**
79. sagitta: **arrow**
80. argentum: **silver, money**

81. ōrō: **I pray, speak**
82. wealth: **dīvitiae**
83. cibus: **food**
84. germāna: **sister**
85. gaudium: **joy, happiness**
86. pecūnia: **money**
87. parvus: **little, small**
88. nōn: **not**
89. foolish: **stultus**
90. īnsula: **island**
91. habitō: **I live, dwell**
92. ōceanus: **ocean**
93. ambulō: **I walk**
94. dominus: **lord, master**
95. hasta: **spear**
96. mundus: **world**
97. ad: (+ **acc.**) **to, toward**
98. pugnō: **I fight**
99. regnum: **kingdom**
100. often: **saepe**
101. patria: **native land**
102. caldus: **warm**
103. bēstia: **beast**
104. I attack: **oppugnō**
105. creō: **I create**
106. now: **nunc**
107. ugly: **foedus**
108. fātum: **fate**
109. anger: **īra**
110. blessed: **beātus**

111. Deus: **God**
112. rēgia: **palace**
113. ferus: **fierce, wild**
114. superō: **I conquer**
115. harēna: **sand, beach**
116. avārus: **greedy**
117. there: **ibī**
118. clāmō: **I shout**
119. multus: **much, many**
120. semper: **always**
121. poēta: **poet**
122. magnus: **large, big, great**
123. terra: **earth, land**
124. occupō: **I seize**
125. nāvigō: **I sail**
126. crās: **tomorrow**
127. sed: **but**
128. boy: **puer**
129. pauca: **few**
130. narrō: **I tell**
131. wine: **vīnum**
132. therefore: **itaque**
133. laetum: **happy, joyful**
134. silva: **forest**
135. pulchrum: **beautiful**
136. bene: **well**
137. I wait for: **exspectō**
138. I burn: **cremō**
139. wretched: **miser**
140. in: (+ **acc.**) **into, against**
    (+ **abl.**) **in, on**

B. Grammar

1. Decline *foolish generation*.

	LATIN SINGULAR	LATIN PLURAL
NOM.	saeculum stultum	saecula stulta
GEN.	saeculī stultī	saeculōrum stultōrum
DAT.	saeculō stultō	saeculīs stultīs
ACC.	saeculum stultum	saecula stulta
ABL.	saeculō stultō	saeculīs stultīs

2. Decline *handsome pirate*.

	LATIN SINGULAR	LATIN PLURAL
NOM.	pīrāta pulcher	pīrātae pulchrī
GEN.	pīrātae pulchrī	pīrātārum pulchrōrum
DAT.	pīrātae pulchrō	pīrātīs pulchrīs
ACC.	pīrātam pulchrum	pīrātās pulchrōs
ABL.	pīrātā pulchrō	pīrātīs pulchrīs

3. Decline *wretched beast*.

	LATIN SINGULAR	LATIN PLURAL
NOM.	misera bēstia	miserae bēstiae
GEN.	miserae bēstiae	miserārum bestiārum
DAT.	miserae bēstiae	miserīs bēstiīs
ACC.	miseram bēstiam	miserās bēstiās
ABL.	miserā bestiā	miserīs bēstiīs

4. Decline *blessed man*.

	LATIN SINGULAR	LATIN PLURAL
NOM.	vir beātus	virī beātī
GEN.	virī beātī	virōrum beātōrum
DAT.	virō beātō	virīs beātīs
ACC.	virum beātum	virōs beātōs
ABL.	virō beātō	virīs beātīs

5. Do a synopsis of *navigō* in the first person singular.

	LATIN	ENGLISH
PRESENT ACT.	nāvigō	I sail, am sailing, do sail
IMPERFECT ACT.	nāvigābam	I was sailing
FUTURE ACT.	nāvigābō	I will sail

6. Do a synopsis of *laudō* in the first person plural.

	LATIN	ENGLISH
PRESENT ACT.	laudāmus	we praise
IMPERFECT ACT.	laudābāmus	we were praising
FUTURE ACT.	laudābimus	we will praise

7. Do a synopsis of *habitō* in the second person singular.

	LATIN	ENGLISH
PRESENT ACT.	habitās	you live
IMPERFECT ACT.	habitābās	you were living
FUTURE ACT.	habitābis	you will live

8. Do a synopsis of *cremō* in the second person plural.

	LATIN	ENGLISH
PRESENT ACT.	cremātis	you (pl.) burn
IMPERFECT ACT.	cremābātis	you (pl.) were burning
FUTURE ACT.	cremābitis	you (pl.) will burn

9. Do a synopsis of *creō* in the third person singular.

	LATIN	ENGLISH
PRESENT ACT.	creat	he/she/it creates
IMPERFECT ACT.	creābat	he/she/it was creating
FUTURE ACT.	creābit	he/she/it will create

10. Do a synopsis of *pugnō* in the third person plural.

	LATIN	ENGLISH
PRESENT ACT.	pugnant	they fight
IMPERFECT ACT.	pugnābant	they were fighting
FUTURE ACT.	pugnābunt	they will fight

C. Memorization

See if you can write out the entire Lord's Prayer in Latin from memory.

Pater noster, quī es in caelīs,

Sanctificētur nōmen tuum. Adveniat regnum tuum.

Fīat voluntās tua, sīcut in caelō et in terrā.

Pānem nostrum quotīdiānum dā nōbīs hodiē,

et dīmitte nōbīs dēbita nostra

sīcut et nōs dīmittimus dēbitōribus nostrīs.

Et nē nōs indūcās in tentātiōnem, sed līberā nōs ā malō. Āmēn.

D. English to Latin Translation

Translate each sentence from English to Latin.

1. The girls were looking at the ugly goat in the field and were screaming well.

   Puellae caprum foedum in agrō spectābant et bene ululābant.

2. God was always giving good words to men and women, but we are wicked.

   Deus virīs et fēminīs bona verba semper dabat, sed malī sumus.

3. The pirate was seizing the little boys' cookies in the forest and will eat the food there.

   Pīrāta crustula puerōrum parvōrum in silvā occupābat et cibum ibī mandūcābit.

4. The wretched farmer was singing tales about joy and fate to the pretty woman, but she will never love the farmer.

   Agricola miser pulchrae fēminae fābulās dē gaudiō et fātō cantābat, sed agricolam numquam amābit.

5. There are evil sailors and pirates on the beach; therefore the queen is in her castle.

   Sunt malī nautae et pīrātae in harēnā; itaque rēgīna in castellō est.

6. The ancient man loves silver and the moon, but you boys love gold and crowns.

   <u>Vir antīquus argentum et lūnam amat, sed puerī aurum et corōnās amātis.</u>

7. The horse will carry the teacher or the student to the town, but the camel carries nothing.

   <u>Equus magistrum/magistram aut discipulum/discipulam ad oppidum portābit, sed camēlus nihil portat.</u>

8. You (sg.) love much gold and wealth, and so you will always be waiting for happiness.

   <u>Multum aurum et [multās] dīvitiās amās, itaque gaudium semper exspectābis.</u>

9. The small sister is greedy and with many words was asking about the cookies.

   <u>Parva germāna avāra est et multīs verbīs dē crustulīs rogābat.</u>

10. They sailed from a distant island to the good farmers' land, and they will attack many towns with swords.

    <u>Ab īnsulā longinquā ad terram/patriam agricolārum bonōrum nāvigābant, et multa oppida gladiīs oppugnābunt.</u>

E. Latin to English Translation

1   Ōlim vir iūstus in magnō oppidō habitābat. Multī virī ab terrā longinquā nāvigābant et oppidum cremābant; itaque vir ab oppidō festīnābat[1] et parvum fīlium servābat. In ōceanō nāvigābant et multa perīcula, multōs bonōs virōs, et multōs malōs virōs spectābant. In longinquā terrā iūstus vir rēgīnam pulchram amābat. Et rēgīna virum amābat, sed deī virō narrābant: "Nāvigābis ab terrā rēgīnae ad
5   Ītaliam.[2] Ibī magnum rēgnum rēgnābis." Itaque vir ab terrā rēgīnae nāvigābat et rēgīna misera sē[3] in pyrā[4] cremābat. Dea iūstum virum nōn amat, et virō multa perīcula dat. Dēnique[5] ad Ītaliam nāvigat, multōs virōs pugnat et superat, et rēgnum nunc creābit. Cūr est magna īra in deīs et deābus?

Glossary
1. *festīnō* (1): I hasten, hurry
2. *Ītalia, -ae* (f): Italy
3. *sē*: himself, herself, itself, accusative reflexive pronoun (points back to the subject)
4. *pyra, -ae* (f): funeral pyre
5. *dēnique*: finally

<u>Once upon a time there lived a just man in a great town. Many men sailed from a distant land and burned the town; therefore the man hastened from the town and saved [his] small son. They sailed on the ocean and saw many dangers, many good men, and many bad men. In a distant land the just man loved a beautiful queen. The queen also loved the man, but the gods told the man, "You will sail from the queen's land to Italy. There you will rule over a great kingdom." Therefore the man sailed from the</u>

queen's land and the wretched queen burned herself upon a pyre. A goddess does not love the just man, and she gives the man many dangers. Finally he sails to Italy, fights and defeats many men, and now will create [his] kingdom. Why is there great anger among [lit., in] the gods and goddesses?

Unit 1 Test (116 points)

A. Vocabulary (25 points)

Translate the following words. Give case(s) for prepositions.

1. nunc: **now**
2. aut: **or**
3. herī: **yesterday**
4. ex: (+ **abl.**) **out of, from**
5. bene: **well**
6. et: **and, even, also**
7. in: (+ **acc.**) **into, against**;
   (+ **abl.**) **in, on**
8. sed: **but**
9. numquam: **never**
10. cūr: **why**
11. per: (+ **acc.**) **through**
12. itaque: **and so, therefore**
13. ab: (+ **abl.**) **from, away from**
14. hodiē: **today**
15. ad: (+ **acc.**) **to, toward**
16. male: **badly, ill, wrongly**
17. crās: **tomorrow**
18. dē: (+ **abl.**) **from, down from, concerning**
19. ibī: **there, at that place; then**
20. semper: **always**
21. saepe: **often**
22. ōlim: **once upon a time, formerly, then**
23. nōn: **not**
24. regnum: **kingdom**
25. rēgia: **palace**

B. Grammar (20 points)

1. Conjugate and translate *sum* in the present active indicative.

	LATIN SINGULAR	ENGLISH SINGULAR
1ST	sum	I am
2ND	es	you are
3RD	est	he/she/it is

	LATIN PLURAL	ENGLISH PLURAL
	sumus	we are
	estis	you (pl.) are
	sunt	they are

2. Give a synopsis of *amō* in the second person plural.

	LATIN	ENGLISH
PRESENT ACT.	amātis	you (pl.) love
IMPERFECT ACT.	amābātis	you (pl.) were loving
FUTURE ACT.	amābitis	you (pl.) will love

3. Give a synopsis of *necō* in the third person plural.

	LATIN	ENGLISH
PRESENT ACT.	necant	they kill
IMPERFECT ACT.	necābant	they were killing
FUTURE ACT.	necābunt	they will kill

4. Decline *ugly sailor*.

	LATIN SINGULAR	LATIN PLURAL
NOM.	nauta foedus	nautae foedī
GEN.	nautae foedī	nautārum foedōrum
DAT.	nautae foedō	nautīs foedīs
ACC.	nautam foedum	nautās foedōs
ABL.	nautā foedō	nautīs foedīs

C. Translation (46 points)

Translate this story from Latin into English.

1 Bēstia antīqua et calda sum. Magna et foeda et fera sum. Mala sum. Aurum et argentum, dīvitiās et pecūniam amō. Ōlim in spēluncā magnā in silvā mīrā habitābam. Multa oppida oppugnābam, et dīvitiās virōrum et fēminārum occupābam. Et castellum rēgīnae pulchrae oppugnābam et corōnās et aurum occupābam. Multās villās parvās ibī cremābam. Fēminae miserae oppidī virīs gladiōs dabant, sed virī
5 oppidī nōn oppugnābant. Sed puer parvus et fīdus stābat et sagittīs pugnābat, et mē[1] vulnerābat. Narrābat: "Oppidum nōn oppugnābis! Ad spēluncam in silvā ambulābis!" Itaque, ad spēluncam ambulābam, et ibī hodiē habitō. Oppidum parvī puerī fidī nōn oppugnābō, sed aurum pulchrum semper amābō.

Glossary
1. *mē*: accusative of the first person pronoun *ego*: I, me

I am an ancient and fiery beast. I am large and horrible and fierce. I am wicked. I love gold and silver, riches and money. Once upon a time I was living in a large cave in a wonderful forest. I was attacking many towns, and seizing the men and women's wealth. I was also attacking the beautiful queen's castle and seizing [her] crowns and gold. I was burning many small farmhouses there. The wretched women of the town were giving swords to the men, but the men of the town were not attacking. But a small and faithful boy was standing and fighting with arrows, and he wounded me. He was saying: "You will not

attack the town! You will walk to the cave in the forest!" Therefore, I was walking to the cave, and I live there today. I will not attack the small faithful boy's town, but I will always love beautiful gold.

D. Memorization (25 points)

Write the Lord's Prayer in Latin.

Pater noster, quī es in caelīs,

Sanctificētur nōmen tuum. Adveniat regnum tuum.

Fīat voluntās tua, sīcut in caelō et in terrā.

Pānem nostrum quotīdiānum dā nōbīs hodiē,

et dīmitte nōbīs dēbita nostra

sīcut et nōs dīmittimus dēbitōribus nostrīs.

Et nē nōs indūcās in tentātiōnem, sed līberā nōs ā malō. Āmēn.

2 Unit Two

Unit 2 Goals

Lessons 9–16

By the end of Unit 2, students should be able to . . .

- Understand how to use both first and second conjugation verbs
- Understand how to form and use imperatives
- Understand how to use the complementary infinitive
- Chant from memory the endings for perfect, pluperfect, and future perfect active indicative verbs
- Conjugate a first or second conjugation verb in any tense in the active indicative: present, imperfect, future, perfect, pluperfect, or future perfect
- Chant from memory the endings of third declension masculine/feminine and third declension neuter nouns
- Decline third declension nouns of any gender
- Form and use the vocative case in first, second, or third declension nouns
- Understand how to use and translate substantive adjectives
- Translate sentences using all of the concepts learned in Units 1 and 2
- Know all the vocabulary from Lessons 9-16
- Write out from memory the *Magnificat* in Latin

LESSON 9 (Student Edition p. 75)

Second Conjugation: Present, Imperfect & Future Active Indicative / Substantive Adjectives

1. Word List

From here on out, as you go through the verbs in the vocabulary, have students identify the conjugation of each verb. This lesson's list consists mainly of second conjugation verbs, but there are a couple of first conjugation verbs mixed in—the (1) tends to give them away. This is also a prime opportunity to remind students that it is important to memorize principal parts—knowing the infinitive (second principal part) will help them identify which conjugation the verb belongs to.

As you go through the new second conjugation verbs, note that there are quite a few irregular verbs. Although there is often the pattern of *-ō, -ēre, -uī, -itum,* I will be listing all the principal parts of second conjugation verbs and will *not* be marking the "regular" ones with a (2).

This lesson your students learn the words for "hello" and "goodbye." *Salvē* (sg.) and *salvēte* (pl.) are actually imperatives or commands, ordering the audience "Be well!" If you are speaking to a single person, use *salvē*; if to more than one, *salvēte*. When you come into the classroom, you can say "*Salvēte, discipulī!*" and your class should respond, "*Salvē, magister/magistra!*" *Valeō* is used to bid farewell in the imperative: *valē* (sg.) and *valēte* (pl.). At the end of class, say, "*Valēte, discipulī!*" and they should respond "*Valē, magister/magistra!*" If you think it is odd to use verbs meaning "be well" for greetings, think of our English word "farewell," which literally wishes the audience to "fare (be/do) well." (Students will officially learn imperatives in Lesson 11.)

Finally, some of your students may wonder why a few of the verbs are lacking a fourth principal part (e.g., *iaceō* and *timeō*). Sometimes there is a logical reason for this (such as, it isn't used passively), but sometimes the verb is simply defective. Students will learn all these things in good time.

2. *doceō,* I teach—This verb takes a *double accusative* rather than an accusative and dative. Thus, in English we would say, "The teacher teaches good things to the students" (where *students* is an indirect object). However, the Latin would be *Magister bona* (acc.) *discipulōs* (acc.) *docet.*

5. *iaceō,* I lie (flat), lie down—You may need to go over the difference in English between "lie" and "lay." "Lie" is an intransitive verb (does not take an object) and is used to say

"I'm going to lie down for a nap." One should *not* say "I'm going to lay down" because "lay" is a transitive verb. *Chickens lay eggs, I'm going to lay the baby down for her nap, etc.* The tricky thing is that the English principal parts of "lie" are "lie, lay, have lain" while those of "lay" are "lay, laid, have laid." So you *can* say "Yesterday I lay down for a nap" because in that context "lay" is the past of "lie."

2. Derivatives/Memorization Helps

1. *dēleō*, I destroy: delete
2. *doceō*, I teach: doctor, doctrine
3. *festīnō*, I hasten, hurry: festinate; *Festīnā lentē*, "Make haste slowly," was a motto of the Emperor Augustus.
4. *habeō*, I have, hold: habit, inhabit (*habitō* is derived from it)
5. *iaceō*, I lie (flat), lie down: adjacent
6. *intrō*, I enter: enter, entrance
7. *moneō*, I warn: admonish, monitor
8. *mordeō*, I bite, sting: morsel, mordant
9. *respondeō*, I answer, respond: respond, response
10. *rīdeō*, I laugh, smile: ridicule
11. *salveō*, I am well: salvation
12. *sedeō*, I sit: sedentary, sedimentary, session
13. *teneō*, I hold, possess: intent, tentacle, tenable, tenacity
14. *terreō*, I frighten, terrify: terrify, terror
15. *timeō*, I fear: timid, timorous
16. *valeō*, I am well/strong: valid, validity
17. *videō*, I see: video, visual, vision
18. *cum*, with: Appears as the prefix com-, con-, cor-, col-, or co- (as in complete, correlation, collate);
19. *sine*, without: sinecure; *sine qua non*, "without which not" (a necessary condition)
20. *interim*, meanwhile, in the meantime: interim

3. Memorization—*Magnificat*

During Unit 2, students will memorize Mary's song of praise in Luke 1:46–55, known as the *Magnificat*. It is a bit longer and probably less familiar to your students than the *Pater Noster*, but is another important piece of Latin found in church liturgies and choral music.

In addition, this unit will finish up around Christmastime, so it is an appropriate text for that season. Also note that although *bracchium* is usually spelled with two *c*'s, in line 9, in accordance with ecclesiastical Latin, it is spelled with one *c* and a macron.

One tip: make sure students know the difference between *exsultāvit* in line 2 and *exaltavit* in line 12: just like the English "*exult*" and "*exalt*," the former is intransitive and means "to exult, rejoice," while the latter is transitive (takes an object) and means "to exalt, lift up."

Lesson 1 Magnificat anima mea Dominum,
  My soul magnifies the Lord,
 et exsultāvit spīritus meus in Deō salvātōre meō,
  and my spirit has rejoiced in God my savior,

Lesson 2 quia rēspexit humilitātem ancillae suae.
  because He has regarded the lowliness of His handmaiden.
 Ecce enim ex hōc beātam mē dicent omnēs generātiōnēs,
  For behold, because of this all generations will call me blessed,

Lesson 3 quia fēcit mihi magna,
  because He has done great things for me,
 quī potēns est,
  He Who is powerful,
 et sanctum nōmen eius,
  and His name (is) holy,

Lesson 4 et misericordia eius in prōgeniēs et prōgeniēs timentibus eum.
  and His mercy (is) upon generations and generations of those fearing Him.
 Fēcit potentiam in brāchiō suō,
  He has worked power with His arm,

Lesson 5 dispersit superbōs mente cordis suī;
  He has scattered the proud in the mind of their heart;
 dēposuit potentēs dē sēde
  He has put down the powerful from (their) seat
 et exaltāvit humilēs;
  and has lifted up the humble;

Lesson 6 ēsurientēs implēvit bonīs
  He has filled the hungry with good things
 et dīvitēs dīmīsit inānēs.
  and He has sent the rich away empty.
 Suscēpit Isrāel puerum suum,
  He has received Israel His son,

Lesson 7 recordātus misericordiae,
  remembering (His) mercy,

sīcut locūtus est ad patrēs nostrōs,
just as He spoke to our fathers,
Ābraham et seminī eius in saecula.
to Abraham and his seed forever.

4. Grammar

No new chant this lesson. Review the present, imperfect, and future active indicative endings, because you will be adding them to second conjugation verbs.

Verbs: Second Conjugation

This lesson students will add a new family of verbs to their repertoire: the second conjugation. Begin with what the students know about the first conjugation: How do you know a verb is in the first conjugation? What is the verb's stem? How do you find it? etc. Take our verb *necō*. The principal parts are *necō, necāre, necāvī, necātum*. To find the stem, go to the second principal part (the infinitive), remove the *-re*, and *voilà!* The present stem is *necā-*. The stem vowel is *-ā-*, which tells us that *necō* is a first conjugation verb. To our stem *necā-* we can add the present, imperfect, or future endings.

This process works exactly the same way for second conjugation verbs. *Deleō, delēre, delēvī, delētum* means "I destroy." We go to the second principal part, *delēre*, chop off the *-re*, and lo, we have *delē-*. This is our stem for the present system. The stem vowel is a long *-ē-*, which tells us that this is a second conjugation verb. As mentioned before, the Romans were great recyclers. Thus, we do not have to learn any new endings for a second conjugation verb: we can just slap the endings we've already memorized onto this stem:

Present Active Indicative of *deleō*, second conjugation verb*

	LATIN SINGULAR	ENGLISH SINGULAR	LATIN PLURAL	ENGLISH PLURAL
1ST	deleō	I destroy	delēmus	we destroy
2ND	delēs	you destroy	delētis	you (pl.) destroy
3RD	delet*	he/she/it destroys	delent*	they destroy

Imperfect Active Indicative of *deleō*, second conjugation verb

	LATIN SINGULAR	ENGLISH SINGULAR	LATIN PLURAL	ENGLISH PLURAL
1ST	delēbam	I was destroying	delēbāmus	we were destroying
2ND	delēbās	you were destroying	delēbātis	you (pl.) were destroying
3RD	delēbat	he/she/it was destroying	delēbant	they were destroying

Future Active Indicative of *deleō*, second conjugation verb

* Notice that, as in the First Conjugation, the third person singular and plural in the present active have a short stem vowel.

	LATIN SINGULAR	ENGLISH SINGULAR		LATIN PLURAL	ENGLISH PLURAL
1ST	delēbō	I will destroy		delēbimus	we will destroy
2ND	delēbis	you will destroy		delēbitis	you (pl.) will destroy
3RD	delēbit	he/she/it will destroy		delēbunt	they will destroy

Synopses also work the same way with second conjugation verbs. Here are a few examples:

habeō in the second person singular

	LATIN	ENGLISH
PRESENT ACT.	habēs	you (sg.) have
IMPERFECT ACT.	habēbās	you (sg.) were having
FUTURE ACT.	habēbis	you (sg.) will have

sedeō in the first person plural

	LATIN	ENGLISH
PRESENT ACT.	sedēmus	we sit
IMPERFECT ACT.	sedēbāmus	we were sitting
FUTURE ACT.	sedēbimus	we will sit

Substantive Adjectives

Your students are hopefully becoming more comfortable with adjectives by now. A sentence such as this one will not pose any problems: *Virōs bonōs laudāmus,* "We praise the good men." In Latin (and in English, for that matter), the substantive use of the adjective means that an adjective can stand alone and function as a noun. (Literally, *substantive* means *stands alone.*) We see the English substantive throughout the Beatitudes: "Blessed are the poor" or "Blessed are the meek," when "the meek" is an adjective standing as a noun: "the meek people." In our sample Latin sentence above, we can actually leave out the *virōs* and say *Bonōs laudāmus,* and it means exactly the same thing: "We praise the good men."

Context also matters here. If we have this sentence in isolation, it is safe to translate the masculine plural ending *-ōs* as "men." If it had been *Bonās laudāmus,* we would say "We praise the good women"; and, if it had been *Bona laudāmus,* "We praise the good things." Without a clear context, use "men" as your default masculine substantive, "women" for the feminine, and "things" for the neuter.

However, if the substantive adjective occurs in a story, we must look at the context to see what was the most recent masculine plural entity discussed. If the story were about a bunch of farmers who were working hard and bringing in a big harvest, then the *Bonōs* of *Bonōs laudāmus* would probably refer to those farmers. Thus we could translate it as either "We praise the good men," meaning "the farmers," or even just say, "We praise the good farmers."

5. Worksheet

The vocabulary sections on the worksheets, quizzes, and exams in Unit 2 will only cover the words from this unit. Words from Unit 1 will of course appear in sentences and stories, and so students will be accountable for them in that way; however, students will not be drilled on Unit 1 words directly.

6. Quiz

Administer Quiz 9 when the students are ready.

Lesson 9 Worksheet

A. Vocabulary

Translate the following words from Latin to English or English to Latin as appropriate. For the verbs, also fill in the missing principal parts. For each preposition, include which case(s) it takes.

1. sine (+ **abl.**) without
2. iaceō, **iacēre**, **iacuī**, —: I lie (flat), lie down
3. **videō**, vidēre, **vīdī**, **vīsum**: I see
4. I warn: **moneō**, **monēre**, **monuī**, **monitum**
5. habeō, **habēre**, habuī, **habitum**: I have, hold
6. mordeō, **mordēre**, **momordī**, **morsum**: I bite, sting
7. I teach: **doceō**, **docēre**, **docuī**, **doctum**
8. respondeō, **respondēre**, **respondī**, responsum: I answer, respond
9. timeō, **timēre**, **timuī**, —: I fear
10. Goodbye! **valē(te)** from **valeō**, **valēre**, **valuī**, **valitum**
11. with (+ **abl.**) **cum**
12. **rīdeō**, rīdēre, **rīsī**, **rīsum**: I laugh, smile
13. salveō, **salvēre**, —, —: I am well
14. salvē(te) **Good day! (Be well)**
15. I hasten: **festīnō**, **festīnāre**, **festīnāvī**, **festīnātum**
16. sedeō, **sedēre**, sēdī, **sessum**: I sit
17. intrō, **intrāre**, **intrāvī**, intrātum: I enter
18. meanwhile **interim**
19. **teneō**, tenēre, **tenuī**, tentum: I hold, possess
20. I frighten: **terreō**, **terrēre**, **terruī**, **territum**
21. dēleō, **dēlēre**, **dēlēvī**, dēlētum: I destroy

B. Grammar

Identify the gender (Masc., Fem., or Neut.), number (Sg. or Pl.), and case (Nom., Gen., Dat., Acc., or Abl.)—any possible options—of the following noun and adjective combinations. Then translate them.

	PHRASE	GENDER, NUMBER, CASE	TRANSLATION
1.	verba fera	Neut. Pl. Nom. Neut. Pl. Acc.	wild words (subject) wild words (direct object)
2.	bēstiae pulchrae	Fem. Sg. Gen. Fem. Sg. Dat. Fem. Pl. Nom.	of the beautiful beast, the beautiful beast's to/for the beautiful beast beautiful beasts (subject)
3.	pīrātae antīquī	Masc. Sg. Gen. Masc. Pl. Nom.	of the ancient pirate, the ancient pirate's ancient pirates (subject)
4.	foedī castellī	Neut. Sg. Gen.	of the ugly castle, the ugly castle's
5.	mundō mīrō	Masc. Sg. Dat. Masc. Sg. Abl.	to/for the wonderful world by/with/from the wonderful world
6.	fidīs magistrīs	Masc./Fem. Pl. Dat. Masc./Fem. Pl. Abl.	to/for the faithful teachers by/with/from the faithful teachers
7.	crustula calda	Neut. Pl. Nom. Neut. Pl. Acc.	hot cookies (subject) hot cookies (direct object)
8.	alnō malā	Fem. Sg. Abl.	by/from/with the evil ship

9.	harēna longinqua	Fem. Sg. Nom.	distant sand (subject)
10.	multārum sagittārum	Fem. Pl. Gen.	of many arrows, many arrows'
11.	agrōs beātōs	Masc. Pl. Acc.	blessed fields (direct object)
12.	stultīs deābus	Fem. Pl. Dat. Fem. Pl. Abl.	to/for the foolish goddesses by/with/from the foolish goddesses

13. Conjugate and translate *rīdeō* in the present, imperfect, and future active indicative.

Present

	LATIN SINGULAR	ENGLISH SINGULAR	LATIN PLURAL	ENGLISH PLURAL
1ST	rīdeō	I laugh	rīdēmus	we laugh
2ND	rīdēs	you laugh	rīdētis	you (pl.) laugh
3RD	rīdet	he/she/it laughs	rīdent	they laugh

Imperfect

	LATIN SINGULAR	ENGLISH SINGULAR	LATIN PLURAL	ENGLISH PLURAL
1ST	rīdēbam	I was laughing	rīdēbāmus	we were laughing
2ND	rīdēbās	you were laughing	rīdēbātis	you (pl.) were laughing
3RD	rīdēbat	he/she/it was laughing	rīdēbant	they were laughing

Future

	LATIN SINGULAR	ENGLISH SINGULAR
1ST	rīdēbō	I will laugh
2ND	rīdēbis	you will laugh
3RD	rīdēbit	he/she/it will laugh

	LATIN PLURAL	ENGLISH PLURAL
	rīdēbimus	we will laugh
	rīdēbitis	you (pl.) will laugh
	rīdēbunt	they will laugh

14. Do a synopsis of *intrō* in the third person singular.

	LATIN	ENGLISH
PRESENT ACT.	intrat	he/she/it enters
IMPERFECT ACT.	intrābat	he/she/it was entering
FUTURE ACT.	intrābit	he/she/it will enter

15. Do a synopsis of *terreō* in the second person plural.

	LATIN	ENGLISH
PRESENT ACT.	terrētis	you (pl.) frighten
IMPERFECT ACT.	terrēbātis	you (pl.) were frightening
FUTURE ACT.	terrēbitis	you (pl.) will frighten

C. Memorization

Fill in the blanks.

Magnificat **anima** mea **Dominum**,

et **exsultāvit** spīritus **meus** in **Deō salvatōre** meō

D. English to Latin Translation

Translate each sentence from English to Latin. Use substantive adjectives wherever possible!

1. The good (female) teacher teaches the students many things, but the foolish ones answer the good (woman) nothing. [*Remember:* doceō *takes a double accusative*]

   Magistra bona discipulōs/discipulās multa docet, sed stultī/stultae bonam nihil respondent.

2. The greedy son of the queen was ruling the faithful men and women badly, and they will warn the wicked man.

   Fīlius avārus rēgīnae fīdōs et fīdās male regnābat, et malum monēbunt.

3. The fiery beast was stinging many goats and camels, and will eat the good and the bad.

   Bēstia calda multōs caprōs et camēlōs mordēbat, et bonōs et malōs mandūcābit.

4. The ugly big brother was frightening the little sisters, and they feared the fierce bad boy.

   Germānus foedus [et] magnus germānās parvās terrēbat, et ferum [et] malum timēbant.

5. The beautiful women enter into the town with the happy daughters and will see many things.

   Pulchrae [fēminae] in oppidum cum fīliābus laetīs/beātīs intrant et multa vidēbunt.

6. Men are always evil without the gospel.

   Virī sine ēvangeliō malī semper sunt.

7. The farmer's daughter is carrying cookies out of the farmhouse; and so you all are happy and are smiling.

   Fīlia agricolae crustula ē/ex villā portat; itaque laetī/beātī [*or* laetae/beātae] estis et rīdētis.

8. We are faithful horses and were lying down in the field, but the evil goats were hastening into the farmhouse and biting the small boys.

   Equī fīdī sumus et in agrō iacēbāmus, sed caprī malī in villam festīnābant et parvōs puerōs mordēbant.

9. The fierce pirate saw the handsome sailors and shouted: "You are strong but I will destroy many!"

   Pīrāta ferus pulchrōs nautās vidēbat et clamābat: "Valētis sed multōs delēbō!"

10. The queen has much gold and silver and many crowns, but the wretched woman is not happy.

    Rēgīna multum aurum et argentum et multās corōnās habet, sed misera laeta nōn est.

E. Latin to English Translation

1 Ōlim erat[1] bēstia calda et mala, et fera multōs terrēbat. Virōs et fēminās, rēgīnās et agricolās, equōs et camēlōs terrēbat. Misera in spēluncā sedēbat et miserōs rīdēbat, aut mala verba lūnae ululābat. Interim Oswaldus Magnanimus[2] in oppidum intrābat et rogābat, "Cūr multī timent?" Respondēbant, "Bēstiam caldam et malam timēmus. Oppidum dēlēbit et cremābit!" Oswaldus Magnanimus respondēbat, "Malam dēlēbō!"

5 Itaque Oswaldus Magnanimus ad spēluncam foedam in silvā miserā festīnābat. Bēstiam feram vidēbat, et fera Oswaldum spectābat. Calda ululābat, sed Oswaldus nōn timēbat. Bēstiam gladiō bonō et magnō oppugnābat. Nunc bēstia nōn rīdēbat, et dēnique[3] timēbat. Oswaldus malam dēlēbat, sīcut[4] turbīs oppidī narrābat.

Glossary
1. *erat*: third person singular, imperfect active indicative of *sum*: he, she, it was; there was
2. *magnanimus, -a, -um*: brave, bold, noble
3. *dēnique*: finally
4. *sīcut*: just as

Once upon a time there was a fiery and evil beast, and the fierce [one] frightened many [people]. He frightened men and women, queens and farmers, horses and camels. The wretched [creature] sat in [his] cave and laughed at the wretched [people], or he howled bad words to/at the moon. Meanwhile Oswald the Brave entered into the town and asked, "Why are many [people] afraid?" They responded, "We fear the fiery and evil beast. He will destroy [our] town and burn [it] with fire!" Oswald the Brave responded, "I will destroy the evil [beast]!" Therefore Oswald the Brave hastened to the horrible cave in the wretched wood. He saw the fierce beast, and the fierce [beast] looked at Oswald. The fiery [one] howled, but Oswald was not afraid. He attacked the beast with [his] good and great sword. Now the beast was not laughing, and finally feared. Oswald destroyed the evil [one], just as he told the crowds of the town.

Lesson 9 Quiz (42 points)

A. Vocabulary (10 points)

Translate the following words.

1. I have: **habeō**
2. iaceō: **I lie (flat), lie down**
3. doceō: **I teach**
4. interim: **meanwhile, in the meantime**
5. I bite: **mordeō**
6. timeō: **I fear**
7. terreō: **I frighten, terrify**
8. cum: (+ **abl**.) **with**
9. without: (+ **abl**.) **sine**
10. salveō: **I am well**

B. Grammar (15 points)

1. Give a synopsis of *moneō* in the second person singular.

	LATIN	ENGLISH
PRESENT ACT.	monēs	you warn
IMPERFECT ACT.	monēbās	you were warning
FUTURE ACT.	monēbis	you will warn

2. Give a synopsis of *festīnō* in the first person plural.

	LATIN	ENGLISH
PRESENT ACT.	festināmus	we hasten
IMPERFECT ACT.	festinābāmus	we were hastening
FUTURE ACT.	festinābimus	we will hasten

C. Translation (11 points)

Translate each sentence.

1. The ugly sailors say "Hello!" but the pretty women say "Goodbye!"

   Nautae foedī "Salvēte!" narrant, sed pulchrae [fēminae] "Valēte!" narrant.

2. Cibum et crustula teneō, et parvīs dabō.

   I am holding food and cookies, and I will give [them] to the little ones.

3. Multum vīnum pōtābātis, et nautae laetī nunc estis.

   You were drinking much wine, and now you are happy sailors.

D. Memorization (6 points)

Write out the first two lines of the *Magnificat* in Latin.

Magnificat anima mea Dominum,

et exsultāvit spīritus meus in Deō salvātōre meō

Lesson 10 (Student Edition p. 75)

Verbs: *Sum*, Imperfect & Future

1. Word List

5. *cētus*, sea monster, kraken, whale—*Cētus* occasionally appears in the neuter or with some forms borrowed from its Greek origin, but for simplicity I will treat *cētus* as a regular 2nd declension masculine noun.

6. *inimīcus*, enemy—Note that in English we can use either "enemies" or "enemy" to express the plural of this Latin noun: *inimīcī oppugnant*, "The enemies are attacking" or "The enemy is attacking" (depending on the nuance we are going for). Also, notice that it is the opposite of the word for "friend," *amīcus* (coming up in Lesson 15). Your *inimīcus* is your "non-friend."

20. *-que, and*—An *enclitic* is a little "word" that never appears solo but is always attached to the end of another word. The enclitic *-que* means "and," differing from *et* because it usually implies a closer connection. Think of how we shorten "and" in English to 'n' as in "half-n-half." The enclitic *-que* also attaches to the second word of the pair being joined: *Puerī puellaeque*, "boys and girls."

2. Derivatives/Memorization Helps

1. *āla*, wing: ala is used in anatomy and biology
2. *centaurus*, centaur: centaur
3. *cervus*, stag, deer: cervine; Cervy the stag is a character in C.S. Lewis's *The Horse and His Boy*
4. *geminus*, twin: Gemini (constellation and Zodiac sign)
5. *cētus*, sea monster, kraken, whale
6. *inimīcus*, (personal) enemy: inimical
7. *līberī*, children
8. *porcus*, pig: porcine, Porky the Pig
9. *scūtum*, shield: scute, scutate
10. *unda*, wave: undulate
11. *venēnum*, poison: venom, venomous
12. *captō*, I hunt: see *capiō* [Lesson 31]
13. *dēclārō*, I declare, make clear, explain: declare, declaration
14. *maneō*, I remain: mansion, permanent, remain
15. *obsideō*, I besiege, remain near: obsession, obsessive, see *sedeō* [Lesson 9]
16. *volō*, I fly: volatile
17. *dēnique*, finally-
18. *repentē*, suddenly: memory help—"Suddenly they repented."
19. *-que*, and (enclitic)
20. *quod*, because

3. Memorization—*Magnificat*

This lesson's new lines are:

> quia rēspexit humilitātem ancillae suae.
> *because He has regarded the lowliness of His handmaiden.*
>
> Ecce enim ex hōc beātam mē dicent omnēs generātiōnēs,
> *For behold, because of this all generations will call me blessed,*

4. Grammar

Sum Imperfect and Future

This lesson students will learn the imperfect and future of *sum*. Although *sum* is an irregular verb, point out to the students that the endings are still regular: -m/-ō, -s, -t, -mus, -tis, -nt. If students need help distinguishing the two, point out the imperfect *eram* chant has "a" throughout, just like -bam, -bās, -bat, -bāmus, -bātis, -bant and the future *erō* has the same vowel pattern as -bō, -bis, -bit, -bimus, -bitis, -bunt. (Also, notice that the *eram* chant has long vowels in the same places as the -*bam* chant: second person singular, first person plural, and second person plural.)

Present Active Indicative of *sum*

	LATIN SINGULAR	ENGLISH SINGULAR		LATIN PLURAL	ENGLISH PLURAL
1ST	sum	I am		sumus	we are
2ND	es	you are		estis	you (pl.) are
3RD	est	he/she/it is		sunt	they are

Imperfect Active Indicative of *sum*

	LATIN SINGULAR	ENGLISH SINGULAR		LATIN PLURAL	ENGLISH PLURAL
1ST	eram	I was		erāmus	we were
2ND	erās	you were		erātis	you (pl.) were
3RD	erat	he/she/it was		erant	they were

Future Active Indicative of *sum*

	LATIN SINGULAR	ENGLISH SINGULAR		LATIN PLURAL	ENGLISH PLURAL
1ST	erō	I will be		erimus	we will be
2ND	eris	you will be		eritis	you (pl.) will be
3RD	erit	he/she/it will be		erunt	they will be

The imperfect and future of *sum* function just like the present does: they are linking verbs, and so nouns, pronouns, or adjectives on either side must be in the nominative. For example, if you wanted to say "Oswald was a just boy," you should say *Oswaldus erat puer iūstus,* **not** *Oswaldus erat puerum iūstum.* And, just like *est* and *sunt* in the present, if the third person singular or plural appears (especially at the beginning of the sentence), you can translate it as "there" instead of "he/she/it/they": *Crās erunt in villā paucae fēminae,* "Tomorrow there will be few women in the farmhouse." *Ōlim erat rēgīna pulchra . . . ,* "Once upon a time there was a beautiful queen . . . ."

5. Worksheet

Follow the directions given to complete the worksheet.

6. Quiz

Administer Quiz 10 when the students are ready.

Lesson 10 Worksheet

A. Vocabulary

Translate the following words from Latin to English or English to Latin as appropriate. For the verbs, also fill in the missing principal parts. For each preposition, include which case(s) it takes.

1. volō, volāre, **volāvī**, **volātum**: **I fly**
2. finally: **dēnique**
3. captō, **captāre**, captāvī, **captātum**: **I hunt**
4. āla: **wing**
5. because: **quod**
6. centaurus: **centaur**
7. meanwhile: **interim**
8. obsideō, **obsidēre**, **obsēdī**, obsessum: **I besiege, remain near**
9. children: **līberī**
10. geminus: **twin**
11. sine: (+ abl.) **without**
12. I declare: **dēclārō**, **declārāre**, **declārāvī**, **declārātum**
13. cētus: **kraken**
14. suddenly: **repentē**
15. inimīcus: **(personal) enemy**
16. doceō, docēre, **docuī**, **doctum**: **I teach**
17. porcus: **pig**
18. cervus: **stag, deer**
19. with: **cum (+ abl.)**
20. scūtum: **shield**
21. -que: **and**
22. unda: **wave**
23. rīdeō, **rīdēre**, **rīsī**, **rīsum**: **I laugh, smile**
24. maneō, **manēre**, **mansī**, mansum: **I remain**
25. poison: **venēnum**

B. Grammar

1. Do a synopsis of *sum* in the third person plural.

	LATIN	ENGLISH
PRESENT ACT.	sunt	they are
IMPERFECT ACT.	erant	they were
FUTURE ACT.	erunt	they will be

2. Do a synopsis of *sum* in the second person plural.

	LATIN	ENGLISH
PRESENT ACT.	estis	you (pl.) are
IMPERFECT ACT.	erātis	you (pl.) were
FUTURE ACT.	eritis	you (pl.) will be

3. Do a synopsis of *sum* in the first person plural.

	LATIN	ENGLISH
PRESENT ACT.	sumus	we are
IMPERFECT ACT.	erāmus	we were
FUTURE ACT.	erimus	we will be

4. Do a synopsis of *sum* in the third person singular.

	LATIN	ENGLISH
PRESENT ACT.	est	he/she/it is
IMPERFECT ACT.	erat	he/she/it was
FUTURE ACT.	erit	he/she/it will be

5. Do a synopsis of *sum* in the second person singular.

	LATIN	ENGLISH
PRESENT ACT.	es	you are
IMPERFECT ACT.	erās	you were
FUTURE ACT.	eris	you will be

6. Do a synopsis of *sum* in the first person singular.

	LATIN	ENGLISH
PRESENT ACT.	sum	I am
IMPERFECT ACT.	eram	I was
FUTURE ACT.	erō	I will be

7. Decline *wretched fate*.

	LATIN SINGULAR	LATIN PLURAL
NOM.	fātum miserum	fāta misera
GEN.	fātī miserī	fātōrum miserōrum
DAT.	fātō miserō	fātīs miserīs
ACC.	fātum miserum	fāta misera
ABL.	fātō miserō	fātīs miserīs

8. Decline *handsome farmer*.

	LATIN SINGULAR	LATIN PLURAL
NOM.	agricola pulcher	agricolae pulchrī
GEN.	agricolae pulchrī	agricolārum pulchrōrum
DAT.	agricolae pulchrō	agricolīs pulchrīs
ACC.	agricolam pulchrum	agricolās pulchrōs
ABL.	agricolā pulchrō	agricolīs pulchrīs

C. Memorization

Fill in the blanks.

Magnificat **anima** mea **Dominum**,

et **exsultāvit** spīritus **meus** in **Deō** **salvātōre** **meō**,

quia rēspexit **humilitātem** **ancillae** suae.

Ecce **enim** ex hōc **beātam** mē **dicent** omnēs **generātiōnēs**,

UNIT TWO \\ LESSON 10

D. English to Latin Translation

Translate each sentence from English to Latin. Use substantive adjectives wherever possible.

1. The wild pigs were large but we were hunting the horrible [ones].

   Porcī ferī erant magnī, sed foedōs captābāmus.

2. Yesterday I was a greedy woman, today I am queen, and tomorrow I will be unhappy.

   Herī [fēmina] avāra eram, hodiē rēgīna sum, et crās misera erō.

3. The teacher was explaining many things to the students, and so now the children will not be foolish.

   Magister/magistra discipulīs multa dēclārābat, nunc itaque līberī stultī nōn erunt.

4. The great man and the fierce centaur were enemies, and the centaur suddenly attacked the great [one] with arrows of poison.

   [Vir] magnus et centaurus ferus inimīcī erant, et centaurus magnum sagittīs venēnī repente oppugnābat.

5. Because you were small children you were not hunting horrible krakens in the waves.

   Quod līberī parvī erātis cētōs foedōs in undīs nōn captābātis.

6. We were small fiery beasts and used to walk, but we will be great and fly with great wings and will destroy many things.

   Bēstiae parvae [et] caldae erāmus et ambulābāmus, sed magnae erimus et ālīs magnīs volābimus et multa delēbimus.

7. We were hunting the ancient stag and finally we were capturing the great beast.

   Cervum antīquum captābāmus et dēnique magnam bēstiam [or magnum] occupābāmus.

8. The enemies were fierce and kept on besieging the good queen's castle with spears and shields.

   Inimīcī erant ferī et castellum rēgīnae bonae hastīs scūtīsque [or et scūtīs] obsidēbant.

9. The sailors were twins and the brothers were always drinking and fighting.

   Nautae geminī erant et germānī semper pōtābant et pugnābant [or pugnābantque].

10. The wild deer were lying down in the fields and we looked at the deer and were happy.

    Cervī ferī in agrīs iacēbant et cervōs spectābāmus et laetī/laetae erāmus.

E. Latin to English Translation

1 Nunc antīquī iūstīque nautae sumus, sed ōlim malī stultīque pīrātae erāmus. Multa oppida et multōs virōsque fēmināsque līberōsque oppugnābāmus. In multīs patriīs manēbāmus et multa castella magna obsidēbāmus. Porcōs ferōs et cervōs in silvīs captābāmus. Ferī inimīcī bestiārum, servōrum, dominōrum, et rēgīnārum erāmus. Perīcula et bona malaque rīdēbāmus. In spēluncīs in insulīs parvīs habitābāmus
5 et cībum mandūcābāmus et multum vīnum pōtābāmus. Semper dēclārābāmus: "Magnī sumus! Laetī et avārī semper erimus! Miserī numquam erimus!" Ōlim in undīs ōceanī nāvigābāmus et repente bēstiam foedam in aquā vidēbāmus. Erat cētus magnus malusque. Cētus alnum vidēbat et oppugnābat. Bēstiam timēbāmus et sīcīs gladiīsque pugnābāmus. Cētus multōs pīrātās ex alnō necābat mandūcābatque. Dēnique paucī pīrātae ad insulam pulchram effugiēbāmus,[1] et dēclārābāmus: "Stultī malīque pīrātī
10 sumus. Bonī erimus et virōs fēmināsque līberōsque nōn oppugnābāmus. Iūstī nautae erimus!"

Glossary
1. *effugiō, -ere, -fūgī, -fugitus*: I escape

Now we are ancient and righteous sailors, but once we were evil and foolish pirates. We attacked many towns and many men, women, and children. We remained in many lands and besieged many great castles. We hunted wild pigs and deer in the forests. We were the fierce enemies of beasts, of servants, of lords, and of queens. We laughed at dangers and good things and evil things [*or, I suppose,* good and evil dangers]. We lived in caves on small islands and ate food and drank much wine. We would always declare: "We are great! We will always be happy and greedy! We will never be unhappy!" Once we were sailing on the ocean's waves and suddenly we saw a horrible beast in the water. It was a great and evil kraken. The kraken saw the ship and attacked. We feared the beast and fought with daggers and swords. The kraken killed and devoured many pirates out of the ship. Finally a few [of us] pirates escaped to a beautiful island, and we declared, "We are foolish and evil pirates. We will be good and will not attack men and women and children. We will be righteous sailors!"

Lesson 10 Quiz (48 points)

A. Vocabulary (10 points)

Translate the following words.

1. geminus: **twin**
2. I hunt: **captō**
3. maneō: **I fly**
4. sedeō: **I sit**
5. obsideō: **I besiege, remain near**
6. centaur: **centaurus**
7. līberī: **children**
8. unda: **wave**
9. cervus: **deer**
10. repentē: **suddenly**

B. Grammar (10 points)

Give a synopsis of *videō* in the second person singular.

	LATIN	ENGLISH
PRESENT ACT.	vidēs	you see
IMPERFECT ACT.	vidēbās	you were seeing
FUTURE ACT.	vidēbis	you will see

C. Translation (15 points)

Translate each sentence.

1. The beast was fiery and was flying with great wings.

   Bēstia calda erat et ālīs magnīs volābat.

2. Pirātās amābam quod pulchrī erant.

   I loved pirates because they were handsome.

3. Puerī bonī nunc estis et virī magnī eritis.

   You are good boys now and you will be great men.

D. Memorization (13 points)

Write out the first four lines of the *Magnificat* in Latin.

Magnificat anima mea Dominum,

et exsultāvit spīritus meus in Deō salvātōre meō,

quia rēspexit humilitātem ancillae suae.

Ecce enim ex hōc beātam mē dicent omnēs generātionēs,

LESSON 11 (Student Edition p. 92)

Verbs: *Possum*—Present, Imperfect & Future / Complementary Infinitives / Imperatives; Nouns: Case Usage—Vocative Case

1. Word List

This lesson, you may need to point out that the possessive adjectives #11 *meus*, #12 *noster*, #13 *tuus,* and #14 *vester* are just like other adjectives and match the nouns they modify in gender, number, and case—no matter who the speaker is. Thus if Oswald says, "I love my sister," the Latin would be *Amō meam germānam,* with *meam* in the feminine to match *germānam*—it does not matter that Oswald is masculine. Although *meam* refers to Oswald, it modifies and therefore matches *germānam*. If your students have studied any modern Romance languages this concept should be no problem! Some students have no difficulty with this, but those who start overthinking it may get confused.

Also, for some reason students tend to confuse *noster* and *vester.* Point out that last unit's memorization, the *Pater Noster,* means "Our Father" not "Your Father." You can also use the phrase (which middle schoolers tend to enjoy) "Where's *your vest*room?" to remember *vester*—because of course you would never ask where "our restroom" is, because you'd know.

2. Derivatives/Memorization Helps

1. *apostolus*, apostle: apostle, apostolic
2. *Biblia Sacra,* Holy Bible
3. *ecclēsia*, church: ecclesiastical
4. *liber*, book: library
5. *populus*, people, nation: populace, popular
6. *stella*, star: constellation, stellar
7. *tenēbrae*, darkness, gloomy place, shadows: tenebrous, tenebrific
8. *via*, road, way: via, viaduct, trivia
9. *victōria*, victory: victory, victorious, Victoria
10. *vīta*, life: viable, vital, vitamin
11. *meus*, my, mine
12. *noster*, our, ours
13. *tuus*, your (sg.), yours
14. *vester*, your (pl.), yours
15. *audeō*, I dare: audacious, audacity
16. *dēbeō*, I owe, ought: debit, debt
17. *lūceō*, I shine, am bright: translucent
18. *possum*, I am able, can: potent, potency, omnipotent
19. *contrā*, against: the prefix contra-, as in contradiction, contraband
20. *trāns*, across: the prefix trans- as in transfer, transport

3. Memorization—*Magnificat*

This lesson's new lines are:

quia fēcit mihi magna,	*Because He has done great things for me*
quī potēns est,	*He Who is powerful,*
et sanctum nōmen eius,	*And His name (is) holy,*

4. Grammar

Possum and Complementary Infinitives

This lesson includes a nice miscellany of items. First off, we will begin with a compound verb of *sum: possum, posse, potuī,* ——, which means "I am able" or "I can." It is irregular, obviously, just as *sum* is. Its stem is basically *pot-*, but whenever that *pot-* runs into an initial *-s*, it is assimilated and becomes another *s*. Thus, *potsum* becomes *possum* and *potsumus* changes to *possumus*. (Try saying *potsum* a bunch of times fast, and you will see how easily that assimilation occurred!) The infinive *posse* is a condensed form of *potesse*.

Freely point out to your students that they are not really learning a new chant this lesson: they are merely applying the *sum* chants they have already learned. (This technique does not always console them, but it certainly leaves them without excuse should they not take the trouble to master it!)

	LATIN SINGULAR	ENGLISH SINGULAR	LATIN PLURAL	ENGLISH PLURAL
1ST	possum	I am able	possumus	we are able
2ND	potes	you are able	potestis	you (pl.) are able
3RD	potest	he/she/it is able	possunt	they are able

	LATIN SINGULAR	ENGLISH SINGULAR	LATIN PLURAL	ENGLISH PLURAL
1ST	poteram	I was able	poterāmus	we were able
2ND	poterās	you were able	poterātis	you (pl.) were able
3RD	poterat	he/she/it was able	poterant	they were able

	LATIN SINGULAR	ENGLISH SINGULAR	LATIN PLURAL	ENGLISH PLURAL
1ST	poterō	I will be able	poterimus	we will be able
2ND	poteris	you will be able	poteritis	you (pl.) will be able
3RD	poterit	he/she/it will be able	poterunt	they will be able

Note that there are two common ways of expressing the meaning of *possum* in English: "I am able" or "I can." For example, the sentences "Oswald is able to kill the fiery beast" and "Oswald can kill the fiery beast" mean virtually the same thing. English is full of helping verbs such as "can" which don't have an exact Latin equivalent. In our first example, notice how our verb "is able" is followed immediately by an infinitive "to kill." The main verb is stating Oswald's ability, and this main verb is filled out, or completed, by the infinitive "to kill." We don't usually just say "he is able" and then stop—we must complete the verb: able to do what? This infinitive is called the **complementary infinitive**, because *it complements, or completes, the main verb.*

Ask students if they know any Latin infinitives, and they should hopefully answer "Yes!"—because for every verb they have learned thus far, they have learned the present active infinitive of that verb, otherwise known as the second principal part. The sentence "Oswald is able to kill the fiery beast" in Latin would then be *Oswaldus bēstiam caldam necāre potest*. We do not add any endings to the infinitive, because of course as an "infinite" form, it is not bound by person and number; we can just plunk it down and it will fill out any person and number it needs to.

Make sure your students will not be confused by the English use of "can," because our Latin sentence above also means "Oswald can kill the fiery beast." They need to remember that in English, our main verb is "kill" with the helping verb (fancy term: *modal*) "can." In Latin, however, the two roles are reversed and "can" is the main verb, with "kill" as the helping verb. Here are a few more example sentences:

We can sing well.	Bene cantāre possumus.
We could not sing well.	Non bene cantāre poterāmus.

[Note: In English, "could" is the past of "can"; not of course to be confused with the polite form "Could you please pass the salt?" Also note that the infinitive here stays the same even though we are using the imperfect tense of *possum*.]

They will be able to save the girl.	Puellam servāre poterunt.

[The English word "can" also functions as the future, but you'd have to make it explicit by context or using a future-pointing adverb such as "tomorrow"—*Tomorrow they can save the girl*. I only mention this because one of your precocious students will ask about it.]

Imperatives

Your students have already received a small taste of the imperative mood last lesson when they learned *salvē* and *salvēte*, *valē* and *valēte*. Begin by asking the students how many moods there are in Latin and to identify them. Hopefully they will rattle off indicative and infinitive, since they have been dealing with these; you may need to remind them of the imperative, subjunctive, and participle. See if anyone remembers the definition of an **imperative:** *a command*. Maybe, just maybe, one of your students will remember how *salvē*, etc. were formed.

If not, then go ahead and explain from the beginning: to form a present active imperative, find the present stem (of course) by going to the second principal part (present active infinitive) and taking off the *-re*. That stem by itself is the singular present active imperative.

If we had *necō, necāre, necāvī, necātum*, then our stem would be *necā-* and thus the singular imperative, "Kill!" would be *Necā!* To form the plural, simply add *-te* to the stem: *Necāte!* "Kill!" (talking to a plural audience).

This process works the same for all conjugations. *Salvē* and *valē* are second conjugation imperatives; *necā* is a first conjugation. This is a timely opportunity to remind students that this is one of many reasons why learning all four principal parts is so valuable!

Imperatives, like indicative verbs, can take direct and indirect objects and can be modified by adverbs and so on. If we were to command Oswald to "Kill the fiery beast now!" or "Give gold to the queen!" we would form our imperative and then use accusatives, datives, and adverbs as we have already learned to do: *Nunc necā bēstiam caldam!* and *Dā rēgīnae aurum!* [Note: *dō* is a bit irregular, as we have seen, and even though its stem vowel *a* is often short, its singular imperative is *dā*. The plural imperative has a short vowel: *date*, pronounced DAH-tay.]

Vocative Case

Very often when you are commanding someone to do something, you call upon that person by name. This is called "direct address," and a Latin noun used this way takes the the vocative case (from *vocō*, "I call"). For most of the declensions, the vocative is the same as the nominative, and you can use the vocative with proper names, common nouns, and even adjectives. If we wanted to say, "Hello, pirate!" we would use *salvē* (since we are speaking to one person) and then put *pīrāta* in the vocative case, which happily is the same as the nominative: *Salvē, pīrāta!* The same is true of the plural: *Salvēte, pīrātae!* "Hello, pirates!" It is a nice optional touch to add an *Ō* in front of the vocative: *Salvēte, Ō pīrātae!* "Greetings, O pirates!" *I will typically include the Ō in my charts, although your students do not need to.*

The vocative for the second declension singular is not so simple, unfortunately. We have seen three different nominative options for second declension nouns: *-us* (as in *Oswaldus*), *-r* (as in *puer*), and *-ius* (as in *fīlius*). Each of these has a different vocative.

For second declension nouns ending in *-us*, the vocative is *-e*. Thus if we were greeting Oswald, we would say, *Salvē, Oswalde!* The way I remember this is with the noun *dominus*, because my school song was taken from Psalm 115:1—*Nōn nōbīs, Domine, sed nōminī tuō dā glōriam*, "Not to us, O Lord, but to Thy name give glory." Notice we have both a vocative (*Domine*) and an imperative (*dā*) in this song. If your students have sung any other sacred music, *Domine* or *Christe* have probably appeared in it.

For second declension nouns ending in *-r*, the vocative is simply *-r*: *Salvē, Ō puer!* "Greetings, boy!"

For second declension nouns ending in *-ius* in the singular, the vocative is *-ī*: *Salvē, Ō fīlī!* "Greetings, son!"

Conveniently, the vocative plural of all second declension nouns, regardless of their nominative singular form, is the same as the nominative plural:

Salvēte, dominī! Greetings, lords!

Salvēte, puerī! Greetings, boys!

Salvēte, fīliī! Greetings, sons! (Note the extra i to distinguish the plural from the singular)

What about the second declension neuter, you might ask? Breathe easy—the vocative for both singular and plural is the same as the nominative. If, for some reason, you wanted to speak to a castle, you would say, *Salvē, Ō castellum!* "Greetings, O castle!"

Here is a handy chart setting forth all of the singular vocatives; you may want to have your students flip back to these three declension chants (Lessons 2, 4, and 5, respectively) and write them in underneath:

	1ST DECLENSION	2ND DECLENSION			2ND DECLENSION NEUTER
NOMINATIVE	-a	-us	-r	-ius	-um
VOCATIVE	-a	-e	-r	-ī	-um
NOM. EXAMPLE	fēmina	germānus	magister	gladius	fātum
VOC. EXAMPLE	Ō fēmina	Ō germāne	Ō magister	Ō gladī	Ō fātum

Vocative of *meus*: Because *me-* + *-e* would give us the awkward *mee*, those two vowels contract to form a long *-ī*: *mī*. Thus you would say *Ō mī fīlī*, "O my son," and in the plural *Ō meī fīliī*, "O my sons." The vocatives of the feminine and neuter forms are completely regular: the vocative of *mea* is simply *mea*, and that of *meum* is *meum*.

5. Worksheet

Exercise D6: O my son and O my daughter, always love the words of God and the faithful church. *Ō mī fīlī et Ō mea fīlia, semper amāte verba Deī et ecclēsiae fīdae.*

This sentence is a bit ambiguous in English: Does it mean "love the words of God and the words of the faithful church"? or "love the words of God and love the faithful church"? If the former meaning is implied, then *ecclēsiae fīdae* is correct; if the latter, then it should read *ecclēsiam fīdam*.

D7. The faithful teacher was able to teach the Holy Bible to my children. *Magister fīdus [or Magistra fīda] meōs līberōs Bibliam Sacram docēre poterat.*

Remember that *doceō* takes a double accusative, even though English says "to my children."

E. *Nōmina Animālium*: Your students should enjoy this extra assignment, even if they have to ask you for help on a few of the names. After they try it on their own, go through it as a class and let them know the meaning of the words in some of the more interesting scientific names (i.e. *bos prīmigenius* means something pretty close to "the original cow," and a cougar is "the one-colored panther").

6. Quiz

Administer Quiz 11 when the students are ready.

Lesson 11 Worksheet

A. Vocabulary

Translate the following words from Latin to English or English to Latin as appropriate. For the verbs, also fill in the missing principal parts. For each preposition, include which case(s) it takes.

1. book: **liber**
2. because: **quod**
3. vester: **your (pl.), yours**
4. noster: **our, ours**
5. apostle: **apostolus**
6. audeō, **audēre**, ausus sum: **I dare**
7. wave: **unda**
8. ecclēsia: **church**
9. possum, **posse**, **potuī**, —: **I am able, can**
10. without: **sine (+ abl.)**
11. Biblia Sacra: **Holy Bible**
12. populus: **people, nation**
13. trāns: **(+ acc.) across**
14. star: **stella**
15. victōria: **victory**
16. contrā: **(+ acc.) against**
17. dēnique: **finally**
18. dēbeō, **dēbēre**, debuī, **debitum**: **I owe, ought**
19. via: **road, way**
20. tuus: **your (sg.), yours**
21. vīta: **life**
22. I lie down: **iaceō**, **-ēre**, **-uī**, —
23. shadows: **tenēbrae**
24. meus: **my, mine**
25. lūceō, **lūcēre**, **lūxī**, —: **I shine, am bright**

B. Grammar

Translate these verbs and phrases into Latin..

1. they were able: **poterant**
2. we are: **sumus**
3. O children, love!: **Ō līberī, amāte!**
4. you (sg.) will be able: **poteris**
5. she can: **potest**
6. Farewell, shadows!: **Valēte, [Ō] tenēbrae!**
7. I could: **poteram**
8. I can: **possum**
9. you (pl.) are able: **potestis**
10. we were able: **poterāmus**
11. they will be able: **poterunt**
12. he was able: **poterat**
13. O star, shine!: **Ō stella, lūcē!**
14. I will be: **erō**
15. you (sg.) are: **es**

C. Memorization

Fill in the blanks.

Magnificat anima mea Dominum,

et exsultāvit spīritus meus in Deō salvātōre meō,

quia **rēspexit** **humilitātem** ancillae **suae**.

Ecce enim **ex** **hōc** **beātam** mē dicent **omnēs** **generātiōnēs**,

quia fēcit **mihi** **magna**,

quī **potēns** **est**,

et sanctum **nōmen** eius,

D. English to Latin Translation

Translate each sentence from English to Latin. Use substantive adjectives wherever possible.

1. The disciples and apostles were suddenly daring to speak the gospel to the foolish and wicked crowds.
   <u>Discipulī apostolīque [or Discipulī et apostolī] turbīs stultīs malīsque [or stultīs et malīs] ēvangelium ōrāre/narrāre repente audēbant.</u>

2. The moon and stars are beautiful and are shining in the shadows.
   <u>Lūna stellaeque [or lūna et stellae] pulchrae sunt et in tenebrīs lūcent.</u>

3. Your son loves our daughter, but she will not love your son because he does not love the church.
   <u>Vester fīlius nostram fīliam amat, sed vestrum fīlium nōn amābit quod ecclēsiam nōn amat. [Note: The context of noster could imply vester, but tuus would also be acceptable.]</u>

4. Christ is the way and the life and He shines in the darkness of our world.
   <u>Christus est via et vīta [or via vītaque] et in tenebrīs nostrī mundī lūcet.</u>

5. The foolish boy cannot conquer the fiery beast and save the queen's daughter, but Oswald can.
   <u>Puer stultus bēstiam caldam superāre et fīliam rēgīnae servāre nōn potest, sed Oswaldus potest.</u>

6. O my son and O my daughter, always love the words of God and the faithful church.
   <u>Ō mī fīlī et Ō mea fīlia, semper amāte verba Deī et ecclēsiae fīdae [or ecclēsiam fīdam].</u>

7. The faithful teacher was able to teach the Holy Bible to my children.
   <u>Magister fīdus [or Magistra fīda] meōs līberōs Bibliam Sacram docēre poterat.</u>

8. The wicked apostle was speaking many things against the church because he loves the gold and silver of the world.
   <u>Apostolus malus multa contrā ecclēsiam ōrābat/narrābat quod aurum argentumque [or aurum et argentum] mundī amat.</u>

9. My master, I am your good servant; therefore, give your help to my wretched children.
   <u>Mī domine, tuus bonus servus sum; itaque, dā meīs līberīs miserīs tuum auxilium.</u>

10. O farmer, your wicked pig is my enemy and you ought to destroy the horrible beast.
    <u>Ō agricola, tuus porcus malus meus inimīcus est et bēstiam foedam delēre dēbēs.</u>

E. Latin to English Translation

1 Ōlim erant puellae geminae, Iūlia Iūniaque,[1] et in villā ad ōceanum habitābant. Iūlia erat bona sed Iūnia mala erat. Iūlia laeta erat et mundum, agrōs, lūnam, et stellās amābat; et bene cantāre et multīs bēstiīs ōrāre poterat. Sed Iūnia avāra erat. Et porcōs et equōs et caprōs lūdere[2] audēbat; itaque Iūniam miseram malamque nōn amābant. Ōlim geminae in harēnā ambulābant, et alnum pīrātārum vidēbant. Iūnia
5 pīrātīs ōrābat: "Dā mihi[3] multum aurum, et germānam meam dabō—serva vestra esse potest." Pīrātae Iūniae ōrābant: "Aurum dabimus, et tuam germānam ad alnum nostram portābimus." Iūlia clāmābat: "Iuvāte!"[4] Oswaldus interim bēstiās ferās in silvā ad harēnam captābat et Iuliam audiēbat.[5] Ad harēnam festinābat et pīrātās superāre et Iūliam servāre poterat. Iūliam ad villam portābat et parentibus[6] multa ōrābat. Nōn laetī erant sed iūstī, et Iūnia serva nunc est et aquam ad agrōs portābit. Sed porcī et equī
10 et caprī dē poenā[7] cōgitant . . . .

Glossary
1. *Iūlia, -ae* (f) and *Iūnia, -ae* (f) are both first declension names. You can translate them as *Iulia* and *Iunia* or *Julia* and *Junia*.
2. *lūdō, -ere, lūsī, lūsum* (third conjugation): I tease
3. *mihi*: dative singular of the first person pronoun *ego*: I, me
4. *iuvō, iuvāre, iūvī, iūtum*: I help
5. *audiō, -īre, -īvī, -ītum* (fourth conjugation): I hear
6. *parentibus*: dative plural of *parens, -ntis* (m/f) parent
7. *poena, -ae* (f): revenge; penalty, punishment

<u>Once there were twin girls, Iulia and Iunia, and they lived in a farmhouse by the sea. Iulia was good but Iunia was evil. Iulia was happy and loved the world, the fields, the moon, and the stars; she could also sing and speak well to many beasts. But Iunia was greedy. She also dared to tease the pigs and horses and goats, and so they did not love the evil and wretched Iunia. Once the twins [twin girls] were walking on the beach and saw a pirate ship [ship of pirates]. Iunia said to the pirates: "Give me much gold and I will give [you] my sister; she can be your slave." The pirates said to Iunia: "We will give [you] gold and will carry your sister to our ship." Iulia shouted: "Help!" Meanwhile, Oswald was hunting wild beasts in the forest near the beach and heard Iulia. He hastened to the beach and was able to defeat the pirates and save Iulia. He carried Iulia to the farmhouse and told the parents many things. They were not happy but just and now Iunia is a servant and will carry water to the fields. But the pigs and horses and goats are thinking about revenge . . . .</u>

F. For Fun: *Nōmina Animālium*

How well do you know the scientific names of the following animals? Give it your best shot.

1. __d__ cat
2. __g__ chicken
3. __k__ cougar
4. __b__ cow
5. __m__ dog
6. __i__ donkey
7. __o__ goat
8. __l__ goldfish
9. __f__ horse
10. __a__ jaguar
11. __j__ leopard
12. __c__ lion
13. __h__ pig
14. __e__ sheep
15. __n__ tiger

a. panthera onca
b. bos prīmigenius
c. panthera leō
d. felis catus
e. ovis aries
f. equus ferus caballus
g. gallus gallus domesticus
h. sus domesticus
i. equus africanus asinus
j. panthera pardus
k. puma concolor
l. carassius auratus auratus
m. canis lupus familiaris
n. panthera tigris
o. capra aegagrus hircus

Lesson 11 Quiz (62 points)

A. Vocabulary (10 points)

Translate the following words.

1. quod: **because**
2. populus: **people, nation**
3. contrā: (+ **acc.**) against
4. dēbeō: **I owe, ought**
5. liber: **book**
6. I shine: **lūceō**
7. unda: **wave**
8. vīta: **life**
9. tenēbrae: **darkness, gloomy place, shadows**
10. via: **road, way**

B. Grammar (18 points)

1. Give a synopsis of *possum* in the first person plural.

	LATIN	ENGLISH
PRESENT ACT.	possumus	we are able, can
IMPERFECT ACT.	poterāmus	we were able, could
FUTURE ACT.	poterimus	we will be able [can]

2. How is an imperative formed? Give an example.

   Go to the second principal part, the present active infinitive, and take off the *-re*. That leaves you with the present stem of the verb, which also happens to be the singular imperative. *Necāre* becomes *Necā!* "Kill!" For the plural imperative, add *-te*: *Necāte!* "Kill [you pl.]!" [Obviously, you will get a variety of answers and examples from your students. Exercise wisdom as you grade, and give partial credit as you see fit.]

C. Translation (15 points)

Translate each sentence.

1. The faithful students were finally able to explain the book's words.

   Discipulī fīdī [*or* discipulae fīdae] verba librī dēnique dēclārāre poterant.

2. Nostrīs fīliābus vestra crustula herī nōn dabātis.

   You (pl.) were not giving your cookies to our daughters yesterday.

D. Memorization (19 points)

Write out the first seven lines of the *Magnificat* in Latin.

Magnificat anima mea Dominum,

et exsultāvit spīritus meus in Deō salvātōre meō,

quia rēspexit humilitātem ancillae suae.

Ecce enim ex hōc beātam mē dicent omnēs generātiōnēs,

quia fēcit mihi magna,

quī potēns est,

et sanctum nōmen eius,

LESSON 12 (Student Edition p. 101)

Nouns: Third Declension Masculine/Feminine

1. Word List

18. *autem* (postpositive conj.), "however, moreover."—"Postpositive" literally means "placed after," so a postpositive conjunction does not appear as the first word of a sentence; it must be placed after the first word. Usually it comes second (but could appear later in the sentence too). *Pīrātae autem in spēluncam intrābunt*, "However, the pirates will enter into the cave" [*or*, "The pirates, however, will . . . "].

2. Derivatives/Memorization Helps

1. *draco*, dragon: Draco (constellation)
2. *frāter*, brother: fraternal, fraternity, fratricide
3. *homō*, man, human being: homicide; not prefix homo-, "same," which is from Greek
4. *labor*, work, toil, labor, hardship: labor, elaborate
5. *leō*, lion: leonine, Leo (constellation and Zodiac sign)
6. *lūx*, light: lucid; see *lūceō* [Lesson 11]
7. *māter*, mother: maternal, maternity, matrimony
8. *mīles*, soldier: military, militia
9. *pater*, father: paternal, paternity
10. *rex*, king: regal, regicide
11. *sōl*, sun: solar, parasol
12. *soror*, sister: sorority, sororicide
13. *tigris*, tiger: tiger, tigress
14. *virgō*, maiden, young woman: virgin, virginal, Virginia
15. *virtūs*, manliness, courage, strength: virtue
16. *caveō*, I guard against, beware (of): caveat
17. *domō*, I tame, subdue: indomitable
18. *autem* (postpositive conj.), however, moreover
19. *quandō*, when?, ever, since, because
20. *ubi*, where?, when: ubiquitous; memory help—"*Ibī* there, *ubi* where?" (although this could be a hindrance to correct classical pronunciation)

3. Memorization—*Magnificat*

This lesson's new lines are:

> et misericordia eius in prōgeniēs et prōgeniēs timentibus eum.
>> *and His mercy (is) upon generations and generations of those fearing Him.*
>
> Fēcit potentiam in brāchiō suō,
>> *He has worked power with His arm,*

4. Grammar

Third Declension Masculine/Feminine

This lesson students will learn a new declension. The third declension is merely another family of nouns, and nouns in this declension function just like nouns of the first or second declension. A third declension noun in the nominative case will act as the subject, just as other nominatives. Third declension nouns also have gender and number.

	LATIN SINGULAR	ENGLISH SINGULAR	LATIN PLURAL	ENGLISH PLURAL
NOMINATIVE	X	a/the *noun* [subject]	-ēs	the *nouns* [subject]
GENITIVE	-is	of the *noun*, the *noun's*	-um	of the *nouns*, the *nouns'*
DATIVE	-ī	to/for the *noun*	-ibus	to/for the *nouns*
ACCUSATIVE	-em	a/the *noun* [object]	-ēs	the *nouns* [object]
ABLATIVE	-e	by/with/from the *noun*	-ibus	by/with/from the *nouns*
VOCATIVE	X	O *noun*	-ēs	O *nouns*

The third declension poses a few new challenges, however. For one thing, the nominative singular is not predictable. If you glance down the Word List, you can see that these nouns end in *-ō, -er, -or, -x, -es, -l, is,* and *-us*. This is why I have put an **X** in the nominative singular box in the chart above. It does not represent the letter *x*, but rather should be thought of as the *x* in an algebra equation—basically, "whatever-the-nominative-ending-happens-to-be."

Because the nominative singular is not predictable, it is even more important for students to learn the genitive singular of these nouns. The genitive singular will tell us not only what declension our noun is in, but also the stem of the noun. (Remember that we find the stem of the noun by removing the genitive singular ending, which in this declension is *-is*.) Thus, the stem of *draco* is *dracōn-*, and not *drac-*. If we were merely to glance at *frāter* or *pater*, we might assume that they are second declension nouns like *puer* or *ager*. However, a look at the genitive singular reveals the folly of such an assumption: *frāter* becomes *frātris*, and that *-is* tells us it is a third declension noun. We also see that our stem is *frātr-*. Similarly, a student might assume that *virtūs* is second declension, but the genitive *virtūtis* tells us otherwise.

Knowing which declension a noun is born into is very important. Take this opportunity to remind students that just as people are born into families and cannot switch families willy-nilly, so Latin nouns are born into particular declensions. If a student sees the word *rēgum* in a sentence, he may be tempted to read it as an accusative since *-um* can be the accusative singular ending of the second declension. However, since *rex* is a third and not a second declension noun, the *-um* is actually the genitive plural: "of the kings."

Another unpredictable feature of third declension nouns is their gender. In the first declension, most nouns were feminine with a few masculine vocational nouns here and there. In the second declension, most nouns were masculine with the very rare feminine. And the second neuter comfortingly consisted of all neuters. However, the third declension is a mixed bag of masculine and feminine nouns. (There is a third declension neuter consisting of all neuters, and that will debut next lesson.) The general rules of gender still apply: a biologically male entity (like *pater* or *frāter*) will be masculine; *māter* and *soror*, feminine. And abstract concepts are almost always feminine: *virtūs*, despite meaning "manliness," is an abstract noun and therefore feminine.

The vocative for both masculine and feminine nouns in the third declension is the same as the nominative.

And now it's time to decline a few of these.

māter, mātris (f) *mother*

	LATIN SINGULAR	ENGLISH SINGULAR	LATIN PLURAL	ENGLISH PLURAL
NOMINATIVE	māter	a/the mother [subject]	mātrēs	the mothers [subject]
GENITIVE	mātris	of the mother, the mother's	mātrum	of the mothers, the mothers'
DATIVE	mātrī	to/for the mother	mātribus	to/for the mothers
ACCUSATIVE	mātrem	the mother [object]	mātrēs	the mothers [object]
ABLATIVE	mātre	by/with/from the mother	mātribus	by/with/from the mothers
VOCATIVE	Ō māter	O mother	Ō mātrēs	O mothers

rex, rēgis (m) *king*

	LATIN SINGULAR	ENGLISH SINGULAR	LATIN PLURAL	ENGLISH PLURAL
NOMINATIVE	rex	a/the king [subject]	rēgēs	the kings [subject]
GENITIVE	rēgis	of the king, the king's	rēgum	of the kings, the kings'
DATIVE	rēgī	to/for the king	rēgibus	to/for the kings
ACCUSATIVE	rēgem	the king [object]	rēgēs	the kings [object]
ABLATIVE	rēge	by/with/from the king	rēgibus	by/with/from the kings
VOCATIVE	Ō rex	O king	Ō rēgēs	O kings

A note on adjectives: third declension nouns can of course be modified by adjectives belonging to the first or second declension. Why? Because adjectives modify nouns in gender, number, and case—*but not necessarily* in declension. The nouns declined above are given below with adjectives:

māter laeta, *joyful mother*

	LATIN SINGULAR	LATIN PLURAL
NOM.	māter laeta	mātrēs laetae
GEN.	mātris laetae	mātrum laetārum
DAT.	mātrī laetae	mātribus laetīs
ACC.	mātrem laetam	mātrēs laetās
ABL.	mātre laetā	mātribus laetīs
VOC.	Ō māter laeta	Ō mātrēs laetae

rex bonus, *good king*

	LATIN SINGULAR	LATIN PLURAL
NOM.	rex bonus	rēgēs bonī
GEN.	rēgis bonī	rēgum bonōrum
DAT.	rēgī bonō	rēgibus bonīs
ACC.	rēgem bonum	rēgēs bonōs
ABL.	rēge bonō	rēgibus bonīs
VOC.	Ō rex bone	Ō rēgēs bonī

Having students decline noun-adjective pairs is very helpful, since they can see the same cases of different declensions working together. Also be sure and point out how helpful adjectives can be in eliminating confusion. Remember how distressed your students were that the *-ae* of the first declension could be genitive singular, dative singular, or nominative plural? Well, now they can rejoice. If a first declension adjective is paired with a third declension noun, we don't have that ambiguity: *mātris laetae* can only be "of the joyful mother" (genitive); *mātrī laetae* can only be the dative "to/for the joyful mother;" and *mātrēs laetae* must be the nominative plural, "joyful mothers."

5. Worksheet

Follow the directions given and complete the worksheet.

6. Quiz

Administer Quiz 12 when the students are ready.

Lesson 12 Worksheet

A. Vocabulary

Translate the following words from Latin to English or English to Latin as appropriate. For the verbs, also fill in the missing principal parts.

1. I am able: **possum**, **posse**, **potuī**, ———
2. domō, **domāre**, **domuī**, **domitum**: **I tame, subdue**
3. tiger: **tigris**
4. lūx: **light**
5. where?: **ubi**
6. homō: **man, human being**
7. virgō: **maiden, young woman**
8. I fly: **volō**, **volāre**, **volāvī**, **volātum**
9. courage: **virtūs**
10. when?: **quandō**
11. mīles: **soldier**
12. cervus: **stag, deer**
13. frāter: **brother**
14. pater: **father**
15. however: **autem**
16. sōl: **sun**
17. lion: **leō**
18. soror: **sister**
19. māter: **mother**
20. I bite: **mordeō**, **mordēre**, **momordī**, **morsum**
21. liber: **book**
22. dragon: **draco**
23. labor: **work, toil, labor, hardship**
24. I beware: **caveō**, **cavēre**, **cāvī**, **cautum**
25. rex: **king**

B. Grammar

1. Decline *ancient dragon*.

	LATIN SINGULAR	LATIN PLURAL
NOM.	draco antīquus	dracōnēs antīquī
GEN.	dracōnis antīquī	dracōnum antīquōrum
DAT.	dracōnī antīquō	dracōnibus antīquīs
ACC.	dracōnem antīquum	dracōnēs antīquōs
ABL.	dracōne antīquō	dracōnibus antīquīs
VOC.	[Ō] draco antīque	[Ō] dracōnēs antīquī

2. Decline *beautiful light*.

	LATIN SINGULAR	LATIN PLURAL
NOM.	lūx pulchra	lūcēs pulchrae
GEN.	lūcis pulchrae	lūcum pulchrārum
DAT.	lūcī pulchrae	lūcibus pulchrīs
ACC.	lūcem pulchram	lūcēs pulchrās
ABL.	lūce pulchrā	lūcibus pulchrīs
VOC.	[Ō] lūx pulchra	[Ō] lūcēs pulchrae

3. Give a synopsis of *caveō* in the second person singular.

	LATIN	ENGLISH
PRESENT ACT.	cavēs	you guard against, beware (of)
IMPERFECT ACT.	cavēbās	you were guarding against
FUTURE ACT.	cavēbis	you will guard against

C. Memorization

Fill in the blanks.

Magnificat anima mea Dominum,

et exsultāvit spīritus meus in Deō salvātōre meō,

quia rēspexit humilitātem ancillae suae.

Ecce enim ex hōc beātam mē dicent omnēs generātiōnēs,

quia **fēcit** **mihi** magna,

quī potēns **est**,

et **sanctum** **nōmen** eius,

et misericordia **eius** **in** **prōgeniēs** et prōgeniēs **timentibus** eum.

Fēcit **potentiam** in **brāchiō** suō,

D. English to Latin Translation

Translate each sentence from English to Latin.

1. Dragons and sea serpents are distant brothers but dragons are fiery, have wings, and live in caves.
   Dracōnēs hydrīque [*or* dracōnēs et hydrī] frātrēs [*or* germanī, *but your students should really be practicing their third declension*] longinquī sunt, sed dracōnēs caldī sunt, ālās habent, et in spēluncīs habitant.

2. When will the great king besiege and conquer the enemy's castle?
   Quandō/ubi rex magnus castellum inimīcī obsidēbit et superābit?

3. God created the fiery sun and it was giving light to humans and beasts.
   Deus solem caldum creābat et hominibus et bēstiīs [*or* hominibus bēstiīsque] lūcem dābat.

4. Children, beware of horrible lions and wild pigs when you walk in the Forest of Darkness.
   [Ō] līberī, cavēte leōnēs foedōs et porcōs ferōs [*or* porcōsque] ubi/quandō in Silvā Tenebrārum ambulātis.

5. The good and faithful mother was giving food and cookies to the little sons and daughters.
   Māter bona et fīda parvīs fīliīs fīliābusque [*or* et fīliābus] cibum et crustula dabat.

6. The greedy tigers were attacking the farmhouses and seizing goats and pigs.

    Tigridēs avārī villās oppugnābant et caprōs porcōsque [*or* et porcōs] occupābant.

7. We were seeing your sisters in town, where they were speaking words of life to the crowds.

    Vestrās/tuās sorōrēs in oppidō vidēbāmus, ubi turbīs verba vītae ōrābant/narrābant.

8. The king's brother is great and can tame fierce lions and tigers.

    Frāter [*or* germānus] rēgis magnus est et ferōs leōnēs tigridēsque [*or* et tigridēs] dōmāre potest.

9. Moreover, our fathers were fighting against the evil dragon and finally were able to save the maidens of the town.

    Nostrī patrēs autem contrā malum dracōnem pugnābant et virginēs oppidī dēnique servāre poterant.

10. You all will remain with the disciple's brother because he is a faithful servant of the Lord.

    Cum frātre discipulī manēbitis quod fīdus servus Dominī est.

E. Latin to English Translation

1   Ōlim erat regnum pulchrum in patriā trāns ōceanum. Rex antīquus et fīdus et bonus erat, sed fīliōs nōn habēbat—sōlam[1] fīliam pulchram. Rex autem et regnum laetī nōn erant. Draco malus patriam saepe oppugnābat, et bēstiās, multum aurum, līberōs parvōs, et virginēs occupābat. Nunc draco ālīs foedīs ad castellum volābat, et ululābat: "Dā mihi[2] fīliam rēgis aut vestram patriam dēlēbō!" Rex miser
5   erat, et multōs magnōs ad castellum vocābat: "Pugnāte et malum dracōnem necāte, aut meam fīliam caldō dare dēbēbō. Festināte!" Magnī ab castellō ad spēluncam dracōnis malī festinābant, sed draco nōn timēbat. Draco hominēs aut bēstiās, centaurōs aut cētōs, leōnēs aut tigridēs nōn timēbat. Magnī dracōnem magnum malumque oppugnābant, sed crēmābat. Nunc rex optiōnem[3] nōn habēbat, et fīliam ad spēluncam dracōnis portābat. Sed Oswaldus ad rēgem festinābat, et clāmābat: "Malum dracōnem
10 necābō, et tuam fīliam servābō!" Oswaldus caldum Gladiō Magnō Virtūtis pugnābat, et malum dracōnem dēnique necābat. Fīlia rēgis laeta erat. Et rex laetus erat, et fīliam Oswaldō in mātrimōniō[4] dabat. Nunc Oswaldus rex regnī laetī pulchrīque erit.

Glossary
1. *sōlus, -a, -um*: only, single
2. *mihi*: dative singular of the first person pronoun *ego*: I, me
3. *optio, optiōnis* (f): choice
4. *mātrimōnium, -ī* (n): You should be able to guess this one from the context! (If you can't, look it up in your Latin dictionary.)

Once upon a time there was a beautiful kingdom in a land across the ocean. The king was old and wise and good, but he did not have sons [had no sons]—only a beautiful daughter. However, the king and the kingdom were not happy. An evil dragon was often attacking the land, and seized beasts, much gold, little children, and maidens. Now the dragon was flying to the castle with [its] horrible wings and howled: "Give me the king's daughter or I will destroy your land!" The king was sad and summoned many great men to the castle: "Fight and kill the evil dragon, or I will have to give my daughter to the fiery [one]. Hasten!" The great men hastened from the castle to the evil dragon's cave, but the dragon did not fear [them]. The dragon did not fear men or beasts, centaurs or krakens, lions or tigers. The great men attacked the huge and evil dragon, but he consumed [them] with fire. Now the king had no choice [did not have a choice], and carried [his] daughter to the dragon's cave. But Oswald hastened to the king, and shouted: "I will kill the evil dragon, and save your daughter!" Oswald fought the fiery [one] with [his] Great Sword of Courage, and finally slew the wicked dragon. The king's daughter [princess] was happy. The king also was happy and gave [his] daughter to Oswald in marriage. Now Oswald will be king of the happy and beautiful kingdom.

Lesson 12 Quiz (67 points)

A. Vocabulary (10 points)

Translate the following words.

1. virtūs: **manliness, courage, strength**
2. human being: **homō**
3. lūx: **light**
4. pater: **father**
5. hardship: **labor**
6. repentē: **suddenly**
7. tiger: **tigris**
8. soror: **sister**
9. caveō: **I guard against, beware (of)**
10. quandō: **when?, ever; since, because**

B. Grammar (15 points)

1. Decline *little brother*. Use *frāter*.

	LATIN SINGULAR	LATIN PLURAL
NOM.	frāter parvus	frātrēs parvī
GEN.	frātris parvī	frātrum parvōrum
DAT.	frātrī parvō	frātribus parvīs
ACC.	frātrem parvum	frātrēs parvōs
ABL.	frātre parvō	frātribus parvīs
VOC.	[Ō] frāter parve	[Ō] frātrēs parvī

2. Give a synopsis of *domō* in the third person plural.

	LATIN	ENGLISH
PRESENT ACT.	domant	they tame, subdue
IMPERFECT ACT.	domābant	they were taming
FUTURE ACT.	domābunt	they will tame

C. Translation (17 points)

Translate each sentence.

1. Good kings ought to be able to slay dragons.

    Rēgēs bonī dracōnēs necāre posse dēbent.

2. Mea soror magna leōnēs ferōs semper timēbat.

    My big sister was always fearing [afraid of] fierce lions.

D. Memorization (25 points)

Write out the first nine lines of the *Magnificat* in Latin.

Magnificat anima mea Dominum,

et exsultāvit spīritus meus in Deō salvātōre meō,

quia rēspexit humilitātem ancillae suae.

Ecce enim ex hōc beātam mē dicent omnēs generātiōnēs,

quia fēcit mihi magna,

quī potēns est,

et sanctum nōmen eius,

et misericordia eius in prōgeniēs et prōgeniēs timentibus eum.

Fēcit potentiam in brāchiō suō,

Lesson 13 (Student Edition p. 110)

Nouns: Third Declension Neuter

1. Word List

Introduce the Word List for Lesson 13.

2. Derivatives/Memorization Helps

1. *caput*, head: captain, chapter
2. *carmen*, song, chant, poem, prophecy: charm
3. *cor*, heart: cordial; a section of some church liturgies is called the *Sursum Corda* ("Lift up your hearts")
4. *corpus*, body: corpse, corps, corporal, corporeal
5. *flūmen*, river: flume
6. *grāmen*, grass, greenery: gramineous, graminivorous
7. *iter*, journey, road, route, trek: itinerary
8. *lac*, milk: prefix lac-, as in lactose, lactate, lactic
9. *lītus*, shore, shoreline: littoral (I remember this word by thinking of litter on a beach)
10. *nōmen*, name: noun, nominate, nominal, denomination (and nominative, of course!)
11. *onus*, burden, load, weight: onerous
12. *ōra*, shore
13. *ōs*, mouth: oral
14. *tempus*, time: tempo, temporary, extemporaneous
15. *vulnus*, wound: see *vulnerō* [Lesson 1]
16. *cārus*, dear, beloved: cherish, charity
17. *doctus*, learned, wise, skilled: see *doceō* [Lesson 9]
18. *horrendus*, dreadful, awful, fearful: horrendous
19. *diū*, for a long time: memory help—think of that short little word with a really *long* meaning
20. *statim*, immediately: stat!

3. Memorization—*Magnificat*

This lesson's new lines are:

> dispersit superbōs mente cordis suī;
>> *He has scattered the proud in the mind of their heart;*
>
> dēposuit potentēs dē sēde
>> *He has put down the powerful from (their) seat*
>
> et exaltāvit humilēs;
>> *and has lifted up the humble;*

In line 12, students encounter *exaltavit*. They will be tempted to confuse this with *exsultāvit* from the first line. Explain that the difference between the two verbs is the same as in English: *exalt* is transitive (it can take an object) and means "to lift up," while *exult* is intransitive (does not take an object) and means "to rejoice."

4. Grammar

Third Declension Neuter

This lesson students will add the third declension neuter to their noun repertoire. First review the third declension masculine/feminine. When you introduce the new neuter chant, point out the differences and see if the students notice a trend. Perhaps some of them will remember the two rules of the neuter that were introduced during the second declension neuter lesson in Unit 1, Lesson 5:

1. The nominative and accusative are the same.

2. The plural nominative and accusative end in *-a*.

Thus our algebraic **X** ending for the nominative means that whatever the nominative happens to be, that shall the accusative singular be also. *Iter* in the accusative will be *iter*, *grāmen* will be *grāmen*, and so on.

	LATIN SINGULAR	ENGLISH SINGULAR	LATIN PLURAL	ENGLISH PLURAL
NOMINATIVE	X	a/the *noun* [subject]	-a	the *nouns* [subject]
GENITIVE	-is	of the *noun*, the *noun's*	-um	of the *nouns*, the *nouns'*
DATIVE	-i	to/for the *noun*	-ibus	to/for the *nouns*
ACCUSATIVE	X	a/the *noun* [object]	-a	the *nouns* [object]
ABLATIVE	-e	by/with/from the *noun*	-ibus	by/with/from the *nouns*
VOCATIVE	X	O *noun*	-a	O *nouns*

The vocative for the third declension neuter is the same as the nominative. Thus you may add to the neuter rules above:

3. The nominative and accusative and vocative of neuter nouns are all the same.

Here are some examples declined.

cor, cordis (n) *heart*

	LATIN SINGULAR	ENGLISH SINGULAR	LATIN PLURAL	ENGLISH PLURAL
NOMINATIVE	cor	a/the heart [subject]	corda	the hearts [subject]
GENITIVE	cordis	of the heart, the heart's	cordum	of the hearts, the hearts'
DATIVE	cordī	to/for the heart	cordibus	to/for the hearts
ACCUSATIVE	cor	the heart [direct object]	corda	the hearts [direct object]
ABLATIVE	corde	by/with/from the heart	cordibus	by/with/from the hearts
VOCATIVE	Ō cor	O heart	Ō corda	O hearts

vulnus, vulneris (n) *wound*

	LATIN SINGULAR	ENGLISH SINGULAR	LATIN PLURAL	ENGLISH PLURAL
NOMINATIVE	vulnus	a/the wound [subject]	vulnera	the wounds [subject]
GENITIVE	vulneris	of the wound, the wound's	vulnerum	of the wounds, the wounds'
DATIVE	vulnerī	to/for the wound	vulneribus	to/for the wounds
ACCUSATIVE	vulnus	the wound [direct object]	vulnera	the wounds [direct object]
ABLATIVE	vulnere	by/with/from the wound	vulneribus	by/with/from the wounds
VOCATIVE	Ō vulnus	O wound	Ō vulnera	O wounds

Review

Make sure you review *sum*, *eram*, and *erō* in this lesson, and that you keep practicing your First/Second Declension adjective endings.

5. Worksheet

Exercise D4: You (pl.) were hastening to the town with many soldiers and were singing many songs of victory. *Ad oppidum multīs cum mīlitibus festinābātis et multa carmina victōriae cantābātis.* *Cum* likes to hide, and when its object has an adjective with a noun, it takes refuge between them.

This lesson's Latin to English story is loosely based on the book of Judith from the Apocrypha.

Lines 4–5 read, *Si pugnābitis, oppidum populumque vestrum delēbimus.* "If you will fight, we will destroy your town and people." This is called a Future More Vivid Condition. Notice that both halves in Latin use the future tense, but it actually sounds more natural in English to use the present in the "if" clause: "If you *fight*, we will destroy your town and people." This use of the English present to indicate future action occurs frequently, as in, "My vacation starts tomorrow."

6. Quiz

Administer Quiz 13 when the students are ready.

Lesson 13 Worksheet

A. Vocabulary

Translate the following words from Latin to English or English to Latin as appropriate.

1. wound: **vulnus**
2. venēnum: **poison**
3. caput: **head**
4. moreover: **autem**
5. onus: **burden, load, weight**
6. grāmen: **grass, greenery**
7. diū: **for a long time**
8. carmen: **song, chant, poem, prophecy**
9. journey: **iter**
10. flūmen: **river**
11. ōs: **mouth**
12. ōra: **shore**
13. lītus: **shore, shoreline**
14. wise: **doctus**
15. nōmen: **name**
16. immediately: **statim**
17. suddenly: **repentē**
18. lac: **milk**
19. tempus: **time**
20. interim: **meanwhile, in the meantime**
21. via: **road, way**
22. heart: **cor**
23. cārus: **dear, beloved**
24. corpus: **body**
25. horrendus: **dreadful, awful, fearful**

B. Grammar

1. Decline *evil journey*.

	LATIN SINGULAR	LATIN PLURAL
NOM.	iter malum	itinera mala
GEN.	itineris malī	itinerum malōrum
DAT.	itinerī malō	itineribus malīs
ACC.	iter malum	itinera mala
ABL.	itinere malō	itineribus malīs
VOC.	[Ō] iter malum	[Ō] itinera mala

2. Decline *beloved mother*.

	LATIN SINGULAR	LATIN PLURAL
NOM.	cāra māter	cārae mātrēs
GEN.	cārae mātris	cārārum mātrum
DAT.	cārae mātrī	cārīs mātribus
ACC.	cāram mātrem	cārās mātrēs
ABL.	cārā mātre	cārīs mātribus
VOC.	[Ō] cāra māter	[Ō] cārae mātrēs

3. Decline *dreadful time*.

	LATIN SINGULAR	LATIN PLURAL
NOM.	tempus horrendum	tempora horrenda
GEN.	temporis horrendī	temporum horrendōrum
DAT.	temporī horrendō	temporibus horrendīs
ACC.	tempus horrendum	tempora horrenda
ABL.	tempore horrendō	temporibus horrendīs
VOC.	[Ō] tempus horrendum	[Ō] tempora horrenda

C. Memorization

Fill in the blanks.

Magnificat anima mea Dominum,

et exsultāvit spīritus meus in Deō salvātōre meō,

quia rēspexit humilitātem ancillae suae.

Ecce enim ex hōc beātam mē dīcent omnēs generātiōnēs,

quia fēcit mihi magna,

quī potēns est,

et sanctum nōmen eius,

et misericordia **eius** _____ in **prōgeniēs** _____ et **prōgeniēs** _____ **timentibus** _____ eum.

Fēcit **potentiam** _____ in **brāchiō** _____ suō,

dispersit _____ superbōs **mente** _____ **cordis** _____ suī;

dēposuit **potentēs** _____ **dē** _____ sēde

et **exaltāvit** _____ humilēs;

D. English to Latin Translation

Translate each sentence from English to Latin.

1. Your journey to the castle will be wretched because the woods of darkness are dreadful.
   <u>Tuum/vestrum iter ad castellum miserum erit quod silvae tenēbrārum horrendae sunt.</u>

2. The horses were carrying great burdens from the ships across the shore to the town.
   <u>Equī onera magna ab alnīs trāns ōram/lītus ad oppidum portābant.</u>

3. Our goats eat grass and drink water, but our children eat cookies and drink milk.
   <u>Nostrī caprī grāmen mandūcant et aquam pōtant, sed līberī nostrī crustula mandūcant et lac pōtant.</u>

4. You (pl.) were hastening to the town with many soldiers and were singing many songs of victory.
   <u>Ad oppidum multīs cum mīlitibus festīnābātis et multa carmina victōriae cantābātis.</u>

5. The evil dragon was wounding the king's body with many wounds of poison, and therefore was able to kill the good king.
   <u>Draco malus corpus rēgis multīs vulneribus venēnī vulnerābat, et itaque rēgem bonum necāre poterat.</u>

6. We will hunt lions and tigers across great rivers and in distant caves and through fearful forests.
   <u>Leōnēs tigridēsque [*or* et tigridēs] trāns flumina magna et in spēluncīs longinquīs et per silvīs horrendīs captābimus.</u>

7. The pirates were fighting the soldiers with daggers and bad words; the soldiers were fighting the pirates with swords and arrows.
   <u>Pīrātae mīlitēs sicīs et verbīs malīs [*or* sicīs verbīsque malīs] pugnābant; mīlitēs pīrātās gladiīs sagittīsque [*or* et sagittīs] [pugnābant].</u>

8. O queen, beware of handsome but evil men when you walk from the castle into the town.

   Ō rēgīna, cavē pulchrōs sed malōs [virōs] ubi/quandō ab castellō in oppidum ambulās.

9. The evil soldiers seized the Lord's apostles and immediately gave the men large burdens.

   Mīlitēs malī apostolōs Dominī occupābant et virīs onera magna statim dābant.

10. Will I be able to conquer the ugly king's soldiers and save your town, your children, and your maidens?

    Mīlitēs rēgis foedī superāre poterō et oppidum vestrum/tuum, līberōs vestrōs/tuōs, et virginēs vestrās/tuās servāre [poterō]?

E. Latin to English Translation

1 Multī mīlitēs magnī malīque oppidum nostrum diū obsidēbant. Multum cibum aut multam aquam nōn habēbāmus, et timēbāmus. Pugnāre nōn audēbāmus, et tempora mala erant. Dux[1] malus mīlitum nostrō populō clāmābat: "Dā mihi[2] vestrum oppidum! Līberī vestrī servī nostrī erunt, et bēstiae vestrae aurumque vestrum erunt nostrae! Sī[3] pugnābitis, oppidum populumque vestrum dēlēbimus."
5 Miserī erāmus et ululābāmus: "Heu![4] Malīs mīlitibus nostrum oppidum dare dēbēmus, aut dēlēbunt." Fēmina autem pulchra doctaque respondēbat, "Oppidum nostrum malīs nōn dabimus! Deus oppidum nostrum, līberōs nostrōs, et vītās nostrās servābit. Ad inimīcōs ab oppidō ambulābō." Fēmina Deum virtūtem victōriamque ōrābat, et ad ducem inimīcōrum ambulābat. Et multum cibum bonum vīnumque portābat. Ducī dēclārābat: "Mē trādō[5] quod hominēs oppidī diū pugnābunt et oppidum dēlēbis. Bonum
10 cibum vīnumque portō, et serva tua erō." Dux malus pulchram spectābat, et amābat. Multum cibum mandūcābat et multum vīnum pōtābat, et fēminae multa narrābat. Et vīnum pōtābat. Dēnique ebrius[6] erat et iacēbat. Fēmina gladium magnum virī occupābat et caput gladiō removēbat.[7] Caput inimīcī nostrī ad oppidum portābat, et laetī erāmus. Itaque inimīcōs Deī superāre et oppidum nostrum et līberōs nostrōs et vītās nostrās servāre poterāmus.

Glossary
1. *dux, ducis* (m): leader, guide, general
2. *mihi*: dative singular of the first person pronoun *ego*: I, me
3. *sī*: if
4. *heu*, interjection: alas!
5. *Mē trādō*: "I am surrendering myself"; *trādō* is a compound of *dō*
6. *ēbrius, -a, -um*: drunk, intoxicated
7. *removeō, -ēre, -mōvī, -mōtum*: I remove

Many great and evil soldiers were besieging our town for a long time. We did not have much food or water, and we were afraid. We did not dare to fight, and the times were evil. The evil general of the soldiers shouted to our people: "Give me your town! Your children will be our slaves and your beasts and [your] gold will be ours! If you [will] fight, we will destroy your town and your people." We were wretched and wailed, "Alas! We ought to give our town to the evil soldiers, or they will destroy [it]." However, a beautiful and wise woman responded, "We will not give our town to the evil men! God will save our town, our children, and our lives. I will walk from the town to the enemy." The woman prayed to God for courage and victory, and walked to the leader of the enemy. She was also carrying much good food and wine. She declared [explained] to the leader: "I am surrendering myself because the men of the town will fight for a long time and you will destroy the town. I am carrying good food and wine, and I will be your servant." The evil leader looked at the beautiful woman, and loved [her]. He ate much food and drank much wine and told the woman many things. He also kept drinking wine. Finally he was drunk and lay down. The woman seized the man's huge sword and removed his head with the sword. She carried the head of our enemy to the town, and we were happy. Thus we were able to defeat the enemy [*or* enemies] of God and save our town and our children and our lives.

Lesson 13 Quiz (74 points)

A. Vocabulary (10 points)

Translate the following words.

1. head: **caput**
2. lītus: **shore, shoreline**
3. nōmen: **name**
4. audeō: **I dare**
5. mouth: **ōs**
6. vulnus: **wound**
7. horrendus: **dreadful, awful, fearful**
8. diū: **for a long time**
9. iter: **journey, road, route, trek**
10. statim: **immediately**

B. Grammar (15 points)

1. Decline *big body*.

	LATIN SINGULAR	LATIN PLURAL
NOM.	corpus magnum	corpora magna
GEN.	corporis magnī	corporum magnōrum
DAT.	corporī magnō	corporibus magnīs
ACC.	corpus magnum	corpora magna
ABL.	corpore magnō	corporibus magnīs
VOC.	[Ō] corpus magnum	[Ō] corpora magna

2. Give a synopsis of *narrō* in the third person singular.

	LATIN	ENGLISH
PRESENT ACT.	narrat	he/she/it tells, recounts, relates
IMPERFECT ACT.	narrābat	he/she/it was telling
FUTURE ACT.	narrābit	he/she/it will tell

C. Translation (17 points)

Translate each sentence.

1. My faithful horses were carrying great burdens to the farmhouse.

   Meī equī fīdī onera magna ad villam portābant.

2. Pīrātās malōs pugnāre et superāre nunc dēbēs.

   You ought to fight and defeat the evil pirates now.

D. Memorization (32 points)

Write out the first twelve lines of the *Magnificat* in Latin.

Magnificat anima mea Dominum,

et exsultāvit spīritus meus in Deō salvātōre meō,

quia rēspexit humilitātem ancillae suae.

Ecce enim ex hōc beātam mē dicent omnēs generātiōnēs,

quia fēcit mihi magna,

quī potēns est,

et sanctum nōmen eius,

et misericordia eius in prōgeniēs et prōgeniēs timentibus eum.

Fēcit potentiam in brāchiō suō,

dispersit superbōs mente cordis suī;

dēposuit potentēs dē sēde

et exaltāvit humilēs;

LESSON 14 (Student Edition p. 118)

Verbs: Perfect Active Indicative

1. Word List

7. *āiō*, I say, assert, affirm—*Āiō* is a "defective" verb. A defective verb is one that is missing some of its forms. The verb *āiō* is missing nearly all of its forms, and exists in the following (for the most part):

	PRESENT ACTIVE INDICATIVE		IMPERFECT ACTIVE INDICATIVE	
	SINGULAR	PLURAL	SINGULAR	PLURAL
1ST	āiō	———	āiēbam	āiēbāmus
2ND	ais	———	āiēbās	āiēbātis
3RD	ait	āiunt	āiēbat	āiēbant

2. Derivatives/Memorization Helps

1. *amor*, love: amorous
2. *dux*, leader, guide, general: duke, duchess
3. *senex*, old man: senile, senior, senate
4. *tellūs*, the earth, ground, land: tellurian, telluric
5. *vesper*, evening, evening star: vespers
6. *vōx*, voice: vocal, vociferous; see also *vocō* [Lesson 1]
7. *āiō*, I say, assert, affirm
8. *errō*, I wander, err, am mistaken: err, error, errant (but not errand)
9. *exerceō*, I train, exercise
10. *fleō*, I weep
11. *moveō*, I move: move, motion, emotion
12. *nō*, I swim: natation, natant
13. *nuntiō*, I announce, declare: announce, pronounce, enunciate
14. *parō*, I prepare: prepare, preparation, apparatus
15. *removeō*, I remove, take away: remove; see *moveō* above
16. *reptō*, I crawl, creep: reptile, reptilian
17. *vastō*, I devastate, lay waste: devastate
18. *nec* (neque), and not, nor; *nec...nec*, neither...nor
19. *sub*, under, up under, close to; below, under(neath), at the foot of: prefixes sub-/suc-/suf-/sug-/sup-/sus-, as in submarine
20. *suprā*, above, over

3. Memorization—*Magnificat*

This lesson's new lines are:

ēsurientēs implēvit bonīs	*He has filled the hungry with good things*
et dīvitēs dīmīsit inānēs.	*and He has sent the rich away empty.*
Suscēpit Isrāel puerum suum,	*He has received Israel His son,*

Notice our perfect tense verbs in these lines: *implēvit*, *dīmīsit*, and *suscēpit*.

4. Grammar

Rejoice, for this lesson your students will move on to a new principal part, a new verb stem, and a new tense system. This lesson focuses on the perfect tense, and next lesson will cover the remaining two tenses, pluperfect and future perfect.

Your students doubtless have been diligently memorizing their principal parts. Review how to form the present stem and everything they've learned that can be derived from the stem (found from the second principal part):

Infinitive (the second principal part *is* the present active infinitive): *necāre*

Indicative:

Present Active: *necō*, etc.

Imperfect Active: *necābam*, etc.

Future Active: *necābō*, etc.

Imperative: *necā!* (sg.), *necāte!* (pl.)

Perfect Active Indicative

Now move on to the third principal part, which in our sample verb is *necāvī*. This form is the first person singular, perfect active indicative, "I killed, have killed." (This works just like the first principal part. *Necō* is the first person singular, present active indicative, "I kill.") **To find the stem for the perfect active system, simply remove the -ī:** *necāv-*. To this stem you can add the perfect active endings:

Perfect Active Indicative Verb Endings

	LATIN SINGULAR	ENGLISH SINGULAR	LATIN PLURAL	ENGLISH PLURAL
1ST	-ī	I *verbed*, have *verbed*	-imus	we *verbed*, have *verbed*
2ND	-istī	you *verbed*, have *verbed*	-istis	you (pl.) *verbed*, have *verbed*
3RD	-it	he/she/it *verbed*, has *verbed*	-ērunt	they *verbed*, have *verbed*

Here is *necō* conjugated in the Perfect Active Indicative:

	LATIN SINGULAR	ENGLISH SINGULAR	LATIN PLURAL	ENGLISH PLURAL
1ST	necāvī	I killed, have killed	necāvimus	we killed, have killed
2ND	necāvistī	you killed, have killed	necāvistis	you (pl.) killed, have killed
3RD	necāvit	he/she/it killed, has killed	necāvērunt	they killed, have killed

Before we get too far ahead of ourselves, we should discuss how to translate the perfect. Recall that the imperfect tense is so called because the action is incomplete, continuous, or habitual. In that sense the perfect tense is the opposite of the imperfect, because it signifies completed action. The perfect can signify a simple past action: *Oswald **killed** the dragon yesterday*. It can also portray action that is completed with reference to the present time: *Rejoice, because Oswald **has killed** the dragon!* (In English we call this the present perfect for that reason—the past action in some way affects the present.) You may also say ***did kill*** for emphasis, or, if you are using a negative word such as "not"—*Oswald **did** not **kill***.

One handy aspect of the perfect active system is that it is highly regular, so that even if a verb has wildly irregular principal parts, chances are that the third principal part will end in -ī and can therefore be conjugated regularly. Let's take *sum* and *possum* for example. Even though the principal parts of *sum* are *sum, esse, fuī, futūrum*, the third principle part *fuī* does end in -ī, and therefore the perfect active stem is *fu-*.

Thus *sum* conjugated in the perfect active will look like this:

	LATIN SINGULAR	ENGLISH SINGULAR	LATIN PLURAL	ENGLISH PLURAL
1ST	fuī	I was, have been	fuimus	we were, have been
2ND	fuistī	you were, have been	fuistis	you (pl.) were, have been
3RD	fuit	he/she/it was, has been	fuērunt	they were, have been

Similarly, the principal parts of *possum* are *possum, posse, potuī*, ——, and the perfect stem is therefore *potu-*. The perfect active indicative of *possum* is:

	LATIN SINGULAR	ENGLISH SINGULAR	LATIN PLURAL	ENGLISH PLURAL
1ST	potuī	I was able, have been able	potuimus	we were able, have been able
2ND	potuistī	you were able, have been able	potuistis	you (pl.) were able, have been able
3RD	potuit	he/she/it was able, has been able	potuērunt	they were able, have been able

We can now add another line to our verb synopsis, which will look like this:

	LATIN	ENGLISH
PRESENT ACT.	necās	you kill
IMPERFECT ACT.	necābās	you were killing
FUTURE ACT.	necābis	you will kill
PERFECT ACT.	necāvistī	you killed, have killed

5. Worksheet

Exercise D3: Oswald was a small boy, but he sailed to a distant island and killed a small kraken there. *Oswaldus puer parvus erat, sed ad longinquam insulam nāvigāvit, et cētum parvum ibī necāvit.* *Erat* is probably better than *fuit* here, since Oswald was a boy for a while—thus the continuous imperfect tense rather than the perfect.

The Latin to English story is based on *Beowulf*.

E. *Invenī Verba:* The Word Search is just for fun (though you could assign credit for translating and analyzing).

6. Quiz

Administer Quiz 14 when the students are ready.

Lesson 14 Worksheet

A. Vocabulary

Translate the following words from Latin to English or English to Latin as appropriate. For the verbs, also fill in the missing principal parts. For each preposition, include which case(s) it takes.

1. darkness: **tenēbrae**
2. nuntiō, nuntiāre, **nuntiāvī**, **nuntiātum**: I announce, declare
3. I move: **moveō**, **movēre**, **mōvī**, **mōtum**
4. exerceō, **exercēre**, **exercuī**, **exercitum**: I train, exercise
5. king: **rex**
6. parō, **parāre**, **parāvī**, parātum: **I prepare**
7. leader: **dux**
8. suprā: **(+acc.) above, over**
9. vōx: **voice**
10. I swim: **nō**, **nāre**, **nāvī**, **nātum**
11. vesper: **evening, evening star**
12. reptō, reptāre, reptāvī, reptātum: **I crawl, creep**
13. I say: **āiō**
14. for a long time: **diū**
15. amor: **love**
16. neque: **and not, nor**
17. senex: **old man**
18. -que: **and**
19. I weep: **fleō**, **flēre**, **flēvī**, **flētum**
20. sub: **(+acc.): under, up under, close to;**
    (+abl.) below, under(neath), at the foot of
21. vastō, **vastāre**, vastāvī, **vastātum**: I devastate, lay waste
22. however: **autem**
23. tellūs: **the earth, ground, land**
24. removeō, removēre, **remōvī**, **remōtum**: I remove, take away
25. I wander: **errō**, **errāre**, **errāvī**, **errātum**

B. Grammar

1. Conjugate *parō* in the perfect active indicative in Latin and English.

	LATIN SINGULAR	ENGLISH SINGULAR	LATIN PLURAL	ENGLISH PLURAL
1ST	parāvī	I prepared, have prepared	parāvimus	we prepared, have prepared
2ND	parāvistī	you prepared, have prepared	parāvistis	you (pl.) prepared, have prepared
3RD	parāvit	he/she/it prepared, has prepared	parāvērunt	they prepared, have prepared

2. Conjugate *fleō* in the perfect active indicative in Latin and English.

	LATIN SINGULAR	ENGLISH SINGULAR	LATIN PLURAL	ENGLISH PLURAL
1ST	flēvī	I wept, have wept	flēvimus	we wept, have wept
2ND	flēvistī	you wept, have wept	flēvistis	you (pl.) wept, have wept
3RD	flēvit	he/she/it wept, has wept	flēvērunt	they wept, have wept

3. Give a synopsis of *reptō* in the first person plural.

	LATIN	ENGLISH
PRESENT ACT.	reptāmus	we crawl, creep
IMPERFECT ACT.	reptābāmus	we were crawling
FUTURE ACT.	reptābimus	we will crawl
PERFECT ACT.	reptāvimus	we crawled, have crawled

4. Decline *beautiful earth* (use *tellūs*).

	LATIN SINGULAR	LATIN PLURAL
NOM.	tellūs pulchra	tellūrēs pulchrae
GEN.	tellūris pulchrae	tellūrum pulchrārum
DAT.	tellūrī pulchrae	tellūribus pulchrīs
ACC.	tellūrem pulchram	tellūrēs pulchrās
ABL.	tellūre pulchrā	tellūribus pulchrīs
VOC.	[Ō] tellūs pulchra	[Ō] tellūrēs pulchrae

C. Memorization

Fill in the blanks.

Magnificat anima mea Dominum,

et exsultāvit spīritus meus in Deō salvātōre meō,

quia rēspexit humilitātem ancillae suae.

Ecce enim ex hōc beātam mē dīcent omnēs generātiōnēs,

quia fēcit mihi magna,

quī potēns est,

et sanctum nōmen eius,

et misericordia eius in prōgeniēs et prōgeniēs timentibus eum.

Fēcit potentiam in brāchiō suō,

dispersit **superbōs** mente **cordis** **suī** ;

dēposuit potentēs dē **sēde**

et **exaltāvit** **humilēs** ;

ēsurientēs **implēvit** bonīs

et **dīvitēs** dīmīsit **inānēs** .

Suscēpit Isrāel **puerum** **suum** ,

D. English to Latin Translation

Translate each sentence from English to Latin.

1. Yesterday the dragon flew on great wings over the heads of the crowd.

   Draco ālīs magnīs suprā capita turbae herī volāvit.

2. Many beasts have laid waste our fields, but neither the king nor the leaders will remove the wild [beasts] from the land.

   Multae bēstiae agrōs nostrōs vastāvērunt, sed nec/neque rex nec/neque ducēs ferās ab tellūre/patriā/terrā removēbunt.

3. Oswald was a small boy, but he sailed to a distant island and killed a small kraken there.

   Oswaldus puer parvus erat/fuit, sed ad longinquam īnsulam nāvigāvit, et cētum parvum ibī necāvit.

4. We have wandered to many lands, where we have sung many songs with our beautiful voices to kings and queens, farmers and maidens.

   Ad multās tellūrēs/patriās/terrās errāvimus, ubi rēgibus rēgīnīsque [*or* et rēgīnīs], agricolīs virginibusque [*or* et virginibus] multa carmina nostrīs vocibus pulchrīs cantāvimus.

5. Skilled but evil pirates destroyed the general's ship, and so the old man swam to the island and was waiting there for a long time.

   Pīrātae doctī sed malī navem/alnum ducis dēlēvērunt; itaque senex ad insulam nāvit et ibī diū manēbat.

6. You wept because you gave your love to the beautiful woman, but she has always loved the faithful soldier.

   Flēvistī quod fēminae pulchrae amōrem tuum dedistī, sed mīlitem fīdum semper amāvit. [*Note: Although I suppose the "you" could be plural, singular makes more sense here.*]

7. However, I assert: "I am a great lion, king of beasts, and I have killed many goats and given wounds to many tigers."

   Āiō autem: "Leō magnus sum, rex bestiārum, et multōs caprōs necāvī et multīs tigridibus vulnera dedī."

8. We have prepared burdens for our camels; when will we walk across the sands and look at the evening stars?

   Onera camēlīs nostrīs parāvimus; quandō/ubi trāns harēnās ambulābimus et vesperēs spectābimus?

9. The soldiers were training for a long time in your fields, but finally the general moved the men to the forests.

   Mīlitēs in agrīs vestrīs/tuīs diū exercēbant, sed dux virōs ad silvās dēnique mōvit.

10. At the foot of the castle sat a small boy, and he was giving grass and milk to the little goats.

    Sub castellō puer parvus sēdit, et parvīs caprīs grāmen lacque [*or* et lac] dabat.

E. Latin to English Translation

1   Senex nunc sum, sed mīles magnus ōlim eram. Bene semper pugnāvī, et servus fīdus nostrī ducis rēgisque eram. Inimīcōs spectāvī et nōn timuī, sed timuērunt. Ad īnsulās longinquās nāvī et cum cētīs et bēstiīs ferīs ōceanī pugnāvī. Ōlim ad tellūrem nāvigāvī ubi rex senex erat et populus flēbat. Bēstia foeda horrendaque carmina mīlitum et rēgis et rēgīnae nōn amāvit. Itaque populum oppugnāvit, et
5   multōs necāvit et mandūcāvit. Rex āit, "Servā nostrum populum, Ō mīles magne!" Rēgī āiō: "Tuum populum servābō, et bēstiam malam meīs palmīs¹ nōn gladiō meō necābō!" In tenēbrīs vesperis, bēstiam exspectāvī. In aulam² intrāvit et virum oppugnāvit. Bēstiam palmīs meīs pugnāvī et bracchium³ bēstiae remōvī. Ad palūdem⁴ errāvit et iacuit. Victōria mea fuit, et rex laetus erat. Māter mala bēstiae autem nōn laeta erat, et ab palūde festīnāvit et aulam oppugnāvit. Ab aulā ad palūdem et in spēluncam sub
10 palūde pugnāvimus. Gladium magnum ibī occupāvī et caput matris bēstiae remōvī. Et bēstiam in spēluncā vīdī, et caput gladiō remōvī. Capita bēstiārum ad aulam portāvī. Populus et rex laetī nunc erant. Ad meam tellūrem nāvigāvī, et rex fuī. Nunc draco malus meum populum oppugnat quod servus in spēluncam dracōnis intrāvit et calicem⁵ aurī occupāvit. Senex sum, sed dracōnem necābō et populum meum servābō.

Glossary
1. *palma, -ae* (f): hand
2. *aula, -ae* (f): hall, inner/royal court
3. *bracchium, -i* (n): arm
4. *palus, palūdis* (f): swamp
5. *calix, calicis* (m): goblet

I am an old man now, but once I was a great soldier. I have always fought well and was a faithful servant of our general and of our king. I have looked upon the enemy and did not fear, but they feared. I have swum to distant islands and fought with krakens and fierce beasts of the ocean. Once I sailed to a land where the king was an old man and the people wept. A horrible and dreadful beast did not like the songs of the soldiers and the king and queen. And so he attacked the people and killed and ate many. The king said, "Save our people, great soldier!" I said to the king [lit., say, *but in English be consistent with tenses!*]: "I will save your people, and I will slay the evil beast with my hands and not with my sword!"

In the darkness of evening, I waited for the beast. He entered into the hall and attacked a man. I fought the beast with my hands and tore the beast's arm off [lit., removed, *but "tore off" is more exciting*]. **He wandered back to [his] swamp and lay down dead. The victory was mine, and the king was happy. However, the beast's evil mother was not happy, and she hastened from the swamp and attacked the hall. We fought from the hall to the swamp, and into a cave under the swamp. There I seized a great sword and removed the head of the beast's mother. I also saw the beast in the cave, and removed his head with the sword. I carried the beasts' heads to the hall. The people and the king were now happy. I sailed to my [own] land, and was king. Now an evil dragon is attacking my people because a slave entered the dragon's cave and seized a goblet of gold. I am an old man, but I will kill the dragon and save my people.**

F. For Fun: *Invenī Verba!*

Find the following list of words in the chart below. The words may be forwards, backwards, vertical, or diagonal. If you wish to impress, translate the words as well. If you wish to amaze, translate *and* analyze (parse, etc. as appropriate) the words.

aiunt they say (3rd person pl. pres. act. indic.)

amorem love (masc. sg. acc.)

autem however, moreover

capitis of the head (neut. sg. sg.)

carmina songs (neut. pl. nom. or acc.)

corda hearts (neut. pl. nom. or acc.)

corporis of the body (neut. sg. gen.)

cum with

deleo I destroy (1st person sg. pres. act. indic.)

diu for a long time

doctorum of the learned [ones] (masc. or neut. pl. gen.)

domuimus we [have] tamed (1st person pl. perf. act. indic.)

draconi to/for the dragon (masc. sg. dat.)

dux leader (masc. sg. nom.)

errabat he was wandering (3rd person sg. imperf. act. indic.)

exercebis you will train (2nd person sg. fut. act. indic.)

festinat he hastens (3rd person sg. pres. act. indic.)

flevisti you [have] wept (2nd person sg. perf. act. indic.)

gramen grass (neut. sg. nom. or acc.

hominem man (masc. sg. acc.)

interim meanwhile

intrant they enter (3rd person pl. pres. act. indic.)

iter journey (neut. sg. nom. or acc.)

leoni to/for the lion (masc. sg. dat.)

matre by/with/from the mother (fem. sg. abl.)

militibus to/for [or, by/with/from] the soldiers (masc. pl. dat. or abl.)

movistis you (pl.) [have] moved (2nd person pl. perf. act. indic.)

nabat he was swimming (3rd person sg. imperf. act. indic.)

neque neither

nōminibus to/for [or, by/with/from] the names (neut. pl. dat. or abl.)

noster our (masc. sg. nom.)

nuntiabunt they will announce (3rd person pl. fut. act. indic.)

onus burden (neut. sg. nom. or acc.)

paro I prepare (1st person sg. pres. act. indic.)

pater father (masc. sg. nom.)

poteras you were able (2nd person sg. imperf. act. indic.)

quando when?

quod because

reges you rule (2nd person sg. pres. act. indic.)

removet he removes (3rd person sg. pres. act. indic.)

reptavimus we [have] crawled (1st person pl. perf. act. indic.)

rides you laugh (2nd person sg. pres. act. indic.)

senex old man (masc. sg. nom.)

sororem <u>sister (fem. sg. acc.)</u>

statim <u>immediately</u>

sub <u>under</u>

supra <u>above</u>

telluris <u>of the earth (fem. sg. gen.)</u>

tempore <u>by/with/from the time (neut. sg. abl.)</u>

tigride <u>by/with/from the tiger (masc. sg. abl.)</u>

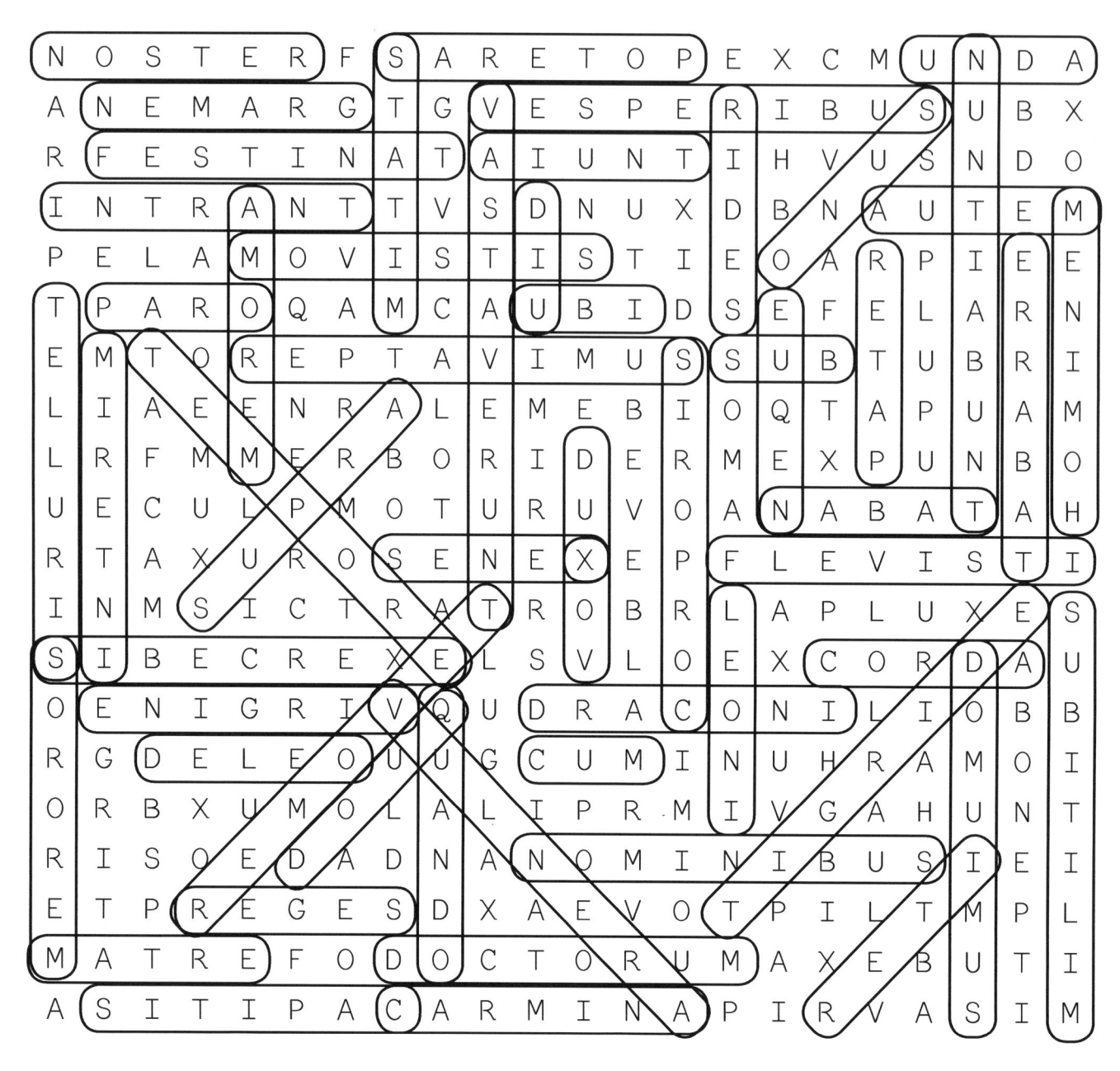

ubi <u>when</u>

unda <u>wave, by/with/from the wave (fem. sg. nom. or abl.)</u>

vastaverunt <u>they [have] devastated (3rd person pl. perf. act. indic.)</u>

vesperibus <u>to/for [or, by/with/from] the evenings (masc. pl. dat. or abl.)</u>

virgine <u>by/with/from the maiden (fem. sg. abl.)</u>

vōx <u>voice (fem. sg. nom.)</u>

vulnera <u>wounds (neut. pl. nom. or acc.)</u>

Lesson 14 Quiz (61 points)

A. Vocabulary (14 points)

Translate the following words. For prepositions, also give the case(s).

1. suprā: (+<u>acc.</u>) <u>above, over</u>
2. exerceō: <u>I train, exercise</u>
3. I prepare: <u>parō</u>
4. vesper: <u>evening, evening star</u>
5. vastō: <u>I devastate, lay waste</u>
6. vōx: <u>voice</u>
7. onus: <u>burden, load, weight</u>
8. āiō: <u>I say, assert, affirm</u>
9. amor: <u>love</u>
10. nor: <u>nec, neque</u>

B. Grammar (22 points)

1. Conjugate *nuntiō* in the perfect active indicative in Latin and English.

	LATIN SINGULAR	ENGLISH SINGULAR	LATIN PLURAL	ENGLISH PLURAL
1ST	nuntiāvī	I (have) announced	nuntiāvimus	we (have) announced
2ND	nuntiāvistī	you (have) announced	nuntiāvistis	you (pl.) (have) announced
3RD	nuntiāvit	he/she/it (has) announced	nuntiāvērunt	they (have) announced

2. Give a synopsis of *moveō* in the first person plural.

	LATIN	ENGLISH
PRESENT ACT.	movēmus	we move
IMPERFECT ACT.	movēbāmus	we were moving
FUTURE ACT.	movēbimus	we will move
PERFECT ACT.	mōvimus	we (have) moved

C. Translation

No sentences this lesson! Be appropriately grateful.

D. Memorization (35 points)

Write out the first fifteen lines of the *Magnificat* in Latin.

Magnificat anima mea Dominum,

et exsultāvit spīritus meus in Deō salvātōre meō,

quia rēspexit humilitātem ancillae suae.

Ecce enim ex hōc beātam mē dicent omnēs generātiōnēs,

quia fēcit mihi magna,

quī potēns est,

et sanctum nōmen eius,

et misericordia eius in prōgeniēs et prōgeniēs timentibus eum.

Fēcit potentiam in brāchiō suō,

dispersit superbōs mente cordis suī;

dēposuit potentēs dē sēde

et exaltāvit humilēs;

ēsurientēs implēvit bonīs

et dīvitēs dīmīsit inānēs.

Suscēpit Isrāel puerum suum,

LESSON 15 (Student Edition p. 130)

Pluperfect & Future Perfect Active Indicative

1. Word List

1. *amīcus/amīca*, friend—Point out that this is the positive opposite of *inimīcus*, "enemy" [Lesson 10].

18. *iam*, now, already; *nōn iam*, no longer—Notice that when used with *nōn*, *iam* has a slightly idiomatic meaning. *Dracōnem nōn iam timeō* literally means, "I do not fear the dragon now" (we don't usually say "I do not fear the dragon already"), but it sounds fine to say, "I no longer fear the dragon."

2. Derivatives/Memorization Helps

1. *amīcus/amīca*, friend: amicable, amiable
2. *bellum*, war: belligerent, rebel
3. *castra*, camp
4. *cōpia*, supply, plenty, abundance; (pl.) troops: copious, cornucopia
5. *crux*, cross: crux, crucify, crucifer
6. *flōs*, flower: floral, florid
7. *frūmentum*, grain; (pl.) crops: frumentaceous, frumenty
8. *gigās*, giant: gigantic, giant
9. *glōria*, fame, glory: glory, glorify, glorious, Gloria
10. *laus*, praise: laud; see also *laudō*, Lesson 1
11. *pāx*, peace: pacify, Pacific Ocean, pacifist
12. *proelium*, battle
13. *aeternus*, eternal: eternal
14. *īrātus*, angry, wrathful: irate; see also *īra*, Lesson 2
15. *appellō*, I name, call
16. *cūrō*, I care for
17. *mereō*, I deserve, earn, am worthy of
18. *iam*, now, already
19. *mox*, soon
20. *tum*, then, at that time; next, thereupon

3. Memorization—*Magnificat*

This lesson's new lines (finishing off the *Magnificat*) are:

recordātus misericordiae,	*remembering (His) mercy,*
sīcut locūtus est ad patrēs nostrōs,	*just as He spoke to our fathers,*
Ābraham et seminī eius in saecula.	*to Abraham and His seed forever.*

Encourage and congratulate your students—this was a lengthy piece of Latin to learn!

4. Grammar

Pluperfect and Future Perfect Tenses

This lesson we will round out the perfect active indicative system by adding two more tenses: the pluperfect and the future perfect. The **pluperfect** tense *expresses an action that is past the past* (think "perfect plus" or "more than perfect"), as in this sentence: "Oswald **had killed** three dragons before he was sixteen years old." Our referent is that "he was sixteen" at a certain point in the past, and before that time, he had killed the dragons.

The future perfect tense is not quite as common and sounds a little funny in isolation, but believe me, you and your students have used it. The **future perfect** refers to *an action that will be completed in the future, but it will be completed in the past of another future event*: "Before he will return to the castle next month, Oswald **will have killed** the evil dragon." Here we have two future events: 1) the return to the castle and 2) the slaying of the dragon. The slaying will happen *before* the return. (To confuse things, the *English* present can also refer to future events. Our example could have read: "Before he returns to the castle next month, Oswald will have killed the dragon." However, as English speakers we all know that the "returns" refers to a future event. We talk this way all the time: "The movie starts at 8:00 tonight," "My plane leaves tomorrow," etc.)

These two tenses are formed from the perfect active stem, which (as you should have one of the students remind the class) is derived by removing the *-ī* from the third principal part. Conveniently (remember what great linguistic recyclers the Romans were?), the pluperfect active indicative endings are identical to the imperfect indicative of *sum*, and the future perfect endings are *almost* identical to the future indicative of *sum*, with one exception in the third person plural:

Pluperfect Active Indicative Verb Endings

	LATIN SINGULAR	ENGLISH SINGULAR	LATIN PLURAL	ENGLISH PLURAL
1ST	-eram	I had *verbed*	-erāmus	we had *verbed*
2ND	-erās	you had *verbed*	-erātis	you (pl.) had *verbed*
3RD	-erat	he/she/it had *verbed*	-erant	they had *verbed*

Future Perfect Active Indicative Verb Endings

	LATIN SINGULAR	ENGLISH SINGULAR	LATIN PLURAL	ENGLISH PLURAL
1ST	-erō	I will have *verbed*	-erimus	we will have *verbed*
2ND	-eris	you will have *verbed*	-eritis	you (pl.) will have *verbed*
3RD	-erit	he/she/it will have *verbed*	**-erint**	they will have *verbed*

Note that the exception is *-erint* in the third person plural. You can help your students remember this by pointing out that the perfect active third person plural ending is *-ērunt*, so of course this one could not be the same and had to be -*erint*. You can also teach them this little saying: "When it's a word, it's *erunt*; when it's an ending, it's -*erint*." (Make sure you emphasize "word" and *erunt* with a nice deep round voice, and "ending" and *erint* in a pinched nasal one—this will get the point across better.)

Here is our sample verb *necō* conjugated in these two new tenses:

Pluperfect Active of *necō*

	LATIN SINGULAR	ENGLISH SINGULAR	LATIN PLURAL	ENGLISH PLURAL
1ST	necāveram	I had killed	necāverāmus	we had killed
2ND	necāverās	you had killed	necāverātis	you (pl.) had killed
3RD	necāverat	he/she/it had killed	necāverant	they had killed

Future Perfect Active of *necō*

	LATIN SINGULAR	ENGLISH SINGULAR	LATIN PLURAL	ENGLISH PLURAL
1ST	necāverō	I will have killed	necāverimus	we will have killed
2ND	necāveris	you will have killed	necāveritis	you (pl.) will have killed
3RD	necāverit	he/she/it will have killed	necāverint	they will have killed

Now that we have all six tenses, our verb synopsis of the active indicative is complete. It will look like this:

Synopsis of *necō* in the second person singular

	LATIN	ENGLISH
PRESENT ACT.	necās	you kill
IMPERFECT ACT.	necābās	you were killing
FUTURE ACT.	necābis	you will kill
PERFECT ACT.	necāvistī	you killed, have killed
PLUPERFECT ACT.	necāverās	you had killed
FUTURE PERF. ACT.	necāveris	you will have killed

One other note: your students now know three past tenses. Thus, when you ask them what tense a verb is, and they say "past," don't let them get away with that—which past? Is it imperfect, perfect, or pluperfect?

5. Worksheet

Follow the directions given and complete the worksheet.

6. Quiz

Administer Quiz 15 when the students are ready.

Lesson 15 Worksheet

A. Vocabulary

Translate the following words from Latin to English or English to Latin as appropriate. For the verbs, also fill in the missing principal parts. For each preposition, include which case(s) it takes.

1. meanwhile: **interim**
2. soon: **mox**
3. laus: **praise**
4. camp: **castra**
5. glōria: **glory**
6. cōpia: **supply, plenty, abundance**; (pl.) **troops**
7. dēnique: **finally**
8. appellō, **appellāre**, **appellāvī**, appellātum: **I name, call**
9. crux: **cross**
10. war: **bellum**
11. kraken: **cētus**
12. flōs: **flower**
13. mereō, **merēre**, **meruī**, meritum: **I deserve, earn, am worthy of**
14. frūmentum: **grain; (pl.) crops**
15. sub: **(+acc.) under, up under, close to; (+abl.) below, under(neath), at the foot of**
16. then: **tum**
17. īrātus: **angry, wrathful**
18. giant: **gigās**
19. caveō, -ēre, cāvī, cautum: **I guard against, beware (of)**
20. proelium: **battle**
21. cūrō, **cūrāre**, cūrāvī, **cūrātum**: **I care for**
22. eternal: **aeternus**
23. iam: **now, already**
24. pāx: **peace**
25. amīca: **friend**

B. Grammar

1. Conjugate *mereō* in the perfect active indicative.

	LATIN SINGULAR	ENGLISH SINGULAR	LATIN PLURAL	ENGLISH PLURAL
1ST	meruī	I (have) deserved	meruimus	we (have) deserved
2ND	meruistī	you (have) deserved	meruistis	you (pl.) (have) deserved
3RD	meruit	he/she/it (has) deserved	meruērunt	they (have) deserved

2. Conjugate *appellō* in the pluperfect active indicative.

	LATIN SINGULAR	ENGLISH SINGULAR	LATIN PLURAL	ENGLISH PLURAL
1ST	appellāveram	I had called	appellāverāmus	we had called
2ND	appellāverās	you had called	appellāverātis	you (pl.) had called
3RD	appellāverat	he/she/it had called	appellāverant	they had called

3. Conjugate *lūceō* in the future perfect active indicative.

	LATIN SINGULAR	ENGLISH SINGULAR	LATIN PLURAL	ENGLISH PLURAL
1ST	lūxerō	I will have shone	lūxerimus	we will have shone
2ND	lūxeris	you will have shone	lūxeritis	you (pl.) will have shone
3RD	lūxerit	he/she/it will have shone	lūxerint	they will have shone

C. Memorization

Fill in the blanks to complete the *Magnificat*.

Magnificat anima mea Dominum,

et exsultāvit spīritus meus in Deō salvātōre meō,

quia rēspexit humilitātem ancillae suae.

Ecce enim ex hōc beātam mē dicent omnēs generātiōnēs,

quia fēcit mihi magna,

quī potēns est,

et sanctum nōmen eius,

et misericordia eius in prōgeniēs et prōgeniēs timentibus eum.

Fēcit potentiam in brāchiō suō,

dispersit superbōs mente cordis suī;

dēposuit potentēs dē sēde

et exaltāvit humilēs;

ēsurientēs **implēvit** **bonīs**

et **dīvitēs** dīmīsit **inanēs**.

Suscēpit **Isrāel** **puerum** suum,

recordātus misericordiae,

sīcut **locūtus** est **ad** **patrēs** nostrōs,

Ābraham et **seminī** **eius** in saecula.

D. English to Latin Translation

Translate each sentence from English to Latin.

1. The wise old centaur had hastened from the cave to the town and then sang prophecies there.

   Centaurus doctus [et] antīquus ab spēluncā ad oppidum festīnāverat et carmina ibī tum cantāvit.

2. The boy will give flowers to the girl, but she will have already given [her] love to the sailor.
   Puer puellae flōrēs dabit, sed nautae amōrem iam dederit.

3. Christ carried the burden of the cross; and so we will give great glory and praise to God.
   Christus onus crucis portāvit; itaque Deō magnam glōriam laudemque [*or* et laudem] dabimus.

4. The evil soldiers had burned the crops and then the angry farmers fought the troops in the camp.
   Mīlitēs malī frūmenta cremāverant et agricolae īrātī cōpiās in castrīs tum pugnāvērunt.

5. Soon you (sg.) will have named your faithful servant your son, and you will then give the good man your wealth.
   Tuum servum fīdum tuum fīlium mox appellāveris, et bonō tuās dīvitiās tum dabis.

6. The great giants were laying waste many towns and castles; they will even attack the gods in heaven.
   Gigantēs magnī multa oppida castellaque [*or* et castella] vastābant; et deōs in caelō oppugnābunt.

7. Because the foolish farmer's evil goats had eaten the woman's flowers, she shouted many bad words and names concerning goats.
   Quod caprī malī agricolae stultī flōrēs fēminae mandūcāverant, multa verba nōminaque [*or* et nōmina] [mala] dē caprīs clāmāvit.

8. We will hasten and attack the castle tomorrow, but our leader will have sat and thought about the battle for a long time.
   Festīnābimus et castellum crās oppugnābimus, sed dux noster sēderit et dē proeliō diū cōgitāverit.

9. You (pl.) moved the troops out of the camp to the beach, where they were able to fight the pirates.
   Cōpiās ex castrīs ad harēnam mōvistis, ubi/quandō pīrātās pugnāre potuērunt/poterant.

10. My mother and father had often given silver and gold to the church, and food to the wretched.
    Mea māter et [meus] pater [*or* paterque] ecclēsiae argentum aurumque [*or* et aurum] saepe dederant, et miserīs cibum [dederant].

E. Latin to English Translation

1 Ambulāverāmus et pīrātās malōs in harēnā vīderāmus. Itaque ad oppidum nostrum festīnāverāmus et virōs fēmināsque līberōsque ibī monuerāmus. Tum omnēs[1] ad castellum festīnāverāmus. Ibī sēderāmus et mānserāmus, et pīrātae in nostrum oppidum et agrōs nostrōs tum intrāvērunt et cremāvērunt. Miserī erāmus; et rēx noster et rēgīna flēvērunt. Pīrātae āiunt, "Nunc date[2] oppidum vestrum!" Respondimus,
5 "Nōn dabimus!" Tum dux pīrātārum dēclārāvit, "Oppidum vestrum obsidēbimus. Dabitis postquam[3] vestrum cibum frūmentumque bēstiāsque mandūcāveritis!" Itaque diū flēvimus. Pīrātās nōn superāre potuimus, quod multum cibum frūmentumque in castellō nōn parāverāmus. Et misera erat fīlia rēgis, et in turrī[4] castellī ambulābat et deōs ōrābat. Dux pīrātārum virginem pulchram vīdit, et amor in cor intrāvit. Pīrātīs āit: "Castellum nōn iam oppugnāre dēbēmus. Amō fīliam rēgis!" Pīrātae laetī nōn
10 erant, quod avārī erant et aurum argentumque servōsque amābant. Dux autem pulcher pīrātīs dēnique persuādēre[5] potuit quod avārīs multum aurum dedit. Tum rēgī in castellō clāmāvit: "Castellum tuum nōn iam obsidēbimus, quod fīliam tuam amō. Valē." Fīlia rēgis dē verbīs ducis cōgitāvit, et pīrātam pulchrum spectāvit. Et amor in cor intrāvit, et ab castellō ad ducem festīnāvit. Hodiē pāx est inter[6] oppidum nostrum et pīrātās.

Glossary
1. *omnēs*: nom. pl. adj. from *omnis*: all, every
2. *date*: in this context, *dō* is better translated "to give up" or "surrender."
3. *postquam*: conj., after
4. *turrī*: abl. sg. of *turris, -is* (f): tower
5. *persuādēre*: infinitive of *persuadeō*, it takes the dative case rather than accusative, and you should be able to guess what it means.
6. *inter* (+ acc.): between, among

<u>We had been walking and had seen the evil pirates on the beach. Therefore, we had hastened to our town and had warned the men and women and children there. Then we all had hastened to the castle. There we had sat and waited, and then the pirates entered into our town and our fields and burned [them] with fire. We were unhappy; our king and queen wept also [or both the king and queen wept]. The pirates said, "Surrender your city now!" We responded, "We will not surrender [it]!" Then the pirates' leader declared, "We will besiege your town. You will surrender after you will have eaten your food and grain and beasts!" Therefore, we wept for a long time. We were not able to defeat the pirates, because we had not prepared much food and grain in the castle. The king's daughter [or princess] was also sad, and she was walking upon a tower of the castle and kept praying to the gods. The pirates' leader saw the beautiful maiden, and love entered into his heart. He said to the pirates: "We ought not to attack the castle any longer [*special use of* iam]. I love the king's daughter!" The pirates were not happy, because they were greedy and loved gold and silver and slaves. However, the handsome leader was finally able to persuade the pirates because he gave the greedy men much gold. Then he shouted to the king in the castle: "We</u>

will no longer besiege your castle, because I love your daughter! Farewell." The king's daughter thought about the leader's words, and looked at the handsome pirate. Love also entered into [her] heart, and she hastened from the castle to the leader. Today there is peace between our town and the pirates.

Lesson 15 Quiz (76 points)

A. Vocabulary (10 points)

Translate the following words.

1. already: **iam**
2. frūmentum: **grain; (pl.) crops**
3. mox: **soon**
4. cōpia **supply, plenty, abundance; (pl.) troops**
5. cūrō: **I care for**
6. āiō: **I say, assert, affirm**
7. war: **bellum**
8. pāx: **peace**
9. tum: **then, at that time; next, thereupon**
10. aeternus: **eternal**

B. Grammar (15 points)

Give a synopsis of *appellō* in the third person plural.

	LATIN	ENGLISH
PRESENT ACT.	appellant	they call, name
IMPERFECT ACT.	appellābant	they were calling
FUTURE ACT.	appellābunt	they will call
PERFECT ACT.	appellāvērunt	they (have) called
PLUPERFECT ACT.	appellāverant	they had called
FUTURE PERF. ACT.	appellāverint	they will have called

C. Translation (13 points)

Translate each sentence.

1. The man of God had declared love and the gospel to the crowds.

    Vir Deī turbīs amōrem ēvangeliumque [*or* et ēvangelium] nuntiāverat/dēclārāverat.

2. Fuit bellum in castrīs et inimīcī ducem nostrum necāvērunt.

    There was war in the camp and the enemy [-mies] killed our leader.

D. Memorization (38 points)

Write out the entire *Magnificat* in Latin from memory.

Magnificat anima mea Dominum,

et exsultāvit spīritus meus in Deō salvātōre meō,

quia rēspexit humilitātem ancillae suae.

Ecce enim ex hōc beātam mē dicent omnēs generātiōnēs,

quia fēcit mihi magna,

quī potēns est,

et sanctum nōmen eius,

et misericordia eius in prōgeniēs et prōgeniēs timentibus eum.

Fēcit potentiam in brāchiō suō,

dispersit superbōs mente cordis suī;

dēposuit potentēs dē sēde

et exaltāvit humilēs;

ēsurientēs implēvit bonīs

et dīvitēs dīmīsit inānēs.

Suscēpit Isrāel puerum suum,

recordātus misericordiae,

sīcut locūtus est ad patrēs nostrōs,

Ābraham et seminī eius in saecula.

Lesson 16 (Student Edition p. 140)

Review & Test

1. Word List

There is no new Word List this lesson. Remember, in the vocabulary section on the Unit 2 test your students will be responsible only for Unit 2 words, although they should be able to translate Unit 1 words in sentences and stories. Review all Unit 2 words, and make sure the students are able to use words from Unit 1.

2. Derivatives/Memorization Helps

There won't be any derivatives on the Unit 2 Test. However, you may want to review derivatives if you feel it will assist your students in remembering their vocabulary.

3. Memorization—*Magnificat*

There is no new memorization this lesson. Review the entirety of the *Magnificat*.

4. Grammar

There is no new chant this lesson. To prepare for the test, review the following:
- how to form verbs in the second conjugation
- verb chants for the perfect, pluperfect, and future perfect active indicative
- irregular verbs *sum* and *possum*
- how to form imperatives
- noun chants for the third declension and third declension neuter
- it would behoove you to review the first and second declension as well

5. Worksheet

Since there are so many exercises, have multiple students write up their answers on the board simultaneously: #1-5, nouns; #6-11, verb synopses; and #12, full verb conjugations.

Instead of the usual sentences and story, this lesson you will be focusing on individual verbs and noun-adjective phrases to help prepare your students for the test.

6. Quiz

There is no quiz this lesson.

7. Test

Administer Unit Test 2 when the students are ready.

Lesson 16 Worksheet

A. Vocabulary

Translate the following words from Latin to English or English to Latin as appropriate. Give case(s) for prepositions.

1. autem: **however, moreover**
2. contrā: (+**acc.**) **against**
3. cum: (+ **abl.**) **with**
4. finally: **dēnique**
5. diū: **for a long time**
6. now, already: **iam**
7. interim: **meanwhile, in the meantime**
8. soon: **mox**
9. nec (neque): **and not, nor**
10. quandō: **when?, ever; since, because**
11. -que: **and**
12. because: **quod**
13. repentē: **suddenly**
14. sine: (+ **abl.**) **without**
15. immediately: **statim**
16. sub: (+**acc.**) **(up) under, close to**
17. sub: (+**abl.**) **below, under(neath), at the foot of**
18. suprā: (+**acc.**) **above, over**
19. trāns: (+**acc.**) **across**
20. tum: **then, at that time; next, thereupon**
21. when?, where: **ubi**
22. āiō: **I say, assert, affirm**
23. appellō: **I name, call**
24. audeō: **I dare**
25. I hunt: **captō**
26. caveō: **I guard against, beware (of)**
27. I care for: **cūrō**
28. dēbeō: **I owe, ought**
29. dēclārō: **I declare, make clear, explain**
30. dēleō: **I destroy**
31. I teach: **doceō**
32. domō: **I tame, subdue**
33. errō: **I wander, err, am mistaken**
34. exerceō: **I train, exercise**
35. festīnō: **I hasten, hurry**
36. I weep: **fleō**
37. habeō: **I have, hold**
38. iaceō: **I lie (flat), lie down**
39. I enter: **intrō**
40. lūceō: **I shine, am bright**
41. maneō: **I remain**
42. mereō: **I deserve, earn, am worthy of**
43. moneō: **I warn**
44. mordeō: **I bite, sting**
45. moveō: **I move**
46. I swim: **nō**

47. nuntiō: **I announce, declare**
48. obsideō: **I besiege, remain near**
49. parō: **I prepare**
50. possum: **I am able, can**
51. removeō: **I remove, take away**
52. reptō: **I crawl, creep**
53. respondeō: **I answer, respond**
54. I laugh, smile: **rīdeō**
55. salveō: **I am well**
56. sedeō: **I sit**
57. teneō: **I hold, possess**
58. terreō: **I frighten, terrify**
59. timeō: **I fear**
60. valeō: **I am well/strong**
61. vastō: **I devastate, lay waste**
62. videō: **I see**
63. I fly: **volō**
64. āla: **wing**
65. amīca: **friend**
66. amor: **love**
67. apostolus: **apostle**
68. war: **bellum**
69. Biblia Sacr: **Holy Bible**
70. caput: **head**
71. carmen: **song, chant, poem, prophecy**
72. castra: **camp**
73. centaurus: **centaur**
74. cervus: **stag, deer**
75. cōpia: **supply, plenty, abundance; (pl.) troops**
76. heart: **cor**
77. corpus: **body**
78. crux: **cross**
79. draco: **dragon**
80. dux: **leader, guide, general**
81. ecclēsia: **church**
82. flower: **flōs**
83. flūmen: **river**
84. frāter: **brother**
85. frūmentum: **grain; (pl.) crops**
86. geminus: **twin**
87. giant: **gigās**
88. glōria: **fame, glory**
89. grāmen: **grass, greenery**
90. homō: **man, human being**
91. cētus: **kraken**
92. inimīcus: **(personal) enemy**
93. iter: **journey, road, route, trek**
94. labor: **work, toil, labor, hardship**
95. milk: **lac**
96. laus: **praise**
97. leō: **lion**
98. liber: **book**
99. līberī: **children**
100. lītus: **shore, shoreline**
101. lūx: **light**
102. māter: **mother**
103. mīles: **soldier**
104. name: **nōmen**
105. onus: **burden, load, weight**

106. ōra: **shore**

107. ōs: **mouth**

108. pater: **father**

109. pāx: **peace**

110. populus: **people, nation**

111. porcus: **pig**

112. proelium: **battle**

113. king: **rex**

114. scūtum: **shield**

115. senex: **old man**

116. sōl: **sun**

117. soror: **sister**

118. star: **stella**

119. tellūs: **the earth, ground, land**

120. tempus: **time**

121. tenēbrae: **darkness, gloomy place, shadows**

122. tigris: **tiger**

123. unda: **wave**

124. poison: **venēnum**

125. vesper: **evening, evening star**

126. road, way: **via**

127. victōria: **victory**

128. virgō: **maiden, young woman**

129. virtūs: **manliness, courage, strength**

130. vīta: **life**

131. voice: **vōx**

132. vulnus: **wound**

133. meus: **my, mine**

134. noster: our, **ours**

135. tuus: **your (sg.), yours**

136. vester: **your (pl.), yours**

137. dear, beloved: **cārus**

138. doctus: **learned, wise, skilled**

139. horrendus: **dreadful, awful, fearful**

140. aeternus: **eternal**

141. angry, wrathful: **īrātus**

B. Grammar

1. Decline *my enemy*.

	LATIN SINGULAR	LATIN PLURAL
NOM.	meus inimīcus	meī inimīcī
GEN.	meī inimīcī	meōrum inimīcōrum
DAT.	meō inimīcō	meīs inimīcīs
ACC.	meum inimīcum	meōs inimīcōs
ABL.	meō inimīcō	meīs inimīcīs
VOC.	[Ō] mī inimīce	[Ō] meī inimīcī

2. Decline *wretched farmer*.

	LATIN SINGULAR	LATIN PLURAL
NOM.	agricola miser	agricolae miserī
GEN.	agricolae miserī	agricolārum miserōrum
DAT.	agricolae miserō	agricolīs miserīs
ACC.	agricolam miserum	agricolās miserōs
ABL.	agricolā miserō	agricolīs miserīs
VOC.	[Ō] agricola miser	[Ō] agricolae miserī

3. Decline *great shield*.

	LATIN SINGULAR	LATIN PLURAL
NOM.	scūtum magnum	scūta magna
GEN.	scūtī magnī	scūtōrum magnōrum
DAT.	scūtō magnō	scūtīs magnīs
ACC.	scūtum magnum	scūta magna
ABL.	scūtō magnō	scūtīs magnīs
VOC.	[Ō] scūtum magnum	[Ō] scūta magna

4. Decline *faithful courage*.

	LATIN SINGULAR	LATIN PLURAL
NOM.	virtūs fīda	virtūtēs fīdae
GEN.	virtūtis fīdae	virtūtum fīdārum
DAT.	virtūtī fīdae	virtūtibus fīdīs
ACC.	virtūtem fīdam	virtūtēs fīdās
ABL.	virtūte fīdā	virtūtibus fīdīs
VOC.	[Ō] virtūs fīda	[Ō] virtūtēs fīdae

5. Decline *angry mouth*.

	LATIN SINGULAR	LATIN PLURAL
NOM.	ōs īrātum	ōra īrāta
GEN.	ōris īrātī	ōrum īrātōrum
DAT.	ōrī īrātō	ōribus īrātīs
ACC.	ōs īrātum	ōra īrāta
ABL.	ōre īrātō	ōribus īrātīs
VOC.	[Ō] ōs īrātum	[Ō] ōra īrāta

6. Give a synopsis of *festīnō* in the third person plural.

	LATIN	ENGLISH
PRESENT ACT.	festīnant	they hasten, are hastening
IMPERFECT ACT.	festīnābant	they were hastening
FUTURE ACT.	festīnābunt	they will hasten
PERFECT ACT.	festīnāvērunt	they (have) hastened
PLUPERFECT ACT.	festīnāverant	they had hastened
FUTURE PERF. ACT.	festīnāverint	they will have hastened

7. Give a synopsis of *iaceō* in the first person singular.

	LATIN	ENGLISH
PRESENT ACT.	iaceō	I lie (down), am lying
IMPERFECT ACT.	iacēbam	I was lying
FUTURE ACT.	iacēbō	I will lie
PERFECT ACT.	iacuī	I lay, have lain
PLUPERFECT ACT.	iacueram	I had lain
FUTURE PERF. ACT.	iacuerō	I will have lain

8. Give a synopsis of *timeō* in the second person plural.

	LATIN	ENGLISH
PRESENT ACT.	timētis	you (pl.) fear
IMPERFECT ACT.	timēbātis	you (pl.) were fearing
FUTURE ACT.	timēbitis	you (pl.) will fear
PERFECT ACT.	timuistis	you (pl.) (have) feared
PLUPERFECT ACT.	timuerātis	you (pl.) had feared
FUTURE PERF. ACT.	timueritis	you (pl.) will have feared

9. Give a synopsis of *possum* in the third person singular.

	LATIN	ENGLISH
PRESENT ACT.	potest	he/she/it is able, can
IMPERFECT ACT.	poterat	he was able, could
FUTURE ACT.	poterit	he will be able, [can]
PERFECT ACT.	potuit	he was able, has been able, could
PLUPERFECT ACT.	potuerat	he had been able
FUTURE PERF. ACT.	potuerit	he will have been able

10. Give a synopsis of *dō* in the second person singular.

	LATIN	ENGLISH
PRESENT ACT.	dās	you give
IMPERFECT ACT.	dabās	you were giving
FUTURE ACT.	dabis	you will give
PERFECT ACT.	dedistī	you gave, have given
PLUPERFECT ACT.	dederās	you had given
FUTURE PERF. ACT.	dederis	you will have given

11. Give a synopsis of *parō* in the first person plural.

	LATIN	ENGLISH
PRESENT ACT.	parāmus	we prepare
IMPERFECT ACT.	parābāmus	we were preparing
FUTURE ACT.	parābimus	we will prepare
PERFECT ACT.	parāvimus	we (have) prepared
PLUPERFECT ACT.	parāverāmus	we had prepared
FUTURE PERF. ACT.	parāverimus	we will have prepared

12. Fully conjugate *moneō* in Latin and English.

Present Active Indicative

	LATIN SINGULAR	ENGLISH SINGULAR
1ST	moneō	I warn, am warning, do warn
2ND	monēs	you warn
3RD	monet	he/she/it warns

	LATIN PLURAL	ENGLISH PLURAL
	monēmus	we warn
	monētis	you (pl.) warn
	monent	they warn

Imperfect Active Indicative

	LATIN SINGULAR	ENGLISH SINGULAR
1ST	monēbam	I was warning
2ND	monēbās	you were warning
3RD	monēbat	he/she/it was warning

	LATIN PLURAL	ENGLISH PLURAL
	monēbāmus	we were warning
	monēbātis	you (pl.) were warning
	monēbant	they were warning

Future Active Indicative

	LATIN SINGULAR	ENGLISH SINGULAR
1ST	monēbō	I will warn
2ND	monēbis	you will warn
3RD	monēbit	he/she/it will warn

	LATIN PLURAL	ENGLISH PLURAL
	monēbimus	we will warn
	monēbitis	you (pl.) will warn
	monēbunt	they will warn

Perfect Active Indicative

	LATIN SINGULAR	ENGLISH SINGULAR
1ST	monuī	I (have) warned
2ND	monuistī	you (have) warned
3RD	monuit	he/she/it (has) warned

LATIN PLURAL	ENGLISH PLURAL
monuimus	we (have) warned
monuistis	you (pl.) (have) warned
monuērunt	they (have) warned

Pluperfect Active Indicative

	LATIN SINGULAR	ENGLISH SINGULAR
1ST	monueram	I had warned
2ND	monuerās	you had warned
3RD	monuerat	he/she/it had warned

LATIN PLURAL	ENGLISH PLURAL
monuerāmus	we had warned
monuerātis	you (pl.) had warned
monuerant	they had warned

Future Perfect Active Indicative

	LATIN SINGULAR	ENGLISH SINGULAR
1ST	monuerō	I will have warned
2ND	monueris	you will have warned
3RD	monuerit	he/she/it will have warned

LATIN PLURAL	ENGLISH PLURAL
monuerimus	we will have warned
monueritis	you (pl.) will have warned
monuerint	they will have warned

C. Memorization

Below is the first word from each line of the *Magnificat*. Fill in the rest.

Magnificat <u>anima mea Dominum,</u>

et <u>exsultāvit spīritus meus in Deō salvātōre meō,</u>

quia <u>rēspexit humilitātem ancillae suae.</u>

Ecce <u>enim ex hōc beatam mē dicent omnēs generātiōnēs,</u>

quia <u>fēcit mihi magna,</u>

quī <u>potēns est,</u>

et <u>sanctum nōmen eius,</u>

et <u>misericordia eius in prōgeniēs et prōgeniēs timentibus eum.</u>

Fēcit <u>potentiam in brāchiō suō,</u>

dispersit **superbōs mente cordis suī;**

dēposuit **potentēs dē sēde**

et **exaltāvit humilēs;**

ēsurientēs **implēvit bonīs**

et **dīvitēs dīmīsit inānēs.**

Suscēpit **Isrāel puerum suum,**

recordātus **misericordiae,**

sīcut **locūtus est ad patrēs nostrōs,**

Ābraham **et seminī eius in saecula.**

D. English to Latin Translation

Parse and translate each verb. To parse a verb, list its attributes: person, number, tense, voice, and mood if it is an indicative verb; if it is an infinitive, give tense, voice, and mood only. Then give the first principal part of the verb it comes from. (Abbreviate but keep your meaning is clear.) An example is given below.

	VERB	PERSON	NO.	TENSE	VOICE	MOOD	1ST PRIN. PART.	TRANSLATION
	cūrāverās	2nd	Sg.	Plupf.	Act.	Ind.	cūrō	you had cared for
1.	dēbuerāmus	1st	Pl.	Plupf.	Act.	Ind.	dēbeō	we had owed
2.	momordērunt	3rd	Pl.	Perf.	Act.	Ind.	mordeō	they bit, have bitten
3.	audēbātis	2nd	Pl.	Impf.	Act.	Ind.	audeō	you (pl.) were daring
4.	docuerō	1st	Sg.	Fut. Perf.	Act.	Ind.	doceō	I will have taught
5.	habētis	2nd	Pl.	Pres.	Act.	Ind.	habeō	you have
6.	flēvit	3rd	Sg.	Perf.	Act.	Ind.	fleō	he/she/it (has) wept
7.	āiunt	3rd	Pl.	Pres.	Act.	Ind.	āiō	they say
8.	manserant	3rd	Pl.	Plupf.	Act.	Ind.	maneō	they had remained
9.	obsēderis	2nd	Sg.	Fut. Perf.	Act.	Ind.	obsideō	you will have besieged
10.	dēlēs	2nd	Sg.	Pres.	Act.	Ind.	dēleō	you destroy
11.	errābimus	1st	Pl.	Fut.	Act.	Ind.	errō	we will wander

12.	reptāre	—	—	Pres.	Act.	Inf.	reptō	to crawl
13.	cāvit	3rd	Sg.	Perf.	Act.	Ind.	caveō	he/she/it (has) guarded against
14.	lūxerās	2nd	Sg.	Plupf.	Act.	Ind.	lūceō	you had shone
15.	nābam	1st	Sg.	Impf.	Act.	Ind.	nō	I was swimming
16.	captāverint	3rd	Pl.	Fut. Perf.	Act.	Ind.	captō	they will have hunted
17.	remōvimus	1st	Pl.	Perf.	Act.	Ind.	removeō	we (have) removed
18.	vastāveram	1st	Sg.	Plupf.	Act.	Ind.	vastō	I had devastated, laid waste
19.	rīdēre	—	—	Pres.	Act.	Inf.	rīdeō	to laugh
20.	domāvistī	2nd	Sg.	Perf.	Act.	Ind.	domō	you (have) tamed

Identify all possible gender, number, and case combinations for the following phrases and translate them. An example is given below.

	PHRASE	GENDER, NUMBER, CASE	TRANSLATION
	bonīs patribus	Masc. Pl. Dat. Masc. Pl. Abl.	to/for the good fathers by/with/from the good fathers
21.	rēge cārō	**Masc. Sg. Abl.**	**by/with/from the beloved king**
22.	amorī aeternō	**Masc. Sg. Dat.**	**to/for eternal love**
23.	gigantēs horrendōs	**Masc. Pl. Acc.**	**dreadful giants (object)**
24.	pāx beāta	**Fem. Sg. Nom.**	**blessed peace (subject)**
25.	tua vulnera	**Neut. Pl. Nom.** **Neut. Pl. Acc.**	**your wounds (subject)** **your wounds (object)**

26.	centaurī ferī	**Masc. Sg. Gen.** **Masc. Pl. Nom.**	of the fierce centaur fierce centaurs (subject)
27.	senex avārus	**Masc. Sg. Nom.**	the greedy old man (subject)
28.	dracōnem caldum	**Masc. Sg. Acc.**	the fiery dragon (object)
29.	flūmen īrātum	**Neut. Sg. Nom.** **Neut. Sg. Acc.**	the angry river (subject) the angry river (object)
30.	pulchra nōmina	**Neut. Pl. Nom.** **Neut. Pl. Acc.**	beautiful names (subject) beautiful names (object)
31.	corpore foedō	**Neut. Sg. Abl.**	by/with/from the ugly body
32.	magnā laude	**Fem. Sg. Abl.**	by/with/from great praise
33.	meīs amīcīs	**Masc./Fem. Pl. Dat.** **Masc./Fem. Pl. Abl.**	to/for my friends by/with/from my friends
34.	bellī iūstī	**Neut. Sg. Gen.**	of the just war
35.	ōrīs antīquīs	**Fem. Pl. Dat.** **Fem. Pl. Abl.**	to/for the ancient shores by/with/from the ancient shores
36.	capitum vestrōrum	**Neut. Pl. Gen.**	of your heads

37.	itineribus stultīs	**Neut. Pl. Dat.** **Neut. Pl. Abl.**	to/for the foolish journeys by/with/from the foolish journeys
38.	castrōrum malōrum	**Neut. Pl. Gen.**	of the evil camp
39.	matris doctae	**Fem. Sg. Gen.**	of the wise mother
40.	cōpiae nostrae	**Fem. Sg. Gen.** **Fem. Sg. Dat.** **Fem. Pl. Nom.**	of our supply to/for our supply our troops (subject)

Unit 2 Test (153 points)

A. Vocabulary (25 points)

Translate the following words.

1. mereō: **I deserve, earn, am worthy of**
2. sine: **(+ abl.) without**
3. mīles: **soldier**
4. āla: **wing**
5. repentē: **suddenly**
6. amīcus: **friend**
7. moveō: **I move**
8. habeō: **I have, hold**
9. vīta: **life**
10. cētus: **kraken**
11. mox: **soon**
12. contrā: **(+ acc.) against**
13. homō: **man, human being**
14. quandō: **when?, ever; since, because**
15. corpus: **body**
16. nōmen: **name**
17. statim: **immediately**
18. liber: **book**
19. trāns: **(+ acc.) across**
20. vastō: **I devastate, lay waste**
21. neque: **and not, nor**
22. rīdeō: **I laugh, smile**
23. castra: **camp**
24. suprā: **(+ acc.) above, over**
25. autem: **however, moreover**

B. Grammar (35 points)

1. Give a synopsis of *sum* in the second person plural.

	LATIN	ENGLISH
PRESENT ACT.	estis	you (pl.) are
IMPERFECT ACT.	erātis	you (pl.) were
FUTURE ACT.	eritis	you (pl.) will be
PERFECT ACT.	fuistis	you (pl.) were, have been
PLUPERFECT ACT.	fuerātis	you (pl.) had been
FUTURE PERF. ACT.	fueritis	you (pl.) will have been

2. Decline *good time*.

	LATIN SINGULAR	LATIN PLURAL
NOM.	tempus bonum	tempora bona
GEN.	temporis bonī	temporum bonōrum
DAT.	temporī bonō	temporibus bonīs
ACC.	tempus bonum	tempora bona
ABL.	tempore bonō	temporibus bonīs
VOC.	[Ō] tempus bonum	[Ō] tempora bona

C. Translation (55 points)

1 Camēlum antīquum mortis[1] captō. Draco nōn est; nōn cremat—hominēs bēstiāsque spectat et timent. Foedus et horrendus semper fuit. Quandō parvus erat, cor camēlī īrātum erat et multās bēstiās parvās in oppidō nostrō et silvā nostrā oppugnāverat. Tum camēlum captāveram, sed īrātum nōn oppugnāre potueram quod parvus eram et camēlus in spēluncam tenebrārum semper festīnāverat. Tempora mala
5 erant, et camēlus mortis[1] onus magnum in terrā nostrā erat. Et grāmen flōrēsque spectāvit, et timuērunt. Tum līberōs nostrōs oppugnāvit; itaque bellum meum ad camēlum portō. Malum mortis[1] in agrīs et silvīs captāvī, et nunc in spēluncam tenebrārum dēnique intrō. Ibī diū pugnāmus, et dēnique camēlum mortis[1] Meō Gladiō Magnō Fātī necāre possum. Nunc grāmen flōrēsque laetī sunt, et nostra terra beāta est.

Glossary
1. *mortis:* gen. sg. of *mors, -tis* (f): death

<u>I am hunting the ancient camel of death. He is not a dragon; he does not burn with fire—he looks at men and beasts and they are afraid. He has always been horrible and horrendous. When he was small, the camel's heart was angry and he had attacked many small beasts in our town and our forest. I had hunted the camel then, but I had not been able to attack the angry [one] since I was small and the camel had always hastened into a cave of darkness. Times were evil, and the camel of death was a great burden in/on our land. He even looked at the grass and flowers, and they feared. Then he attacked our children; therefore I am carrying my war to the camel. I have hunted the evil [one] of death in fields and forests, and now I am finally entering into the cave of darkness. There we fight for a long time, and finally I am able to kill the camel of death with my Great Sword of Fate. Now the grass and flowers are happy, and our land is blessed.</u>

D. Memorization (38 points)

Write out all eighteen lines of the *Magnificat* from memory.

Magnificat anima mea Dominum,

et exsultāvit spīritus meus in Deō salvātōre meō,

quia rēspexit humilitātem ancillae suae.

Ecce enim ex hōc beātam mē dicent omnēs generātiōnēs,

quia fēcit mihi magna,

quī potēns est,

et sanctum nōmen eius,

et misericordia eius in prōgeniēs et prōgeniēs timentibus eum.

Fēcit potentiam in brāchiō suō,

dispersit superbōs mente cordis suī;

dēposuit potentēs dē sēde

et exaltāvit humilēs;

ēsurientēs implēvit bonīs

et dīvitēs dīmīsit inānēs.

Suscēpit Isrāel puerum suum,

recordātus misericordiae,

sīcut locūtus est ad patrēs nostrōs,

Ābraham et seminī eius in saecula.

Unit Three

UNIT 3 GOALS

Lessons 17–24

By the end of Unit 3, students should be able to . . .

- Decline first, second, and third person personal pronouns
- Decline and identify third declension i-stem nouns
- Decline third declension adjectives
- Know basic Latin numerals, both cardinal and ordinal
- Conjugate a first or second conjugation verb in the present, imperfect, future, perfect, pluperfect, and future perfect passive indicative
- Translate sentences using all of the concepts learned in Units 1–3
- Know all vocabulary from Lessons 17-24
- Write out from memory the *Symbolum Nicaenum* (Nicene Creed)

LESSON 17 (Student Edition p. 155)

Personal Pronouns

1. Word List

There are a number of colors in this lesson's vocabulary. The Romans did not use our neat ROYGBIV color spectrum, so don't be surprised if the range of colors is a bit different from what you are used to. I have not given every color word out there, but have tried to list the words that are found in the *Vulgate* and in Vergil—the words that your students will more likely encounter. Take note of the following words:

16. *viridis, -e*: green; fresh, young, vigorous—This is a third declension adjective, which your students will learn about in Lesson 19. (I could have waited until then to include it, but I wanted it to be with the other colors.) For now, just have them learn the meaning of the word and tell them they will be learning how to use it soon.

18. *torreō, -ēre, torruī, tostum*: I burn, parch, dry up—This is an intransitive verb, meaning it does not take a direct object. Thus you could use it to say, "I am burning up with a fever," but you would use the transitive verb *cremō* to say "The dragon burned up the village."

21. *enim* (postpositive conj.): indeed, truly, certainly; for—"Postpositive" simply means that this conjunction does not appear first in the sentence and is placed after the first word (remember *autem*?). It usually comes second or third in the sentence. See if your students recognize *enim* (and *ecce*) from the *Magnificat*: *Ecce enim ex hōc beatam . . . .*

2. Derivatives/Memorization Helps

1. *ego*, I: ego, egotistic
2. *nōs*, we
3. *is, ea, id*, he, she it, they; this, that: i.e. = *id est*, "that is" (don't confuse this abbreviation with e.g., *exempli gratia*, "for example")
4. *tū*, you (sg.)
5. *vōs*, you (pl.)
6. *albus*, (dead) white: albino, albumen, album
7. *argenteus*, silver: see *argentum*, Lesson 5
8. *āter*, (dead) black, dark: atrabilious
9. *aureus*, golden, gold: aureole; see *aurum*, Lesson 5
10. *caeruleus*, blue: cerulean
11. *candidus*, (glittering) white: candid, candidate
12. *hyacinthinus*, blue, purplish-blue, violet: hyacinth (flower)

13. *niger*, (shining) black, dark-colored: nigrescence, nigrosine
14. *purpureus*, purple; dark red, dark violet, dark brown: purple (from the related word *purpura*)
15. *ruber*, red, ruddy: rubric
16. *viridis*, green; fresh, young, vigorous: virid, viridity, viridescent, viridian
17. *flōreō*, I flourish: flourish, fl. = *floruit*, "he flourished" (usually used to describe the period when a historical figure was active and produced most of his work, especially when the dates of birth and death are unknown or uncertain)
18. *torreō*, I burn, parch, dry up: torrid, torrent, toast
19. *enim*, indeed, truly, certainly; for
20. *ante*, before: a.m. = *ante meridiem*, "before noon"; prefix ante- as in antecedent, antediluvian
21. *post*, after, behind: p.m. = *post meridiem*, "after noon"; posterity; prefix post-; post mortem
22. *ecce*, behold!

3. Memorization—*Symbolum Nicaenum* (Nicene Creed)

This unit's memorization is the Nicene Creed, one of the great confessions of historic Christendom. Adopted by the Council of Nicea in AD 325 and revised at the Council of Constantinople in AD 381, this creed is a bit longer and more specific than the earlier Apostles' Creed. At the time the church was divided by the Arian heresy, which denied the full deity of Christ. Therefore, the Nicene Creed upholds the human and divine nature of Christ. I also chose this creed over the Apostles' Creed as this unit's memorization because it is a bit more poetic (especially line 5). In addition, there are numerous choral versions of this creed set to music, so choose one (or more) to play for the class while they follow along.

The full text of the Creed with translation is as follows:

Lesson 17 Crēdō in ūnum Deum, Patrem omnipotentem, Factōrem caelī et terrae, vīsibilium omnium et invīsibilium.

> *I believe in one God, the Father Almighty, Maker of heaven and earth, of all things visible and invisible.*

Et in ūnum Dominum Iēsum Christum, Fīlium Deī Ūnigenitum,

> *And in one Lord Jesus Christ, the only-begotten Son of God,*

Lesson 18 Et ex Patre nātum ante omnia saecula.

> *Begotten also of the Father before all worlds/ages.*

Deum dē Deō, Lūmen dē Lūmine, Deum vērum dē Deō vērō,

> *God of God, Light of Light, very God of very God,*

Lesson 19 Genitum, nōn factum, consubstantiālem Patrī: per quem omnia facta sunt;

> *Begotten, not made, [being] of one substance with the Father: by whom all things were made;*

Quī propter nōs hominēs et propter nostram salūtem dēscendit dē caelīs,

> *Who for us men and for our salvation descended from heaven,*

Lesson 20   Et incarnātus est dē Spīritū Sanctō ex Marīā virgine, et homō factus est.

> *And was incarnate by the Holy Ghost of the virgin Mary, and was made man.*

Crucifīxus etiam prō nōbīs sub Pontiō Pīlātō; passus, et sepultus est,

> *He was crucified also for us under Pontius Pilate; suffered, and was buried,*

Lesson 21   Et resurrēxit tertiā diē, secundum Scriptūrās, et ascendit in caelum, sedet ad dexteram Patris.

> *And He rose again on the third day, according to the Scriptures, and ascended into heaven, [and] sits at the right hand of the Father.*

Et iterum ventūrus est cum glōriā, iūdicāre vīvōs et mortuōs, cuius regnī nōn erit fīnis.

> *And He will come again with glory, to judge the living and the dead, whose kingdom shall have no end.*

Lesson 22   Et in Spīritum Sanctum, Dominum et vīvificantem: Quī ex Patre Fīliōque prōcēdit.

> *And [I believe] in the Holy Ghost, the Lord and Giver of Life: Who proceeds from the Father and the Son.*

Quī cum Patre et Fīliō simul adōrātur et conglōrificātur: Quī locūtus est per prophētās.

> *Who with the Father and the Son together is worshiped and glorified: Who spoke by the prophets.*

Lesson 23   Et ūnam, sanctam, catholicam, et apostolicam ecclēsiam.

> *And in one, holy, catholic, and apostolic church.*

Confiteor ūnum baptisma in remissiōnem peccātōrum.

> *I confess one baptism for the remission of sins.*

Et expectō resurrectiōnem mortuōrum, et vītam ventūrī saeculī. Āmēn.

> *And I look for the resurrection of the dead, and the life of the world to come. Amen.*

Grading tip: I recommend not taking off points for lack of capitalization except for proper names, of course. If students don't capitalize the first word of each line, for example, don't sweat it. Just be excited that they are getting words down! This goes for macrons as well—my advice is to let them go, since your students have plenty of other things to memorize.

4. Grammar

Personal Pronouns

During the first half of this year, you have perhaps felt hampered by the lack of pronouns (as did I). It gets awkward saying, "The king is good. The people love the king and they give honor to the king"—where the pronoun "him" would make this flow so much better. **Pronouns** (which *take the place of a noun*) are extremely handy. In this lesson your students will learn the personal pronouns—that is, pronouns for first, second, and third person. I have already sprinkled a few of these into their translations, and they have encountered some of them in their memorizations.

Pronouns function the same way as nouns—they have gender, number, and case. The gender of course is dependent upon the pronoun's antecedent (which is the word the pronoun takes the place of). If a teacher were talking about a girl, the teacher would say, *Ea discipula est*; about a boy, the teacher would say, *Is discipulus est*. In the first example ea is feminine, while in the second is is masculine.

Let's begin with the first and second person pronouns.

First Person Personal Pronouns

	LATIN SINGULAR	ENGLISH SINGULAR	LATIN PLURAL	ENGLISH PLURAL
NOMINATIVE	ego	I [subject]	nōs	we [subject]
GENITIVE	meī	of me	nostrum	of us
DATIVE	mihi	to/for me	nōbīs	to/for us
ACCUSATIVE	mē	me [object]	nōs	us [object]
ABLATIVE	mē	by/with/from me	nōbīs	by/with/from us

Second Person Personal Pronouns

	LATIN SINGULAR	ENGLISH SINGULAR	LATIN PLURAL	ENGLISH PLURAL
NOMINATIVE	tū	you [subject]	vōs	you (pl.) [subject]
GENITIVE	tuī	of you	vestrum	of you (pl.)
DATIVE	tibī	to/for you	vōbīs	to/for you (pl.)
ACCUSATIVE	tē	you [object]	vōs	you (pl.) [object]
ABLATIVE	tē	by/with/from you	vōbīs	by/with/from you (pl.)

If you or your students have studied any modern Romance languages (French, Spanish, Italian, etc.), these pronouns should look quite familiar and be fairly easy to memorize. Sometimes students are tempted to confuse *nōs* and *vōs*, so you will need to help them keep these two straight. Remember our memory devices for *noster* and *vester*: *Pater Noster* means "Our Father" not "Your Father," and the phrase, "Where's **your** *vestrum*?"

When you chant these pronouns out loud with your students, it is more rhythmical to chant through the singulars first and then the plurals, rather than sticking with first person singular and plural, then second person singular and plural: *ego, meī, mihi, mē, mē! tū, tuī, tibī, tē, tē! nōs, nostrum, nōbīs, nōs, nōbīs! vōs, vestrum, vōbīs, vōs, vōbīs!* (If you don't believe me, try doing it *ego-nōs, tū-vōs,* and you will find that I am right.)

One very important thing to note about the first and second personal pronouns is that **their genitives** (*meī, tuī, nostrum,* and *vestrum*) **are *not* used to show possession.** If I wanted to say "my king" or "your daughter," I would use the possessive adjectives that we have already learned (*meus, tuus, noster, vester*): *meus rex* or *tua filia*. So what are these genitives used for? We have not really discussed uses of the genitive other than possession, but there are other usages which will be mentioned later on as they come up. For now you can just tell your students *not* to use the genitive of these pronouns to show possession, because they are used to show other things, such as the partitive genitive (e.g., if you wanted to say "Part of me wants to go to the movie," then you would use *meī*). Another usage would be the objective genitive, where the genitive is an "object" of a noun: "Out of his love *of the princess,* Oswald killed the dragon." "Princess" is the object of the noun "love"; the "his" is the possessive.

One of your precocious students may ask why we need the nominatives of these pronouns, since Latin verb endings already contain a subject pronoun. We have been able to say "I love" or "you do not love" for months now without having to use *ego* or *tū*. These nominative pronouns were often added to express emphasis. If we want to make some sort of contrast, we can throw them in: *Ego amō, sed tū nōn amās.* "I love, but *you* do not love." Of course very often this emphasis cannot be translated into English without using italics or underlining the words or with intonation, but that's why you want your students to read things in their original Latinic glory, is it not?

And now to the third person pronouns. This chart may look a bit intimidating to your students because it has lots of tiny little words. However, you can calm their fears immediately by pointing out that they know most all of these endings already. Except for the forms in bold below, all you have to do is put a first or second declension ending onto an *e*, and you have your pronoun.

Third Person Personal Pronouns—Singular

	MASCULINE	FEMININE	NEUTER	
	he/his/him	she/hers/her	it/its (this/that)	ENGLISH
NOM.	**is**	ea	**id**	he/she/it
GEN.	**eius**	**eius**	**eius**	of him/his, of her/hers, of it/its
DAT.	**eī**	**eī**	**eī**	to/for him, to/for her, to/for it
ACC.	eum	eam	**id**	him/her/it
ABL.	eō	eā	eō	by/with/from him/her/it

Third Person Personal Pronouns—Plural

	MASCULINE	FEMININE	NEUTER	ENGLISH
	they	they	they	
NOM.	eī	eae	ea	they
GEN.	eōrum	eārum	eōrum	of them, their
DAT.	eīs	eīs	eīs	to/for them
ACC.	eōs	eās	ea	them
ABL.	eīs	eīs	eīs	by/with/from them

When you chant this one out loud with your students, it flows better if you go horizontally first rather than vertically: *is, ea, id! eius, eius, eius! eī, eī, eī! eum, eam, id!* etc. You may want to practice this chart every day as you go through this lesson by putting up portions of it on the board. Then at the beginning of class, call on various students to come and fill in the blanks.

The third person pronoun is quite handy, because not only does it function as a personal pronoun, but it can also be used as an adjective where it means "this, that" (making it what is called a demonstrative adjective). Here are a few examples to illustrate: *Ego eam amō*, "I love her." *Ego eam fēminam amō*, "I love this woman."

And what about the genitive of this pronoun? Rest easy—it is a normal old genitive of possession. Thus we would say, *Ego fīliam eius amō*, "I love his daughter" (or "her daughter," depending on the context).

Note: Demonstrative adjectives simply do not have a vocative (perhaps they don't need it because they are already pointing to the noun in question), so when your students are declining a noun/adjective phrase (such as on this lesson's worksheet), they can leave out the vocative of *is, ea,* and *id*.

5. Worksheet

Follow the directions given and complete the worksheet.

6. Quiz

Administer Quiz 17 when the students are ready.

Lesson 17 Worksheet

A. Vocabulary

Translate the following words from Latin to English or English to Latin as appropriate. For the verbs, also fill in the missing principal parts. For each preposition, include which case(s) it takes.

1. golden: **aureus**

2. vōs: **you (pl.)**

3. āter: **(dead) black, dark**

4. you (sg.): **tū**

5. ecce: **behold!**

6. caeruleus: **blue**

7. flōreō, flōrēre, **flōruī**, **——** : **I flourish**

8. (glittering) white: **candidus**

9. is: **he, she, it, they; this, that**

10. violet: **hyacinthinus**

11. enim: **indeed, truly, certainly; for**

12. before: **ante (+ acc.)**

13. niger: **(shining) black, dark-colored**

14. post: **(+ acc.) after**

15. purple: **purpureus**

16. I: **ego**

17. ruber: **red, ruddy**

18. argenteus: **silver**

19. albus: **(dead) white**

20. green: **viridis**

21. I parch: **torreō, torrēre, torruī, tostum**

22. nōs: **we**

23. Get the colored pencils out. Choose five of your new color adjectives and draw an object in each color in the space below. Write the Latin color word in the space below each drawing.

Answers will vary; award creativity!				

B. Grammar

Fill in the charts (from memory, if possible).

1. First Person Personal Pronouns

	LATIN SINGULAR	LATIN PLURAL
NOMINATIVE	ego	nōs
GENITIVE	meī	nostrum
DATIVE	mihi	nōbīs
ACCUSATIVE	mē	nōs
ABLATIVE	mē	nōbīs

2. Second Person Personal Pronouns

	LATIN SINGULAR	LATIN PLURAL
NOMINATIVE	tū	vōs
GENITIVE	tuī	vestrum
DATIVE	tibī	vōbīs
ACCUSATIVE	tē	vōs
ABLATIVE	tē	vōbīs

3. Third Person Personal Pronouns

	SINGULAR			PLURAL		
	MASC.	FEM.	NEUT.	MASC.	FEM.	NEUT.
NOM.	is	ea	id	eī	eae	ea
GEN.	eius	eius	eius	eōrum	eārum	eōrum
DAT.	eī	eī	eī	eīs	eīs	eīs
ACC.	eum	eam	id	eōs	eās	ea
ABL.	eō	eā	eō	eīs	eīs	eīs

Identify and translate all possible options for the following pronouns. An example is given below.

	PRONOUN	GENDER, NUMBER, CASE	TRANSLATION
	eōrum	Masc. Pl. Gen. Neut. Pl. Gen.	their(s), of them their(s), of them
4.	vōbīs	M/F/N Pl. Dat. M/F/N Pl. Abl.	to/for you (pl.) by/with/from you (pl.)
5.	eī	M/F/N Sg. Dat.	to/for him/her/it
6.	eā	Fem. Sg. Abl.	by/with/from her
7.	nōs	M/F/N Pl. Nom. M/F/N Pl. Acc.	we us
8	id	Neut. Sg. Nom. Neut. Sg. Acc.	it [subject] it [object]
9.	eae	Fem. Pl. Nom.	they [subject]
10.	mihi	M/F/N Sg. Dat.	to/for me

11.	nostrum	M/F/N Pl. Gen.	of us
12.	eōs	Masc. Pl. Acc.	them
13.	mē	M/F/N Sg. Acc. M/F/N Sg. Abl.	me by/with/from me

14. Give a synopsis of *torreō* in the second person plural.

	LATIN	ENGLISH
PRESENT ACT.	torrētis	you (pl.) burn, parch, dry up
IMPERFECT ACT.	torrēbātis	you (pl.) were burning
FUTURE ACT.	torrēbitis	you (pl.) will burn
PERFECT ACT.	torruistis	you (pl.) (have) burned
PLUPERFECT ACT.	torruerātis	you (pl.) had burned
FUTURE PERF. ACT.	torrueritis	you (pl.) will have burned

C. Memorization

Fill in the blanks for the first two lines of the *Symbolum Nicaenum*.

Crēdō **in** **ūnum** Deum, **Patrem** omnipotentem, **Factōrem** caelī **et** **terrae**, vīsibilium **omnium** et **invīsibilium**.

Et in ūnum **Dominum** **Iēsum** **Christum**, **Fīlium** Deī **Ūnigenitum**,

D. English to Latin Translation

Translate each sentence from English to Latin. Include subject pronouns wherever possible.

1. Behold, God gave the Son to us and we love and praise Him because He is good.

    Ecce, Deus nōbīs Fīlium dedit et nōs eum amāmus et laudāmus quod is bonus est.

2. The fierce centaur had attacked us and seized our gold and now he will give you our wealth.
   Centaurus ferus nōs oppugnāverat et aurum nostrum occupāverat et nunc vōbīs/tibī dīvitiās nostrās dabit.

3. The sky was blue and the sun was shining but then the purple dragon flew from his dark cave.
   Caelum caeruleum erat et sol lucēbat sed draco purpureus ab/ex spēluncā ātrā tum volāvit.

4. The king gave the queen a silver crown but his crown was gold.
   Rex rēgīnae corōnam argenteam dedit sed corōna eius aurea erat.

5. Then the angry pirate says to us, "Give me your money or your lives!"
   Pīrāta īrātus nōbīs tum aīt, "Dā mihi pecuniam vestram aut vestrās vītās!"

6. Indeed, black horses have carried us from the town but this white horse will carry you to the castle.
   Equī enim nigrī [*I prefer* niger *here over* āter *because horses are usually glossy*] nōs ab oppidō portāvit sed is equus albus [*but white horses aren't glittering*] tē/vōs [*if the horse can carry more than one person*] ad castellum portābit.

7. After the peace with their enemy, their fields and grasses flourished.
   Post pācem cum inimīcō/inimīcīs eōrum/eārum, agrī et grāminā [*or* grāmināque] eōrum/eārum floruērunt.

8. Our mother gives us good cookies and we give her our love.
   Māter nostra nōbīs crustula bona dat et nōs eī amōrem nostrum dāmus.

9. The little girls were holding violet flowers and gave them to you and your queen.
   Puellae parvae flōrēs hyacinthinōs tenēbant et tibī rēgīnaeque [*or* et rēgīnae] tuae eōs dedit.

10. Their brothers were boys before that war, but now they are men and soldiers.
    Frātrēs eōrum puerī ante id bellum erant, sed eī virī mīlitēsque [*or* et mīlitēs] nunc sunt.

E. Latin to English Translation

1 Frāter meus es, sed tē nōn amō. Pater noster agricola erat, et ego fīlius bonus eius sum quod et ego agricola sum. Tū fīlius malus eius est quod tū poēta es. Tū labōrem sōlemque nōn amās, sed lūnam candidam amās et eī noctīque[1] ātrae cantās. Dē stellīs purpureīs et pulchrā lūce candidā eārum cantās. Tū multās fēminās amāvistī, et cum eīs in agrīs errāvistī. Tū eīs flōrēs rubrōs et hyacinthinōs et albōs
5 dedistī, sed eīs aurea aut argentea numquam dare potuistī quod ea nōn tenēs. Ōlim eī pīrātae patriam nostram oppugnābant; itaque tū in spēluncam ātram festīnāvit et exspectāvit. Post proelium tū in oppidum dēnique intrāvit. Tū mīles nōn es, sed ego mīles et vir sum. Pater noster tibī gladium magnum dederat, sed eum gladium nōn amās et itaque ego eum occupāvī. Ego gladiō eius pugnābō. Ego labōrem amābō et multum aurum argentumque tenēbō, et bonam fēminam amābō. Nōs laetī erimus. Tū in tuā
10 spēluncā diū habitābis et carmina creābis, sed laetus eris?

Glossary
1. *noctī*: dative singular of *nox, noctis* (f): night

You are my brother, but I do not love you. Our father was a farmer, and I am his good son because I am a farmer also. You are his bad son because you are a poet. You do not love work and the sun, but you love the glittering white moon and sing to her and [to] the dark night. You sing about the purple stars and their beautiful white light. You have loved many women, and have wandered in the fields with them. You have given them red and violet and white flowers, but you have never been able to give them gold or silver things because you do not possess them. Once these/those pirates were attacking our land, and so you hastened into a dark cave and waited. After the battle you finally entered the town. You are not a soldier, but I am a soldier and a man. Our father had given you a great sword, but you do not love this sword and therefore I seized it. I will fight with his sword. I will love work and possess much gold and silver, and I will love a good woman. We will be happy. You will live in your cave for a long time and create songs, but will you be happy?

Lesson 17 Quiz (57 points)

A. Vocabulary (10 points)

Translate the following words. Give case(s) for prepositions.

1. I flourish: **flōreō**
2. before: **ante (+ acc.)**
3. after: **post (+ acc.)**
4. enim: **indeed, truly, certainly; for**
5. ecce: **behold!**
6. I dry up: **torreō**

Finish the sentences using the Latin colors from this lesson.

7. Roses are **ruber** and violets are **hyacinthinus**, but grapes are **purpureus**.
8. What a beautiful day—the sky is **caeruleus** with fluffy **albī [or candidī]** clouds and the grass is **viridis**.
9. The lights went out suddenly and the room was very **āter**.
10. Second place gets a(n) **argenteus** medal, but first place a(n) **aureus** one.

B. Grammar (15 points)

1. Give a synopsis of *laudō* in the first person singular.

	LATIN	ENGLISH
PRESENT ACT.	laudō	I praise
IMPERFECT ACT.	laudābam	I was praising
FUTURE ACT.	laudābō	I will praise
PERFECT ACT.	laudāvī	I (have) praised
PLUPERFECT ACT.	laudāveram	I had praised
FUTURE PERF. ACT.	laudāverō	I will have praised

2. Decline the second person pronoun in the singular and plural, Latin only.

	LATIN SINGULAR	LATIN PLURAL
NOMINATIVE	tū	vōs
GENITIVE	tuī	vestrum
DATIVE	tibī	vōbīs
ACCUSATIVE	tē	vōs
ABLATIVE	tē	vōbīs

C. Translation (17 points)

Translate each sentence.

1. I love his daughter, but she loves the pirate and he loves her.

    Ego fīliam eius amō, sed [ea] pīrātam amat et [is] eam amat.

2. Lūx lūnae erat candida, et ea in poētā et carminibus eius lūcēbat.

    The light of the moon was [shining/glittering] white, and it was shining upon the poet and his songs.

D. Memorization (15 points)

Write out the first two lines of the *Symbolum Nicaenum*.

Crēdō in ūnum Deum, Patrem omnipotentem, Factōrem caelī et terrae, vīsibilium omnium et invīsibilium.

Et in ūnum Dominum Iēsum Christum, Fīlium Deī Ūnigenitum,

LESSON 18 (Student Edition p. 165)

Third Declension i-stems

1. Word List

The words in this lesson are all third declension i-stems, but don't tell your students this yet. You'll learn the rules for determining this in the "Grammatical Concepts" section.

13. *turris, -is* (f), "tower, turret"—Be aware that this word has irregularities in the accusative and ablative singular, often becoming *turrim* instead of *turrem*, and *turrī* instead of *turre*.

2. Derivatives/Memorization Helps

1. *animal*, animal: animal, animalian, animate; see *animus*, Lesson 29
2. *avis*, bird: aviary, avian, aviation, aviator
3. *canis*, dog: canine
4. *hostis*, enemy (of the state): hostile, hostility
5. *ignis*, fire: ignite, ignition, igneous
6. *mare*, sea: marine, mariner, submarine
7. *moenia*, fortifications, city walls: munitions, ammunition
8. *mōns*, mountain: mount, mountain, Montana
9. *mors*, death: mortal, immortal, post mortem
10. *nāvis*, ship: navy, naval; see *nauta* and *navigō*
11. *nox*, night: nocturne, nocturnal, equinox
12. *nūbēs*, cloud, gloom: nubilous
13. *turris*, tower, turret: tower, turret
14. *urbs*, city: urban, urbane, suburban
15. *vallēs*, valley, vale: valley
16. *vestis*, clothing, garment: vest, vestments, invest, investment (but not investigate)
17. *ergō*, therefore, then, consequently, accordingly
18. *quia*, because, since
19. *sī*, if
20. *prō*, before, in front of; for (the sake of) instead of: pros and cons; prefix prō-

3. Memorization—*Symbolum Nicaenum* (Nicene Creed)

This lesson's new lines are:

> Et ex Patre nātum ante omnia saecula.
> *Begotten also of the Father before all worlds.*
> Deum dē Deō, Lūmen dē Lūmine, Deum vērum dē Deō vērō,
> *God of God, Light of Light, very God of very God,*

4. Grammar

Third Declension i-Stems

Happily, third declension i-stem nouns aren't all that much different from regular old third declension nouns. They just have an extra *i* sprinkled here and there. Masculine and feminine i-stem nouns have an *i* in the genitive plural, making the ending *-ium* rather than *-um*, while neuter nouns have an *-ī* instead of an *-e* in the ablative singular, *-ia* instead of *-a* in the nominative and accusative (and vocative) plural, and the *-ium* in the genitive plural. (Once in a while, masculine/feminine i-stems will also have *-ī* in the ablative singular.) Thus:

Third Declension Masculine/Feminine i-Stem

	LATIN SG.	ENGLISH SINGULAR	LATIN PL.	ENGLISH PLURAL
NOMINATIVE	X	a/the *noun* [subject]	-ēs	the *nouns* [subject]
GENITIVE	-is	of the *noun*, the *noun's*	**-ium**	of the *nouns*, the *nouns'*
DATIVE	-ī	to/for the *noun*	-ibus	to/for the *nouns*
ACCUSATIVE	-em	a/the *noun* [direct object]	-ēs	the *nouns* [direct object]
ABLATIVE	**-e/-ī**	by/with/from the *noun*	-ibus	by/with/from the *nouns*
VOCATIVE	X	[O] *noun*!	-ēs	[O] *nouns*!

Third Declension Neuter i-Stem

	LATIN SG.	ENGLISH SINGULAR	LATIN PL.	ENGLISH PLURAL
NOMINATIVE	X	a/the *noun* [subject]	**-ia**	the *nouns* [subject]
GENITIVE	-is	of the *noun*, the *noun's*	**-ium**	of the *nouns*, the *nouns'*
DATIVE	-ī	to/for the *noun*	-ibus	to/for the *nouns*
ACCUSATIVE	X	a/the *noun* [object]	**-ia**	the *nouns* [object]
ABLATIVE	**-ī**	by/with/from the *noun*	-ibus	by/with/from the *nouns*
VOCATIVE	X	[O] *noun*!	**-ia**	[O] *nouns*!

Start out by reviewing the regular third declension and third neuter (pick two students to write them up on the board). Then all you have to do is make the new additions (in a different colored marker, of course)—that way the students do not think that they have to learn a whole new declension. This is simply a variation. In fact, if I had slipped in any third declension i-stems in the Latin translations earlier, the students probably would have translated them without batting an eye.

How do you know if a third declension noun is an i-stem or not? Believe it or not, there actually are guidelines for determining this:

IF THE NOUN IS	IT'S AN I-STEM IF ...	EXAMPLES
Masculine or Feminine	1. The nominative ends in -*is* or -*ēs* and the nominative and genitive have the same number of syllables (called "parisyllabic").	canis, canis (m/f) *dog* nūbēs, nūbis (f) *cloud, gloom*
	2. The nominative ends in -*s* or -*x* and the noun stem ends in two consonants. (The nominatives of most of these nouns are one syllable.)	mors, mortis (m) *death* nox, noctis (f) *night*
Neuter	3. The nominative ends in -*al*, -*ar*, or -*e*.	animal, -ālis (n) *animal* mare, maris (n) *sea*

The first two rules may look a bit complicated, but they actually are pretty straightforward. From now on, have your students analyze each third declension noun in their vocab lists to see if it is an i-stem or not. **When you are figuring out the declension of a noun, you have to look at *both* the nominative and the genitive singular,** because of course the genitive not only gets you started on the correct chant, but it also gives you the stem. Similarly, have your students look first at the nominative of the third declension noun. If it ends with -*ēs* or -*is*, such as *canis*, then they should look at the genitive. If the genitive "rhymes" with the nominative (i.e., has two syllables if the nominative has two syllables), then it's an i-stem.

With the second rule, you again need to look at both the nominative and the genitive. Say the nominative ends in -*s* or -*x*, as with *nox*. Look at the genitive singular, and take off the -*is* to find the stem: *noct*-. If the stem ends in two consonants (which *noct*- does), then it's an i-stem. Compare *nox* to *rex*. Yes, the nominative does end in -*x*, but if you look at the genitive *rēgis*, the stem *rēg*- does not end in two consonants, and therefore *rex* is not an i-stem.

The rule for neuter i-stems is much easier, because you don't even need to look at the genitive (for once). If the nominative ends in -*al*, -*ar*, or -*e*, then it's an i-stem. Simple!

Now go over the new nouns with your students (these words all happen to be third declension i-stems), and have them use the above guidelines to tell you how they know each one is an i-stem.

5. Worksheet

Follow the directions given and complete the worksheet.

6. Quiz

Administer Quiz 18 when the students are ready.

Lesson 18 Worksheet

A. Vocabulary

Translate the following words from Latin to English or English to Latin as appropriate. For the verbs, also fill in the missing principal parts. For each preposition, include which case(s) it takes.

1. death: **mors**
2. urbs: **city**
3. torreō, -ēre, **torruī**, **tostum**: **I burn, parch, dry up**
4. sea: **mare**
5. vestis: **clothing, garment**
6. avis: **bird**
7. mōns: **mountain**
8. animal: **animal**
9. red: **ruber**
10. nāvis: **ship**
11. sī: **if**
12. fortifications: **moenia**
13. nūbēs: **cloud, gloom**
14. dog: **canis**
15. enim: **indeed, truly, certainly, for**
16. turris: **tower, turret**
17. ergō: **therefore, then, consequently, accordingly**
18. fire: **ignis**
19. prō: (+ **abl.**) **before, in front of; for (the sake of), instead of**
20. nox: **night**
21. valley: **vallēs**
22. quia: **because, since**
23. purpureus: **purple; dark-red, dark-violet, dark-brown**
24. hostis: **enemy (of the state)**
25. green: **viridis**

B. Grammar

1. Decline "that dark night," *ea nox ātra*.

	LATIN SINGULAR	LATIN PLURAL
NOM.	ea nox ātra	eae noctēs ātrae
GEN.	eius noctis ātrae	eārum noctium ātrārum
DAT.	eī noctī ātrae	eīs noctibus ātrīs
ACC.	eam noctem ātram	eās noctēs ātrās
ABL.	eā nocte ātrā	eīs noctibus ātrīs
VOC.	Ō nox ātra	Ō noctēs ātrae

2. Decline "this blue sea," *id mare caeruleum*.

	LATIN SINGULAR	LATIN PLURAL
NOM.	id mare caeruleum	ea maria caerulea
GEN.	eius maris caeruleī	eōrum marium caeruleōrum
DAT.	eī marī caeruleō	eīs maribus caeruleīs
ACC.	id mare caeruleum	ea maria caerulea
ABL.	eō marī caeruleō	eīs maribus caeruleīs
VOC.	Ō mare caeruleum	Ō maria caerulea

3. Give a synopsis of *vastō* in the third person plural.

	LATIN	ENGLISH
PRESENT ACT.	vastant	they devastate
IMPERFECT ACT.	vastābant	they were devastating
FUTURE ACT.	vastābunt	they will devastate
PERFECT ACT.	vastāvērunt	they (have) devastated
PLUPERFECT ACT.	vastāverant	they had devastated
FUTURE PERF. ACT.	vastāverint	they will have devastated

C. Memorization

Fill in the blanks.

<u>Crēdō</u> <u>in</u> <u>ūnum</u> Deum, **Patrem** <u>omnipotentem</u>,

Factōrem **caelī** <u>et</u> <u>terrae</u>, vīsibilium **omnium** <u>et</u> <u>invīsibilium</u>.

<u>Et</u> <u>in</u> ūnum **Dominum** <u>Iēsum</u> Christum, **Fīlium** <u>Deī</u> Ūnigenitum,

<u>Et</u> ex **Patre** nātum **ante** <u>omnia</u> saecula.

<u>Deum</u> dē Deō, Lūmen <u>dē</u> <u>Lūmine</u>, Deum **vērum** <u>dē</u> <u>Deō</u> vērō,

D. English to Latin Translation

Translate each sentence from English to Latin. Use subject pronouns wherever possible.

1. I have always loved the blue seas and the wild songs of the birds there.

   <u>Maria caerulea et carmina fera avium ibī semper amāvī.</u>

2. Oswald had killed the fiery dragon of fire before the king and therefore had saved his daughter in the turret.

   <u>Oswaldus dracōnem caldum ignis prō rēge necāverat et ergō/itaque fīliam eius in turre [*or* turrī] servāverat.</u>

3. Our clothing was black and silver but theirs was purple and gold.

   <u>Vestis nostra ātra argenteaque [*or* et argentea] erat sed vestis eōrum purpurea aureaque [*or* et aurea] erat. [*Or* vestis *can be plural; change adjectives and verbs accordingly:* Vestēs nostrae ātrae argenteaeque erant sed vestēs eōrum purpureae aureaeque erant.]</u>

4. His dogs are faithful and he gives them good food, and so they hunt many deer well.

   <u>Canēs eius fīdī sunt et is eīs bonum cibum dat, itaque eī multōs cervōs bene captant.</u>

5. If wild animals and birds hasten from the dark forest, then the dragon is flying from the purple mountains to the forest.

   <u>Sī animālia fera et avēs [ferae] ab/ex silvā ātrā festinant, ergō/tum draco ab/ex montibus purpureīs ad silvam volat.</u>

6. Before the great battle of the twin seas, the enemies' black ships had sailed to our land and attacked our shores.

   <u>Ante proelium magnum marium geminōrum, nāvēs ātrae hostium ad patriam/terram nostram nāvigāverant et ōrās nostrās oppugnāverant [*or, I suppose*, oppugnāverunt].</u>

7. We declared the word of God to them and to their children, but they were foolish and laughed at us.
   Nōs eīs et līberīs [*or* līberīsque] eōrum/eārum verbum Deī dēclārāvimus, sed stultī erant [*or* fuērunt] et nōs rīsērunt.

8. Grasses were flourishing in the valleys but then the dragon flew over them and burned them.
   Grāmina in vallibus flōrēbant sed tum draco suprā ea volāvit et ea cremāvit.

9. The silvery castle with the fortifications and turrets was beautiful in front of the purplish-blue mountains.
   Castellum argenteum cum moenibus et turribus [turribusque] pulchrum erat [*or* fuit] prō montibus hyacinthīnīs.

10. After the death of my faithful old dog, I sat in the dark night and wept under the silvery moon.
    Post mortem canis meī fīdī antīquī, in nocte ātrā sēdī et sub lūnā argenteā flēvī.

E. Latin to English Translation

1   **Dē Fātō Pīrātae Īrātī**

Ōlim erat pīrāta īrātus. Is īrātus semper fuerat. Magnam nāvem ātram habēbat et cor eius ātrum erat. Vestēs eius ātrae rubraeque erant, et cibus eius bellum erat. Is oppida vestra et moenia urbium nostrārum oppugnābat. Is pīrāta cum bonīs malīsque pugnābat. Multa animālia ab eīs terrīs occupābat et pīrātīs
5   ea prō cibō dabat. Fēmīnās autem et puellās occupābat et eās ad nāvem ātram portābat. Ūnā[1] nocte, is multum vīnum pōtābat et pīrātīs dēclārāvit: "Ego magnus vir et bonus pīrāta sum! Aurum argentumque teneō; fēminās et vīnum et carmen habeō. Ego deus sum!" Sed tum dormīvit[2] et somniāvit:[3] Camēlus Magnus et Horrendus Mortis ab Montibus Purpureīs Tenēbrārum festīnāverat, et in diaetam[4] eius in nāve intrāvit. "Stulte!" āit. "Tū deus nōn es. Ego Mors sum, et ad tē festīnō. Tē ad meōs Montēs
10 Purpureōs Tenēbrārum portābō." Ergō Camēlus Mortis pīrātam superbum[5] et īrātum occupāvit, et eum in tenēbrās montium portāvit. Nōs eum iterum[6] numquam vīdimus, et terra pācem habuit.

Glossary
1. *ūnus, -a, -um*: one; here it is in the ablative matching *nocte*, which is showing "time when"
2. *dormiō, -īre, -īvī, -ītum*: I sleep
3. *somniō (1)*: I dream
4. *diaeta, -ae (f)*: cabin (of a ship)
5. *superbus, -a, -um*: proud, haughty
6. *iterum*: again

Concerning the Fate of the Angry Pirate

Once upon a time there was an angry pirate. He had always been angry. He had a great black ship and his heart was black. His clothes were black and red, and his food was war. He attacked your towns and the fortifications of our cities. This pirate fought with good people and bad. He seized many animals from these lands and gave them to the pirates as/for food. He moreover seized women and girls and carried them to the black ship. One night, he was drinking much wine and declared to the pirates: "I am a great man and a good pirate! I possess gold and silver; I have women, wine, and song. I am a god!" But then he slept and dreamed: A Great and Dread Camel of Death had hastened from the Purple Mountains of Darkness, and entered into his cabin on the ship. "Fool!" he said. "You are not a god. I am Death, and I am hastening to you. I will carry you to my Purple Mountains of Darkness." Therefore the Camel of Death seized the proud and angry pirate, and took him into the darkness of the mountains. We never saw him again, and the land had peace.

Lesson 18 Quiz (66 points)

A. Vocabulary (10 points)

Translate the following words.

1. urbs: **city**
2. ignis: **fire**
3. enim: **indeed, truly, certainly; for**
4. animal: **animal**
5. fortifications: **moenia**
6. nūbēs: **cloud, gloom**
7. ergō: **therefore, then, consequently, accordingly**
8. mōns: **mountain**
9. sī: **if**
10. dog: **canis**

B. Grammar (18 points)

1. Decline *this evil death*.

	LATIN SINGULAR	LATIN PLURAL
NOM.	ea mors mala	eae mortēs malae
GEN.	eius mortis malae	eārum mortium malārum
DAT.	eī mortī malae	eīs mortibus malīs
ACC.	eam mortem malam	eās mortēs malās
ABL.	eā morte malā	eīs mortibus malīs
VOC.	[Ō] mors mala	[Ō] mortēs malae

2. Give a synopsis of *videō* in the first person plural.

	LATIN	ENGLISH
PRESENT ACT.	vidēmus	we see
IMPERFECT ACT.	vidēbāmus	we were seeing
FUTURE ACT.	vidēbimus	we will see
PERFECT ACT.	vīdimus	we saw, have seen
PLUPERFECT ACT.	vīderāmus	we had seen
FUTURE PERF. ACT.	vīderimus	we will have seen

C. Translation (21 points)

Translate each sentence.

1. The purple dragon seized their horses under the darkness of night.

   Draco purpureus equōs eōrum/eārum sub tenēbrīs noctis occupāvit.

2. Nōs eīs dōna aurea herī dedimus.

   Yesterday we gave them golden gifts [gifts of gold].

D. Memorization (17 points)

Write out the first four lines of the *Symbolum Nicaenum*.

Crēdō in ūnum Deum, Patrem omnipotentem, Factōrem caelī et terrae, vīsibilium omnium et invīsibilium.

Et in ūnum Dominum Iēsum Christum, Fīlium Deī Ūnigenitum,

Et ex Patre nātum ante omnia saecula.

Deum dē Deō, Lūmen dē Lūmine, Deum vērum dē Deō vērō,

LESSON 19 (Student Edition p. 173)

Third Declension Adjectives

1. Word List

Have the students identify which conjugation each verb is from and what declension each noun belongs to (including third declension i-stems).

14. *omnis*, every, all—Sometimes in English it will sound better to put an "of" between *omnis* and the noun it modifies, but the phrase will be in the same case in Latin. For example, *omnēs fēminae* could be translated either as "all women" or "all of the women." We would not need to put *fēminae* in the genitive.

2. Derivatives/Memorization Helps

1. *asinus*, donkey: asinine
2. *bōs*, cow, bull, ox; (pl.) cattle: bovine
3. *elephantus*, elephant: elephantine, elephantiasis
4. *piscis*, fish: piscine
5. *altus*, high, lofty, deep: altitude, alto, altimeter
6. *brevis*, short, small, brief: brevity, abbreviate
7. *celer*, swift, quick: celerity, accelerate
8. *dulcis*, sweet: dulcet, dulcimer
9. *fēlix*, lucky, fortunate, happy: felicity, Felix
10. *fortis*, strong, brave: fortitude, forte
11. *infēlix*, unlucky, unfortunate, miserable: see *felix*
12. *ingēns*, huge, vast, enormous
13. *mediōcris*, ordinary: mediocre, mediocrity
14. *omnis*, every, all: prefix omni-, as in omniscient, omnipotent, omnipresent, omnibus, etc.
15. *potēns*, powerful: potent, potential, omnipotent
16. *augeō*, I increase: auction, augment
17. *vexō*, I vex, ravage, annoy: vex
18. *inter*, between, among: prefix inter-, as in intercept, international
19. *paene*, almost: peninsula
20. *prope*, near, next to

3. Memorization—*Symbolum Nicaenum* (Nicene Creed)

Omnia, one of this lesson's adjectives, appears substantively in line 5: *per quem omnia facta sunt*, "through whom all things were made." This lesson's new lines are:

Genitum, nōn factum, consubstantiālem Patrī: per quem omnia facta sunt.

> *Begotten, not made, [being] of one substance with the Father: by whom all things were made.*

Quī propter nōs hominēs et propter nostram salūtem dēscendit dē caelīs.

> *Who for us men and for our salvation descended from heaven.*

4. Grammar

Third Declension Adjectives

We will continue to reinforce and expand the use of the third declension as students learn third declension adjectives this lesson. Thus far all adjectives have been first/second declension adjectives, such as *bonus, -a, -um* or *ruber, -bra, -brum*. Third declension adjectives can be a little intimidating because their nominatives vary, but once you get into the chant, they are pretty normal. They decline like third declension i-stems, except that the masculine/feminine ablative singular has an *-ī* like the neuter (in bold):

	SINGULAR		PLURAL	
	MASC./FEM.	NEUTER	MASC./FEM.	NEUTER
NOM.	X	X	-ēs	-ia
GEN.	-is	-is	-ium	-ium
DAT.	-ī	-ī	-ibus	-ibus
ACC.	-em	X	-ēs	-ia
ABL.	**-ī**	-ī	-ibus	-ibus
VOC.	X	X	-ēs	-ia

As I mentioned, the only tricky thing with these adjectives is getting past the nominatives. They are sorted into three categories: **three termination**, **two termination**, and **single termination.** "Termination" is simply a fancy grammatical term for "ending." All the first/second declension adjectives you have learned were three termination—because the dictionary listing gave three nominative endings, one each for masculine, feminine, and neuter: *-us, -a, -um*. **Three termination third declension adjectives generally end in** *-r***, -is, -e.** The adjective *celer, celeris, celere* ("swift") is from this lesson's vocabulary list and is declined as follows:

	SINGULAR			PLURAL		
	MASCULINE	FEMININE	NEUTER	MASCULINE	FEMININE	NEUTER
NOM.	celer	celeris	celere	celerēs	celerēs	celeria
GEN.	celeris	celeris	celeris	celerium	celerium	celerium
DAT.	celerī	celerī	celerī	celeribus	celeribus	celeribus
ACC.	celerem	celerem	celere	celerēs	celerēs	celeria
ABL.	celerī	celerī	celerī	celeribus	celeribus	celeribus
VOC.	celer	celeris	celere	celerēs	celerēs	celeria

Notice how besides the nominative (and vocative), the masculine and feminine columns are exactly the same. Thus, they don't need to be written out separately unless your students are dying to have the review! Just make sure you remind them that the left column represents both masculine and feminine forms.

Two termination third declension adjectives generally end in *-is, -e.* This means that the masculine and feminine adjectives share the same form in the nominative, ending in *-is,* and the neuter nominative ends in *-e.* Your students have already learned a two termination adjective: *viridis, -e,* "green." It would be declined as follows:

	SINGULAR		PLURAL	
	MASC./FEM.	NEUTER	MASC./FEM.	NEUTER
NOM.	viridis	viride	viridēs	viridia
GEN.	viridis	viridis	viridium	viridium
DAT.	viridī	viridī	viridibus	viridibus
ACC.	viridem	viride	viridēs	viridia
ABL.	viridī	viridī	viridibus	viridibus
VOC.	viridis	viride	viridēs	viridia

Single termination third declension adjectives will vary in their nominative. Because masculine, feminine, and neuter all share the same nominative, the dictionary will usually list the genitive so that you can find the stem. *Ingēns, -entis* means "huge" and is declined as follows:

	SINGULAR		PLURAL	
	MASC./FEM.	NEUTER	MASC./FEM.	NEUTER
NOM.	ingēns	ingēns	ingentēs	ingentia
GEN.	ingentis	ingentis	ingentium	ingentium
DAT.	ingentī	ingentī	ingentibus	ingentibus
ACC.	ingentem	ingēns	ingentēs	ingentia
ABL.	ingentī	ingentī	ingentibus	ingentibus
VOC.	ingēns	ingēns	ingentēs	ingentia

The masculine/feminine and neuter do share many of the same forms, but they are given separately in the chart above because of those few important differences. Notice how the third declension neuter adjectives follow our two neuter rules:

1. The nominative, accusative, and vocative endings are the same.

2. The nominative and accusative plurals end in *-a*.

As with third declension nouns, the vocative of third declension adjectives—whether masculine, feminine, or neuter—is just the same as the nominative (see examples).

All of these adjectives, no matter what their termination, can modify nouns of any declension. Remember that **an adjective must match the noun it modifies in gender, number, and case, but not necessarily in declension.** We have already seen this with first/second declension nouns modifying nouns of first, second, or third declension: *agricola malus, vir malus, draco malus*. Similarly, a third declension adjective can modify a first declension noun: *nauta celer,* "swift sailor"; a second declension noun: *equus celer,* "swift horse"; or a third declension noun: *draco celer,* "swift dragon." The adjective simply must match the noun in gender, number, and case.

Here are a few example noun-adjective phrases fully declined. If you have enough boards in your classroom, pick several students to write these out all at the same time—you can even have one do the singular and another work on the plural. That way they get more involved, and afterwards you can involve even more students by calling on others to tell you if the first group wrote it out correctly.

draco celer, "swift dragon" (masculine)

	LATIN SINGULAR	LATIN PLURAL
NOM.	draco celer	dracōnēs celerēs
GEN.	dracōnis celeris	dracōnum celerium
DAT.	dracōnī celerī	dracōnibus celeribus
ACC.	dracōnem celerem	dracōnēs celerēs
ABL.	dracōne celerī	dracōnibus celeribus
VOC.	Ō draco celer	Ō dracōnēs celerēs

id crustulum ingēns, "that huge cookie"

	LATIN SINGULAR	LATIN PLURAL
NOM.	id crustulum ingēns	ea crustula ingentia
GEN.	eius crustulī ingentis	eōrum crustulōrum ingentium
DAT.	eī crustulō ingentī	eīs crustulīs ingentibus
ACC.	id crustulum ingēns	ea crustula ingentia
ABL.	eō crustulō ingentī	eīs crustulīs ingentibus
VOC.	Ō crustulum ingēns	Ō crustula ingentia

fēmina fēlix, "lucky woman"

	LATIN SINGULAR	LATIN PLURAL
NOM.	fēmina fēlix	fēminae fēlicēs
GEN.	fēminae fēlicis	fēminārum fēlicium
DAT.	fēminae fēlicī	fēminīs fēlicibus
ACC.	fēminam fēlicem	fēminās fēlicēs
ABL.	fēminā fēlicī	fēminīs fēlicibus
VOC.	Ō fēmina fēlix	Ō fēminae fēlicēs

Finally, keep in mind that third declension adjectives are capable of all the things adjectives are capable of—they can act as substantives and predicates.

Substantive examples: *Omnēs Oswaldum dracōnemque vidērunt,* "All [people] saw Oswald and the dragon." Here *omnēs* is masculine or feminine, nominative plural, and is acting as a noun (substantive). Another example would be *Omnia dēclārāvit,* "He declared all [things]"—*omnia* is neuter plural accusative.

Predicate examples: *Fēlix sum,* "I am happy." *Mīlitēs fortēs erant,* "The soldiers were brave."

5. Worksheet

The title for this lesson's Latin to English story, *Pons Asinōrum,* is the phrase used to refer to one of Euclid's geometry propositions and also by extension can be employed to describe a difficult challenge that will separate the weak from the strong. The riddle is based on the riddle of the Sphinx in the story of Oedipus.

E. *Litterae Mixtae Comparātaeque* (Letters Mixed and Matched): This for-fun exercise deals with matching adjectives.

6. Quiz

Administer Quiz 19 when the students are ready.

Lesson 19 Worksheet

A. Vocabulary

Translate the following words from Latin to English or English to Latin as appropriate. For the verbs, also fill in the missing principal parts. For each preposition, include which case(s) it takes.

1. almost: **paene**
2. bōs: **cow, bull, ox; (pl.) cattle**
3. augeō, **augēre**, **auxī**, **auctum**: **I increase**
4. ecce: **behold!**
5. fish: **piscis**
6. fēlix: **lucky, fortunate, happy**
7. brevis: **short, small, brief**
8. donkey: **asinus**
9. swift: **celer**
10. sea: **mare**
11. ingēns: **huge, vast, enormous**
12. prope: (+ **acc.**) **near, next to**
13. ergō: **therefore, then, consequently, accordingly**
14. unlucky: **infēlix**
15. dulcis: **sweet**
16. enim: **indeed, truly, certainly; for**
17. altus: **high, lofty, deep**
18. strong: **fortis**
19. between: **inter (+ acc.)**
20. mediōcris: **ordinary**
21. I annoy: **vexō**, **vexāre**, **vexāvī**, **vexātum**
22. quia: **because, since**
23. all: **omnis**
24. potēns: **powerful**
25. elephantus: **elephant**

B. Grammar

1. Give a synopsis of *vexō* in the second person plural.

	LATIN	ENGLISH
PRESENT ACT.	vexātis	you (pl.) vex, ravage, annoy
IMPERFECT ACT.	vexābātis	you (pl.) were vexing
FUTURE ACT.	vexābitis	you (pl.) will vex
PERFECT ACT.	vexāvistis	you (pl.) (have) vexed
PLUPERFECT ACT.	vexāverātis	you (pl.) had vexed
FUTURE PERF. ACT.	vexāveritis	you (pl.) will have vexed

2. Decline *this brave king*.

	LATIN SINGULAR	LATIN PLURAL
NOM.	is rex fortis	eī rēgēs fortēs
GEN.	eius rēgis fortis	eōrum rēgum fortium
DAT.	eī rēgī fortī	eīs rēgibus fortibus
ACC.	eum rēgem fortem	eōs rēgēs fortēs
ABL.	eō rēge fortī	eīs rēgibus fortibus
VOC.	Ō rex fortis	Ō rēgēs fortēs

3. Decline *green grass*.

	LATIN SINGULAR	LATIN PLURAL
NOM.	grāmen viride	grāmina viridia
GEN.	grāminis viridis	grāminum viridium
DAT.	grāminī viridī	grāminibus viridibus
ACC.	grāmen viride	grāmina viridia
ABL.	grāmine viridī	grāminibus viridibus
VOC.	Ō grāmen viride	Ō grāmina viridia

4. Decline *powerful pirate*.

	LATIN SINGULAR	LATIN PLURAL
NOM.	pīrāta potēns	pīrātae potentēs
GEN.	pīrātae potentis	pīrātārum potentium
DAT.	pīrātae potentī	pīrātīs potentibus
ACC.	pīrātam potentem	pīrātās potentēs
ABL.	pīrātā potentī	pīrātīs potentibus
VOC.	Ō pīrāta potēns	Ō pīrātae potentēs

Identify and translate all possible options for the following pronouns. An example is given below.

	PHRASE	GENDER, NUMBER, CASE	TRANSLATION
	vallī mediocrī	Fem. Sg. Dat. Fem. Sg. Abl.	to/for the ordinary valley by/with/from the ordinary valley
5.	fortēs asinōs	Masc. Pl. Acc.	the brave donkeys (object)
6.	amōre fēlīcī	Masc. Sg. Abl.	by/with/from the lucky love
7.	omnium urbium	Fem. Pl. Gen.	of all the cities
8.	crustula dulcia	Neut. Pl. Nom. Neut. Pl. Acc.	sweet cookies (subject) sweet cookies (object)
9	bōs celeris	Fem. Sg. Nom.	swift cow (subject)
10.	populum potentem	Masc. Sg. Acc.	powerful people (object)
11.	proeliō brevī	Neut. Sg. Dat. Neut. Sg. Abl.	to/for the short battle by/with/from the short battle

12.	ōrīs infēlicibus	Fem. Pl. Dat. Fem. Pl. Abl.	to/for the unlucky shores by/with/from the unlucky shores
13.	turrēs altās	Fem. Pl. Acc.	lofty towers (object)
14.	piscis celeris	Masc. Sg. Gen.	of the swift fish Note: this phrase can't be nominative because *piscis* is masculine and therefore the nominative adjective form would be *celer*.
15.	mare ingēns	Neut. Sg. Nom. Neut. Sg. Acc.	huge sea (subject) huge sea (object)
16.	gigās fēlix	Masc. Sg. Nom.	happy giant (subject)
17.	fēminae dulcis	Fem. Sg. Gen.	of the sweet woman
18.	flōrī rubrō	Masc. Sg. Dat.	to/for the red flower
19.	avis nigra	Fem. Sg. Nom.	black bird (subject)

C. Memorization

Fill in the blanks.

<u>Crēdō in ūnum Deum, Patrem omnipotentem, Factōrem caelī et terrae, vīsibilium omnium et invīsibilium.</u>

<u>Et in ūnum Dominum Iēsum Christum, Fīlium Deī Ūnigenitum,</u>

Et **ex** Patre nātum **ante** omnia **saecula** .

Deum **dē** **Deō** , **Lūmen** dē Lūmine, **Deum** vērum dē Deō **vērō** ,

Genitum , **nōn** factum, **consubstantiālem** **Patrī** : per **quem** omnia **facta** sunt;

Quī **propter** **nōs** hominēs et **propter** nostram **salūtem** **dēscendit** dē caelīs,

D. English to Latin Translation

Translate each sentence from English to Latin.

1. All the animals of the green forest loved the lucky man and sat at his feet.

   Omnia animālia silvae viridis fēlīcem [virum] amābant/amāvērunt et sub eum sedēbant/sēdērunt.

2. Indeed, his donkeys kept ravaging our fields and therefore we seized his grain and swift horses.

   Asinī enim eius agrōs nostrōs vexābant et ergō [nōs] frūmentum eius equōsque [*or* et equōs] celerēs eius occupāvimus.

3. The deep blue sea is huge and powerful, and you (pl.) fear it.

   Mare altum [et] caeruleum ingēns potēnsque [*or* et potēns] est, et [vōs] id timētis.

4. I watched the sweet daughter of the farmer when she was watching all his cattle, and I loved her.

   [Ego] fīliam dulcem agricolae spectāvī/spectābam ubi/quandō [ea] omnēs bovēs eius spectābat, et [ego] eam amāvī/amābam.

5. The turrets of the castle were high and beautiful, and from them the king could see all his kingdom.

   Turrēs castellī altae pulchraeque [*or* et pulchrae] erant/fuērunt, et ab eīs rex omne regnum eius vidēre poterat/potuit.

6. The brave man had hunted tigers and elephants in the black forest because he loved the powerful king's daughter.

   Fortis [vir] tigridēs et elephantōs in silvā ātrā captāverat quod/quia [is] fīliam rēgis potentis amāvit/amābat.

7. We saw many swift fish where they were swimming in the waves of the sea.

   [Nōs] multōs piscēs celerēs vīdimus ubi in undīs maris nābant.

8. The king's and queen's garments were purple and gold and glittering white, and their crowns shone.

   Vestēs rēgis rēgīnaeque [*or* et rēgīnae] purpureae et aureae et candidae [*or* aureaeque candidaeque] erant/fuērunt, et corōnae eōrum lūcēbant/lūxērunt.

9. I am the fierce enemy of your kingdom; fear me, everyone!

   [Ego] hostis ferus regnī vestrī/tuī sum; timēte mē, omnēs!

10. Grasses are green, the sky is blue; cookies are sweet, and I love you.

    Grāmina viridia sunt, caelum caeruleum est; crustula dulcia sunt, et ego tē amō.

E. Latin to English Translation

1. **Pons[1] Asinōrum**

Ōlim erant trēs[2] frātres: Iūlius, Fabius, et Oswaldus.[3] Iūlius postnatus[4] et mīles fortis erat. Is cum mīlitibus rēgis in terrā longinquā diū pugnāverat. Fabius medius[5] frāter erat, et is poēta infēlix erat. Nec pugnāvit nec labōrāvit, sed semper sedēbat et pōtābat et carmina misera dulciaque cantābat. Oswaldus iuvenissimus[6] fīlius erat, et is cum matre eōrum viduātā[7] in agrō semper laborābat. Tempora mala in terrā erant, et eī nec cibum neque pecūniam nōn habuērunt. Ergō māter eōrum eīs āit: "Festīnāte ab agrō et trāns Pontem Asinōrum. Ibī gigās brevis sed foedus sub ponte habitat, et omnibus enigma[8] rogat. Sī eī bene respondent, eīs multum aurum dat. Sī eī male respondent, eōs necat et mandūcat. Bene eī respondēte, meī fīliī, et tum pecūniam cibumque habēbimus!" Sed Fabius in vīllā sēdit et pōtāvit; itaque Oswaldus ad pontem festīnāvit. Ibī stetit gigās brevis sed foedus, et rogāvit: "Quid[9] quattuor[10] crūrēs[11] mane,[12] duo[13] crūrēs merīdiē,[14] et trēs crūrēs vespere[14] habet?" Oswaldus cōgitāvit, et tum respondit: "Homō." Gigās īrātus erat, sed eī aurum dedit quod bene responderat. Itaque Oswaldus et māter frūmentum et cibum habēre potuērunt, sed Fabius pōtābat.

Glossary
1. *pons, pontis* (m): bridge (so, is it an i-stem?)
2. *trēs*: three
3. *Iūlius, Fabius,* and *Oswaldus* are all second declension names
4. *postnatus, -i* (m): oldest [son]
5. *medius, -a, -um*: middle (of)
6. *iuvenissimus, -a, -um*: youngest
7. *viduātā*: widowed, from the verb *viduō*
8. *enigma, -matis* (n): riddle
9. *quid*: what?
10. *quattuor*: four
11. *crūs, crūris* (m): leg
12. *mane*: in the morning
13. *duo*: two
14. *merīdiē*: at noon
15. *vespere*: ablative of time when

<u>Bridge of Donkeys</u>

<u>Once upon a time there were three brothers: Iulius, Fabius, and Oswaldus. Iulius was the oldest and a brave soldier. He had been fighting with the king's solders in a far away land for a long time. Fabius was the middle brother, and he was an unlucky poet. He neither fought nor worked, but always sat and drank and sang sweet, sad songs. Oswald was the youngest son, and he always worked with their widowed mother on the farm. Times were evil in the land, and they did not have food or money. Therefore, their mother said to them: "Hasten from the field and across the Bridge of Donkeys. There a short but horrible giant lives under the bridge, and he asks all [men] a riddle. If they answer him well, he gives them much gold. If they answer badly, he kills and eats them. Answer him well, my sons, and then we will have money and food!" But Fabius sat in the farmhouse and drank; and so Oswald hastened to the bridge. There the short but horrible giant stood, and asked: "What has four legs in the morning, two at noon, and three in the evening?" Oswald thought, and then answered, "Man." The giant was angry, but gave him the gold because he had answered well. Therefore Oswald and his mother were able to have grain and food, but Fabius kept drinking.</u>

E. For Fun: *Litterae Mixtae Comparātaeque*

Unscramble the letters in the left column to form a Latin adjective, then pair it with a noun from the list on the right column to make a sensible phrase. You must use logic to match them all correctly since each adjective and noun can only be used once!

	SCRAMBLED LETTERS	UNSCRAMBLED LATIN ADJECTIVE	MATCHING NOUN
1.	bauls	**albus**	elephantus
2.	mārutār	**ātrārum**	avibus
3.	urōpperu	**purpureō**	piscī
4.	ilercse	**celeris**	nox
5.	divīir	**viridī**	igne
6.	caddian	**candida**	moenia
7.	aeīur	**aureī**	piscis
8.	ēsculd	**dulcēs**	vallēs
9.	lsrceeīua	**caeruleīs**	avibus
10.	ōuumbrrr	**rubrōrum**	hostium

nox
moenia
hostium
navium
avibus
piscī
vallēs
elephantus
piscis
igne

Lesson 19 Quiz (73 points)

A. Vocabulary (10 points)

Translate the following words. Give case(s) for prepositions.

1. prope: (+ <u>acc.</u>) <u>near, next to</u>
2. ingēns: <u>huge, vast, enormous</u>
3. candidus: <u>(glittering) white</u>
4. ox: <u>bōs</u>
5. brevis: <u>short, small, brief</u>
6. dulcis: <u>sweet</u>
7. swift: <u>celer</u>
8. paene: <u>almost</u>
9. fortis: <u>strong, brave</u>
10. altus: <u>high, lofty, deep</u>

B. Grammar (18 points)

1. Give a synopsis of *augeō* in the third person singular.

	LATIN	ENGLISH
PRESENT ACT.	auget	he/she/it increases
IMPERFECT ACT.	augēbat	he was increasing
FUTURE ACT.	augēbit	he will increase
PERFECT ACT.	auxit	he (has) increased
PLUPERFECT ACT.	auxerat	he had increased
FUTURE PERF. ACT.	auxerit	he will have increased

2. Decline *unfortunate queen*.

	LATIN SINGULAR	LATIN PLURAL
NOM.	rēgīna infēlix	rēgīnae infēlīcēs
GEN.	rēgīnae infēlīcis	rēgīnārum infēlīcium
DAT.	rēgīnae infēlīcī	rēgīnīs infēlīcibus
ACC.	rēgīnam infēlīcem	rēgīnās infēlīcēs
ABL.	rēgīnā infēlīcī	rēgīnīs infēlīcibus
VOC.	[Ō] rēgīna infēlix	[Ō] rēgīnae infēlīcēs

C. Translation (21 points)

Translate each sentence.

1. I sit between the king and queen, but I am ordinary.

   [Ego] inter rēgem et rēgīnam [*or* rēgīnamque] sedeō, sed [ego] mediōcris sum.

2. Fortis leōnem pugnāvit et pulchram servāvit.

   The brave man fought the lion and saved the beautiful woman.

D. Memorization (24 points)

Write out the first six lines of the *Symbolum Nicaenum*.

Crēdō in ūnum Deum, Patrem omnipotentem, Factōrem caelī et terrae, vīsibilium omnium et invīsibilium.

Et in ūnum Dominum Iēsum Christum, Fīlium Deī Ūnigenitum,

Et ex Patre nātum ante omnia saecula.

Deum dē Deō, Lūmen dē Lūmine, Deum vērum dē Deō vērō,

Genitum, nōn factum, consubstantiālem Patrī: per quem omnia facta sunt;

Quī propter nōs hominēs et propter nostram salūtem dēscendit dē caelīs,

LESSON 20 (Student Edition p. 185)

Verbs: Present, Imperfect & Future Passive Indicative

1. Word List

Run through the adjectives aloud and have students identify if they are first/second declension adjectives or third declension adjectives. Take note of the following words:

3. *epulae, -ārum* (f, pl.) feast—Note that this noun comes in the plural only, like *tenēbrae* or *dīvitiae*.

4. *eques, -quitis* (m) knight, horseman, cavalryman—This noun is similar to *equus*, because the *eques* rode upon an *equus*. Your students should avoid confusing the two, of course—but happily *eques* is third declension and its stem is *equit-*, so that should help.

6. *pastor, pastōris* (m) shepherd—Although we today see the word "pastor" and immediately think "preacher," it originally meant "shepherd." This original sense is most commonly retained in the adjective "pastoral," as in "pastoral landscape" (a countryside dotted with sheep or the like).

15. *ardeō, ardēre, arsī*, I burn, blaze—This verb is intransitive, like *torreō* and unlike the transitive *cremō*.

2. Derivatives/Memorization Helps

1. *arbor*, tree: arbor, arboretum
2. *cēna*, dinner, meal: cenacle
3. *epulae*, feast
4. *eques*, knight, horseman, cavalryman: equitant; see *equus*, Lesson 4
5. *matrimōnium*, marriage: matrimony, matrimonial; see *māter*, Lesson 12
6. *pastor*, shepherd: pastor, pastoral, pastorale
7. *ācer*, sharp, eager; fierce: acrid, eager
8. *difficilis*, difficult: difficult
9. *facilis*, easy: facile, facility, facilitate
10. *fessus*, tired, weary
11. *lātus*, wide, broad: latitude
12. *longus*, long: longitude

13. *tristis*, sad, gloomy, dismal: triste, trustful; memory help—"The story of *Tristan* and Isolde is a *sad* one."

14. *vīvus*, living: vivid, convivial

15. *ardeō*, I burn, blaze: ardent, ardor, arson

16. *mūtō*, I change: mutable, mutant, mutate

17. *properō*, I hurry, rush

18. *certātim*, eagerly

19. *minūtātim*, gradually, bit by bit

20. *sīcut*, as, just as, like

3. Memorization—*Symbolum Nicaenum* (Nicene Creed)

This lesson's new lines are:

> Et incarnātus est dē Spīritū Sanctō ex Marīā virgine, et homō factus est.
>
> *And was incarnate by the Holy Ghost of the virgin Mary, and was made man.*
>
> Crucifīxus etiam prō nōbīs sub Pontiō Pīlātō; passus, et sepultus est,
>
> *He was crucified also for us under Pontius Pilate; suffered, and was buried,*

4. Grammar

Present, Imperfect, and Future Passive Indicative

This is rather an important lesson for the students since they will be introduced to the passive voice in three of the six tenses. Recall that a verb has five attributes: person, number, tense, voice, and mood. So far your students have learned all persons (first, second, and third) and both numbers (singular and plural). They have studied all six tenses (present, imperfect, future, perfect, pluperfect, future perfect) but only in the active voice. They have also learned several moods (indicative, imperative, and infinitive). Now it is time to learn about the passive voice.

Give your students a sentence such as "Oswald killed the dragon" and see if they can turn that sentence into a passive, conveying similar meaning. The correct answer would be "The dragon was killed by Oswald" or "The dragon has been killed by Oswald." If someone suggests "Oswald was killed by the dragon," you need to point out that this is actually the *opposite* of "Oswald killed the dragon." **When a verb is in the active voice, the subject *performs* the action. When a verb is passive, the subject *receives* the action.**

Now have your students turn a verb of each tense from active into the passive:

Oswald loves the princess.

The princess is loved [is being loved] by Oswald.

The pirates were singing many songs.

Many songs were being sung by the pirates.

The enemy will attack our town.

Our town will be attacked by the enemy.

The king gave the princess to Oswald in marriage.

The princess was given [has been given] by the king to Oswald in marriage.

The angry goddess had changed him into a dog.

He had been changed into a dog by the angry goddess.

The donkey will have carried great burdens to town.

Great burdens will have been carried to town by the donkey.

This lesson we will focus on the present passive system: present, imperfect, and future passive. Here are the chants:

Present Passive Indicative

	LATIN SINGULAR	ENGLISH SINGULAR	LATIN PLURAL	ENGLISH PLURAL
1ST	-r	I am (being) *verbed*	-mur	we are (being) *verbed*
2ND	-ris	you are (being) *verbed*	-minī	you (pl.) are (being) *verbed*
3RD	-tur	he/she/it is (being) *verbed*	-ntur	they are being *verbed*

Imperfect Passive Indicative

	LATIN SINGULAR	ENGLISH SINGULAR	LATIN PLURAL	ENGLISH PLURAL
1ST	-bar	I was (being) *verbed*	-bāmur	we were (being) *verbed*
2ND	-bāris	you were (being) *verbed*	-bāminī	you (pl.) were (being) *verbed*
3RD	-bātur	he/she/it was (being) *verbed*	-bantur	they were (being) *verbed*

Future Passive Indicative

	LATIN SINGULAR	ENGLISH SINGULAR	LATIN PLURAL	ENGLISH PLURAL
1ST	-bor	I will be *verbed*	-bimur	we will be *verbed*
2ND	-beris	you will be *verbed*	-biminī	you (pl.) will be *verbed*
3RD	-bitur	he/she/it will be *verbed*	-buntur	they will be *verbed*

Before the students can bewail how much they have to memorize this lesson, quickly point out to them yet again the virtue of Roman recycling: Once the students learn the present passive chant, they are well on their way to knowing the other two because the *-r, -ris, -tur,* etc. is found at the end of the imperfect and future passive endings. They should also note the similarities to the active endings: *-ba-* is the sign of the imperfect, whether active or passive, and *-bo-, -bi-,* and *-bu-* appear in the future in the same places (with the exception of *-beris* versus *-bis* in the second person singular).

To form the present, imperfect, or future passive, simply follow the method for forming their active equivalents. Go to the second principal part (the present active infinitive), remove the *-re,* and you have the present stem. Then you can add any of the endings above. *Necāre* and *vidēre* are conjugated below as examples from the first and second conjugations. As with the present active in the first conjugation, the *ā* contracts with the *ō* and remains simply *ō: amō* (not *amaō*), "I love" and *amor* (not *amāor*), "I am loved." The stem vowel *ē* of the second conjugation, however, does not contract: *videō* becomes *videor,* etc.

Necō—First Conjugation Verb
Present Passive Indicative

	LATIN SINGULAR	ENGLISH SINGULAR	LATIN PLURAL	ENGLISH PLURAL
1ST	necor	I am (being) killed	necāmur	we are (being) killed
2ND	necāris	you are (being) killed	necāminī	you (pl.) are (being) killed
3RD	necātur	he/she/it is (being) killed	necantur	they are (being) killed

Imperfect Passive Indicative

	LATIN SINGULAR	ENGLISH SINGULAR	LATIN PLURAL	ENGLISH PLURAL
1ST	necābar	I was (being) killed	necābāmur	we were (being) killed
2ND	necābāris	you were (being) killed	necābāminī	you (pl.) were (being) killed
3RD	necābātur	he/she/it was (being) killed	necābantur	they were (being) killed

Future Passive Indicative

	LATIN SINGULAR	ENGLISH SINGULAR	LATIN PLURAL	ENGLISH PLURAL
1ST	necābor	I will be killed	necābimur	we will be killed
2ND	necāberis	you will be killed	necābiminī	you (pl.) will be killed
3RD	necābitur	he/she/it will be killed	necābuntur	they will be killed

Videō—Second Conjugation Verb*

Present Passive Indicative

	LATIN SINGULAR	ENGLISH SINGULAR	LATIN PLURAL	ENGLISH PLURAL
1ST	videor	I am (being) seen, I seem	vidēmur	we are (being) seen, we seem
2ND	vidēris	you are (being) seen, you seem	vidēminī	you (pl.) are (being) seen, you (pl.) seem
3RD	vidētur	he/she/it is (being) seen, he/she/it seems	videntur	they are being seen, they seem

Imperfect Passive Indicative

	LATIN SINGULAR	ENGLISH SINGULAR	LATIN PLURAL	ENGLISH PLURAL
1ST	vidēbar	I was (being) seen, I was seeming	vidēbāmur	we were (being) seen, we were seeming
2ND	vidēbāris	you were (being) seen, you were seeming	vidēbāminī	you (pl.) were (being) seen, you (pl.) were seeming
3RD	vidēbātur	he/she/it was (being) seen, he/she/it was seeming	vidēbantur	they were (being) seen, they were seeming

Future Passive Indicative

	LATIN SINGULAR	ENGLISH SINGULAR	LATIN PLURAL	ENGLISH PLURAL
1ST	vidēbor	I will be seen, I will seem	vidēbimur	we will be seen, we will seem
2ND	vidēberis	you will be seen, you will seem	vidēbiminī	you (pl.) will be seen, you (pl.) will seem
3RD	vidēbitur	he/she/it will be seen, he/she/it will seem	vidēbuntur	they will be seen, they will seem

One more concept that goes hand-in-hand with the passive: **ablative of agent** (with *ab*). All of the English examples above had an agent: Something was done *by* someone. To express that someone (the agent), use *ā* or *ab* plus the ablative (use *ab* if the word following begins with a vowel; either *ā* or *ab* if a consonant): *Draco ab Oswaldō necābātur*, "The dragon was being killed by Oswald." Remember that if it is a thing—not a person—performing the passive action, we can use our good old ablative of means/instrument: *Draco gladiō necābātur*, "The dragon was being killed by the sword."

Have your students translate the following sentences with active verbs into Latin, and then put the same meaning into the passive. Notice that we have a couple English translation options for the present and imperfect passive, just as we had with their active equivalents. For example, *necō* can mean "I am killing" (progressive), and *necor* can mean "I am killed" (simple) or "I am being killed" (progressive). Our favorite verb exercise, the synopsis, will now look a bit different:

---

* Note the special passive meaning of *videō*. It makes sense with an example such as: "He is seen to be happy" which is basically the same as "He seems to be happy."

ACTIVE	PASSIVE
The enemy will destroy our great city. Hostēs [Hostis] nostram urbem magnam dēlēbunt [dēlēbit].	*Our great city will be destroyed by the enemy.* Nostra urbs magna ab hostibus [hostī] dēlēbitur.
He was taming the wild horse yesterday. [Is] equum ferum herī domābat.	*The wild horse was being tamed by him yesterday.* Equus ferus ab eō herī domābātur.
That woman is singing many songs. Ea fēmina multa carmina cantant.	*Many songs are being sung by that woman.* Multa carmina ab eā fēminā cantantur.

Our favorite verb exercise, the synopsis, will now look a bit different:

	ACTIVE		PASSIVE	
	LATIN	ENGLISH	LATIN	ENGLISH
PRES.	necāmus	we kill	necāmur	we are (being) killed
IMPF.	necābāmus	we were killing	necābāmur	we were (being) killed
FUT.	necābimus	we will kill	necābimur	we will be killed
PERF.	necāvimus	we (have) killed		
PLUPF.	necāverāmus	we had killed		
FT. PF.	necāverimus	we will have killed		

The perfect, pluperfect, and future perfect passives are in gray because they will not be taught until Lesson 22. When a portion of the synopsis is blacked out (i.e., in black, not gray), it means that that particular form does not exist in Latin.

Review

Be sure to review the third declension i-stem nouns and the adjective endings. Also, keep reviewing your pronouns.

5. Worksheet

Follow the directions given and complete the worksheet. The Latin to English translation is simplified and adapted from Ovid's *Metamorphoses* I.452–567.

6. Quiz

Administer Quiz 20 when the students are ready.

Lesson 20 Worksheet

A. Vocabulary

Translate the following words from Latin to English or English to Latin as appropriate. For the verbs, also fill in the missing principal parts.

1. mūtō, **mūtāre**, **mūtāvī**, **mūtātum**: **I change**
2. ācer: **sharp, eager; fierce**
3. feast: **epulae**
4. ardeō, **ardēre**, **arsī**, —— : **I burn, blaze**
5. fessus: **tired, weary**
6. paene: **almost**
7. tree: **arbor**
8. longus: **long**
9. (dead) black: **āter**
10. marriage: **matrimōnium**
11. minūtātim: **gradually, bit by bit**
12. facilis: **easy**
13. shepherd: **pastor**
14. sī: **if**
15. difficult: **difficilis**
16. cēna: **dinner, meal**
17. lātus: **wide, broad**
18. properō, **properāre**, properāvī, **properātum**: **I hurry, rush**
19. sīcut: **as, just as, like**
20. night: **nox**
21. vīvus: **living**
22. omnis: **all, every**
23. knight: **eques**
24. certātim: **eagerly**
25. tristis: **sad, gloomy, dismal**

B. Grammar

Identify whether the main verbs of the following sentences are active or passive.

1. You had been eating ice cream for two hours. — active
2. His mother was sending many messengers to the faraway land. — active
3. I will not be seen by anyone. — passive
4. After that we were told the truth. — passive
5. The queen will listen to the bard's song. — active
6. By then I will have received the reward for capturing the pirate. — active
7. You were taken to the castle dungeon by the soldiers. — passive
8. The grass is being trampled by the neighbor's goats. — passive
9. He has been wounded horribly in the battle. — passive
10. We have been poor but happy. — active

11. Give a synopsis of *mūtō* in the second person plural.

	ACTIVE		PASSIVE	
	LATIN	ENGLISH	LATIN	ENGLISH
PRES.	mutātis	you (pl.) change	mutāminī	you (pl.) are changed
IMPF.	mutābātis	you (pl.) were changing	mutābāminī	you (pl.) were (being) changed
FUT.	mutābitis	you (pl.) will change	mutābiminī	you (pl.) will be changed
PERF.	mutāvistis	you (pl.) (have) changed		
PLUPF.	mutāverātis	you (pl.) had changed		
FT. PF.	mutāveritis	you (pl.) will have changed		

12. Give a synopsis of *vastō* in the first person singular.

	ACTIVE		PASSIVE	
	LATIN	ENGLISH	LATIN	ENGLISH
PRES.	vastō	I devastate, lay waste	vastor	I am (being) devastated, laid waste
IMPF.	vastābam	I was devastating	vastābar	I was (being) devastated
FUT.	vastābō	I will devastate	vastābor	I will be devastated
PERF.	vastāvī	I (have) devastated		
PLUPF.	vastāveram	I had devastated		
FT. PF.	vastāverō	I will have devastated		

13. Give a synopsis of *moveō* in the third person plural.

	ACTIVE		PASSIVE	
	LATIN	ENGLISH	LATIN	ENGLISH
PRES.	movent	they move	moventur	they are (being) moved
IMPF.	movēbant	they were moving	movēbantur	they were (being) moved
FUT.	movēbunt	they will move	movēbuntur	they will be moved
PERF.	mōvērunt	they (have) moved		
PLUPF.	mōverant	they had moved		
FT. PF.	mōverint	they will have moved		

C. Memorization

Fill in the blanks.

Crēdō in ūnum Deum, Patrem omnipotentem, Factōrem caelī et terrae, vīsibilium omnium et invīsibilium.

Et in ūnum Dominum Iēsum Christum, Fīlium Deī Ūnigenitum,

Et ex Patre nātum ante omnia saecula.

Deum **dē** **Deō**, **Lūmen** dē Lūmine, **Deum** vērum dē **Deō** **vērō**,

Genitum, nōn **factum**, **consubstantiālem** Patrī: **per** **quem**

omnia facta **sunt**;

Quī **propter** **nōs** hominēs **et** **propter** nostram **salūtem**

dēscendit **dē** **caelīs**,

Et incarnātus **est** dē Spīritū **Sanctō** ex Marīā **virgine**, et **homō**

factus est.

Crucifīxus etiam prō **nōbīs** sub **Pontiō** Pīlātō; **passus**, et sepultus **est**,

D. English to Latin Translation

Translate each sentence from English to Latin.

1. Our land was being burned by the dragon; the trees were blazing and the fields dried up.

   <u>Patria/Terra/Tellūs nostra ab/ā dracōne cremābātur; arborēs ardēbant et agrī [*or* agrīque] torrēbant.</u>

2. The river is wide, the road is long, and the journey will seem difficult.

   <u>Flūmen lātum est, via longa [est], et iter difficile vidēbuntur.</u>

3. I love the handsome pirate, but I am not loved by him.

   <u>[Ego] pīrātam pulchrum amō, sed [ego] ab eō nōn amor.</u>

4. Bit by bit all of the huge dinner is being eaten by the short and small boy.

   <u>Omnis cēna magna ab puerō brevī et parvō [*or* parvōque] minūtātim mandūcātur.</u>

5. When will glory and praise be given to the true king

   <u>Quando/Ubi glōria lausque [et laus] rēgī vērō dabuntur?</u>

6. The bad sailor was drinking much wine and then purple elephants were seen by him.

   <u>Nauta malus vīnum multum pōtābat et elephantī purpureī ab eō tum vidēbantur.</u>

7. There will be a marriage between you and the king's daughter, and a great feast will be eaten.

   <u>Erit matrimōnium inter tē et fīliam [*or* fīliamque] rēgis, et epulae magnae mandūcābuntur. *[Make sure that* epulae *is the subject of a plural verb because it is plural in Latin, even though its English meaning is singular.]*</u>

8. The great battle was being fought and now all the knights and soldiers are weary.

   <u>Proelium magnum pugnābātur et nunc omnēs equitēs mīlitēsque [*or* et mīlitēs] fessī sunt.</u>

9. Great and horrible things were predicted by the strange woman in the dark cave.

   <u>Magna foedaque [*or* et foeda] ā/ab fēminā mīrā in spēluncā ātrā cantābantur.</u>

10. On the high mountain we were being hunted by the giant, and therefore we hastened eagerly to the castle.

    <u>In monte altō [nōs] ā/ab gigante captābāmur, et [nōs] ergō ad castellum certātim festīnāvimus/festīnābāmus.</u>

E. Latin to English Translation

1 **Apollō et Daphne**

Ōlim erat nympha[1] pulchra, fīlia deī flūminis. Daphne[2] appellābātur. Ea virōs nōn amābat, quod Cupīdō,[3] deus amōris, eam in corde sagittā plumbeā[4] petīverat.[5] Ea autem ab Apolline[6] certātim amābātur, quod is ab Cupīdine sagittā aureā petēbātur. Sīcut Diāna,[7] soror Apollinis, Daphne silvās
5 amāvit et in eīs semper erat. Apollō ad eam ibī festīnāvit et eī verba amōris cantāvit: "Ō Daphne pulchra, ego nec agricola nec miser sum—deus sum! Ego tibī amōre ardeō! Erit mātrimōnium inter nōs?" Daphne eī nōn respondit, sed ab eō festīnāvit. Et Apollō properāvit, et eam captāvit sīcut leō cervum captat. Ea fessa erat, et victōria Apollinī ab Cupīdine dabātur, sed Daphne patrī deō flūminis clamāvit: "O pater! Mē nunc servā!" Clāmor[8] eius audiēbātur,[9] et ea in arborem pulchrum
10 minūtātim mutābātur. Apollō, "Tū esse uxor[10] mea nōn potes," āit, "sed tū arbor meus eris! Folia[11] tua sīcut corōna multīs dabuntur, et tū laudem glōriamque dāberis." Itaque laurus[12] arbor Apollinis semper erit.

Glossary
1. *nympha, -ae* (f): nymph
2. *Daphne, -ēs* (f): Daphne
3. *Cupīdō, -dinis* (m): Cupid (son of Venus and god of love)
4. *plumbeus, -a, -um*: leaden, of lead
5. *petō, -ere, -īvī, -ītum*: I shoot
6. *Apollō, -inis* (m): Apollo (god of prophesy, music, archery, the sun, etc.)
7. *Diāna, -ae* (f): Diana, virgin goddess of the moon and hunting
8. *clāmor, -ōris* (m): shout, cry
9. *audiō, -īre, -īvī, -ītum*: I hear
10. *uxor, -ōris* (f): wife
11. *folium, -ī* (n): leaf
12. *laurus, -ī* (f): laurel-tree

Apollo and Daphne

Once upon a time there was a beautiful nymph, the daughter of a river god [lit., a god of the river]. She was called Daphne. She did not love men, because Cupid, the god of love, had shot her in the heart with an arrow of lead. However, she was eagerly loved by the god Apollo, because he was shot by Cupid with an arrow of gold. Just like Diana, Apollo's sister, Daphne loved the forests and was always in them. Apollo hastened to her there and sang words of love to her: "O beautiful Daphne, I am not a farmer nor wretch [wretched man]—I am a god! I burn with love for you! Will there be a marriage between us?" Daphne did not answer him, but hastened away from him. Apollo hastened too, and hunted her as a lion hunts a deer. She was weary, and victory was being given [to] Apollo by Cupid, but Daphne shouted to [her] father the river god: "O father! Save me now!" Her cry was heard, and she was changed bit by bit into a beautiful tree. Apollo said, "You cannot be my wife, but you will be my tree! Your leaves will be given as a crown to many, and you will be given praise and glory." Thus the laurel will always be the tree of Apollo.

Lesson 20 Quiz (77 points)

A. Vocabulary (10 points)

Translate the following words.

1. certātim: **eagerly**
2. paene: **almost**
3. facilis: **easy**
4. shepherd: **pastor**
5. ruber: **red, ruddy**
6. ardeō: **I burn, blaze**
7. turris: **tower, turret**
8. feast: **epulae**
9. fessus: **tired, weary**
10. tristis: **sad, gloomy, dismal**

B. Grammar (15 points)

1. Give a synopsis of *amō* in the third person singular.

	ACTIVE			PASSIVE	
	LATIN	ENGLISH		LATIN	ENGLISH
PRES.	amat	he/she/it loves		amātur	he is [being] loved
IMPF.	amābat	he was loving		amābātur	he was [being] loved
FUT.	amābit	he will love		amābitur	he will be loved
PERF.	amāvit	he [has] loved			
PLUPF.	amāverat	he had loved			
FT. PF.	amāverit	he will have loved			

C. Translation (21 points)

Translate each sentence.

1. The animals will rush into the sea because the fire will be seen by them.

   Animālia in mare properābunt quia ignis ab eīs vidēbitur.

2. Multī piscēs turbīs ab Pastōre Bonō dabantur.

   Many fish were given to the crowds by the Good Shepherd.

D. Memorization (31 points)

Write out the first eight lines of the *Symbolum Nicaenum*.

Crēdō in ūnum Deum, Patrem omnipotentem, Factōrem caelī et terrae, vīsibilium omnium et invīsibilium.

Et in ūnum Dominum Iēsum Christum, Fīlium Deī Ūnigenitum,

Et ex Patre nātum ante omnia saecula.

Deum dē Deō, Lūmen dē Lūmine, Deum vērum dē Deō vērō,

Genitum, nōn factum, consubstantiālem Patrī: per quem omnia facta sunt;

Quī propter nōs hominēs et propter nostram salūtem dēscendit dē caelīs,

Et incarnātus est dē Spīritū Sanctō ex Marīā virgine, et homō factus est.

Crucīfixus etiam prō nōbīs sub Pontiō Pīlātō; passus, et sepultus est,

LESSON 21 (Student Edition p. 196)

Numerals / Review of Present Passive System

1. Word List

This lesson your students will learn twenty-five important numerals. They will learn the cardinals this lesson—the "counting" numbers (one, two, three, etc.). In two lessons they'll learn how to order things with the ordinal numerals (first, second, third, etc.).

Review Roman numerals if necessary—this is a good opportunity to play a game on the board doing speed math problems using Roman numerals. (You can mix the new cardinals in, too!)

Note: The easiest number to misspell is *quattuor* (students will frequently leave out the second *u* and write "quattor"). *Vīgintī* is often confused with *virgō* (this can lead to odd and amusing translations).

2. Derivatives/Memorization Helps

1. *ūnus*, one: unity, union; prefix uni-, as in unicorn
2. *duo*, two: duet, duo; prefix duo-
3. *trēs*, three: triple, triplet; prefix tri-
4. *quattuor*, four: quatrain
5. *quīnque*, five: quinquinnial, quinquinnium
6. *sex*, six: sextet; prefix sex-, "six" (but the word "sex" is from *sexus*)
7. *septem*, seven: September, septennial, septenarius
8. *octō*, eight: October, octet
9. *novem*, nine: November, novena
10. *decem*, ten: December, decimal, decimate
11. *ūndecim*, eleven
12. *duodecim*, twelve
13. *tredecim*, thirteen
14. *quattuordecim*, fourteen
15. *quīndecim*, fifteen
16. *sēdecim*, sixteen
17. *septendecim*, seventeen
18. *duodēvīgintī*, eighteen
19. *ūndēvīgintī*, nineteen
20. *vīgintī*, twenty: vigintillion
21. *vīgintī ūnus*, twenty-one
22. *quīnquāgintā*, fifty: quinquagenarian, Quinquagesima (Shrove Sunday)
23. *centum*, one hundred: cent, centipede, century
24. *quīngentī*, five hundred
25. *mīlle*, one thousand: millennium, million, millipede

3. Memorization—*Symbolum Nicaenum* (Nicene Creed)

This lesson's new lines are:

> Et resurrēxit tertiā die, secundum Scriptūrās, et ascendit in caelum, sedet ad dexteram Patris.
>
> *And He rose on the third day, according to the Scriptures, and ascended into heaven, [and] sits at the right hand of the Father.*
>
> Et iterum ventūrus est cum glōriā, iūdicāre vīvōs et mortuōs, cuius regnī nōn erit fīnis.
>
> *And He will come again with glory, to judge the living and the dead, whose kingdom shall have no end.*

4. Grammar

Numerals

Happily, most cardinal numerals are indeclinable. This means that your students only need to learn the chants for *ūnus, duo, trēs,* and the plural of *mīlle,* and that's it! First off, ask your class what part of speech numbers are, and hopefully they will answer "adjective." Then show them how these four numbers, although slightly irregular, follow the declensions students have already learned. As adjectives, numbers will match the nouns they modify in gender, number, and case.

Here are the declensions of these numbers, with the odd forms in bold:

	SINGULAR			PLURAL		
	MASCULINE	FEMININE	NEUTER	MASCULINE	FEMININE	NEUTER
NOM.	ūnus	ūna	ūnum	**duo**	duae	**duo**
GEN.	**ūnīus**	**ūnīus**	**ūnīus**	duōrum	duārum	duōrum
DAT.	**ūnī**	**ūnī**	**ūnī**	duōbus	duābus	duōbus
ACC.	ūnum	ūnam	ūnum	duōs	duās	**duo**
ABL.	ūnō	ūnā	ūnō	duōbus	duābus	duōbus

Notice that *ūnus* has a genitive and dative similar to *ille*. The other forms are fairly regular. Also—although this probably should go with saying—*ūnus* only has a singular because it means "one" (which cannot be plural), and *duo* and the rest only have plurals because, well, they are plural.

	PLURAL		SINGULAR	PLURAL
	M/F	N	M/F/N	N
NOM.	trēs	tria	mīlle	mīlia
GEN.	trium	trium	mīlle	mīlium
DAT.	tribus	tribus	mīlle	mīlibus
ACC.	trēs	tria	mīlle	mīlia
ABL.	tribus	tribus	mīlle	mīlibus

Note that although in the singular *mīlle* is indeclinable, in the plural it is not (and it loses one *l*). Also, the singular *mīlle* functions as an adjective while the plural *mīlia* is a third declension neuter i-stem noun. Just as in English, we say "thousands of his soldiers," in Latin you can use a genitive (called the partitive genitive or genitive of the whole)—*mīlia mīlitum eius*. With other cardinals you will generally employ a preposition such as *ex* or *dē*—*ūnus ex mīlitibus eius*, "one of his soldiers."

5. Worksheet

Follow the directions given and complete the worksheet.

C. *Lūdus Numerōrum*: Time for some Latin sudoku! Thanks to www.sudokukingdom.com for the arabic numeral version of this sudoku puzzle (although I did solve it my very own self).

E. Translation: The Latin to English story is a simplified version of the Io myth found in Ovid's *Metamorphoses* I. 587–746.

6. Quiz

Administer Quiz 21 when the students are ready.

Lesson 21 Worksheet

A. Vocabulary

Read each problem *carefully* and answer with the correct number in the correct format.

1. Count to twenty in Latin using only *even cardinal* numbers:

   duo, quattuor, sex, octō, decem, duodecim, quattuordecim, sēdecim, duodēvīgintī, vīgintī

2. Count to twenty-one in Latin using only *odd Roman* numerals:

   I, III, V, VII, IX, XI, XIII, XV, XVII, XIX [or XVIIII], XXI

3. My neighbor Iulius was born in MCMLIX, and his wife Livia in MCMLXIII. Who is older? By how much?

   Iulius, born in 1959, is four years older than Livia, who was born in 1963.

4. In what year were you born? (Give Roman and Arabic numerals.)

   Answers will vary

5. How old are you? (Answer with a Latin cardinal number.)

   Answers will vary

6. If your favorite book were written in 1818, in Roman numerals that year would be

   MDCCCXVIII.

7. *Duodēvīgintī* plus *quīngentī* plus *septem* minus *quattuor* equals (give Latin cardinal):

   quīngentī (et) vīgintī ūnus [ūnus et vīgintī]

8. God gave **Decem/X** Commandments to Moses for the **duodecim/XII** tribes to observe (give both Latin cardinals and Roman numerals).

9. L minus XXXVII plus CIX minus VI equals (give Roman numeral):

   CXVI

10. There are **quīnque** pennies to a nickel,

    duo nickels to a dime,

    quattuor quarters to a dollar, and

    quīndecim minutes in a quarter of an hour (give Latin cardinals only).

B. Grammar

1. Decline *one turret*.

	LATIN SINGULAR
NOM.	ūna turris
GEN.	ūnīus turris
DAT.	ūnī turrī
ACC.	ūnam turrem [turrim]
ABL.	ūnā turre [turrī]
VOC.	Ō ūna turris

2. Decline *two shepherds*.

	LATIN PLURAL
NOM.	duo pastōrēs
GEN.	duōrum pastōrum
DAT.	duōbus pastōribus
ACC.	duōs pastōrēs
ABL.	duōbus pastōribus
VOC.	Ō duo pastōrēs

3. Decline *three wounds*.

	LATIN PLURAL
NOM.	tria vulnera
GEN.	trium vulnerum
DAT.	tribus vulneribus
ACC.	tria vulnera
ABL.	tribus vulneribus
VOC.	Ō tria vulnera

4. Give a synopsis of *oppugnō* in the second person plural.

	ACTIVE		PASSIVE	
	LATIN	ENGLISH	LATIN	ENGLISH
PRES.	oppugnātis	you attack	oppugnāminī	you are (being) attacked
IMPF.	oppugnābātis	you were attacking	oppugnābāminī	you were (being) attacked
FUT.	oppugnābitis	you will attack	oppugnābiminī	you will be attacked
PERF.	oppugnāvistis	you (have) attacked		
PLUPF.	oppugnāverātis	you had attacked		
FT. PF.	oppugnāveritis	you will have attacked		

C. Memorization

Fill in the blanks.

Crēdō in ūnum Deum, Patrem omnipotentem, Factōrem caelī et terrae, vīsibilium omnium et invīsibilium.

Et in ūnum Dominum Iēsum Christum, Fīlium Deī Ūnigenitum,

Et ex Patre nātum ante omnia saecula.

Deum dē Deō, Lūmen dē Lūmine, Deum vērum dē Deō vērō,

Genitum, nōn factum, consubstantiālem Patrī: per quem omnia facta sunt;

Quī propter nōs hominēs et propter nostram salūtem dēscendit dē caelīs,

Et incarnātus est dē Spīritū Sanctō ex Marīā virgine, et homō factus est.

Crucifīxus etiam prō nōbīs sub Pontiō Pīlātō; passus, et sepultus est,

Et <u>resurrēxit</u>   tertiā <u>diē</u>   , secundum <u>Scrīptūrās</u>   , et <u>ascendit</u>

in <u>caelum</u>   , <u>sedet</u>   <u>ad</u>   dexteram <u>Patris</u>   .

<u>Et</u>   iterum <u>ventūrus</u>   est cum <u>glōriā</u>   , iūdicāre <u>vīvōs</u>

et <u>mortuōs</u>   , cuius <u>rēgnī</u>   nōn erit <u>fīnis</u>   .

D. Translation

Translate each sentence from English to Latin.

1. You will give five beautiful black horses to the king, and they will be praised by him.

    <u>[Tū/vōs] rēgī equōs quīnque pulchrōs [et] nigrōs dabis/dabitis, et [eī] ab eō laudābuntur.</u>

2. All the king's horses and all the king's men could not save this one wretched man.

    <u>Omnēs equī rēgis et omnēs [virī] rēgis eum ūnum miserum [virum] servāre nōn poterant/</u>
    <u>potuērunt.</u>

3. Two of his daughters were seen in the forest by three soldiers.

    <u>Duae ē/ex fīliābus eius ab tribus mīlitibus in silvā vidēbantur.</u>

4. Our Lord gave food to thousands and then good words were spoken by Him.

    <u>Dominus noster mīlibus cibum dedit [dabat] et bona verba ab eō tum ōrābantur.</u>

5. The blessed farmer lived at the foot of the purple mountains and had one beautiful wife, six happy children, and eight large dogs.

    <u>Agricola beātus sub montibus purpureīs habitābat/habitāvit et ūnam fēminam pulchram, sex līberōs</u>
    <u>laetōs/beātōs, et octō canēs magnōs tenēbat/tenuit/habēbat/habuit].</u>

6. Five hundred cookies were eaten by the greedy children in your town yesterday.

    <u>Quīngentī crustula ab līberīs avārīs in oppidō vestrō/tuō herī mandūcābantur.</u>

7. The king and queen will give a great feast to fifty of the knights because three ugly giants were killed by them.

    <u>Rēx rēgīnaque quīnquāgintā ex equitibus epulās magnās dabunt quod trēs gigantēs foedī ab eīs</u>
    <u>necābantur.</u>

8. There are twenty tall turrets in my castle, but five of them are gloomy.

   Sunt vīgintī turrēs altae in castellō meō, sed quīnque ex eīs tristēs sunt.

9. We were hunting twelve deer in the dark forest but were seen by one of them and they all hastened away from us.

   Duodecim cervōs in silvā ātrā captābāmus sed ab ūnō ex eīs vidēbāmur, et [eī] omnēs ab nōbīs festīnābant/festīnāvērunt.

10. I am a beautiful woman and am loved by two farmers; however, my one heart will be given to the handsome pirate.

    Fēmina pulchra [ego] sum et ab duōbus agricolīs amor; ūnum autem cor meum pīrātae pulchrō dabitur.

E. Latin to English Translation

1 **Fābula Iōnis**

Ōlim erat deus flūminis, nomine Īnachus.[1] Multōs līberōs tenēbat—fortasse[2] quīnque, fortasse septem. Ūna ex filiābus eius erat Īō[3] pulchra. Ea ab Iove[4] amābātur et certātim captābātur, sed ab eō festīnāvit. Nōn autem occultāre[5] potuit et ab eō occupābātur. Iuppiter Iūnōnem timuit, et Īō ergō in candidam
5 bovem pulchram mūtābātur. Iūnō[6] bovem vīdit et suspīciōsa[7] erat—itaque dēclārāvit: "Dā mihi eam bovem!" Quod Iuppiter eam timuit, eī Īōnem bovem dedit. Īō ab Argō,[8] gigante antīquō centum cum oculīs, tum spectābātur. Duo ad montem longinquum horrendumque ambulāvērunt ubi Argus eam semper spectābat. Īō misera erat, et miser Iuppiter. Ergō Mercuriō[9] rogāvit: "Tū Īōnem servābis? Argum necā!" Mercurius ad montem volāvit, et in pastōrem mūtābātur. Is Argō avēnīs[10] cantāvit. Ūnus ex centum
10 oculīs dormīvit,[11] tum alius.[12] Dēnique omnēs centum oculī dormīvērunt. Tum Mercurius Argum gladiō necāvit et Īō liberābātur. Iūnō tristis erat, et oculōs Argī in caudā[13] avis cārae, pāvōnis,[14] collocāvit.[15] Et īrāta erat, et Īōnem miseram per mundum captābat. Dēnique Iuppiter Iūnōnem clēmentiam[16] rogāvit. Et quattuor crūra[17] bovis in duo crūra hominis mūtābantur—et Īō fēmina nunc erat.

Glossary
1. *Īnachus, -ī* (m): Inachus, god of the Inachus River in Argos
2. *fortasse*: perhaps
3. *Īō, -ōnis* (f): Io, a beautiful nymph and daughter of Inachus
4. *Iuppiter, Iovis* (m): Jupiter/Jove, king of the gods; called Zeus by the Greeks
5. *occultō* (1): I hide
6. *Iūnō, -ōnis* (f): Juno, queen of the gods and wife of Jupiter; called Hera by the Greeks
7. *suspīciosus, -a, -um*: suspicious
8. *Argus, -ī* (m): Argus, a hundred-eyed giant (*oculus, -ī* (m): eye)
9. *Mercurius, -ī* (m): Mercury, the messenger god
10. *avēna, -ae* (f): pan pipe, shepherd's pipe
11. *dormiō, -īre, -īvī, ītum*: I sleep
12. *alius, alia, aliud*: another, other
13. *cauda, -ae* (f): tail
14. *pāvō, -ōnis* (m): peacock
15. *collocō* (1): I place, set, arrange
16. *clēmentia, -ae* (f): mercy, clemency
17. *crūs, crūris* (n): leg

The Story of Io

Once upon a time there was a river god [lit., god of a river], Inachus by name. He had many children—perhaps five, perhaps seven. One of his daughters was the beautiful Io. She was loved and eagerly hunted by Jove, but hastened away from him. However, she was not able to hide and was seized by him. Jove feared Juno and therefore Io was changed into a beautiful white cow. Juno saw the cow and was suspicious; thus she declared: "Give me that cow!" Because Jupiter feared her, he gave Io the cow to her. Io was then watched by Argus, an ancient giant with one hundred eyes. The two walked to a distant and dreadful mountain where Argus watched her always. Io was wretched, and Jove was wretched. Therefore he asked Mercury: "Will you save Io? Kill Argus!" Mercury flew to the mountain, and was changed into a shepherd. He played [on] the pipes for Argus. One of the hundred eyes slept, then another. Finally all one hundred eyes slept. Mercury then killed Argus with a sword and Io was set free. Juno was sad and placed Argus's eyes in the tail of (her) beloved bird, the peacock. She was also angry, and hunted poor Io through the world. Finally, Jove asked Juno for mercy. And the four legs of the cow were changed into the two legs of a human—and Io was now a woman.

F. Lūdus Numerōrum

To play:

1. The numbers I–IX must appear once in each column.
2. I–IX must also appear once in each row.
3. I–IX can only appear once in each 3x3 box in the grid.

IX	I	V	VI	III	VIII	VII	II	IV
VI	VII	III	IX	IV	II	V	VIII	I
II	IV	VIII	I	VII	V	III	VI	IX
IV	II	VII	VIII	V	I	VI	IX	III
VIII	V	I	III	IX	VI	II	IV	VII
III	IX	VI	IV	II	VII	VIII	I	V
VII	III	IV	II	VI	IX	I	V	VIII
I	VI	IX	V	VIII	III	IV	VII	II
V	VIII	II	VII	I	IV	IX	III	VI

Thanks to www.sudokukingdom.com for the arabic numeral version of this puzzle.

Lesson 21 Quiz (95 points)

A. Vocabulary (20 points)

Count to twenty in Latin: ūnus [ūna, ūnum], duo [duae, duo], trēs [tria], quattuor, quīnque, sex, septem, octō, novem, decem, ūndecim, duodecim, tredecim, quattuordecim, quīndecim, sēdecim, septendecim, duodēvīgintī, ūndēvīgintī, vīgintī

B. Grammar (21 points)

1. Decline *mīlle*.

	SINGULAR	PLURAL
	M/F/N	N
NOM.	mīlle	mīlia
GEN.	mīlle	mīlium
DAT.	mīlle	mīlibus
ACC.	mīlle	mīlia
ABL.	mīlle	mīlibus

2. Give a synopsis of *videō* in the first person plural.

	ACTIVE		PASSIVE	
	LATIN	ENGLISH	LATIN	ENGLISH
PRES.	vidēmus	we see	vidēmur	we are (being) seen, we seem
IMPF.	vidēbāmus	we were seeing	vidēbāmur	we were (being) seen, seemed
FUT.	vidēbimus	we will see	vidēbimur	we will be seen, will seem
PERF.	vīdimus	we (have) seen		
PLUPF.	vīderāmus	we had seen		
FT. PF.	vīderimus	we will have seen		

C. Translation (15 points)

Translate each sentence.

1. I ate four cookies yesterday.

   [Ego] quattuor crustula herī mandūcāvī.

2. Iō in bovem ab deō mūtābātur.

   Io was changed into a cow by the/a god.

D. Memorization (39 points)

Write out the first ten lines of the *Symbolum Nicaenum*.

Crēdō in ūnum Deum, Patrem omnipotentem, Factōrem caelī et terrae, vīsibilium omnium et invīsibilium.

Et in ūnum Dominum Iēsum Christum, Fīlium Deī Ūnigenitum,

Et ex Patre nātum ante omnia saecula.

Deum dē Deō, Lūmen dē Lūmine, Deum vērum dē Deō vērō,

Genitum, nōn factum, consubstantiālem Patrī: per quem omnia facta sunt.

Quī propter nōs hominēs et propter nostram salūtem dēscendit dē caelīs.

Et incarnātus est dē Spīritū Sanctō ex Marīā virgine, et homō factus est.

Crucīfīxus etiam prō nōbīs sub Pontiō Pīlātō; passus, et sepultus est,

Et resurrēxit tertiā die, secundum Scriptūrās, et ascendit in caelum, sedet ad dexteram Patris.

Et iterum ventūrus est cum glōriā, iūdicāre vīvōs et mortuōs, cuius regnī nōn erit fīnis.

LESSON 22 (Student Edition p. 206)

Perfect, Pluperfect & Future Perfect Passive Indicative

1. Word List

This lesson's list includes various family members—notice how precise the Romans were in distinguishing relatives on the mother's versus the father's side! English does not do this (although other languages besides Latin do).

2. Derivatives/Memorization Helps

1. *amita*, aunt
2. *avia*, grandmother
3. *avunculus*, uncle (mother's brother): avuncular
4. *avus*, grandfather, ancestor
5. *coniūnx*, husband, wife: conjugal
6. *consōbrīnus/consōbrīna*, cousin (mother's side)
7. *familia*, household, family: familial, familiar
8. *mulier*, woman: muliebrity
9. *orbus/orba*, orphan
10. *patruēlis*, cousin (father's side)
11. *patruus*, uncle (father's brother)
12. *vidua*, widow
13. *orbus*, deprived of parents or children, bereft
14. *vērus*, true: veracity, veracious
15. *iuvō*, I help: aid, adjutant
16. *gaudeō*, I rejoice: gaudy, gaud, gaudery
17. *labōrō*, I work: labor, laboratory; see *labor* [Lesson 12]
18. *occultō*, I hide, conceal: occultation; occult from related verb *occulō*
19. *deinde*, from that place, then, thereupon, next: memory help—"In *dē Inde* 500, the cars go around, *then* they go around again, *then* they go around again...."
20. *etiam*, even, also, besides, still
21. *heu (eheu)*, alas! oh!: It's an onomatopoeia!

3. Memorization—*Symbolum Nicaenum* (Nicene Creed)

Notice that there are a few perfect passives in the Nicene Creed (bolded).

> Genitum, nōn factum, consubstantiālem Patrī: per quem omnia **facta sunt.**
>
> Et **incarnātus est** dē Spīritū Sanctō ex Marīā virgine, et homō **factus est.**
>
> **Crucifīxus** etiam prō nōbīs sub Pontiō Pīlātō; **passus**, et **sepultus est,**

Notice that the *est* is implied for *crucifīxus est* and *passus est* and is only given once at the end of the line. We do this sort of thing in English as well: "The dragon was hunted, wounded, and finally killed." The "was" is only said once but implied for all three verbs—"was hunted," "was wounded," and "was killed." This lesson's new lines are:

> Et in Spīritum Sanctum, Dominum et vīvificantem: Quī ex Patre Fīliōque prōcēdit.
> *And [I believe] in the Holy Ghost, the Lord and Giver of Life: Who proceeds from the Father and the Son.*

> Quī cum Patre et Fīliō simul adōrātur et conglōrificātur: Quī locūtus est per prophētās.
> *Who with the Father and the Son together is worshipped and glorified: Who spoke by the prophets.*

4. Grammar

Perfect, Pluperfect, and Future Perfect Passive Indicative

By now your students should be fairly solid on the present passive system—present, imperfect, and future tense. This lesson we add the perfect passive system—perfect, pluperfect, and future perfect.

Review the four principal parts, and have the students list what verbs can be formed from each part. Doubtless they have all kept the handy chart you gave them at the beginning of the year close by (see Introduction, pages XIV–XVI):

	FIRST	SECOND	THIRD	FOURTH
	necō	necāre	necāvī	necātum
DEFINITION/ FUNCTION	1st Sg. Present Active Indicative—*I kill* Helps identify conjugations and shows if present stem vowel has contracted	Present Active Infinitive—*to kill*; Present Stem: *necā-*	1st. Sg. Perfect Active Indicative—*I killed, have killed* Perfect Active Stem: *necāv-*	Neuter Sg. Nom. Perfect Passive Participle—*killed, having been killed* Forms Perfect Passives, so in that sense may be considered Perfect Passive "stem"
INDICATIVE		**Present Active Present Passive Imperfect Active Imperfect Passive Future Active Future Passive**	**Perfect Active Pluperfect Active Future Perfect Active**	Perfect Passive Pluperfect Passive Future Perfect Passive
IMPERATIVE		**Present Active** Present Passive Future Active Future Passive		
INFINITIVE		**Present Active Present Passive**	Perfect Active	Perfect Passive Future Active Future Passive
SUBJUNCTIVE		Present Active Present Passive Imperfect Active Imperfect Passive	Perfect Active Pluperfect Active	Perfect Passive Pluperfect Passive
PARTICIPLE		Present Active Future Passive		Perfect Passive Future Active

The bolded moods/tenses are those you have already covered up to this point. So far your students have been acquainted with the first three principal parts; now it is time to meet the fourth.

The fourth principal part is the perfect passive participle, and it is used to form the perfect passive verb system. A participle is a verbal adjective, and thus can modify a noun or pronoun in gender, number, and case. The full form of the perfect passive participle is actually *necātus, -a, -um* (masculine, feminine, and neuter—looks like an adjective, doesn't it?). For convenience, in this book I have listed the neuter form by way of abbreviation; some dictionaries will simply give the masculine form.

Take a moment to consider some English passive indicatives: *The dragon was killed, the dragon had been killed, the dragon will have been killed.* Notice that English requires the use of helping verbs to form the passive: *was* for the perfect, *had* and *been* for the pluperfect, and the whopping *will have been* for the future perfect. Also, note that in each tense the word *killed* is used (yes, it's a participle). Similarly, Latin perfect passives will use the "helping verb" *sum* along with the fourth principal part.

For the perfect tense, simply take the fourth principal part of the verb, and conjugate it with the present chant of *sum*:

Perfect Passive Indicative of *necō*

	LATIN SINGULAR	ENGLISH SINGULAR	LATIN PLURAL	ENGLISH PLURAL
1ST	necātus/a/um sum	I was/have been killed	necātī/ae/a sumus	we were/have been killed
2ND	necātus/a/um es	you were/have been killed	necātī/ae/a estis	you (pl.) were/have been killed
3RD	necātus/a/um est	he/she/it was/has been killed	necātī/ae/a sunt	they were/have been killed

Notice that we will only use the nominative forms of the participle, because these adjectives are functioning as predicate adjectives with *sum*—they must agree with the case of the pronoun subject (which will always be nominative). They must also agree with the subject in number; thus the plurals have the plural nominative form of the adjective—*necātī, -ae, -a*. And finally, these verbs show us the gender of their subjects (which can be very helpful). A few examples:

Draco necātus est.	*The dragon has been killed.*
Avis necāta est.	*The bird has been killed.*
Animal necātum est.	*The animal has been killed.*
Dracōnēs necātī sunt.	*The dragons have been killed.*
Avēs necātae sunt.	*The birds have been killed.*
Animālia necāta sunt.	*The animals have been killed.*
Animālia necāta sunt.	*The animals have been killed.*

Once your students are comfortable with this idea of a compound verb, the next two tenses should follow easily and logically. The pluperfect passive will be conjugated with the imperfect of *sum,* and the future perfect passive with the future of *sum.*

Pluperfect Passive Indicative of *necō*

	LATIN SINGULAR	ENGLISH SINGULAR	LATIN PLURAL	ENGLISH PLURAL
1ST	necātus/a/um eram	I had been killed	necātī/ae/a erāmus	we had been killed
2ND	necātus/a/um erās	you had been killed	necātī/ae/a erātis	you (pl.) had been killed
3RD	necātus/a/um erat	he/she/it had been killed	necātī/ae/a erant	they had been killed

Future Perfect Passive Indicative of *necō*

	LATIN SINGULAR	ENGLISH SINGULAR	LATIN PLURAL	ENGLISH PLURAL
1ST	necātus/a/um erō	I will have been killed	necātī/ae/a erimus	we will have been killed
2ND	necātus/a/um eris	you will have been killed	necātī/ae/a eritis	you (pl.) will have been killed
3RD	necātus/a/um erit	he/she/it will have been killed	necātī/ae/a erunt	they will have been killed

And now our example sentences using these tenses:

Draco necātus erat.	*The dragon had been killed.*
Avis necāta erat.	*The bird had been killed.*
Animal necātum erat.	*The animal had been killed.*
Dracōnēs necātī erant.	*The dragons had been killed.*
Avēs necātae erant.	*The birds had been killed.*
Animālia necāta erant.	*The animals had been killed.*
Draco necātus erit.	*The dragon will have been killed.*
Avis necāta erit.	*The bird will have been killed.*
Animal necātum erit.	*The animal will have been killed.*
Dracōnēs necātī erunt.	*The dragons will have been killed.*
Avēs necātae erunt.	*The birds will have been killed.*
Animālia necāta erunt.	*The animals will have been killed.*

A reminder on the future perfect passive, third person plural: Take this opportunity to remind your students that when *erō* is a *word,* the third person plural is *erunt;* when it's an *ending,* it's *-erint* (say *word* and *erunt* in a nice deep voice, and make *ending* and *-erint* sound nasal).

Our verb synopsis in the indicative is now complete, and will look like this:

	ACTIVE		PASSIVE	
	LATIN	ENGLISH	LATIN	ENGLISH
PRES.	necō	I kill	necor	I am (being) killed
IMPF.	necābam	I was killing	necābar	I was (being) killed
FUT.	necābō	I will kill	necābor	I will be killed
PERF.	necāvī	I (have) killed	necātus/a/um sum	I was/have been killed
PLUPF.	necāveram	I had killed	necātus/a/um eram	I had been killed
FT. PF.	necāverō	I will have killed	necātus/a/um erō	I will have been killed

5. Worksheet

Follow the directions given and complete the worksheet.

6. Quiz

Administer Quiz 22 when the students are ready.

Lesson 22 Worksheet

A. Vocabulary

Translate the following words from Latin to English or English to Latin as appropriate.

1. aunt: **amita**
2. sixteen: **sēdecim**
3. gaudeō: **I rejoice**
4. I hide: **occultō**
5. mother's brother: **avunculus**
6. father's brother: **patruus**
7. vestis: **clothing, garment**
8. avus: **grandfather, ancestor**
9. I help: **iuvō**
10. sweet: **dulcis**
11. female cousin (mother's side): **consōbrīna**
12. labōrō: **I work**
13. mulier: **woman**
14. etiam: **even, also, besides**
15. grandmother: **avia**
16. male cousin (father's side): **patruēlis**
17. orphan: **orbus/orba**
18. sīcut: **as, just as, like**
19. alas: **heu (eheu)**
20. vidua: **widow**
21. true: **vērus**
22. coniūnx: **husband, wife**
23. deinde: **from that place, then, thereupon, next**
24. hyacinthinus: **blue, purplish-blue, violet**
25. household: **familia**

B. Grammar

1. Give a synopsis of *iuvō* in the third person plural.

	ACTIVE		PASSIVE	
	LATIN	ENGLISH	LATIN	ENGLISH
PRES.	iuvant	they help	iuvantur	they are (being) helped
IMPF.	iuvābant	they were helping	iuvābantur	they were (being) helped
FUT.	iuvābunt	they will help	iuvābuntur	they will be helped
PERF.	iūvērunt	they (have) helped	iūtī/ae/a sunt	they were (have been) helped
PLUPF.	iūverant	they had helped	iūtī/ae/a erant	they had been helped
FT. PF.	iūverint	they will have helped	iūtī/ae/a erunt	they will have been helped

2. Give a synopsis of *removeō* in the second person singular.

	ACTIVE		PASSIVE	
	LATIN	ENGLISH	LATIN	ENGLISH
PRES.	removēs	you remove	removēris	you are (being) removed
IMPF.	removēbās	you were removing	removēbāris	you were (being) removed
FUT.	removēbis	you will remove	removēberis	you will be removed
PERF.	remōvistī	you (have) removed	remōtus/a/um es	you were (have been) removed
PLUPF.	remōverās	you had removed	remōtus/a/um erās	you had been removed
FT. PF.	remōveris	you will have removed	remōtus/a/um eris	you will have been removed

3. Draw your family tree below. Label your mother, father, grandparents, aunts, uncles, and cousins using your Latin family vocabulary. **Answers will vary.**

4. Count to twenty twice—first with Roman numerals, then with Latin cardinals.

Roman numerals: <u>I, II, III, IV [IIII], V, VI, VII, VIII, IX, X, XI, XII, XIII, XIV [XIIII], XV, XVI, XVII, XVIII, XIX, XX</u>

Latin cardinals: <u>ūnus [ūna, ūnum], duo [duae, duo], trēs [tria], quattuor, quīnque, sex, septem, octō, novem, decem, ūndecim, duodecim, tredecim, quattuordecim, quīndecim, sēdecim, septendecim, duodēvīgintī, ūndēvīgintī, vīgintī</u>

C. Memorization

Fill in the blanks.

<u>Crēdō in ūnum Deum, Patrem omnipotentem, Factōrem caelī et terrae, vīsibilium omnium et invīsibilium.</u>

<u>Et in ūnum Dominum Iēsum Christum, Fīlium Deī Ūnigenitum,</u>

<u>Et ex Patre nātum ante omnia saecula.</u>

<u>Deum dē Deō, Lūmen dē Lūmine, Deum vērum dē Deō vērō,</u>

<u>Genitum, nōn factum, consubstantiālem Patrī: per quem omnia facta sunt;</u>

<u>Quī propter nōs hominēs et propter nostram salūtem dēscendit dē caelīs,</u>

<u>Et incarnātus est dē Spīritū Sanctō ex Marīā virgine, et homō factus est.</u>

<u>Crucifīxus etiam prō nōbīs sub Pontiō Pīlātō; passus, et sepultus est,</u>

<u>Et</u> resurrēxit tertiā **die**, **secundum** Scriptūrās, <u>et</u> <u>ascendit</u> in **caelum**, sedet ad **dexteram** Patris.

<u>Et</u> iterum **ventūrus** est cum **glōriā**, iūdicāre **vīvōs** et mortuōs, <u>cuius</u> regnī nōn **erit** **fīnis**.

Et <u>in</u> Spīritum **Sanctum**, **Dominum** et vīvificantem: **Quī** ex Patre **Fīliōque** **prōcēdit**.

<u>Quī</u> cum **Patre** et Fīliō **simul** adōrātur **et** **conglōrificātur**: Quī **locūtus** est per **prophētās**.

D. English to Latin Translation

Translate each sentence from English to Latin.

1. Three krakens had been seen in the dark and purple waves, but we still sailed to the unlucky island.
   <u>Trēs cētī in undīs ātrīs et purpureīs [or purpureīsque] vīsī erant, sed etiam [nōs] ad īnsulam infēlīcem nāvigāvimus.</u>

2. Tomorrow, if the dragon will have been killed, the king's daughter will be given to the knight in marriage.
   <u>Crās sī draco necātus erit, fīlia rēgis equitī in matrimōniō dabitur.</u>

3. The five wretched orphans were carried to the farmhouse and we helped them there.
   <u>Quīnque orbī/orbae miserī/miserae ad villam portātī/portātae sunt et ibī [nōs] eōs/eās iūvimus.</u>

4. My aunt once watched the centaurs' feast because she had hidden among the tall trees of the forest.
   <u>Amita mea epulās centaurōrum ōlim spectāvit quod inter arborēs altōs silvae occultāverat.</u>

5. Soon all the cookies will have been eaten and all the milk will have been drunk by the nine cousins.
   <u>Mox ab novem consōbrīnīs [or patruēlibus] omnia crustula mandūcāta erunt et omne lac pōtātum [or pōtum] erit.</u>

6. Thousands of eager soldiers rushed to the castle because the enemy's ships had been seen on the shore.
   <u>Mīlia mīlitum ācrium ad castellum properāvērunt quod nāvēs/alnī hostis [or hostium] in lītore/ōrā vīsae erant.</u>

7. My father has four brothers; these men are my uncles and they all work in our fields.
   <u>Pater meus quattuor frātrēs tenet [habet]; eī [virī] meī patruī sunt et omnēs in agrīs nostrīs labōrant.</u>

8. The poor widow's horses had been seized by the evil pirates, and all her gold besides was carried to their cave.
   <u>Equī viduae miserae ab pīrātīs malīs occupātī erant, et omne aurum eius ad spēluncam eōrum etiam portātum est.</u>

9. The weary farmers were rejoicing because the crops had been carried from the fields.
   <u>Agricolae fessī gaudēbant quod frūmenta ab [ex] agrīs portāta erant.</u>

10. You had been seen with the wild sailors by our grandfather, and he was not happy.

   Nautīs cum ferīs ab avō nostrō vīsus erās/vīsa erās/vīsī erātis/vīsae erātis], et [is] laetus/fēlix/beātus nōn erat/fuit.

E. Latin to English Translation

1 **Porcus Mediōcris**

   Mediōcris sum. Mea familia magna est, et in eā multī fortēs potentēsque sunt. Avus meus ūnus ex equitibus rēgis erat, et contrā dracōnēs, gigantēs, et hostēs bene pugnābat. Venēnō cētī dēnique necātus est. Trēs avunculī meī nautae sunt, et in septem maribus nāvigāvērunt. Pater meus mīles magnus est,
5 et māter mea docta mulier et consōbrīna rēgīnae est. Etiam sorōrēs meae duae pulchrae sunt et bene cantant; duōbus dominīs magnīs in patriā in mātrimōniō datae sunt. Sed ego mediōcris sum. Nōmen meum est Eduardus.[1] Spectō porcōs familiae, et eīs cibum dat. Herī autem ūnus ex porcīs mihi ōrāvit: "Tū, puer, mē līberā et tibī multum aurum dabō!" Respondī, "Porcus es. Quōmodo[2] aurum tenēre potes?" Porcus autem ōrāvit, "Mē līberā! Tē ad spēluncam dīvitiārum portābō." Ergō, ab porcō per agrōs et ab
10 villā familiae meae portātus sum. Omnēs rīsērunt; etiam equī bovēsque rīsērunt. Ego cōgitābam, "Sī is porcus vēra nōn ōrat, eum necābō et mandūcābō." Porcus in Silvam Tristem properāvit et mē ad ōs spēluncae portāvit. Intrāvī, et ecce! Mīlia nummōrum[3] aureōrum in spēluncā occultāta erant! "Decem nummī tuī erunt," porcus āit, "sed sī mē pugnābis et necābis, omnēs habēbis." "Tē nec pugnābō nec necābō," respondī. "Laetus cum decem nummīs sum." Porcus in virginem pulchram repentē mutātus
15 est. "Ego," ea āit, "ūnica[4] fīlia rēgis sum. In porcum ab malā novercā[5] meā mutāta sum. Quod avārus nōn erās, carmen[6] dēlētum est!" Nunc ego, Eduardus mediōcris, coniugem pulchram et milia nummōrum aureōrum et regnum teneō.

   Glossary
   1. *Eduardus:* a 2nd declension name
   2. *quōmodo:* how? in what way?
   3. *nummus, -ī* (m): coin
   4. *ūnicus, -a, -um:* one, only, sole
   5. *noverca, -ae* (f): step-mother
   6. *carmen* can also mean "spell, enchantment"

<u>**The Ordinary Pig**</u>

I am ordinary. My family is large, and there are many brave and powerful people in it. My grandfather was one of the king's knights, and fought well against dragons, giants, and enemies. He was finally killed by the poison of a kraken. My three uncles are sailors, and have sailed on the seven seas. My father is a great soldier, and my mother is a wise woman and the queen's cousin. Even my two sisters are beautiful and sing well; they were given in marriage to two great lords in the land. But I am ordinary. My name is Edward. I watch the family's pigs, and give food to them. However, yesterday one of the pigs spoke to me: "You, boy, set me free and I will give you much gold!" I replied, "You are a pig. How can you possess

gold?" However, the pig said, "Set me free! I will carry you to a cave of wealth." Therefore, I was carried by the pig through the fields and away from my family's farmhouse. Everyone laughed; even the horses and cows laughed. I was thinking, "If this pig does not speak true things, I will kill him and eat him." The pig rushed into the Gloomy Forest and carried me to the mouth of a cave. I entered, and behold! Thousands of gold coins had been hidden in the cave! "Ten coins will be yours," said the pig, "but if you fight and kill me, you will have all." "I will not fight nor kill you," I replied. "I am happy with ten coins." Suddenly the pig was changed into a beautiful maiden. "I am the king's only daughter," she said. "I was changed into a pig by my evil stepmother. Because you were not greedy, the spell has been destroyed!" Now I, ordinary Edward, have a beautiful wife, thousands of gold coins, and a kingdom.

Lesson 22 Quiz (93 points)

A. Vocabulary (10 points)

Translate the following words.

1. gaudeō: **I rejoice**
2. grandmother: **avia**
3. ignis: **fire**
4. etiam: **even, also, besides**
5. widow: **vidua**
6. patruēlis: **cousin (father's side)**
7. coniūnx: **husband, wife**
8. true: **vērus**
9. avus: **grandfather, ancestor**
10. deinde: **from that place, then, thereupon, next**

B. Grammar (20 points)

1. Give a synopsis of *occultō* in the third person singular.

	ACTIVE		PASSIVE	
	LATIN	ENGLISH	LATIN	ENGLISH
PRES.	occultat	he/she/it hides	occultātur	he is (being) hidden
IMPF.	occultābat	he was hiding	occultābātur	he was (being) hidden
FUT.	occultābit	he will hide	occultābitur	he will be hidden
PERF.	occultāvit	he hid (has hidden)	occultātus est	he was (has been) hidden
PLUPF.	occultāverat	he had hidden	occultātus erat	he had been hidden
FT. PF.	occultāverit	he will have hidden	occultātus erit	he will have been hidden

C. Translation (15 points)

Translate each sentence.

1. The evil dragon had been killed by the brave knight.

    Draco malus ab equite fortī necātus erat.

2. "Eheu!" clāmat mulier, "Ego ab pīrātīs īrātīs occupāta sum!"

    "Alas!" shouts the woman, "I have been seized by angry pirates!"

D. Memorization (48 points)

Write out the first twelve lines of the *Symbolum Nicaenum*.

Crēdō in ūnum Deum, Patrem omnipotentem, Factōrem caelī et terrae, vīsibilium omnium et invīsibilium.

Et in ūnum Dominum Iēsum Christum, Fīlium Deī Ūnigenitum,

Et ex Patre nātum ante omnia saecula.

Deum dē Deō, Lūmen dē Lūmine, Deum vērum dē Deō vērō,

Genitum, nōn factum, consubstantiālem Patrī: per quem omnia facta sunt;

Quī propter nōs hominēs et propter nostram salūtem dēscendit dē caelīs,

Et incarnātus est dē Spīritū Sanctō ex Marīā virgine, et homō factus est.

Crucifīxus etiam prō nōbīs sub Pontiō Pīlātō; passus, et sepultus est,

Et resurrēxit tertiā die, secundum Scriptūrās, et ascendit in caelum, sedet ad dexteram Patris.

Et iterum ventūrus est cum glōriā, iūdicāre vīvōs et mortuōs, cuius regnī nōn erit fīnis.

Et in Spīritum Sanctum, Dominum et vīvificantem: Quī ex Patre Fīliōque prōcēdit.

Quī cum Patre et Fīliō simul adōrātur et conglōrificātur: Quī locūtus est per prophētās.

Lesson 23 (Student Edition p. 216)

More Numerals: Ordinals

1. Word List

Introduce this lesson's Word List. If you or any of your students have studied another modern language (especially one of the Romance languages), this would be a perfect opportunity to compare Latin numerals to numerals in other languages.

2. Derivatives/Memorization Helps

1. *prīmus*, first: primary, primal
2. *secundus*, second: second, secondary
3. *tertius*, third: tertian, tertiary, tertium quid
4. *quārtus*, fourth: quarter
5. *quīntus*, fifth: quintet, quintessential
6. *sextus*, sixth: see *sex* [Lesson 21]
7. *septimus*, seventh: see *septem* [Lesson 21]
8. *octāvus*, eighth: octave
9. *nōnus*, ninth: nonagenarian
10. *decimus*, tenth: see *decem* [Lesson 21]
11. *ūndecimus*, eleventh
12. *duodecimus*, twelfth
13. *tertius decimus*, thirteenth
14. *quārtus decimus*, fourteenth
15. *quīntus decimus*, fifteenth
16. *sextus decimus*, sixteenth
17. *septimus decimus*, seventeenth
18. *duodēvīcēsimus*, eighteenth
19. *ūndēvīcēsimus*, nineteenth
20. *vīcēsimus*, twentieth: see *vīgintī* [Lesson 21]
21. *vīcēsimus prīmus*, twenty-first
22. *quīnquāgēsimus*, fiftieth
23. *centēsimus*, one hundredth: see *centum* [Lesson 21]
24. *quīngentēsimus*, five hundredth: see *quīnquāgintā* [Lesson 21]
25. *mīllēsimus*, one thousandth: see *mille* [Lesson 21]

3. Memorization—*Symbolum Nicaenum* (Nicene Creed)

This lesson's new lines are:

Et ūnam, sanctam, catholicam et apostolicam ecclēsiam.

And in one, holy, catholic, and apostolic church.

Confiteor ūnum baptisma in remissiōnem peccātōrum.

I confess one baptism for the remission of sins.

Et expectō resurrectiōnem mortuōrum, et vītam ventūrī saeculī. Āmēn.

And I look for the resurrection of the dead, and the life of the world to come. Amen.

4. Grammar

Ordinal Numbers

In order to let the passive voice settle in, this lesson is a cinch. Your students have already learned cardinal numbers for counting (*ūnus, duo, trēs*, etc.); now they will add the ordinal numbers, which are for putting things in their proper order: first, second, third, and so on. They do all decline, but simply as *-us, -a, -um* adjectives, so nothing too worrisome there. (Note on the Word List Chart: I listed the *-us, -a, -um* only for *prīmus, -a, -um,* but of course it applies to *secundus* on down.)

You may need to remind students that these are adjectives, *not* adverbs. (Nor are they fractions! *Tertius* means "third" as in "third place," not as in "one-third cup of flour.") Thus, if they wanted to say "First I did this, and second I did that," they would need to use adverbs (*prīmum* or *prīmo* for "first," *secundō* or *deinde* for "second").

There is no new chant this lesson. Solidify your numbers, your passives, and the Creed!

Review

Be sure to review your numbers, as well as your passive forms. Also go over Third Declension i-stem nouns and adjective endings if you're rusty. Rehashing these old forms will help you prepare for your test.

5. Worksheet

Follow the directions given and complete the worksheet. The Latin to English story is based on an actual historic figure, the famous charioteer Scorpus (and, I confess, I discovered him on Wikipedia).

6. Quiz

Administer Quiz 23 when the students are ready.

Lesson 23 Worksheet

A. Vocabulary

Translate the following words from Latin to English or English to Latin as appropriate.

1. twentieth: **vīcēsimus**
2. fish: **piscis**
3. septimus: **seventh**
4. third: **tertius**
5. octāvus: **eighth**
6. thirteenth: **tertius decimus**
7. quārtus: **fourth**
8. decimus: **tenth**
9. moenia: **fortifications, city walls**
10. quīntus: **fifth**
11. eleventh: **ūndecimus**
12. prīmus: **first**
13. amita: **aunt**
14. duodecimus: **twelfth**
15. sixth: **sextus**
16. vīcēsimus prīmus: **twenty-first**
17. fourteenth: **quārtus decimus**
18. quīngentēsimus: **five hundredth**
19. quīntus decimus: **fifteenth**
20. ninth: **nōnus**
21. ūndēvīgintī: **nineteen**
22. sextus decimus: **sixteenth**
23. seventeenth: **septimus decimus**
24. mīllēsimus: **one thousandth**
25. ūndēvīcēsimus: **nineteenth**
26. fiftieth: **quīnquāgēsimus**
27. duodēvīcēsimus: **eighteenth**
28. centēsimus: **one hundredth**
29. bit by bit: **minūtātim**
30. secundus: **second**

B. Grammar

1. Give a synopsis of *dēleō* in the third person plural.

	ACTIVE		PASSIVE	
	LATIN	ENGLISH	LATIN	ENGLISH
PRES.	dēlent	they destroy	dēlentur	they are (being) destroyed
IMPF.	dēlēbant	they were destroying	dēlēbantur	they were (being) destroyed
FUT.	dēlēbunt	they will destroy	dēlēbuntur	they will be destroyed
PERF.	dēlēvērunt	they (have) destroyed	dēlētī/ae/a sunt	they were, have been destroyed
PLUPF.	dēlēverant	they had destroyed	dēlētī/ae/a erant	they had been destroyed
FT. PF.	dēlēverint	they will have destroyed	dēlētī/ae/a erunt	they will have been destroyed

2. Match each Roman numeral with both of the appropriate cardinal and ordinal numbers from the lists on the right.!

ROMAN NUMERAL	LETTERS OF CORRECT MATCHES
I	F, e
II	N, l
III	W, o
IV (IIII)	Q, k
V	K, y
VI	L, f
VII	R, g
VIII	Y, w
IX	O, i
X	J, u
XI	T, v
XII	A, c
XIII	S, m
XIV (XIIII)	B, x
XV	V, h
XVI	H, p
XVII	E, a
XVIII	G, r
XIX (XVIIII)	M, j
XX	D, t
XXI	X, s
L	I, b
C	C, q
D	U, n
M	P, d

A. duodecim
B. quattuordecim
C. centum
D. vīgintī
E. septendecim
F. ūnus
G. duodēvīgintī
H. sēdecim
I. quīnquāgintā
J. decem
K. quīnque
L. sex
M. ūndēvīgintī
N. duo
O. novem
P. mīlle
Q. quattuor
R. septem
S. tredecim
T. ūndecim
U. quīngentī
V. quīndecim
W. trēs
X. vīgintī ūnus
Y. octō

a. septimus decimus
b. quīnquāgēsimus
c. duodecimus
d. mīllēsimus
e. prīmus
f. sextus
g. septimus
h. quīntus decimus
i. nōnus
j. ūndēvīcēsimus
k. quārtus
l. secundus
m. tertius decimus
n. quīngentēsimus
o. tertius
p. sextus decimus
q. centēsimus
r. duodēvīcēsimus
s. vīcēsimus prīmus
t. vīcēsimus
u. decimus
v. ūndecimus
w. octāvus
x. quārtus decimus
y. quīntus

C. Memorization

Fill in the blanks.

Crēdō in ūnum Deum, Patrem omnipotentem, Factōrem caelī et terrae, vīsibilium omnium et invīsibilium.

Et in ūnum Dominum Iēsum Christum, Fīlium Deī Ūnigenitum,

Et ex Patre nātum ante omnia saecula.

Deum dē Deō, Lūmen dē Lūmine, Deum vērum dē Deō vērō,

Genitum, nōn factum, consubstantiālem Patrī: per quem omnia facta sunt.

Quī propter nōs hominēs et propter nostram salūtem dēscendit dē caelīs.

Et incarnātus est dē Spīritū Sanctō ex Marīā virgine, et homō factus est.

Crucifīxus etiam prō nōbīs sub Pontiō Pīlātō; passus, et sepultus est,

Et resurrēxit tertiā die, secundum Scriptūrās, et ascendit in caelum, sedet ad dexteram Patris.

Et iterum ventūrus est cum glōriā, iūdicāre vīvōs et mortuōs, cuius regnī nōn erit fīnis.

Et in Spīritum Sanctum, Dominum et vīvificantem: Quī ex Patre Fīliōque prōcēdit.

Quī cum Patre et Fīliō simul adōrātur et conglōrificātur: Quī locūtus est per prophētās.

Et ūnam, sanctam, catholicam et apostolicam ecclēsiam.

Confiteor ūnum baptisma in remissiōnem peccātōrum.

Et expectō resurrectiōnem mortuōrum, et vītam ventūrī saeculī.

Āmēn.

D. English to Latin Translation

Translate each sentence from English to Latin.

1. The happy farmer has three cows—the first is white, the second black, and the third golden.

   Agricola beātus/fēlix/laetus trēs bovēs tenet/habet—prīmus albus/candidus est, secundus niger/āter [est], et tertius aureus [est].

2. Our castle will have been besieged for a long time by the hundred black ships on the shore.
   Castellum nostrum ab centum nāvibus ātrīs in ōrā/harēnā/lītore diū obsessum erit.

3. Farewell, my son! Farewell, my daughters! Behold, I hasten to a distant land where beasts and giants will be hunted and great wealth will be seized.
   Valē, mī fīlī! Valēte, meae fīliae! Ecce, [ego] ad terram/patriam/tellūrem longinquam festīnō ubi bēstiae et gigantēs captābuntur et dīvitiae magnae occupābuntur.

4. The five hundredth fiery dragon flew to our city with wings of death, and was also slain by the brave knight.
   Quīngentēsimus draco caldus ad urbem nostram ālīs mortis volāvit, et ab equite fortī etiam necātus est.

5. We have been summoned to the king's feast and therefore our beautiful purple and blue garments are being prepared for us.
   [Nōs] ad epulās rēgis vocātī/vocātae sumus et ergō nostrae vestēs pulchrae purpureae caeruleaeque nōbīs [*or* prō nōbīs] parantur.

6. You had once been loved by two pirates, but you have been given by your father in marriage to the trustworthy sailor.
   [Tū] ab duōbus pīrātīs ōlim amāta erās, sed [tū] nautae fīdō in matrimōniō ab patre tuō data es.

7. Our fourth son was terrified by the old widow's goat and fought it with a little dagger.
   Quārtus fīlius noster ab caprō viduae antīquae territus est, et eum sīcō parvō pugnāvit.

8. The large woman sang songs badly, and all the dogs howled and crept away from the palace.
   Magna fēmina/mulier carmina male cantāvit, et omnēs canēs ululāvērunt et ab rēgiā reptāvērunt.

9. The sad moon and thousands of glittering white stars were shining, and so we stood on the high tower and watched them through the night.
   Lūna tristis [*or* misera] et mīlia stellārum candidārum lūcēbant, itaque [nōs] in turre altā stetimus et eās per noctem spectāvimus.

10. The unlucky sailor was swimming in the deep sea and was seized by a kraken; you (pl.) were unable to save him.
    Nauta infēlix in marī altō nābat et ab cētō occupātus est; [vōs] eum servāre nōn potuistis [*or* poterātis].

E. Latin to English Translation

1. **Scorpus[1] Maximus**

Ōlim erat certāmen[2] magnum in Circō Maximō[3] in Rōmā.[4] Mīlia et mīlia hominum spectābant. Duodecim quadrīgae[5] post carcerēs[6] stetērunt. Ūnus ex duodecim aurīgīs[7] erat Scorpus, vir fortis et doctus. In duo mille certāminibus superāverat, et nihil timet. Trēs, duo, ūnus—ecce! mappa[8] deiecta est[9]
5 et quadrīgae ex carceribus properāvērunt! Omnēs aurīgae bene gubernant.[10] Scorpus decimus est, nunc octāvus, nunc quīntus! Ad mētam[11] appropinquant.[12] Eheu! Quadrīgae secundae in prīmās quadrīgās gubernātae sunt, et naufragium[13] magnum est! Nunc Scorpus tertius aurīga est, et curriculum[14] prīmum bene perficit.[15] Erunt septem curricula. Post curriculum secundum et tertium et quārtum, Scorpus tertius etiam est. Superāre poterit? In curriculō quīntō, in spīnā[16] ab aurīgā quārtō paene gubernātur, sed
10 ab equīs eius fortibus līberātur. In curriculō sextō, aurīgam secundum appropinquat, et eum ad mētam superat! Nunc est Gaius, aurīga prīmus. Scorpus ab Gaiō[17] rīdētur et vexātur, sed fortis est et certātim gubernat. Dēnique mēta curriculī septimī! Scorpus equīs bona verba clāmat, et deōs ōrat. Gaius retrō[18] spectat, et spīnam nōn videt. In spīnam gubernat, et naufragium paene habet. Scorpus prīmus nunc est, et omnēs superat! Turbae clāmant ululantque. Nunc multās dīvitiās et fāmam[19] magnam habēbit.

Glossary
1. *Scorpus* is a second declension name.
2. *certāmen, -minis* (n): contest, race
3. *Circus Maximus, Circī Maximī* (m): the Circus Maximus, a famous racetrack at the foot of the Palatine Hill in Rome
4. *Roma, -ae* (f): Rome
5. *quadrīgae, -ārum* (f): four-horse chariot
6. *carcer, -eris* (m): prison; generally in pl., starting gates (of a horse race)
7. *aurīga, -ae* (m/f): charioteer, driver
8. *mappa, -ae* (f): starting flag (lit., "a napkin")
9. *dēiciō, -icere, -iēci, -iectum*: I throw down, cast down, hurl down
10. *gubernō* (1): I steer, direct, govern
11. *mēta, -ae* (f): turning-post, goal
12. *appropinquō* (1): I approach, draw near
13. *naufragium, -ī* (n): wreck, crash (lit., "shipwreck")
14. *curriculum, -ī* (n): lap (of a race), course
15. *perficiō, -ere, -fēci, -fectum*: I complete, finish
16. *spīna, -ae* (f): barrier (lit., "spine," the wall dividing the race course in half lengthwise)
17. *Gaius* is a second declension noun.
18. *retrō*: back(ward), behind
18. *fāma, -ae* (f): report, reputation, fame

<u>**Scorpus the Greatest**</u>

<u>Once there was a great race in the Circus Maximus in Rome. Thousands and thousands of people were watching. Twelve four-horse chariots stood behind the starting gates. One of the twelve charioteers was Scorpus, a brave and skilled man. He had won [lit., conquered] in two thousand races, and fears nothing. Three, two, one—behold, the starting flag has been thrown down and the chariots have rushed from the gates! All [of] the charioteers are driving [lit., steering] well. Scorpus is tenth, now [he is] eighth, and now fifth! They are approaching the turning post. Alas! The second (place) chariot has been steered into the first (place) chariot, and there is a great wreck! Now Scorpus is the third charioteer, and he finishes the first lap well. There will be seven laps. After the second, third, and fourth laps Scorpus is still third. Will he be able to conquer? In the fifth lap, he is almost steered into the barrier by the fourth charioteer, but is set free by his strong horses. In the sixth lap, he approaches the second</u>

place charioteer, and defeats him at the turning post! Now there is Gaius, the first charioteer. Scorpus is mocked and harassed by Gaius, but he is strong and drives eagerly. Finally, the turning post of the seventh lap! Scorpus shouts good words to [his] horses, and prays to the gods. Gaius looks back, and does not see the barrier. He drives into the barrier and nearly has a wreck. Scorpus is now first, and conquers everyone! The crowds shout and scream. Now he will have much wealth and great fame.

Lesson 23 Quiz (100 points)

A. Vocabulary (10 points)

Translate the following words.

1. quārtus decimus: **fourteenth**
2. vīgintī ūnus: **twenty-one**
3. quīnquāgēsimus: **fiftieth**
4. mīllēsimus: **one thousandth**
5. nōnus: **ninth**
6. prīmus: **first**
7. duodēvīcēsimus: **eighteenth**
8. duodecimus: **twelfth**
9. quīntus: **fifth**
10. tertius: **third**

B. Grammar (20 points)

Give a synopsis of *iuvō, iuvāre, iūvi, iūtum* in the third person singular.

	ACTIVE		PASSIVE	
	LATIN	ENGLISH	LATIN	ENGLISH
PRES.	iuvat	he/she/it helps	iuvātur	he is (being) helped
IMPF.	iuvābat	he was helping	iuvābātur	he was (being) helped
FUT.	iuvābit	he will help	iuvābitur	he will be helped
PERF.	iūvit	he (has) helped	iūtus/a/um est	he was (has been) helped
PLUPF.	iūverat	he had helped	iūtus erat	he had been helped
FT. PF.	iūverit	he will have helped	iūtus erit	he will have been helped

C. Translation (15 points)

Translate each sentence.

1. The seventh son of the king had been wounded by a small dragon.

   Fīlius septimus rēgis ab dracōne parvō vulnerātus erat.

2. Ego ā pīrātā brevī amāta sum, sed eum nōn amāvī.

   <u>I was loved by a short pirate, but I did not love him.</u>

D. Memorization (55 points)

Write out the entire *Symbolum Nicaenum* from memory.

<u>Crēdō in ūnum Deum, Patrem omnipotentem, Factōrem caelī et terrae, vīsibilium omnium et</u>
   <u>invīsibilium.</u>

<u>Et in ūnum Dominum Iēsum Christum, Fīlium Deī Ūnigenitum,</u>

<u>Et ex Patre nātum ante omnia saecula.</u>

<u>Deum dē Deō, Lūmen dē Lūmine, Deum vērum dē Deō vērō,</u>

<u>Genitum, nōn factum, consubstantiālem Patrī: per quem omnia facta sunt;</u>

<u>Quī propter nōs hominēs et propter nostram salūtem dēscendit dē caelīs,</u>

<u>Et incarnātus est dē Spīritū Sanctō ex Marīā virgine, et homō factus est.</u>

<u>Crucifīxus etiam prō nōbīs sub Pontiō Pīlātō; passus, et sepultus est,</u>

<u>Et resurrēxit tertiā diē, secundum Scriptūrās, et ascendit in caelum, sedet ad dexteram Patris.</u>

<u>Et iterum ventūrus est cum glōriā, iūdicāre vīvōs et mortuōs, cuius regnī nōn erit fīnis.</u>

<u>Et in Spīritum Sanctum, Dominum et vīvificantem: Quī ex Patre Fīliōque prōcēdit.</u>

<u>Quī cum Patre et Fīliō simul adōrātur et conglōrificātur: Quī locūtus est per prophētās.</u>

<u>Et ūnam, sanctam, catholicam et apostolicam ecclēsiam.</u>

<u>Confiteor ūnum baptisma in remissiōnem peccātōrum.</u>

<u>Et expectō resurrectiōnem mortuōrum, et vītam ventūrī saeculī. Āmēn.</u>

Lesson 24 (Student Edition p. 224)

Review & Test

1. Word List

There is no new Word List this lesson. Remind students that they will be responsible for Unit 3 words in the vocabulary portion of the test, as well as Unit 1 and 2 words in translation.

2. Derivatives/Memorization Helps

There won't be any derivatives on the Unit 3 Test. However, you may want to review derivatives if you feel it will assist your students in remembering their vocabulary.

3. Memorization—*Symbolum Nicaenum* (Nicene Creed)

There is no new memorization this lesson. Review the entirety of the *Symbolum Nicaenum*.

4. Grammar

There is no new chant this lesson. Students should review all of their chants because of the cumulative nature of the Latin language! Be sure to review:

first, second, third, and third i-stem declension nouns

first/second and third declension adjectives

personal pronouns

cardinal and ordinal numerals

the entire active indicative verb system

the entire passive indicative verb system

5. Worksheet

Follow the directions given and complete the worksheet. If you don't have time to go over the conjugation of *iuvō* on the board, at least go over it orally, calling on as many students as you can.

This lesson, instead of the usual English to Latin sentences and Latin to English story, your students will have to translate fifteen sentences from Latin and then parse the verbs. I like to tell students who aren't too keen on parsing that this is a slow-motion exercise (like practicing a karate move) that will help their brain translate like lightning (like doing the karate move instinctively when attacked). When your brain translates *necātus est* as "he was killed," it has already parsed for you—third person singular, "he"; passive and perfect and indicative "was killed." Thus parsing is not torture for torture's sake; think of it as the torture of a really good workout.

D.14.c.—Parse *cavē*: [second person] singular present active imperative of *caveō*. Remember that just as in English, the subject of a Latin imperative is an implied "you" (second person). In this sentence, the grandfather is saying, "(You) beware!" We know that it is singular from the ending *-ē* rather than the plural *-ēte*.

6. Quiz

There is no quiz this lesson.

7. Test

Administer Unit Test 3 when the students are ready.

Lesson 24 Worksheet

A. Vocabulary

Translate the following words from Latin to English or English to Latin as appropriate. Include case(s) for prepositions.

1. facilis: **easy**
2. eighteen: **duodēvīgintī**
3. argenteus: **silver**
4. prope: (+ **acc.**) **near**
5. fourteenth: **quārtus decimus**
6. urbs: **city**
7. minūtātim: **gradually**
8. eight: **octō**
9. ante: **(+ acc.) before**
10. mūtō: **I change**
11. fifth: **quīntus**
12. brevis: **short**
13. eighteenth: **duodēvīcēsimus**
14. green: **viridis**
15. marriage: **matrimōnium**
16. dulcis: **sweet**
17. thirteen: **tredecim**
18. shiny white: **candidus**
19. eighth: **octāvus**
20. nāvis: **ship**
21. twenty-first: **vīcēsimus prīmus**
22. ergō: **therefore**
23. twenty-one: **vīgintī ūnus**
24. elephant: **elephantus**
25. all, every: **omnis**
26. 500: **quīngentī**
27. ecce: **behold**
28. third: **tertius**
29. augeō: **I increase**
30. tree: **arbor**
31. sixteen: **sēdecim**
32. golden: **aureus**
33. fortis: **strong, brave**
34. family: **familia**
35. sharp: **ācer**
36. dog: **canis**
37. thirteenth: **tertius decimus**
38. wide: **lātus**
39. albus: **(dead) white**
40. iuvō: **I help**
41. vīvus: **living**
42. in front of: (+ **abl.**) **prō**
43. avus: **grandfather**
44. huge: **ingēns**
45. seventh: **septimus**
46. hostis: **enemy (of the state)**
47. widow: **vidua**
48. four: **quattuor**
49. quia: **because**
50. is: **he/she/it, this, that**

51. (dead) black: **āter**
52. twelve: **duodecim**
53. post: (+ **acc.**) **after**
54. six: **sex**
55. 100th: **centēsimus**
56. epulae: **feast**
57. high: **altus**
58. ninth: **nōnus**
59. sīcut: **as, just as**
60. purpureus: **purple**
61. difficult: **difficilis**
62. fourth: **quārtus**
63. death: **mors**
64. fifty: **quīnquāgintā**
65. properō: **I hurry, rush**
66. tenth: **decimus**
67. vallēs: **valley**
68. fifteenth: **quīntus decimus**
69. ardeō: **I burn**
70. nineteen: **ūndēvīgintī**
71. violet: **hyacinthus**
72. between: **inter (+ acc.)**
73. seventeenth: **septimus decimus**
74. one: **ūnus**
75. nūbēs: **cloud**
76. 1,000: **mīlle**
77. cow: **bōs**
78. fourteen: **quattuordecim**
79. ego: **I**
80. avia: **grandmother**
81. cēna: **dinner**

82. 500th: **quīngentēsimus**
83. turris: **tower**
84. nineteenth: **ūndēvīcēsimus**
85. tristis: **sad, gloomy**
86. second: **secundus**
87. flōreō: **I flourish**
88. consōbrīna: **cousin (mother's side)**
89. ten: **decem**
90. infēlix: **unlucky**
91. etiam: **even, also**
92. fire: **ignis**
93. patruus: **uncle (father's side)**
94. eagerly: **certātim**
95. alas!: **heu/eheu!**
96. vōs: **you (pl.)**
97. long: **longus**
98. aunt: **amita (mother's side)**
99. moenia: **fortifications**
100. twelfth: **duodecimus**
101. celer: **swift**
102. potēns: **powerful**
103. fifteen: **quīndecim**
104. fessus: **tired**
105. I parch: **torreō**
106. twenty: **vīgintī**
107. night: **nox**
108. labōrō: **I work**
109. seven: **septem**
110. caeruleus: **blue**
111. fiftieth: **quīnquāgēsimus**
112. fēlix: **lucky, happy**

113. first: **prīmus**
114. vestis: **clothing**
115. avunculus: **uncle (mother's side)**
116. ordinary: **mediōcris**
117. twentieth: **vīcēsimus**
118. mare: **sea**
119. knight: **eques**
120. sixteenth: **sextus decimus**
121. asinus: **donkey**
122. nine: **novem**
123. I rejoice: **gaudeō**
124. paene: **almost**
125. indeed: **enim**
126. occultō: **I hide**
127. two: **duo**
128. avis: **bird**
129. five: **quīnque**
130. patruēlis: **cousin**
131. niger: **(shining) black**

132. sixth: **sextus**
133. piscis: **fish**
134. seventeen: **septendecim**
135. mulier: **woman**
136. red: **ruber**
137. one hundred: **centum**
138. pastor: **shepherd**
139. eleventh: **ūndecimus**
140. mōns: **mountain**
141. orbus: **orphan**
142. three: **trēs**
143. if: **sī**
144. coniūnx: **husband, wife**
145. eleven: **ūndecim**
146. true: **vērus**
147. animal: **animal**
148. 1,000th: **mīllēsimus**
149. vexō: **I vex**
150. next: **deinde**

B. Grammar

1. Give the principal parts for *iuvō*:

   iuvō, iuvāre, iūvī, iūtum

Now fully conjugate *iuvō*.

Present Active Indicative

	LATIN SINGULAR	ENGLISH SINGULAR
1ST	iuvō	I help
2ND	iuvās	you help
3RD	iuvat	he/she/it helps

LATIN PLURAL	ENGLISH PLURAL
iuvāmus	we help
iuvātis	you (pl.) help
iuvant	they help

Present Passive Indicative

	LATIN SINGULAR	ENGLISH SINGULAR	LATIN PLURAL	ENGLISH PLURAL
1ST	iuvor	I am (being) helped	iuvāmur	we are helped
2ND	iuvāris	you are helped	iuvāminī	you (pl.) are helped
3RD	iuvātur	he is helped	iuvantur	they are helped

Imperfect Active Indicative

	LATIN SINGULAR	ENGLISH SINGULAR	LATIN PLURAL	ENGLISH PLURAL
1ST	iuvābam	I was helping	iuvābāmus	we were helping
2ND	iuvābās	you were helping	iuvābātis	you (pl.) were helping
3RD	iuvābat	he was helping	iuvābant	they were helping

Imperfect Passive Indicative

	LATIN SINGULAR	ENGLISH SINGULAR	LATIN PLURAL	ENGLISH PLURAL
1ST	iuvābar	I was (being) helped	iuvābāmur	we were (being) helped
2ND	iuvābāris	you were (being) helped	iuvābāminī	you (pl.) were (being) helped
3RD	iuvābātur	he was (being) helped	iuvābantur	they were (being) helped

Future Active Indicative

	LATIN SINGULAR	ENGLISH SINGULAR	LATIN PLURAL	ENGLISH PLURAL
1ST	iuvābō	I will help	iuvābimus	we will help
2ND	iuvābis	you will help	iuvābitis	you (pl.) will help
3RD	iuvābit	he will help	iuvābunt	they will help

Future Passive Indicative

	LATIN SINGULAR	ENGLISH SINGULAR	LATIN PLURAL	ENGLISH PLURAL
1ST	iuvābor	I will be helped	iuvābimur	we will be helped
2ND	iuvāberis	you will be helped	iuvābiminī	you (pl.) will be helped
3RD	iuvābitur	he will be helped	iuvābuntur	they will be helped

Perfect Active Indicative

	LATIN SINGULAR	ENGLISH SINGULAR	LATIN PLURAL	ENGLISH PLURAL
1ST	iūvī	I (have) helped	iūvimus	we helped
2ND	iūvistī	you helped	iūvistis	you (pl.) helped
3RD	iūvit	he helped	iūvērunt	they helped

Perfect Passive Indicative

	LATIN SINGULAR	ENGLISH SINGULAR	LATIN PLURAL	ENGLISH PLURAL
1ST	iūtus/a/um sum	I was/have been helped	iūtī/ae/a sumus	we were helped
2ND	iūtus es	you were helped	iūtī estis	you (pl.) were helped
3RD	iūtus est	he was helped	iūtī sunt	they were helped

Pluperfect Active Indicative

	LATIN SINGULAR	ENGLISH SINGULAR	LATIN PLURAL	ENGLISH PLURAL
1ST	iūveram	I had helped	iūverāmus	we had helped
2ND	iūverās	you had helped	iūverātis	you (pl.) had helped
3RD	iūverat	he had helped	iūverant	they had helped

Pluperfect Passive Indicative

	LATIN SINGULAR	ENGLISH SINGULAR	LATIN PLURAL	ENGLISH PLURAL
1ST	iūtus/a/um eram	I had been helped	iūtī/ae/a erāmus	we had been helped
2ND	iūtus erās	you had been helped	iūtī erātis	you (pl.) had been helped
3RD	iūtus erat	he had been helped	iūtī erant	they had been helped

Future Perfect Active Indicative

	LATIN SINGULAR	ENGLISH SINGULAR	LATIN PLURAL	ENGLISH PLURAL
1ST	iūverō	I will have helped	iūverimus	we will have helped
2ND	iūveris	you will have helped	iūveritis	you (pl.) will have helped
3RD	iūverit	he will have helped	iūverint	they will have helped

Future Perfect Passive Indicative

	LATIN SINGULAR	ENGLISH SINGULAR		LATIN PLURAL	ENGLISH PLURAL
1ST	iūtus/a/um erō	I will have been helped		iūtī/ae/aerimus	we will have been helped
2ND	iūtus eris	you will have been helped		iūtī eritis	you (pl.) will have been helped
3RD	iūtus erit	he will have been helped		iūtī erunt	they will have been helped

2. Decline *green field*.

	LATIN SINGULAR	LATIN PLURAL
NOM.	ager viridis	agrī viridēs
GEN.	agrī viridis	agrōrum viridium
DAT.	agrō viridī	agrīs viridibus
ACC.	agrum viridem	agrōs viridēs
ABL.	agrō viridī	agrīs viridibus
VOC.	[Ō] ager viridis	[Ō] agrī viridēs

3. Decline *ugly ship (use alnus)*.

	LATIN SINGULAR	LATIN PLURAL
NOM.	alnus foeda	alnī foedae
GEN.	alnī foedae	alnōrum foedārum
DAT.	alnō foedae	alnīs foedīs
ACC.	alnum foedam	alnōs foedās
ABL.	alnō foedā	alnīs foedīs
VOC.	[Ō] alne foeda	[Ō] alnī foedae

4. Decline *swift animal*.

	LATIN SINGULAR	LATIN PLURAL
NOM.	celere animal	celeria animālia
GEN.	celeris animālis	celerium animālium
DAT.	celerī animālī	celeribus animālibus
ACC.	celere animal	celeria animālia
ABL.	celerī animālī	celeribus animālibus
VOC.	[Ō] celere animal	[Ō] celeria animālia

5. Decline the first person personal pronoun.

	LATIN SINGULAR	LATIN PLURAL
NOM.	ego	nōs
GEN.	meī	nostrum
DAT.	mihi	nōbīs
ACC.	mē	nōs
ABL.	mē	nōbīs

6. Decline the second person personal pronoun.

	LATIN SINGULAR	LATIN PLURAL
NOM.	tū	vōs
GEN.	tuī	vestrum
DAT.	tibī	vōbīs
ACC.	tē	vōs
ABL.	tē	vōbīs

3. Decline the third person personal pronoun.

	SINGULAR			PLURAL		
	MASC.	FEM.	NEUT.	MASC.	FEM.	NEUT.
NOM.	is	ea	id	eī	eae	ea
GEN.	eius	eius	eius	eōrum	eārum	eōrum
DAT.	eī	eī	eī	eīs	eīs	eīs
ACC.	eum	eam	id	eōs	eās	ea
ABL.	eō	eā	eō	eīs	eīs	eīs

C. Memorization

Write out the entire *Symbolum Nicaenum* from memory.

Crēdō in ūnum Deum, Patrem omnipotentem, Factōrem caelī et terrae, vīsibilium omnium et invīsibilium.

Et in ūnum Dominum Iēsum Christum, Fīlium Deī Ūnigenitum,

Et ex Patre nātum ante omnia saecula.

Deum dē Deō, Lūmen dē Lūmine, Deum vērum dē Deō vērō,

Genitum, nōn factum, consubstantiālem Patrī: per quem omnia facta sunt;

Quī propter nōs hominēs et propter nostram salūtem dēscendit dē caelīs,

Et incarnātus est dē Spīritū Sanctō ex Marīā virgine, et homō factus est.

Crucīfixus etiam prō nōbīs sub Pontiō Pīlātō; passus, et sepultus est,

Et resurrēxit tertiā diē, secundum Scriptūrās, et ascendit in caelum, sedet ad dexteram Patris.

Et iterum ventūrus est cum glōriā, iūdicāre vīvōs et mortuōs, cuius regnī nōn erit fīnis.

Et in Spīritum Sanctum, Dominum et vīvificantem: Quī ex Patre Fīliōque prōcēdit.

Quī cum Patre et Fīliō simul adōrātur et conglōrificātur: Quī locūtus est per prophētās.

Et ūnam, sanctam, catholicam et apostolicam ecclēsiam.

Confiteor ūnum baptisma in remissiōnem peccātōrum.

Et expectō resurrectiōnem mortuōrum, et vītam ventūrī saeculī. Āmēn.

D. English to Latin Translation

Translate each sentence and then parse the selected verbs. For indicative and imperative, give person, number, tense, voice, and mood; for infinitive, tense, voice and mood. Also identify the first principal part.

Example:

Draco ab Oswaldō necātus est.

a. Translation: **The dragon was [or has been] killed by Oswald.**

b. Parse *necātus est*: **third person singular perfect passive indicative of *necō***

1. Avia nostra līberīs crustula vīgintī dedērunt et ea omnia ab eīs certātim mandūcāta sunt.

    a. Translation: **Our grandmother gave [or has given] the children twenty cookies and they were all eaten [or have been eaten] eagerly by them.**

    b. Parse *dedērunt*: **third person plural perfect active indicative of *dō***

    c. Parse *mandūcāta sunt*: **third person plural perfect passive indicative of *mandūcō***

2. Mundus lūnaque sōlque stellaeque ā Deō omnēs creātī sunt, et eōs cūrat.

    a. Translation: **The world and moon and sun and stars were all created by God, and He cares for them.**

    b. Parse *creātī sunt*: **third person plural perfect passive indicative of *creō***

    c. Parse *cūrat*: **third person singular present active indicative of *cūrō***

3. Nōs diū nāvigāverāmus, et dominum pīrātārum dēnique rogāvimus, "Ubi sumus?"

    a. Translation: **We had been sailing for a long time, and finally asked the lord of the pirates, "Where are we?"**

    b. Parse *nāvigāverāmus*: **first person plural pluperfect active indicative of *nāvigō***

    c. Parse *sumus*: **first person plural present active indicative of *sum***

4. Fābulae horrendae dē dracōne caldō narrātae erant, et in caelō suprā montibus ātrīs nunc vidētur.

   a. Translation: <u>Dreadful stories had been told about the fiery dragon, and now he is seen in the sky above the dark mountains.</u>

   b. Parse *narrātae erant*: <u>third person plural pluperfect passive indicative of *narrō*</u>

   c. Parse *vidētur*: <u>third person singular present passive indicative of *videō*</u>

5. Amita mea ab tuīs caprīs tribus vexāta est quod eōs domāre nōn potuistī.

   a. Translation: <u>My [paternal] aunt has been harassed [*or* was harassed] by your three goats because you have not been able to tame them [*or* were not able to tame or could not tame].</u>

   b. Parse *domāre*: <u>present active infinitive of *domō*</u>

   c. Parse *potuistī*: <u>second person singular perfect active indicative of *possum*</u>

6. Equus eius nōnus et asinus duodecimus in agrīs iacēbant quia multa magna ab eīs herī portāta erant.

   a. Translation: <u>His ninth horse and twelfth donkey were lying down in the fields because many large things had been carried by them yesterday.</u>

   b. Parse *iacēbant*: <u>third person plural imperfect active indicative of *iaceō*</u>

   c. Parse *portāta erant*: <u>third person plural pluperfect passive indicative of *portō*</u>

7. In Silvā Ātrā ā centaurō malō oppugnātus sum, sed eum meō Gladiō Ingentī Fātī dēlēvī.

   a. Translation: <u>I was attacked in the Black Forest by an evil centaur, but I destroyed him with my Huge Sword of Fate.</u>

   b. Parse *oppugnātus sum*: <u>first person singular perfect passive indicative of *oppugnō*</u>

   c. Parse *dēlēvī*: <u>first person singular perfect active indicative of *dēleō*</u>

8. Sī omnēs servī miserī līberātī erunt, eī gaudēbunt et dominum bonum iūstumque laudābunt.

   a. Translation: <u>If all the wretched slaves are [lit., "will have been"] set free, they will rejoice and praise the good and just master.</u>

   b. Parse *līberātī erunt*: <u>third person plural future perfect passive indicative of *līberō*</u>

   c. Parse *gaudēbunt*: <u>third person plural future active indicative of *gaudeō*</u>

9. Patruus avārus meus aurum argentumque auxit et diū flōruit, sed omnēs dīvitiae eius igne magnō herī cremātae sunt.

   a. Translation: <u>My greedy [paternal] uncle increased [his] gold and silver and flourished for a long time, but yesterday all his wealth was consumed by a great fire.</u>

   b. Parse *auxit*: <u>third person singular perfect active indicative of *augeō*</u>

   c. Parse *cremātae sunt*: <u>third person plural perfect passive indicative of *cremō*</u>

10. Puerī stultī nōn bene doctī erant, itaque in ōs Spēluncae Noctis Mortisque errāvērunt.

    a. Translation: <u>The foolish boys had not been taught well, and so they wandered into the mouth of the Cave of Night and Death.</u>

    b. Parse *doctī erant*: <u>third person plural pluperfect passive indicative of *doceō*</u>

    c. Parse *errāvērunt*: <u>third person plural perfect active indicative of *errō*</u>

11. "Leō," semper āiō, "rex bestiārum est et numquam superābitur."

    a. Translation: <u>"The lion," I always assert, "is the king of beasts and will never be defeated."</u>

    b. Parse *āiō*: <u>first person singular present active indicative of *āiō*</u>

    c. Parse *est*: <u>third person singular present active indicative of *sum*</u>

12. Mīlitēs hostium bene exercitī erant, et mīlia ex eīs nostram urbem infēlīcem vastāvērunt.

    a. Translation: <u>The enemy's [or enemies'] soldiers had been trained well, and thousands of them laid waste our unlucky city.</u>

    b. Parse *exercitī erant*: <u>third person plural pluperfect passive indicative of *exerceō*</u>

    c. Parse *vastāvērunt*: <u>third person plural perfect active indicative of *vastō*</u>

13. Frāter malus rēgis corōnam nōn meret; ergō ab eō ea ab rēge vērō servīsque eius fīdīs removēbitur.

    a. Translation: <u>The king's evil brother does not deserve the crown; therefore it will be removed from him by the true king and [his] faithful servants.</u>

    b. Parse *meret*: <u>third person singular present active indicative of *mereō*</u>

    c. Parse *removēbitur*: <u>third person singular future passive indicative of *removeō*</u>

14. Avus meus mē monuit: "Cavē, cavē pīrātam pulchrum quōd malus est, dē malō cōgitat, et multum vīnum pōtat!"

   a. Translation: <u>My grandfather warned me: "Beware, beware the handsome pirate because he is evil, he thinks about evil, and he drinks much wine!"</u>

   b. Parse *monuit*: <u>third person singular perfect active indicative of *moneō*</u>

   c. Parse *cavē*: <u>[second person] singular present active imperative of *caveō*</u>

15. Fīlia tertia rēgis in turre altā habitāvit ubi deōs fātumque ōrābat et amōrem vērum exspectābat.

   a. Translation: <u>The king's third daughter lived in the high tower where she prayed to the gods and [to] fate and awaited [her] true love.</u>

   b. Parse *habitāvit*: <u>third person singular perfect active indicative of *habitō*</u>

   c. Parse *ōrābat*: <u>third person singular imperfect active indicative of *ōrō*</u>

Unit 3 Test (220 points)

A. Vocabulary (25 points)

Translate the following words. Give case(s) for prepositions.

1. nine: **novem**
2. enim: **indeed, truly, certainly; for**
3. pastor: **shepherd**
4. argenteus: **silver**
5. dog: **canis**
6. piscis: **fish**
7. four: **quattuor**
8. ante: **(+ acc.) before**
9. torreō: **I burn, parch, dry up**
10. quīnquāgintā: **fifty**
11. prope: **(+ acc.) near, next to**
12. ūndēvīcēsimus: **nineteenth**
13. I change: **mūtō**
14. minūtātim: **gradually, bit by bit**
15. labōrō: **I work**
16. prō: **(+ abl.) before, in front of; for (the sake of), instead of**
17. uncle (mother's brother): **avunculus**
18. deinde: **from that place, then, thereupon, next**
19. sīcut: **as, just as, like**
20. centēsimus: **one hundredth**
21. fifth: **quīntus**
22. celer: **swift, quick**
23. inter: **(+ acc.) between, among**
24. nūbēs: **cloud, gloom**
25. sī: **if**

B. Grammar (20 points)

1. Give a synopsis of *moveō* in the third person plural.

	ACTIVE		PASSIVE	
	LATIN	ENGLISH	LATIN	ENGLISH
PRES.	movent	they move	moventur	they are (being) moved
IMPF.	movēbant	they were moving	movēbantur	they were (being) moved
FUT.	movēbunt	they will move	movēbuntur	they will be moved
PERF.	mōvērunt	they (have) moved	mōtī/ae/a sunt	they were/have been moved
PLUPF.	mōverant	they had moved	mōtī/ae/a erant	they had been moved
FT. PF.	mōverint	they will have moved	mōtī/ae/a erunt	they will have been moved

2. Decline *that gloomy sea*.

	LATIN SINGULAR	LATIN PLURAL
NOM.	id mare triste	ea maria tristia
GEN.	eius maris tristis	eōrum marium tristium
DAT.	eī marī tristī	eīs maribus tristibus
ACC.	id mare triste	ea maria tristia
ABL.	eō marī tristī	eīs maribus tristibus
VOC.	[Ō] mare triste	[Ō] maria tristia

C. Translation (120 points)

1 Ōlim sorōrēs duae, Iūlia Iūniaque, in Silvam Ātram intrāverant. Ibī eae diū ambulābant—Iūlia flōrēs occupābat sed Iūnia parva animālia captābat et terrēbat. Iūlia paene centum flōrēs habuit et tum Iūniam vidēre nōn potuit. "Ubi es?" ea rogāvit. Iūnia post arborem magnam occultāta erat et germānam repentē terruit. Iūlia clāmāvit et Iūnia rīsit.

5   Iūlia flēvit et "Tū," āit, "mē terrēre nōn dēbēs. Sī mē male terrēbit, tū ab Camēlō Magnō Malō terrēbitur!"

"Nōn est Camēlus Magnus Malus!" āit Iūnia. "Fābulae dē eō nōbīs ā mātre nostrā narrātae sunt, sed nōn vērae sunt!"

Iūlia respondit, "Est Camēlus, et mē iuvābit!"

10   Sed gemina mala iam occultāverat et deinde Iūlia ab eā iterum¹ territa est. "Quis² Camēlum Magnum Malum timet?" rīsit Iūnia. Iūlia flēbat ubi repentē ecce! Camēlus Magnus Malus ad eās ambulābat. Flōrēs Iūliae torrent et caelum ātrum erat. Camēlus Iūniae, "Tū," āit, "Camēlum Magnum Malum *nunc* timēs?" Ea ab eō per silvam tum diū captāta et territa est. Iūnia nec hominēs nec animālia iterum¹ terruit.

Glossary
1. *iterum*: again
2. *quis*: who?

Once upon a time the two sisters, Iulia and Iunia, had entered into the Dark Forest. They walked there for a long time—Iulia was picking [lit., seizing] flowers but Iunia was hunting and scaring small animals. Iulia had nearly one hundred flowers and then could not see Iunia. "Where are you?" she asked. Iunia had been hidden behind a large tree and suddenly frightened (her) sister. Iulia screamed and Iunia laughed.

Iulia wept and said, "You ought not to scare me! If you [will] scare me wrongly, you will be scared by the Big Bad Camel."

"There is no [lit., not a] Big Bad Camel!" asserted Iunia. "Stories about him were told to us by our mother, but they are not true!"

Iulia replied, "There is a Camel, and he will help me!"

But the evil twin had already hidden and thereupon Iulia was scared again by her. "Who's afraid of the Big Bad Camel?" taunted Iunia. Iulia was weeping when suddenly, behold! The Big Bad Camel was walking toward them. Iulia's flowers dried up and the sky was dark. The Camel said to Iunia, "Are you afraid of the Big Bad Camel *now?*" She was then hunted and scared by him through the forest for a long time. Iunia scared neither people nor animals again.

D. Memorization (55 points)

Write out the entire *Symbolum Nicaenum*.

Crēdō in ūnum Deum, Patrem omnipotentem, Factōrem caelī et terrae, vīsibilium omnium et invīsibilium.

Et in ūnum Dominum Iēsum Christum, Fīlium Deī Ūnigenitum,

Et ex Patre nātum ante omnia saecula.

Deum dē Deō, Lūmen dē Lūmine, Deum vērum dē Deō vērō,

Genitum, nōn factum, consubstantiālem Patrī: per quem omnia facta sunt;

Quī propter nōs hominēs et propter nostram salūtem dēscendit dē caelīs,

Et incarnātus est dē Spīritū Sanctō ex Marīā virgine, et homō factus est.

Crucīfīxus etiam prō nōbīs sub Pontiō Pīlātō; passus, et sepultus est,

Et resurrēxit tertiā die, secundum Scriptūrās, et ascendit in caelum, sedet ad dexteram Patris.

Et iterum ventūrus est cum glōriā, iūdicāre vīvōs et mortuōs, cuius regnī nōn erit fīnis.

Et in Spīritum Sanctum, Dominum et vīvificantem: Quī ex Patre Fīliōque prōcēdit.

Quī cum Patre et Fīliō simul adōrātur et conglōrificātur: Quī locūtus est per prophētās.

Et ūnam, sanctam, catholicam et apostolicam ecclēsiam.
Confiteor ūnum baptisma in remissiōnem peccātōrum.
Et expectō resurrectiōnem mortuōrum, et vītam ventūrī saeculī. Āmēn.

Unit Four

Unit 4 Goals

Lessons 25–32

By the end of Unit 4, students should be able to . . .

- Decline fourth declension nouns
- Decline fifth declension nouns
- Decline the demonstrative pronouns *hic*, *ille*, and *iste*
- Conjugate a third, fourth, or third -iō conjugation verb in the present, imperfect, future, perfect, pluperfect, and future perfect active and passive indicative
- Translate sentences using all of the concepts learned in Units 1–4
- Know all vocabulary from Lessons 25–32
- Write out from memory Psalm 23 from the Vulgate

LESSON 25 (Student Edition p. 239)

Fourth Declension Nouns

1. Word List

Take note of word #15, *appropinquō*. This verb can either take the dative, or *ad* + accusative. So if you wanted to say "Oswald approached the dragon," you could either say *Oswaldus dracōnī appropinquāvit* or *Oswaldus ad dracōnem appropinquāvit*.

This verb is a compound word of *ad* + *propinquō*, and although in English we don't usually repeat that preposition, Latin is fond of doing so. When encountering the second sentence above, you don't need to translate the *ad*; you can simply say "Oswald approached the dragon." If you really really feel the need to put in the *ad*, you can say, "Oswald approached unto the dragon," but it sounds a bit stiff.

2. Derivatives/Memorization Helps

1. *cantus*, song, singing: chant, chanson; see *cantō*, Lesson 1
2. *cornū*, horn: cornucopia, cornea, unicorn
3. *domus*, house, home: domicile, domestic, dome
4. *exercitus*, army: exercise; see *exerceō*, Lesson 14
5. *frūctus*, fruit, profit: fructose, frugal, fruit
6. *genū*, knee: genuflect
7. *Iēsus*, Jesus
8. *manus*, hand: manual, manufacture, manuscript
9. *portus*, harbor, port: port (for both a harbor and the left side of the ship); don't confuse with *portō* or *porta*
10. *spīritus*, spirit, breath: spirit, spiritual, conspire, respiratory
11. *tonitrus*, thunder
12. *vultus*, face, expression
13. *salvus*, safe, saved, well, sound: safe, salvific; see *salveō*, Lesson 9
14. *sanctus*, holy, sacred, consecrated: sanctify, sanction, sanctuary; *sanctum sanctōrum* = the Holy of Holies
15. *appropinquō*, I approach, draw near: propinquity
16. *foveō*, I cherish, love, esteem: foment
17. *gubernō*, I steer, direct, govern: govern, governor, government, gubernatorial
18. *iterum*, again, a second time
19. *propter*, because of, on account of, near: The informal fallacy *post hoc ergō propter hoc*, "after this therefore because of this"
20. *quōmodo*, how, in what way

3. Memorization—*Psalmus XXIII*

This unit's memorization is Psalm 23 (although it's Psalm 22 according to the Vulgate numbering system). It is the Latin version translated from the Septuagint, which is the Greek translation of the Hebrew. Thus it is a bit removed from the original text and the literal translation of it (below) will seem quite different in spots from the King James Version that we all know by heart. I wanted to give the students a taste of the Vulgate and a poetic portion at that. As with previous memorizations, I strongly recommend that you do not require students to know all the macrons. They can certainly learn the macrons if they so desire (and macrons will assist with pronunciation), but since students have so many other things to learn, these macrons may well become a millstone around their necks. You don't want to kill their interest in Latin by overemphasizing trifles.

Psalmus XXIII *(Psalm 23 from the Vulgate*)*

Lesson 25   ¹Psalmus Dāvīd.

> *A Psalm of David.*

Dominus reget mē et nihil mihi dēerit.

> *The Lord will guide me and I will lack nothing (lit., "nothing will be lacking to me").*

Lesson 26   ²In locō pascuae ibī mē conlocāvit;

> *In a place of pasture, there He will establish me;*

super aquam refectiōnis ēducāvit mē.

> *beside the water of restoration He will lead me.*

Lesson 27   ³Animam meam convertit.

> *He directs my soul.*

Dēdūxit mē super sēmitās iūstitiae

> *He has led me along paths of righteousness*

propter nōmen suum.

> *because of His name.*

Lesson 28   ⁴Nam et sī ambulāverō in mediō umbrae mortis,

> *For even if I walk (lit., "will have walked") in the midst of the shadow of death,*

nōn timēbō mala quoniam tū mēcum es;

> *I will not fear evils because you are with me;*

virga tua et baculus tuus ipsa mē consōlāta sunt.

> *Your rod and Your staff themselves have comforted me.*

---

* Latin text accessed at http://www.thelatinlibrary.com/bible/psalms.html#22.

Lesson 29 ⁵Parāstī in conspectū meō mensam
> *You have prepared a table in my sight*

adversus eōs quī trībulant mē.
> *against those who trouble me.*

Inpinguāstī in oleō caput meum,
> *You have anointed my head with (lit., "in") oil,*

Lesson 30 et calix meus inēbrians quam praeclārus est.
> *and my cup is intoxicating like splendid [wine].*

⁶Et misericordia tua subsequitur mē
> *And Your mercy follows me*

omnibus diēbus vītae meae,
> *all the days of my life,*

Lesson 31 et ut inhabitem in domō Dominī
> *so that I also may dwell in the house of the Lord*

in longitūdinem diērum.
> *for the length of [my] days.*

4. Grammar

Fourth Declension Noun Endings:

We now introduce the fourth of the five Latin declensions. It's fairly straightforward, and the neuter variant is especially fun to chant. The fourth declension functions exactly like the others, so all that your students need to do is add these endings to their repertoire. As with the third declension, fourth declension masculine and feminine nouns share the same set of endings. Most fourth declension nouns are masculine, with several feminines and a mere handful of neuters (though important ones). And whether masculine, feminine, or neuter, fourth declension nouns are the same in the Vocative and the Nominative. The chants for both are as follows:

Fourth Declension Masculine/Feminine Endings

	LATIN SINGULAR	ENGLISH SINGULAR	LATIN PLURAL	ENGLISH PLURAL
NOMINATIVE	-us	a/the *noun* [subject]	-ūs	the *nouns* [subject]
GENITIVE	-ūs	of the *noun*, the *noun's*	-uum	of the *nouns*, the *nouns'*
DATIVE	-uī	to/for the *noun*	-ibus	to/for the *nouns*
ACCUSATIVE	-um	a/the *noun* [object]	-ūs	the *nouns* [object]
ABLATIVE	-ū	by/with/from the *noun*	-ibus	by/with/from the *nouns*
VOCATIVE	-us	O *noun*	-ūs	O *nouns*

Fourth Declension Neuter Endings

	LATIN SINGULAR	ENGLISH SINGULAR
NOMINATIVE	-ū	a/the *noun* [subject]
GENITIVE	-ūs	of the *noun*, the *noun's*
DATIVE	-ū	to/for the *noun*
ACCUSATIVE	-ū	a/the *noun* [object]
ABLATIVE	-ū	by/with/from the *noun*
VOCATIVE	-ū	O *noun*

	LATIN PLURAL	ENGLISH PLURAL
NOMINATIVE	-ua	the *nouns* [subject]
GENITIVE	-uum	of the *nouns*, the *nouns'*
DATIVE	-ibus	to/for the *nouns*
ACCUSATIVE	-ua	the *nouns* [object]
ABLATIVE	-ibus	by/with/from the *nouns*
VOCATIVE	-ua	O *nouns*

As with nouns in all other declensions, we find the stem of fourth declension from the genitive by taking off the *-ūs*. As mentioned previously, the vocative of all fourth declension nouns (regardless of gender) is the same as the nominative.

In the masculine/feminine chant, notice that the nominative and vocative signular are a short *-us*, while long *ūs* is found in the genitive singular and nominative, accusative, and vocative plurals. Here, taking note of that old macron could be helpful in selecting the correct number and case.

Also notice that fourth declension neuters still follow our neuter noun guidelines:

1. The nominative, accusative, and vocative singulars and plurals are all the same.

2. The plural nominative, accusative, and vocative end in *-a*.

Here are two nouns declined as examples and for edification:

manus, -ūs (f) *hand*

	LATIN SINGULAR	ENGLISH SINGULAR
NOMINATIVE	manus	a/the hand [subject]
GENITIVE	manūs	of the hand, the hand's
DATIVE	manuī	to/for the hand
ACCUSATIVE	manum	a/the hand [object]
ABLATIVE	manū	by/with/from the hand
VOCATIVE	Ō manus	O hand!

	LATIN PLURAL	ENGLISH PLURAL
NOMINATIVE	manūs	the hands [subject]
GENITIVE	manuum	of the hands, the hands'
DATIVE	manibus	to/for the hands
ACCUSATIVE	manūs	the hands [object]
ABLATIVE	manibus	by/with/from the hands
VOCATIVE	-ūs	O hands!

genū, -ūs (n) *knee*

	LATIN SINGULAR	ENGLISH SINGULAR
NOMINATIVE	genū	a/the knee [subject]
GENITIVE	genūs	of the knee, the knee's
DATIVE	genū	to/for the knee
ACCUSATIVE	genū	a/the knee [object]
ABLATIVE	genū	by/with/from the knee
VOCATIVE	Ō genū	O knee!

	LATIN PLURAL	ENGLISH PLURAL
NOMINATIVE	genua	the knees [subject]
GENITIVE	genuum	of the knees, the knees'
DATIVE	genibus	to/for the knees
ACCUSATIVE	genua	the knees [object]
ABLATIVE	genibus	by/with/from the knees
VOCATIVE	Ō genua	O knees!

A note on *domus*: it will sometimes appear with second declension endings in a few of its cases. In the worksheet for this lesson, simply have your students do all fourth endings so that they can practice them, but they should be aware of this phenomenon:

	LATIN SINGULAR	LATIN PLURAL
NOM.	domus	domūs
GEN.	domūs [or domī]	domuum [or domōrum]
DAT.	domuī [or domō]	domibus
ACC.	domum	domūs [or domōs]
ABL.	domū [or domō]	domibus
VOC.	domus	domūs

The declension of *Iesus* is also slightly irregular (as happens with many names in the Vulgate, actually—some do not decline at all!).

	LATIN SINGULAR
NOM.	Iēsus
GEN.	Iēsu
DAT.	Iēsu
ACC.	Iēsum
ABL.	Iēsu
VOC.	Ō Iēsu

Review

Review those passive forms from last term (Lessons 4 and 6), especially the perfects, pluperfects, and future perfects. Also, review pronouns again, since they're so important.

5. Worksheet

Follow the directions given to complete the worksheet.

D.1. Those two disciples of Jesus had been called "Sons of Thunder." *Eī duo discipulī Iēsu Filiī Tonitruī appellātī erant.* Notice that *appellō* functions as a linking verb here, so "Sons" should be translated with the nominative *Filiī*, not accusative *Filiōs*. If the sentence read "Jesus had called those two disciples the 'Sons of Thunder,'" then it would be accusative: *Iēsus eōs duōs discipulōs Filiōs Tonitruī appellāverat.*

6. Quiz

Administer Quiz 25 when the students are ready.

Lesson 25 Worksheet

A. Vocabulary

Translate the following words from Latin to English or English to Latin as appropriate. For the verbs, also fill in the missing principal parts. For each preposition, include which case(s) it takes.

1. holy: **sanctus**
2. cantus: **song, singing**
3. hand: **manus**
4. domus: **house, home**
5. I approach: **appropinquō, -quāre, -quāvī, -quātum**
6. exercitus: **army**
7. vultus: **face, expression**
8. gubernō, **-āre, -āvī, -ātum**: **I steer, direct, govern**
9. iterum: **again, a second time**
10. Jesus: **Iēsus**
11. salvus: **safe, saved, well, sound**
12. how: **quōmodo**
13. harbor: **portus**
14. propter: (+ **acc.**) **because of, on account of, near**
15. foveō, **-ēre, fōvī, fōtum**: **I cherish, love, esteem**
16. spirit: **spīritus**
17. frūctus: **fruit, profit**
18. cornū: **horn**
19. thunder: **tonitrus**
20. genū: **knee**

B. Grammar

1. Decline *my gloomy house*.

	LATIN SINGULAR	LATIN PLURAL
NOM.	mea domus tristis	meae domūs tristēs
GEN.	meae domūs tristis	meārum domuum tristium
DAT.	meae domuī tristī	meīs domibus tristibus
ACC.	meam domum tristem	meās domūs tristēs
ABL.	meā domū tristī	meīs domibus tristibus
VOC.	[Ō] mea domus tristis!	[Ō] meae domūs tristēs

2. Decline *that evil army*.

	LATIN SINGULAR	LATIN PLURAL
NOM.	is exercitus malus	eī exercitūs malī
GEN.	eius exercitūs malī	eōrum exercituum malōrum
DAT.	eī exercituī malō	eīs exercitibus malīs
ACC.	eum exercitum malum	eōs exercitūs malōs
ABL.	eō exercitū malō	eīs exercitibus malīs
VOC.	[Ō] exercitus male	[Ō] exercitūs malī

3. Decline *one ordinary knee*. For the plural, use *two ordinary knees*.

	LATIN SINGULAR	LATIN PLURAL
NOM.	unum genū mediōcre	duo genua mediōcria
GEN.	ūnius genūs mediōcris	duōrum genuum mediōcrium
DAT.	ūnī genū mediōcrī	duōbus genibus mediōcribus
ACC.	ūnum genū mediōcre	duo genua mediōcria
ABL.	ūnō genū mediōcrī	duōbus genibus mediōcribus
VOC.	[Ō] ūnum genū mediōcre	[Ō] duo genua mediōcria

4. Give a synopsis of *foveō* in the first person plural.

	ACTIVE		PASSIVE	
	LATIN	ENGLISH	LATIN	ENGLISH
PRES.	fovēmus	we cherish	fovēmur	we are (being) cherished
IMPF.	fovēbāmus	we were cherishing	fovēbāmur	we were (being) cherished
FUT.	fovēbimus	we will cherish	fovēbimur	we will be cherished
PERF.	fōvimus	we (have) cherished	fōtī/ae/a sumus	we were/have been cherished
PLUPF.	fōverāmus	we had cherished	fōtī/ae/a erāmus	we had been cherished
FT. PF.	fōverimus	we will have cherished	fōtī/ae/a erimus	we will have been cherished

C. Memorization

Fill in the blanks.

¹Psalmus <u>Dāvīd</u>.

<u>Dominus</u> reget <u>mē</u> et <u>nihil</u> mihi <u>dēerit.</u>

D. English to Latin Translation

Translate each sentence from English to Latin.

1. Those two disciples of Jesus had been called "Sons of Thunder."

   <u>Eī duo discipulī Iēsū Fīliī Tonitruī appellātī erant.</u>

2. The leader of the pirates steered their ship into our harbor and then seven homes were burned by their army.

   <u>Dux pīrātārum nāvem eōrum in portum nostrum gubernāvit, et septem domūs ab exercitū eōrum deinde/tum cremātae sunt.</u>

3. The brave knight approached the castle of the wicked queen and asked again concerning the princess [lit., "king's daughter"] in the high tower.

   <u>Eques fortis ad [**N.B. The English does not require an additional preposition, but Latin is fond of that repetition. If** ad **is not used, remember that** appropinquō *takes the dative:* castellō. . . appropinquāvit.] castellum rēgīnae malae appropinquāvit et dē fīliā rēgis in turre/turrī altā iterum rogāvit.</u>

4. Silver and gold had been cherished by the greedy old man for a long time, and now he loves riches, not people.

   <u>Argentum aurumque [*or* et aurum] ab sene avārō diū fota erant, et [is] dīvitiās nōn hōminēs nunc amat.</u>

5. The giant had two big hands, two huge knees, and one ugly face.

   <u>Gigās duās manūs magnās, duo genua ingentia, et unum vultum foedum habēbat/habuit [*or* tenēbat/tenuit].</u>

6. Because of the Holy Spirit, many in the church will help widows and orphans.

   <u>Propter Sanctum Spiritum, multī/multae in ecclēsiā viduās et orbōs/orbās iuvābunt.</u>

7. The poet was singing songs of love to the woman for a long time but he was never loved by her.

   <u>Poēta fēminae cantūs amōris diū cantābat sed [is] ab eā numquam amātus est.</u>

8. How did the deer swim to the distant island in the deep sea?

   Quōmodo cervī ad īnsulam longinquam in marī altō nāvērunt?

9. Because of the great danger of the bull's horns, we hastened out of the field into the farmhouse.

   Propter perīculum magnum cornuum bōvis, [nōs] ex agrō in villam properāvimus [or festīnāvimus].

10. The bad children seized much fruit from your grandmother's tree and carried it into town.

    Līberī malī multum fructum ab arbōre aviae tuae/vestrae occupāvērunt et eum in oppidum portāvērunt.

E. Latin to English Translation

1 **Fābula dē Porcīs Pinguibus**[1]

Cūr, tū rogās, sunt multī porcī magnī pinguēsque in oppidō nostrō? Tibī narrābō. Ōlim exercitus magnus ad patriam nostram appropinquāverat. Rex exercitūs in omnia oppida patriae nostrae intrāvit et clāmāvit: "Vōs omnēs meī servī eritis! Frūmentum vestrum et fructūs et vīnum mihi dabuntur, et
5 multōs ad regnum meum portābō!" Vultūs nostrī miserī erant et genua nostra tremēbant.[2] Manūs nostrās sustulimus[3] et deam nostrī oppidī ōrāvimus. Rex hostium ad castellum in monte prope oppidum nostrum deinde festīnāvit et id obsēdit. Mīlitēs in castellō bene pugnābant, sed castellum dēnique captum est.[4] Rex malus per moenia ad templum[5] properāvit. Simulācrum[6] aureum deae occupāvit et id ē templō portāvit. Omnia sacra aurea ab exercitū eius ex templō tum portāta sunt. Nōs flēvimus
10 ululāvimusque, sed dea īrāta erat. Erant fulgura[7] et tonitrūs dē nūbibus ātrīs in caelīs. Rex malus malī exercitūs dēnique timuit. Ad caelum vīdit, et vōx deae audīta[8] est: "Vōs avārī estis sīcut porcī pinguēs harae;[9] porcī vōs nunc semper eritis!" Et is exercitusque in porcōs statim mūtātī sunt, et eī servī nostrī nunc sunt.

Glossary
1. *pinguis, -e*: fat
2. *tremō, -ere, -uī, —*: I tremble, quake
3. *tollō, -ere, sustulī, sublātum*: I lift up, raise
4. *capiō, -ere, cēpī, captum*: I capture
5. *templum, -ī* (n): temple, shrine
6. *simulācrum, -ī* (n): statue
7. *fulgur, -uris* (n): lightning
8. *audiō, -īre, -īvī, -ītum*: I hear
9. *hara, -ae* (f): pig-sty

The Tale of the Fat Pigs

Why, you ask, are there many big [and] fat pigs in our town? I will tell you. Once upon a time, a great army had approached our land. The king of the army entered [into] all the towns of our land and shouted: "You will all be my servants! Your grain and fruit and wine will be given to me, and I will carry many people to my kingdom!" Our faces were sad and our knees were quaking. We lifted up our hands and prayed to the goddess of our town. The king of the enemy then hastened to the castle on the mountain near our town and besieged it. The soldiers in the castle fought well, but the castle was finally captured. The evil king hastened through fortifications toward the temple. He seized the golden statue of the goddess and carried it out of the temple. Then all the golden and sacred things were carried out of the temple by his army. We wept and wailed, but the goddess was angry. There were lightnings and thunderings from the black clouds in the heavens. The evil king of the evil army finally was afraid. He looked to heaven and the goddess's voice was heard: "You are greedy as fat pigs of the sty; now you will be pigs forever!" And he and his army were immediately changed into pigs, and now they are our servants.

Lesson 25 Quiz (69 points)

A. Vocabulary (10 points)

Translate the following words (include all four principal parts for verbs). Give case(s) for prepositions.

1. cantus: **song, singing**
2. genū: **knee**
3. cornū: **horn**
4. propter: (+ **acc.**) **because of, on account of, near**
5. iterum: **again, a second time**
6. how: **quōmodo**
7. I approach: **appropinquō, -quāre, -quāvī, -quātum**
8. salvus: **safe, saved, well, sound**
9. frūctus: **fruit, profit**
10. thunder: **tonitrus**

B. Grammar (18 points)

Decline *beautiful green fruit.*

	LATIN SINGULAR	LATIN PLURAL
NOM.	pulcher fructus viridis	pulchrī fructūs viridēs
GEN.	pulchrī fructūs viridis	pulchrōrum frūctuum viridium
DAT.	pulchrō frūctuī viridī	pulchrīs frūctibus viridibus
ACC.	pulchrum frūctum viridem	pulchrōs fructūs viridēs
ABL.	pulchrō frūctū viridī	pulchrīs frūctibus viridibus
VOC.	Ō pulcher frūctus viridis	Ō pulchrī fructūs viridēs

C. Translation (20 points)

Translate each sentence.

1. The face of the queen was beautiful, but her voice was sad.

   Vultus rēgīnae pulcher [erat], sed vōx eius misera [*or* tristis] erat.

2. Iēsus discipulīs Sanctum Spīritum dedit, et multōs iūvāvērunt.

   Jesus gave the disciples the Holy Spirit, and they helped many.

D. Memorization (21 points)

Write the first verse of Psalm 23 in Latin.

[1]<u>Psalmus Dāvīd.</u>

<u>Dominus reget mē et nihil mihi dēerit.</u>

LESSON 26 (Student Edition p. 247)

Verbs: Third Conjugation Active & Imperative

1. Word List

Take note of word #5, *medius*. This adjective can mean either "middle" or "middle of." You could say *medius frāter*, "the middle brother." Or you could say *in mediam silvam*, "into the middle of the forest," and you would **not** put *silvam* in the genitive.

6. *novus*, "new"—Make sure students don't confuse this with *nōnus*, "ninth" [Lesson 23].

2. Derivatives/Memorization Helps

Point out how English derivatives come from both the second and fourth principal parts (e.g., "permit" from *mittere* and "permission" from *missus*).

1. *lingua*, language, tongue: linguistics, bilingual, lingo
2. *littera*, letter of the alphabet; (pl.) letter, epistle: literal, (il)literate, letters
3. *metus*, fear, dread: meticulous
4. *tempestās*, weather, storm: tempest, tempestuous
5. *medius*, middle (of), midst (of): median, medium, Mediterranean, medieval
6. *novus*, new: novel, novelty, novice
7. *agō*, I do, act, drive: action, actor, agent, agenda
8. *crēdō*, I believe: credence, (in)credible, creed, credit
9. *currō*, I run: currency, curriculum, current, incur; C.V. = *curriculum vitae*, a resumé
10. *dīcō*, I say, speak: dictate, dictionary, contradict, predict
11. *dūcō*, I lead, guide: induce, produce, reduce, abduct, etc.
12. *lūdō*, I play, tease, trick: ludicrous, illusion; from related noun *ludus*, "game"
13. *mittō*, I send, let go: mission, missile, permit, permission, promise, commit, commission
14. *pōnō*, I put, place: position, deposit, opponent
15. *regō*, I rule: direct, regent, regime, correct
16. *scrībō*, I write: scribe, script, prescription, prescribe, scribble
17. *vincō*, I defeat, conquer: (in)vincible, victory, Victōria, Vincent, convict; see *victoria*, Lesson 11
18. *fortasse*, perhaps

19. *quoniam*, because, since

20. *super* (+ acc./+ abl.), over, above, beyond: prefix super-, as in supercede, superficial, superhuman

3. Memorization—*Psalmus XXIII*

This lesson's lines are:

> ²In locō pascuae ibī mē conlocāvit;
>
> > *In a place of pasture, there He will establish me;*
>
> super aquam refectiōnis ēducāvit mē.
>
> > *beside the water of restoration He will lead me.*

4. Grammar

Third Conjugation Verbs, Active:

Your students have been complacently chugging along using just two of the five Latin conjugations, and it is high time they added another. The third conjugation is a bit trickier than the first and second, but only in the present system. In the perfect system it conjugates just like all the other verbs your students have dealt with thus far.

First, review the first and second conjugation stem vowels. Your class may need a reminder about how to find the stem vowel in the first place: go to the infinitive (second principal part), remove the *-re*, and there it is. Thus for a first conjugation verb like *necō, necāre*, the stem vowel is *ā*, and for a second conjugation verb such as *videō, vidēre*, it is *ē*. This makes conjugating easy, for all one has to do is slap the endings *-ō, -s, -t* or *-bam, -bās, -bat* or *-bō, -bis, -bit* onto that stem.

However, since the stem vowel of the third conjugation is a short *e*, a few interesting things happen. We find this stem in the same way as the other two conjugations—second principal part, take off the *-re*: *mittō, mittere, mīsī, missum*, I send. Our present stem for *mittō* is *mitte-*. That short *e* morphs quite a bit when various endings are added. Here are the present vowels:

	SINGULAR	PLURAL
1ST	-ō	-i-
2ND	-i-	-i-
3RD	-i-	-u-

When conjugated in the present active tense then, *mittō* looks like this:

Present Active Indicative of *mittō*

	LATIN SINGULAR	ENGLISH SINGULAR		LATIN PLURAL	ENGLISH PLURAL
1ST	mittō	I send		mittimus	we send
2ND	mittis	you send		mittitis	you (pl.) send
3RD	mittit	he/she/it sends		mittunt	they send

One of your students will inevitably ask *why* the stem vowel changes like this. Without going into the historical and linguistic reasons, you can point out that short *e* and short *i* are actually quite close phonetically. Have the class say "eh" and "ih" and note how your tongue stays in the same position, but the "eh" is made a little bit more back in the mouth than the "ih."

One way to remember that the third person plural ending is -*unt* and not -*int* is to point out how nasally -*int* sounds. Wouldn't a round, rolling vowel sound better? Of course, you can always have them chant ō, i, i, i, i, u! over and over until it is entrenched.

The imperfect is not as strange; our short *e* stem vowel becomes a long *ē* for the whole chant:

Imperfect Active Indicative of *mittō*

	LATIN SINGULAR	ENGLISH SINGULAR		LATIN PLURAL	ENGLISH PLURAL
1ST	mittēbam	I was sending		mittēbāmus	we were sending
2ND	mittēbās	you were sending		mittēbātis	you (pl.) were sending
3RD	mittēbat	he/she/it was sending		mittēbant	they were sending

The future of the third conjugation is where it really gets interesting. Instead of using -*bō*, -*bis*, -*bit* for the future, third conjugation verbs undergo a vowel change and add regular endings! Here are the vowels of the future:

	SINGULAR	PLURAL
1ST	-a-	-ē-
2ND	-ē-	-ē-
3RD	-e-	-e-

To these vowels, -*m*, -*s*, -*t*, -*mus*, -*tis*, -*nt* are added. If anyone questions why the first person singular is an -*m* rather than an -*ō*, point out that some of their first person singular verbs end in -*m* not -*ō*: -*bam* and *sum*, for example. They can think of it as an alternative first person singular ending. Here is our example verb conjugated in the future:

Future Active Indicative of *mittō*

	LATIN SINGULAR	ENGLISH SINGULAR		LATIN PLURAL	ENGLISH PLURAL
1ST	mittam	I will send		mittēmus	we will send
2ND	mittēs	you will send		mittētis	you (pl.) will send
3RD	mittet	he/she/it will send		mittent	they will send

If it is helpful to your students, they can chant *-am, -ēs, -et, -ēmus, -ētis, -ent!* as an alternate future active chant, rather than *a, ē, e, ē, ē, e.*

Happily, third conjugation verbs are perfectly normal in the perfect system. Simply remove the *-ī* from the third principal part, and add the usual perfect, pluperfect, and future perfect endings:

Perfect Active Indicative of *mittō*

	LATIN SINGULAR	ENGLISH SINGULAR		LATIN PLURAL	ENGLISH PLURAL
1ST	mīsī	I (have) sent		mīsimus	we (have) sent
2ND	mīsistī	you (have) sent		mīsistis	you (pl.) (have) sent
3RD	mīsit	he/she/it (has) sent		mīsērunt	they (have) sent

Pluperfect Active Indicative of *mittō*

	LATIN SINGULAR	ENGLISH SINGULAR		LATIN PLURAL	ENGLISH PLURAL
1ST	mīseram	I had sent		mīserāmus	we had sent
2ND	mīserās	you had sent		mīserātis	you (pl.) had sent
3RD	mīserat	he/she/it had sent		mīserant	they had sent

Future Perfect Active Indicative of *mittō*

	LATIN SINGULAR	ENGLISH SINGULAR		LATIN PLURAL	ENGLISH PLURAL
1ST	mīserō	I will have sent		mīserimus	we will have sent
2ND	mīseris	you will have sent		mīseritis	you (pl.) will have sent
3RD	mīserit	he/she/it will have sent		mīserint	they will have sent

Third conjugation verbs often have more irregular principal parts, and thus you should "encourage" (by whatever means you deem necessary) your students to learn them.

Because there isn't exactly a new "chant" to learn, I have given the students an example verb to look at so they can see the vowels changing in the present system.

Third Conjugation Imperatives

To form a third conjugation singular imperative, follow the known procedure for imperatives of other conjugations: Go to the second principal part. Chop off the *-re*. And there it is. Thus, *mittere* becomes *mitte!* send! However, in the plural, the weight of the *-te* ending squishes that short *e* so that it slims up into an *i*: *mittite* (**not** *mittete*)! send!

A couple of third conjugation verbs have irregular singular imperatives: *dūcō* becomes *dūc* (**not** *dūce*); the imperative of *dīcō* is *dīc* (**not** *dīce*).

5. Worksheet

The Latin to English story this lesson is a simplified paraphrase of Mark 3:1–7. Point out to your students how in the Latin, present and past tenses are both used. In English, however, this would be considered improper, so be consistent in your translation and use a past tense even to translate a present verb.

Follow the directions given to complete the worksheet.

6. Quiz

Administer Quiz 26 when the students are ready.

Lesson 26 Worksheet

A. Vocabulary

Translate the following words from Latin to English or English to Latin as appropriate. For the verbs, also fill in the missing principal parts. For each preposition, include which case(s) it takes.

1. dicō, **dicere**, **dixī**, **dictum**: **I say, speak**
2. I rule: **regō**, **regere**, **rexī**, **rectum**
3. fortasse: **perhaps**
4. middle (of): **medius, -a, -um**
5. tempestās: **weather, storm**
6. lūdō, **lūdere**, **lūsī**, **lūsum**: **I play, tease, trick**
7. agō, **agere**, **ēgī**, **actum**: **I do, act, drive**
8. I send: **mittō**, **mittere**, **mīsī**, **missum**
9. currō, **currere**, **cūcurrī**, **cursum**: **I run**
10. quoniam: **because, since**
11. pōnō, **pōnere**, **posuī**, **positum**: **I put, place**
12. super **(+ acc./+ abl.) over, above, beyond**
13. language: **lingua**
14. I believe: **crēdō**, **credere**, **credidī**, **creditum**
15. littera: **letter of the alphabet; (pl.) letter, epistle**
16. I write: **scrībō**, **scrībere**, **scrīpsī**, **scrīptum**
17. metus: **fear, dread**
18. dūcō, **dūcere**, **dūxī**, **ductum**: **I lead, guide**
19. new: **novus**
20. vincō, **vincere**, **vīcī**, **victum**: **I defeat, conquer**

B. Grammar

1. Conjugate *dūcō* in full in the active indicative.

Present Active Indicative

	LATIN SINGULAR	ENGLISH SINGULAR	LATIN PLURAL	ENGLISH PLURAL
1ST	dūcō	I lead	dūcimus	we lead
2ND	dūcis	you lead	dūcitis	you (pl.) lead
3RD	dūcit	he/she/it leads	dūcunt	they lead

Imperfect Active Indicative

	LATIN SINGULAR	ENGLISH SINGULAR	LATIN PLURAL	ENGLISH PLURAL
1ST	dūcēbam	I was leading	dūcēbāmus	we were leading
2ND	dūcēbās	you were leading	dūcēbātis	you (pl.) were leading
3RD	dūcēbat	he was leading	dūcēbant	they were leading

Future Active Indicative

	LATIN SINGULAR	ENGLISH SINGULAR	LATIN PLURAL	ENGLISH PLURAL
1ST	dūcam	I will lead	dūcēmus	we will lead
2ND	dūcēs	you will lead	dūcētis	you (pl.) will lead
3RD	dūcet	he will lead	dūcent	they will lead

Perfect Active Indicative

	LATIN SINGULAR	ENGLISH SINGULAR	LATIN PLURAL	ENGLISH PLURAL
1ST	dūxī	I (have) led	dūximus	we led
2ND	dūxistī	you led	dūxistis	you (pl.) led
3RD	dūxit	he led	dūxērunt	they led

Pluperfect Active Indicative

	LATIN SINGULAR	ENGLISH SINGULAR	LATIN PLURAL	ENGLISH PLURAL
1ST	dūxeram	I had led	dūxerāmus	we had led
2ND	dūxerās	you had led	dūxerātis	you (pl.) had led
3RD	dūxerat	he had led	dūxerant	they had led

Future Active Indicative

	LATIN SINGULAR	ENGLISH SINGULAR
1ST	dūxerō	I will have led
2ND	dūxeris	you will have led
3RD	dūxerit	he will have led

	LATIN PLURAL	ENGLISH PLURAL
	dūxerimus	we will have led
	dūxeritis	you (pl.) will have led
	dūxerint	they will have led

2. Decline *new fear*.

	LATIN SINGULAR	LATIN PLURAL
NOM.	metus novus	metūs novī
GEN.	metūs novī	metuum novōrum
DAT.	metuī novō	metibus novīs
ACC.	metum novum	metūs novōs
ABL.	metū novō	metibus novīs
VOC.	Ō metus nove	Ō metūs novī

3. Give a synopsis of *pōnō* in the second person plural.

	ACTIVE		PASSIVE	
	LATIN	ENGLISH	LATIN	ENGLISH
PRES.	pōnitis	you (pl.) place		
IMPF.	pōnēbātis	you were placing	*Third conjugation passive still to come!*	
FUT.	pōnētis	you will place		
PERF.	posuistis	you (have) placed		
PLUPF.	posuerātis	you had placed		
FT. PF.	posueritis	you will have placed		

C. Memorization

Fill in the blanks.

[1]**Psalmus Dāvīd.**

Dominus reget mē et nihil mihi dēerit.

²In <u>locō</u> pascuae <u>ibī</u> mē <u>conlocāvit</u> ;
<u>super</u> aquam <u>refectiōnis</u> ēducāvit <u>mē</u> .

D. English to Latin Translation

Translate each sentence from English to Latin.

1. That pirate will do many evil things, and then perhaps he will be killed by a brave sailor in a battle on the sea.
   <u>Is pīrāta multa mala aget, et ā/ab mīlite fortī in proeliō in marī deinde/tum fortasse necābitur.</u>

2. We are running out of the middle of the dark forest because we were teasing a wild pig and now it is hunting us.
   <u>[Nōs] ē/ex mediā silvā ātrā currimus quoniam/quod/quia porcum ferum lūdēbāmus et [is] nōs nunc captat.</u>

3. You (sg.) believe in God the Father, Son, and Holy Spirit, and you will believe in these true things always.
   <u>[Tū] in Deum Patrem, Fīlium, et Spīritum Sanctum crēdis, et in ea vēra semper crēdēs. [N.B. The Latin preposition</u> in <u>takes the accusative when used with</u> crēdō, <u>as you should remember from the Nicene Creed.]</u>

4. I will write a beautiful letter to the poet because I love him and perhaps I will be loved by him.
   <u>[Ego] poētae litterās pulchrās scrībam quoniam/quod/quia eum amō et ab eō fortasse amābor.</u>

5. The old knight could not conquer the dragon because his sword was not new.
   <u>Eques antīquus dracōnem nōn vincere/superāre poterat/potuit quoniam/quod/quia gladius eius novus nōn erat/fuit.</u>

6. The king will send five hundred knights into the middle of the battle with the giants, but will they defeat them?
   <u>Rex quīnquāgentā equitēs in medium proelium cum gigāntibus mittet, sed eōs vincent?</u>

7. There was great fear among the children because of the huge storm and angry thunder.
   <u>Erat metus magnus inter līberōs propter temptestātem ingentem et īrātum tonitrum.</u>

8. You (pl.) disciples were all speaking in seventeen new languages because you were moved by the Holy Spirit.
   <u>Vōs omnēs discipulī in septendecim linguīs novīs dīcēbātis quoniam/quod/quia ab Spīritū Sanctō movēbāminī [or mōtī estis].</u>

9. Jesus will put [His] hands over her and she will be well.

   Iēsus manūs super eam pōnet et [ea] salva erit.

10. Our leaders are leading us again to the port of the king of the pirates, but we are weary and wretched.

    Ducēs nostrī nōs ad portum rēgis pīrātārum iterum dūcunt, sed fessī miserīque [or et miserī] sumus.

E. Latin to English Translation

Mark 3:1–7 (Paraphrase)

1 Et Iēsus intrāvit iterum synagogam¹ et erat ibī homō. Is manum āridam² habet, et Pharisaeī Iēsum spectābant. Etiam invicem³ rogābant, "Cūrābit Iēsus hominem sabbatīs?"⁴—quod eum accūsāre cupiēbant.⁵ Et Iēsus āit hominī manū cum āridā: "Surge⁶ in medium." Et dīcit eīs, "Licet⁷ sabbatīs bene facere⁸ aut male? Animam salvam facere aut perdere?"⁹ Eī autem tacēbant.¹⁰ Iēsus īrātus est quoniam
5 corda eōrum caeca¹¹ erant, et dīcit hominī: "Extende¹² manum tuam." Et eam extendit et manus eius salva est. Pharisaeī autem invicem rogābant, "Quōmodo Iēsum perdēmus?"

Glossary
1. *synagōga, -ae* (f): synagogue
2. *āridus, -a, -um*: dry, withered
3. *invicem*: reciprocally (i.e., "[to] one another")
4. *sabbata, -ōrum* (n, pl.): Sabbath; *sabbatīs* is an ablative of time when, "on the Sabbath"
5. *cupiō, -ere, -īvī, -ītum*: I desire, wish (for)
6. *surgō, -ere, surrēxī, surrēctum*: I rise, arise
7. *licet*: it is permitted/allowed
8. *faciō, -ere, fēcī, factum*: I make, do
9. *perdō, -ere, -didī, -ditum*: I destroy, kill
10. *taceō, -ēre, -uī, -itum*: I am silent
11. *caecus, -a, -um*: blind
12. *extendō, -ere, -tendī, -tensum*: I stretch out, extend

And Jesus entered the synagogue again and there was a man there. This man had [habet *is a historical present*] a withered hand, and the Pharisees were watching Jesus. They were also asking themselves [or one another], "Will Jesus heal a man on the Sabbath?"—because they desired to accuse Him. And Jesus said to the man with the withered hand: "Rise [up] in the midst." And He said to them, "Is it permitted to do good on the Sabbath or evil [lit., to do well or badly]? To make a life whole or to destroy [it]?" But they were silent. Jesus was angry because their hearts were blind, and He said to the man: "Stretch out your hand." And he stretched it out and his hand was whole. The Pharisees, however, kept asking themselves, "How will we destroy Jesus?"

Lesson 26 Quiz (70 points)

A. Vocabulary (10 points)

Translate the following words. Give case(s) for prepositions.

1. I play: **lūdō**
2. super: (**+ acc./+ abl.**) **over, above, beyond**
3. fortasse: **perhaps**
4. quoniam: **because, since**
5. dūcō: **I lead, guide**
6. dīcō: **I say, speak**
7. quōmodo: **how, in what way**
8. medius: **middle (of)**
9. novus: **new**
10. crēdō: **I believe**

B. Grammar (15 points)

Give a synopsis of *pōnō* in the third person singular, active only.

	ACTIVE	
	LATIN	ENGLISH
PRES.	pōnit	he/she/it puts/places
IMPF.	pōnēbat	he was placing
FUT.	pōnet	he will place
PERF.	posuit	he (has) placed
PLUPF.	posuerat	he had placed
FT. PF.	posuerit	he will have placed

C. Translation (17 points)

Translate each sentence.

1. Good kings will always rule well, but evil kings rule badly.

   Rēgēs bonī bene semper regent, sed rēgēs malī male regunt.

2. Multum cibum ad viduās orbōsque mittimus.

   We are sending much food to widows and orphans.

D. Memorization (28 points)

Write Psalm 23:1–2 in Latin.

[1]Psalmus Dāvīd.

Dominus reget mē et nihil mihi dēerit.

[2]in locō pascuae ibī mē conlocāvit;

super aquam refectiōnis ēducāvit mē.

LESSON 27 (Student Edition p. 256)

Verbs: Third Conjugation Passive

1. Word List

12. *grātiās agō* (+ dat.) and 15. *poenās dō*—This lesson includes these two new idioms. If you want to say "We thank God" or "We give thanks to God," then you use *grātiās agimus* (because "we" are the subject) plus the indirect object, "God," in the dative: *Deō grātiās agimus*. When *poenās* appears with any form of *dō*, it means "to pay [not "to give"] the penalty." This seems counterintuitive, but makes sense if you think of someone paying a fine—giving it to the magistrate.

21. *cōram*, in the presence of, before; (adv.) personally, openly: This word can be used both as a preposition with an object, and as an adverb by itself. Both its uses are very closely related.

2. Derivatives/Memorization Helps

1. *arcus*, bow, arch, rainbow: arc, arcade, arch
2. *grātia*, grace, favor, kindness, thanks: grace, gracious, graceful, gratis
3. *lacus*, lake, tub, hollow: lake, lacuna, lagoon
4. *poena*, penalty, punishment: penalty, penal, pain, subpoena
5. *vēritas*, truth: verity, veritable, verify; see *vērus*, Lesson 22
6. *versus*, row, line (of poetry), furrow: verse, version, versification; see *vertō*, Lesson 28
7. *āridus*, dry: arid
8. *caecus*, blind: caecilian, caecum/cecum (part of the large intestine)
9. *grātus*, grateful, pleasing: grateful, gratitude, congratulate, congratulations; see *grātia* above
10. *cadō*, I fall, sink, drop: accident, incident, occasion
11. *frangō*, I break, smash, shatter: frangible, fragile, fracture
12. *grātiās agō*, I give thanks, I thank
13. *iungō*, I join, unite, yoke: junction, juncture; memory help: in the *jung*le, trees are *joined* with vines
14. *perdō*, I destroy, ruin, lose: perdition, Perdita (the name of the mother dog in *The Hundred and One Dalmatians*, whose puppies were *lost*—get it?)
15. *poenās dō*, I pay the penalty
16. *tangō*, I touch, strike: tangible, tactile, tact

17. *vehō*, I carry, convey: vehicle
18. *vīvō*, I live: vivid, vivacious; see *vīvus* [Lesson 20]
19. *atque (ac)*, and, and also
20. *cito*, quickly, fast, speedily: memory help—"I *quickly* killed the mos-*cito*"
21. *cōram*, in the presence of, before; (adv.) personally, openly: *coram Deō*, "in the presence of God"
22. *modo*, only, just, merely, but

3. Memorization—*Psalmus XXIII*

This lesson's lines are:

> [3]Animam meam convertit.
>> *He directs my soul.*
>
> Dēdūxit mē super sēmitās iūstitiae
>> *He has led me along paths of righteousness*
>
> propter nōmen suum
>> *because of His name.*

4. Grammar

Third Conjugation Verbs, Passive:

Like its active counterpart, the third conjugation passive is a bit tricky in the present system (due to those vowels) but perfectly normal in the perfect system. Review the vowel chant from the present active: *ō, i, i, i, i, u!* These will be your vowels for the present passive—with one exception (second person singular):

	SINGULAR	PLURAL
1ST	-ō	-i-
2ND	-e-	-i-
3RD	-i-	-u-

The present passive tense of *mittō* will conjugate like this:

Present Passive Indicative

	LATIN SINGULAR	ENGLISH SINGULAR	LATIN PLURAL	ENGLISH PLURAL
1ST	mittor	I am (being) sent	mittimur	we are sent
2ND	mitteris	you are sent	mittiminī	you (pl.) are sent
3RD	mittitur	he/she/it is sent	mittuntur	they are sent

Again, you can help your students remember this anomaly by emphasizing how bad and nasally it would sound if it were *-iris* (really emphasize the "eeeeeeeris").

The imperfect passive is simple like the active, with that long *-ē-* for the whole chant:

Imperfect Passive Indicative

	LATIN SINGULAR	ENGLISH SINGULAR	LATIN PLURAL	ENGLISH PLURAL
1ST	mittēbar	I was being sent	mittēbāmur	we were being sent
2ND	mittēbāris	you were being sent	mittēbāminī	you (pl.) were being sent
3RD	mittēbātur	he/she/it was being sent	mittēbantur	they were being sent

The future passive of the third conjugation also employs a vowel change rather than using our customary *-bor, -beris, -bitur*. We use the same *a, e, e, e, e, e* pattern, but in the passive the third person singular *-ē-* will be long rather than short as in the active:

	SINGULAR	PLURAL
1ST	-a-	-ē-
2ND	-ē-	-ē-
3RD	-ē-	-e-

To this set of vowels we add our regular, basic passive endings: *-r, -ris, -tur, -mur, -minī, -ntur*:

Future Passive Indicative

	LATIN SINGULAR	ENGLISH SINGULAR	LATIN PLURAL	ENGLISH PLURAL
1ST	mittar	I will be sent	mittēmur	we will be sent
2ND	mittēris	you will be sent	mittēminī	you (pl.) will be sent
3RD	mittētur	he/she/it will be sent	mittentur	they will be sent

If it is helpful to your students, they can chant *-ar, -ēris, -ētur, -ēmur, -ēminī, -entur!* as an alternate future passive chant. Note that the difference between the second person singular present passive and the second singular future passive is that short versus long vowel: *mitteris,* you are being sent; *mittēris,* you will be sent.

We come now to the perfect passive system of the third conjugation, where you may rejoice—they are formed just like the perfect passives we have been practicing. Use the 4th principal part plus the appropriate form of *sum*, and you're set!

Perfect Passive Indicative

	LATIN SINGULAR	ENGLISH SINGULAR	LATIN PLURAL	ENGLISH PLURAL
1ST	missus/a/um sum	I was/have been sent	missī/ae/a sumus	we were/have been sent
2ND	missus/a/um es	you were/have been sent	missī/ae/a estis	you (pl.) were/have been sent
3RD	missus/a/um est	he/she/it was/has been sent	missī/ae/a sunt	they were/have been sent

Pluperfect Passive Indicative

	LATIN SINGULAR	ENGLISH SINGULAR	LATIN PLURAL	ENGLISH PLURAL
1ST	missus/a/um eram	I had been sent	missī/ae/a erāmus	we had been sent
2ND	missus/a/um erās	you had been sent	missī/ae/a erātis	you (pl.) had been sent
3RD	missus/a/um erat	he/she/it had been sent	missī/ae/a erant	they had been sent

Future Perfect Passive Indicative

	LATIN SINGULAR	ENGLISH SINGULAR	LATIN PLURAL	ENGLISH PLURAL
1ST	missus/a/um erō	I will have been sent	missī/ae/a erimus	we will have been sent
2ND	missus/a/um eris	you will have been sent	missī/ae/a eritis	you (pl.) will have been sent
3RD	missus/a/um erit	he/she/it will have been sent	missī/ae/a erunt	they will have been sent

Once again, rather than providing a chant, I have given the students an example verb to study in order to see the vowels changing in the present passive system.

5. Worksheet

The Latin to English stories this lesson and next will tell the tale of King Midas in two parts. He is best known for the "golden touch," which is recounted this lesson.

E. *Mythology Quiz:* This for-fun assignment makes for lots of interesting discussions about mythology.

6. Quiz

Administer Quiz 27 when the students are ready.

Lesson 27 Worksheet

A. Vocabulary

Translate the following words from Latin to English or English to Latin as appropriate. For the verbs, also fill in the missing principal parts. For each preposition, include which case(s) it takes.

1. lacus: **lake, tub, hollow**
2. perdō, **perdere**, **perdidī**, **perditum**: **I destroy, ruin, lose**
3. I fall: **cadō**, **-ere**, **cecidī**, **casum**
4. ac: **and, and also**
5. I touch, strike: **tangō**, **tangere**, **tetigī**, **tactum**
6. arcus: **bow, arch, rainbow**
7. poena: **penalty, punishment**
8. fortasse: **perhaps**
9. grātus: **grateful, pleasing**
10. blind: **caecus**
11. cito: **quickly, fast, speedily**
12. truth: **vēritas**
13. frangō, **frangere**, **frēgī**, **fractum**: **I break, smash, shatter**
14. I ride: **vehō**, **-ere**, **vexī**, **vectum**
15. versus: **row, line (of poetry), furrow**
16. āridus: **dry**
17. tonitrus: **thunder**
18. middle: **medius**
19. grātia: **grace, favor, kindness, thanks**
20. again: **iterum**
21. cōram: **(+ abl.) in the presence of, before; (adv.) personally, openly**
22. I join: **iungō**, **iungere**, **iunxī**, **iunctum**
23. currō, **currere**, **cūcurrī**, **cursum**: **I run**
24. modo: **only, just, merely, but**
25. because of: **propter (+ acc.)**

B. Grammar

1. Conjugate *dūcō* in the passive indicative only.

Present Passive Indicative

	LATIN SINGULAR	ENGLISH SINGULAR
1ST	dūcor	I am (being) led
2ND	dūceris	you are (being) led
3RD	dūcitur	he/she/it is (being) led

	LATIN PLURAL	ENGLISH PLURAL
	dūcimur	we are (being) led
	dūcitur	you (pl.) are (being) led
	dūcuntur	they are (being) led

Imperfect Passive Indicative

	LATIN SINGULAR	ENGLISH SINGULAR
1ST	dūcēbar	I was (being) led
2ND	dūcēbāris	you were (being) led
3RD	dūcēbātur	he/she/it was (being) led

	LATIN PLURAL	ENGLISH PLURAL
	dūcēbāmur	we were (being) led
	dūcēbāminī	you (pl.) were (being) led
	dūcēbantur	they were (being) led

Future Passive Indicative

	LATIN SINGULAR	ENGLISH SINGULAR
1ST	dūcar	I will be led
2ND	dūcēris	you will be led
3RD	dūcētur	he/she/it will be led

	LATIN PLURAL	ENGLISH PLURAL
	dūcēmur	we will be led
	dūcēminī	you (pl.) will be led
	dūcentur	they will be led

Perfect Passive Indicative

	LATIN SINGULAR	ENGLISH SINGULAR
1ST	ductus/a/um sum	I was/have been led
2ND	ductus es	you were led
3RD	ductus est	he was led

	LATIN PLURAL	ENGLISH PLURAL
	ductī/ae/a sumus	we were led
	ductī estis	you (pl.) were led
	ductī sunt	they were led

Pluperfect Passive Indicative

	LATIN SINGULAR	ENGLISH SINGULAR	LATIN PLURAL	ENGLISH PLURAL
1ST	ductus/a/um eram	I had been led	ductī/ae/a erāmus	we had been led
2ND	ductus erās	you had been led	ductī erātis	you (pl.) had been led
3RD	ductus erat	he had been led	ductī erant	they had been led

Future Perfect Passive Indicative

	LATIN SINGULAR	ENGLISH SINGULAR	LATIN PLURAL	ENGLISH PLURAL
1ST	ductus/a/um erō	I will have been led	ductī/ae/a erimus	we will have been led
2ND	ductus eris	you will have been led	ductī eritis	you (pl.) will have been led
3RD	ductus erit	he will have been led	ductī erunt	they will have been led

2. Give a synopsis of *perdō* in the third person plural.

	ACTIVE		PASSIVE	
	LATIN	ENGLISH	LATIN	ENGLISH
PRES.	perdunt	they destroy	perduntur	they are (being) destroyed
IMPF.	perdēbant	they were destroying	perdēbantur	they were (being) destroyed
FUT.	perdent	they will destroy	perdentur	they will be destroyed
PERF.	perdidērunt	they (have) destroyed	perditī/ae/a sunt	they were/have been destroyed
PLUPF.	perdiderant	they had destroyed	perditī/ae/a erant	they had been destroyed
FT. PF.	perdiderint	they will have destroyed	perditī/ae/a erunt	they will have been destroyed

C. Memorization

Fill in the blanks.

[1]<u>Psalmus Dāvīd.</u>

<u>Dominus reget mē et nihil mihi dēerit.</u>

[2]<u>in locō pascuae ibī mē conlocāvit;</u>

<u>super aquam refectiōnis ēducāvit mē.</u>

[3]<u>Animam</u> meam <u>convertit.</u>

Dēdūxit <u>mē</u> super <u>sēmitās</u> iūstitiae

<u>propter</u> nōmen <u>suum</u> .

D. English to Latin Translation

Translate each sentence from English to Latin.

1. We all were afraid in the presence of the evil king, and fell to our faces on the ground.

   <u>[Nōs] omnēs coram rēge malō timuimus [timēbāmus], et ad vultūs nostrōs in terrā cecidimus.</u>

2. Your land will be destroyed if the fiery dragon will fly to it on wings of death.

   <u>Terra/patria/tellūs vestra/tua perdētur sī draco caldus ad eam ālīs mortis volābit.</u>

3. The bad little boy did not speak the truth, and therefore he paid the penalty.

   <u>Puer malus [et] parvus vēritātem nōn dīxit, et/atque ergō poēnās dedit.</u>

4. After the storm a rainbow was seen in the heavens, and beautiful lines of poetry will be written about it.

   <u>Post tempestātem arcus in caelīs vīsus est [vidēbātur], et versūs pulchrī dē eō scrībentur.</u>

5. We had yoked the two cows and then they carried us into the town with our grain.

   <u>Duōs [duās] bovēs iūnxerāmus et [eī/eae] nōs in oppidum cum frūmentō nostrō vexērunt.</u>

6. The beautiful woman smiled at the wretched poet and now songs are being written quickly to her by the grateful man.

   <u>Pulchra [fēmina] poētam miserum rīsit [rīdēbat] et nunc cantūs eī ab grātō [virō] citō scrībuntur.</u>

7. "You are being destroyed by much wine," the pirate's grandmother was telling him, but he only laughed.

   "[Tū] vīnō multō perderis," avia pīrātae eī dīcēbat, sed [is] modo rīsit [rīdēbat].

8. The dry tree is being broken by the storm, but will it also fall over our house?

   Arbor āridus ab tempestāte frangitur, sed [is] super domum nostrum atque/etiam cadet?

9. My aunt and uncle live near a great lake and all their food is carried there in boats.

   Amita mea et avunculus/patruus meus prope lacum magnum vīvunt [*although* habitant *may be better*] et omnis cibus eōrum nāvibus ibī vehitur.

10. A man's withered hand is now whole and many blind can see because of Jesus' grace.

    Manus ārida virī/hominis salva nunc est et multī caecī propter grātiam Iēsū vidēre possunt.

E. Latin to English Translation

1   **Fābula Midae[1] I: Cāsus[2] Infēlix in Alchemiā[3]**

Ōlim Sīlēnus,[4] magister amīcusque Bacchī,[5] multum vīnum pōtāverat et ab Bacchō errāverat. Ab servīs Midae, rex Phrygiae,[6] inventus est.[7] Midās eī epulās multās et magnās dedit, ac eum ad deum vīnī deinde dūxit. Bacchus gaudēbat quoniam Sīlēnus salvus erat et dīxit: "Ō Midās, rogā ūllum[8] prō praemiō[9]
5   tuō et tibi dabō." Midās stultus avārusque erat, et respondit: "Id mihi dā: Quandō ūllum tangam, in aurum mūtābitur." Bacchus tristis erat propter stultitiam[10] Midae, sed dīxit: "Id dātur." Midās ad rēgiam ambulāvit, et lapidem[11] tetigit—in aurum mūtātus est! Deinde arborem tetigit, deinde frūctum—duo nunc aurum erant! Laetus erat. "Dīvitiās," āit, "magnās habēbō." In rēgiā servīs dīxit: "Mihi epulās magnās et multum vīnum portāte!" Cibum in ōs pōnere temptāvit,[12] sed in aurum iam mūtātus erat.
10 Atque vīnum eius in aurum mūtātum est, et id nōn pōtāre potuit. Nunc Midās tristis erat—"Quōmodo vivam sī nec mandūcāre nec pōtāre poterō?" dīxit. "Bacche, mē iuvā!" Itaque Bacchus dīxit, "In flūmine Pactōlō[13] lavā,[14] et salvus eris." Midās ergō ad flūmen cito properāvit et in eō lāvit. Deinde omnia tangere potuit, et in aurum nōn mūtāta sunt. Posteā[15] erat autem semper multum aurum in eō flūmine et prope terram. Midās vītam dīvitiārum tum reliquit[16] et in agrīs montibusque habitāvit.

Glossary
1. *Midās, -ae* (m): Midas, king of Phrygia
2. *casus, -ūs* (m): incident, event; misfortune, downfall
3. *alchemia, -ae* (f): alchemy, the study of how to turn metals into gold
4. *Sīlēnus, -ī* (m): Silenus, pudgy old fellow (usually drunk), former tutor and longtime companion of Bacchus
5. *Bacchus, -ī* (m): Bacchus, the god of wine
6. *Phrygia, -ae* (f): Phrygia, a land in Asia Minor
7. *inveniō, -īre, -vēnī, -ventum*: I find
8. *ūllus, -a, -um*: anyone, anything
9. *praemium, -ī* (n): reward
10. *stultitia, -ae* (f): foolishness, folly
11. *lapis, -idis* (m): stone
12. *temptō* (1): I attempt
13. *Pactōlus, -ī* (m): Pactolus, a river in Lydia in Asia Minor
14. *lavō, -āre, lāvī, lōtum/lavātum*: I wash
15. *posteā*: afterwards
16. *relinquō, -ere, -līquī, -lictum*: I abandon

The Story of Midas I: An Unfortunate Incident in Alchemy

Once upon a time, Silenus, teacher and friend of Bacchus, had been drinking much wine and had wandered away from Bacchus. He was found by the servants of Midas, king of Phrygia. Midas gave him many great feasts, and then led him [back] to the god of wine. Bacchus rejoiced because Silenus was safe, and said, "O Midas, ask anything for your reward and I will give [it] to you." Midas was foolish and greedy, and answered: "Grant me this: When I [will] touch anything, it will be changed into gold." Bacchus was sad because of Midas's folly, but he said, "It is granted." Midas walked to his palace, and touched a stone—it was changed into gold! Then he touched a tree, then a [piece of] fruit—both were now gold! He was happy. "I will have great riches!" he said. In [his] palace he said to [his] servants: "Bring me a great feast and much wine!" He attempted to put food in [his] mouth, but it had already been changed into gold. His wine also was changed into gold, and he could not drink it. Now Midas was sad—"How will I live if I will not be able to eat or drink?" he said. "Bacchus, help me!" And so Bacchus said, "Wash in the Pactolus River and you will be cured." Therefore, Midas quickly hastened to the river and washed in it. Then he could touch all things and they were not changed into gold. Afterwards however there was always much gold in this river and the land nearby. Midas then abandoned [his] life of wealth and lived in the fields and mountains.

F. For Fun: Mythology Matching

How well do you know the major Roman gods? For each god or goddess below, correctly match the deity up with its correct Greek name and description from the lists on the right..

GOD/GODDESS	GREEK NAME	DESCRIPTION
Bacchus	G	10
Ceres	H	4
Diana	K	6
Juno	B	9
Jupiter	D	2
Mars	M	3
Mercury	J	5
Minerva	I	1
Neptune	C	13
Phoebus	L	7
Pluto	F	12
Venus	A	11
Vulcan	E	8

A. Aphrodite
B. Hera
C. Poseidon
D. Zeus
E. Hephaestus
F. Hades
G. Dionysius
H. Demeter
I. Athena
J. Hermes
K. Artemis
L. Apollo
M. Ares

1. goddess of wisdom
2. king of the gods
3. god of war
4. goddess of agriculture
5. messenger god
6. goddess of the hunt
7. god of prophecy
8. god of fire
9. queen of the gods
10. god of wine
11. goddess of love
12. god of the underworld
13. god of the sea

Lesson 27 Quiz (78 points)

A. Vocabulary (10 points)

Translate the following words.

1. cadō: **I fall, sink, drop**
2. vultus: **face, expression**
3. I live: **vīvō**
4. perdō: **I destroy, ruin, lose**
5. lacus: **lake, tub, hollow**
6. versus: **row, line (of poetry), furrow**
7. ac: **and, and also**
8. I join: **iungō**
9. modo: **only, just, merely, but**
10. rainbow: **arcus**

B. Grammar (21 points)

Give a synopsis of *frangō* in the third person singular, active and passive.

	ACTIVE		PASSIVE	
	LATIN	ENGLISH	LATIN	ENGLISH
PRES.	frangit	he/she/it breaks	frangitur	he is (being) broken
IMPF.	frangēbat	he was breaking	frangēbātur	he was (being) broken
FUT.	franget	he will break	frangētur	he will be broken
PERF.	frēgit	he broke, has broken	fractus/a/um est	he was/has been broken
PLUPF.	frēgerat	he had broken	fractus/a/um erat	he had been broken
FT. PF.	frēgerit	he will have broken	fractus/a/um erit	he will have been broken

C. Translation (15 points)

Translate each sentence.

1. Servī miserī cōram rēgīnā vehentur, sed poenās dabunt?

   <u>The wretched servants will be carried before the queen, but will they pay the penalty?</u>

2. The greedy girl quickly ate all the cookies and will not thank [her] mother.

   <u>Puella avāra omnia crustula cito mandūcāvit et mātrī grātiās nōn aget.</u>

D. Memorization (32 points)

Write Psalm 23:1–3 in Latin.

[1]<u>Psalmus Dāvīd.</u>

<u>Dominus reget mē et nihil mihi dēerit.</u>

[2]<u>in locō pascuae ibī mē conlocāvit;</u>

<u>super aquam refectiōnis ēducāvit mē.</u>

[3]<u>Animam meam convertit.</u>

<u>Dēdūxit mē super sēmitās iūstitiae</u>

<u>propter nōmen suum.</u>

LESSON 28 (Student Edition p. 266)

Nouns: Fifth Declension / Time Constructions

1. Word List

9. *cōgō*—As the principal parts make clear, *cōgō* is a compound verb from *agō* (the *cō-* part can mean "together, thoroughly," among other things).

2. Derivatives/Memorization Helps

1. *cāsus*, event, incident; misfortune, downfall: see *cadō*, Lesson 27
2. *diēs*, day, period of time: diary, diurnal, journey, journal, dismal (from *diēs* + *malus*)
3. *faciēs*, shape, form; face; character: face, facet, facial; *primā faciē*, "at first glance, on its appearance"
4. *fidēs*, faith: fidelity, confide, infidel, perfidy
5. *merīdiēs*, noon: meridian; a.m. = *ante merīdiem*, "before noon"; p.m. = *post merīdiem*, "after noon"
6. *rēs*, thing: reify, real, realistic
7. *spēs*, hope: despair, desperation; memory help: "spēs, speī, *hope* and pray"
8. *cēdō*, I go, move, yield: cede, proceed/procession, intercede/intercession, succeed/succession
9. *cōgō*, I drive together, force, compel: cogent, coagulate
10. *dēfendō*, I defend: defend, defense, defensible, fence
11. *dēligō*, I pick, choose: see *legō* below
12. *gerō*, I bear, carry on: belligerent, gestation, gesture, gerund
13. *legō*, I read, choose: elect, (il)legible, legend
14. *relinquō*, I abandon, leave behind: relinquish, relict, delinquent
15. *surgō*, I (a)rise: surge, insurgence, insurrection
16. *vertō*, I turn, change: divorce, convert/conversion, revert/reversion, invert/inversion, pervert/perversion
17. *iūxta*, near (to), close to/by: juxtapose, juxtaposition
18. *postea*, afterwards
19. *quam*, as, than, how
20. *secundum*, after; according to

3. Memorization—*Psalmus XXIII*

This lesson's lines are:

⁴Nam et sī ambulāverō in mediō umbrae mortis
> *For even if I walk (lit., "will have walked") in the midst of the shadow of death*

nōn timēbō mala, quoniam tū mēcum es;
> *I will not fear evils, because you are with me;*

virga tua et baculus tuus ipsa mē consōlāta sunt.
> *Your rod and Your staff themselves have comforted me.*

4. Grammar

Fifth Declension Noun Endings:

Rejoice! You have now reached the fifth and *final* Latin noun declension. Although it does not contain a boatload of nouns, those it does are quite important (e.g., *diēs,* "day" or *rēs,* "thing"). By now your students should be familiar enough with gender, number, and case that learning a new declension will not be difficult—just a few more endings to memorize, that's all!

Most fifth declension nouns are feminine, with the exception of *diēs* and its compound *merīdiēs,* which are (usually) masculine. There are no neuters. Here are the new endings:

	LATIN SINGULAR	ENGLISH SINGULAR	LATIN PLURAL	ENGLISH PLURAL
NOMINATIVE	-ēs	a/the *noun* [subject]	-ēs	the *nouns* [subject]
GENITIVE	-eī/-ēī	of the *noun,* the *noun's*	-ērum	of the *nouns,* the *nouns'*
DATIVE	-eī/-ēī	to/for the *noun*	-ēbus	to/for the *nouns*
ACCUSATIVE	-em	a/the *noun* [object]	-ēs	the *nouns* [object]
ABLATIVE	-ē	by/with/from the *noun*	-ēbus	by/with/from the *nouns*
VOCATIVE	-ēs	O *noun*	-ēs	O *nouns*

As usual, an adjective must match its noun in gender, number, and case (*not* in declension), so a fifth declension noun can of course be modified by a first/second declension adjective or a third declension adjective. (There are no fourth or fifth declension adjectives, in case you were wondering.) Here is the fifth declension noun *fidēs* ("faith") declined with a couple of adjectives:

	LATIN SINGULAR	LATIN PLURAL
NOMINATIVE	antīqua fidēs fortis	antīquae fidēs fortēs
GENITIVE	antīquae fideī fortis	antīquārum fidērum fortium
DATIVE	antīquae fideī fortī	antīquīs fidēbus fortibus
ACCUSATIVE	antīquam fidem fortem	antīquās fidēs fortēs
ABLATIVE	antīquā fidē fortī	antīquīs fidēbus fortibus
VOCATIVE	Ō antīqua fidēs fortis	Ō antīquae fidēs fortēs

Time Constructions

1. **Ablative of Time When and Time Within Which:** In Latin, you can do quite a bit with the ablative without using prepositions. One such usage is expressing the time when something happens (or happened), or the time within which it happened. If you want to say (as in the Creed) that "And He rose again on the third day," you simply put "third day" in the ablative: *Et resurrēxit tertiā diē*. You could also say, "He will rise again within (in) three days": *Tribus diēbus resurget*.

2. **Accusative of Duration of Time:** If you want to express how long it took to do something, you will use the accusative and *not* the ablative: "He remained there for three days" is *Trēs diēs ibī mānsit*. Another example would be "The king waged war for two years"—*Rex bellum duōs annōs gessit*.

5. Worksheet

There are no English to Latin sentences this lesson. Instead, the students will be doing more parsing and noun analysis to firm up the new declensions and conjugation.

6. Quiz

Administer Quiz 28 when the students are ready.

Lesson 28 Worksheet

A. Vocabulary

Translate the following words from Latin to English or English to Latin as appropriate. For the verbs, also fill in the missing principal parts. For each preposition, include which case(s) it takes.

1. dēligō, **dēligere**, **dēlēgī**, **dēlēctum**: **I pick, choose**
2. penalty: **poena**
3. legō, **legere**, **lēgī**, **lēctum**: **I read, choose**
4. I yield: **cēdō**, **-ere**, **cessī**, **cessum**
5. pōnō, **pōnere**, **posuī**, **positum**: **I put, place**
6. than: **quam**
7. iterum: **again, a second time**
8. gerō, **gerere**, **gessī**, **gestum**: **I bear, carry on**
9. surgō, **surgere**, **surrēxī**, **surrēctum**: **I (a)rise**
10. day: **diēs**
11. relinquō, **relinqere**, **relīquī**, **relictum**: **I abandon, leave behind**
12. faciēs: **shape, form; face; character**
13. secundum: **(+ acc.) after; according to**
14. cōgō, **cōgere**, **coēgī**, **coactum**: **I drive together, force, compel**
15. faith: **fidēs**
16. iūxta: **(+ acc.) near (to), close to/by**
17. spēs: **hope**
18. noon: **merīdiēs**
19. cāsus: **event, incident; misfortune, downfall**
20. metus: **fear, dread**
21. rēs: **thing**
22. afterwards: **postea**
23. dēfendō, **dēfendere**, **dēfendī**, **dēfēnsum**: I defend
24. āridus: **dry**
25. cornū: **horn**

B. Grammar

1. Decline *new thing*.

	LATIN SINGULAR	LATIN PLURAL
NOM.	rēs nova	rēs novae
GEN.	reī novae	rērum novārum
DAT.	reī novae	rēbus novīs
ACC.	rem novam	rēs novās
ABL.	rē novā	rēbus novīs
VOC.	Ō rēs nova	Ō rēs novae

2. Decline *unfortunate incident*.

	LATIN SINGULAR	LATIN PLURAL
NOM.	cāsus infēlix	cāsūs infēlicēs
GEN.	cāsūs infēlicis	cāsuum infēlicium
DAT.	cāsuī infēlicī	cāsibus infēlicibus
ACC.	cāsum infēlicem	cāsūs infēlicēs
ABL.	cāsū infēlicī	cāsibus infēlicibus
VOC.	Ō cāsus infēlix	Ō cāsūs infēlicēs

3. Give a synopsis of *cōgō* in the first person plural.

	ACTIVE		PASSIVE	
	LATIN	ENGLISH	LATIN	ENGLISH
PRES.	cōgimus	we compel	cōgimur	we are (being) compelled
IMPF.	cōgēbāmus	we were compelling	cōgēbāmur	we were (being) compelled
FUT.	cōgēmus	we will compel	cōgēmur	we will be compelled
PERF.	cōēgimus	we (have) compelled	cōāctī/ae/a sumus	we were/have been compelled
PLUPF.	cōēgerāmus	we had compelled	cōāctī/ae/a erāmus	we had been compelled
FT. PF.	cōēgerimus	we will have compelled	cōāctī/ae/a erimus	we will have been compelled

C. Memorization

Fill in the blanks.

¹Psalmus Dāvīd.

Dominus reget mē et nihil mihi dēerit.

²In locō pascuae ibī mē conlocāvit;

super aquam refectiōnis ēducāvit mē,

³Animam meam convertit.

Dēdūxit mē super sēmitās iūstitiae

propter nōmen suum.

⁴**Nam** _____ et **sī** _____ ambulāverō in **mediō** _____ **umbrae** _____ mortis,

nōn **timēbō** _____ mala **quoniam** _____ tū **mēcum** _____ **es;** _____

virga _____ tua **et** _____ **baculus** _____ tuus **ipsa** _____ mē **consōlāta** _____ sunt.

D. English to Latin Translation

Parse and translate each verb. To parse a verb, list its attributes: person, number, tense, voice, and mood, if it is an indicative verb; if it is an infinitive, give tense, voice, and mood only. Then give the first principal part of the verb it comes from. (Abbreviate but keep your meaning clear.) An example is given below.

	VERB	PERSON	NBR.	TENSE	VOICE	MOOD	1ST PRIN. PART.	TRANSLATION
	cūrāverās	2nd	Sg.	Plupf.	Act.	Ind.	cūrō	you had cared for
1.	amātī erunt	3rd	Pl.	Fut. Perf.	Pas.	Ind.	amō	they will have been loved
2.	gessit	3rd	Sg.	Perf.	Act.	Ind.	gerō	he/she/it (has) carried
3.	legentur	3rd	Pl.	Fut.	Pas.	Ind.	legō	they will be read
4.	videntur	3rd	Pl.	Pres.	Pas.	Ind.	videō	they are (being) seen, they seem
5.	dūceris	2nd	Sg.	Pres.	Pas.	Ind.	dūcō	you are (being) led
6.	dūcēris	2nd	Sg.	Fut.	Pas.	Ind.	dūcō	you will be led
7.	duxeris	2nd	Sg.	Fut. Perf.	Act.	Ind.	dūcō	you will have led
8.	scrībit	3rd	Sg.	Pres.	Act.	Ind.	scrībō	he/she/it writes

9.	dēfendit	3rd	Sg.	Pres.	Act.	Ind.	dēfendō	he/she/it defends
		3rd	Sg.	Perf.	Act.	Ind.	dēfendō	he/she/it (has) defended
10.	victī erātis	2nd	Pl.	Pluperf.	Pas.	Ind.	vincō	you (pl.) had been conquered
11.	perdor	1st	Sg.	Pres.	Pas.	Ind.	perdō	I am (being) destroyed
12.	regēminī	2nd	Pl.	Fut.	Pas.	Ind.	regō	you (pl.) will be ruled
13.	audēs	2nd	Sg.	Pres.	Act.	Ind.	audeō	you dare
14.	coactae sumus	1st	Pl.	Perf.	Pas.	Ind.	cōgō	we were/have been compelled
15.	cecidistis	2nd	Pl.	Perf.	Act.	Ind.	cadō	you fell, have fallen

Identify and translate all possible options for the following noun/adjective combinations.

	PHRASE	GENDER, NUMBER, CASE	TRANSLATION
1.	lacuum mediōcrium	Masc. Pl. Gen.	of the ordinary lakes
2.	potēns tempestās	Fem. Sg. Nom.	powerful storm (subject)
3.	speī bonae	Fem. Sg. Gen. Fem. Sg. Dat.	of the good hope to/for the good hope
4.	caecī patruī	Masc. Sg. Gen. Masc. Pl. Nom.	of the blind uncle blind uncles (subject)
5.	genū ingentī	Neut. Sg. Dat. Neut. Sg. Abl.	to/for the huge knee by/with/from the huge knee
6.	exercituī stultō	Masc. Sg. Dat.	to/for the foolish army
7.	diēs caldī	Masc. Pl. Nom.	hot days (subject)
8.	mala animālia	Neut. Pl. Nom. Neut. Pl. Acc.	evil animals (subject) evil animals (object)

9.	mediās rēs	Fem. Pl. Acc.	middle [of] things (object)
10.	hostis celeris	Masc. Sg. Gen.	of the swift enemy [Note: The case cannot be nominative, because hostis is masculine, and in the nominative would be paired with the masculine adjective—hostis celer.]
11.	pulchrīs faciēbus	Fem. Pl. Dat. Fem. Pl. Abl.	to/for the beautiful faces by/with/from the beautiful faces
12.	manūs albae	Fem. Sg. Gen. Fem. Pl. Nom.	of the white hand white hands (subject)
13.	linguae mīrae	Fem. Sg. Gen. Fem. Sg. Dat. Fem. Pl. Nom.	of the strange language to/for the strange language strange languages (subject)
14.	fortī fidē	Fem. Sg. Abl.	by/with/from the strong faith
15.	agrī viridēs	Masc. Pl. Nom.	green fields (subject)

E. Latin to English Translation

1 **Fābula Midae II: Aurēs[1] Asīnī**

Post cāsum tactūs[2] aureī, Midās in agrīs montibusque multōs annōs habitābat. Deum Pāna[3] coluit[4] et laetus diū erat. Ōlim autem Apollō[5] ad montēs vēnit.[6] Pān dīxit, "Ego sum mūsicus[7] melior[8] quam Apollō!" sed Apollō dīxit, "Nōn es!" Pān Apollōnī nōn cessit; itaque certāmen[9] dēclārātum est. Tmōlus,[10]
5 deus montis, iūdex[11] appellātus est. Pān calamīs[12] cantāvit,[13] et fīdus Midās stupōre[14] victus est. "Quam pulchrum!" clāmāvit. Sed Apollō lyrā[15] deinde cantāvit, et Tmōlus statim dēclārāvit, "Apollō mūsicus melior est!" Midās dīxit, "Nōn est!" et nōn cēssit. Apollō īrātus erat et dīxit: "Aurēs tuae malae stultaeque sunt! Nunc tū aurēs asinī habēbis!" Aurēs Midae in aurēs asinī statim mūtātae sunt! Tristis erat et postea semper mītram[16] purpuream gessit et eās celāvit.[17] Tonsor[18] eius autem eās vīdit; itaque Midās dīxit:
10 "Sī dē eīs auribus dīcēs, necāberis!" Sed tonsor sēcrētum[19] nōn occultāre potuit, et ergō in terrā fōdit[20] et sēcrētum in eam susurrāvit.[21] Deinde calamī multī flōruērunt, et in ventō[22] susurrant: "Rēx Midās aurēs asinī habet!"

Glossary
1. *auris, -is* (f): ear
2. *tactus, -ūs* (m): touch
3. *Pān, Pānos* (acc. *Pāna*) (m): Pan, the god of woods, shepherds, and flocks
4. *colō, -ere, coluī, cultum*: I cultivate, inhabit, worship
5. *Apollō, -inis* (m): Apollo, the god of prophesy, music, archery, the sun, etc.
6. *veniō, -īre, vēnī, ventūrum*: I come
7. *mūsicus, -ī* (m): musician
8. *melior, -ius*: better
9. *certāmen, -minis* (n): contest
10. *Tmōlus, -ī* (m): Tmolus, a god and a mountain in Lydia
11. *iūdex, -dicis* (m): judge
12. *calamus, -ī* (m): reed, reed-pipe
13. *cantō* can also mean "play"; the musical instrument being played takes the ablative
14. *stupor, -ōris* (m): amazement, astonishment
15. *lyra, -ae* (f): lyre
16. *mītra, -ae* (f): turban
17. *celō* (1): I hide, conceal
18. *tonsor, -ōris* (m): barber
19. *sēcrētum, -ī* (n): secret
20. *fodiō, -ere, fōdī, fossum*: I dig
21. *susurrō* (1): I whisper
22. *ventus, -ī* (m): wind

The Story of Midas II: Donkey's Ears

After the incident of the golden touch, Midas was living in the fields and mountains for many years. He worshipped the god Pan and was happy for a long time. Once, however, Apollo came to the mountains. Pan said, "I am a better musician than Apollo!" but Apollo said, "You are not!" Pan did not yield to Apollo; and so a contest was declared. Tmolus, god of mountain, was named the judge. Pan played [his] pipes, and faithful Midas was overcome with amazement. "How beautiful!" he shouted. But then Apollo played the lyre, and immediately Tmolus declared, "Apollo is the better musician!" Midas said, "He is not!" and he did not yield. Apollo was angry and said, "Your ears are bad and foolish. You will now have donkey's ears!" Immediately Midas's ears were changed into the ears of a donkey! He was sad and afterwards always wore a purple turban and hid them. His barber saw them, however; and so Midas said, "If you [will] speak about these ears, you will be killed!" The barber could not conceal the secret, and therefore he dug in the ground and whispered the secret into it. From that place many reeds flourished, and in the wind the reeds say: "King Midas has donkey's ears!"

Lesson 28 Quiz (87 points)

A. Vocabulary (10 points)

Translate the following words.

1. pōnō: **I put, place**
2. gerō: **I bear, carry on**
3. I arise: **surgō**
4. cōgō: **I drive together, force, compel**
5. I send: **mittō**
6. merīdiēs: **noon**
7. spēs: **hope**
8. postea: **afterwards**
9. dēligō: **I pick, choose**
10. according to: **secundum (+ acc.)**

B. Grammar (24 points)

Give a synopsis of *relinquō* in the second person plural.

	ACTIVE		PASSIVE	
	LATIN	ENGLISH	LATIN	ENGLISH
PRES.	relinquitis	you (pl.) abandon	relinquiminī	you (pl.) are (being) abandoned
IMPF.	relinquēbātis	you (pl.) were abandoning	relinquēbāminī	you (pl.) were (being) abandoned
FUT.	relinquētis	you (pl.) will abandon	relinquēminī	you (pl.) will be abandoned
PERF.	relīquistis	you (pl.) (have) abandoned	relictī/ae/a estis	you (pl.) were, have been abandoned
PLUPF.	relīquerātis	you (pl.) had abandoned	relictī/ae/a erātis	you (pl.) had been abandoned
FT. PF.	relīqueritis	you (pl.) will have abandoned	relictī/ae/a eritis	you (pl.) will have been abandoned

C. Translation (18 points)

Translate each sentence.

1. Discipulī autem fidem fortem nōn habuērunt, et metū magnō victī sunt.

   The disciples, however, did not have strong faith and were conquered by great fear.

2. On the third day after the war, I will see the beautiful faces of my children.

   Tertiā diē post bellum [ego] faciēs pulchrās meōrum līberōrum vidēbō.

D. Memorization (35 points)

Write Psalm 23:1–4 in Latin.

[1]**Psalmus Dāvīd.**

Dominus reget mē et nihil mihi dēerit.

[2]**In locō pascuae ibī mē conlocāvit;**

super aquam refectiōnis ēducāvit mē.

[3]**Animam meam convertit.**

Dēdūxit mē super sēmitās iūstitiae.

propter nōmen suum.

[4]**Nam et sī ambulāverō in mediō umbrae mortis**

nōn timēbō mala quoniam tū mēcum es;

virga tua et baculus tuus ipsa mē consōlāta sunt.

LESSON 29 (Student Edition p. 275)

Verbs: Fourth Conjugation, Active, Passive & Imperative / Irregular Verb *eō*

1. Word List

Introduce the Word List for Lesson 29.

2. Derivatives/Memorization Helps

1. *animus*, mind: animate, animosity, unanimous, magnanimous
2. *pānis*, bread: companion
3. *saxum*, rock: memory help—Think of someone playing a saxaphone made of rock.
4. *ēgregius*, outstanding, excellent: egregious (from *ē/ex* + *grex*, "out of the flock")
5. *famēlicus*, hungry: famine, famished from the related noun *famēs*
6. *improbus*, wicked: improbity
7. *aperiō*, I open, expose: apertif, aperture
8. *audiō*, I hear, listen to: audio, audit, auditorium, (in)audible
9. *colō*, I cultivate, inhabit, worship: cultivate, culture
10. *dormiō*, I sleep: dormitory, dormant, dormer, dormouse
11. *eō*, I go: exit, initial, transit
12. *impediō*, I hinder: impediment, impeach
13. *inveniō*, I come upon, find: invent, invention, inventory
14. *resurgō*, I rise again: resurgence, resurrection; see *surgō* [Lesson 28]
15. *sciō*, I know: science, scientist, conscience
16. *veniō*, I come: intervene/intervention, advent, adventure, covenant, prevent
17. *clam*, secretly: memory help—Try using mental pictures with clams: "He *clams* up to keep the *secret*" or "The *clam secretly* makes a pearl."
18. *magnoperē*, greatly, very much: see *magnus* [Lesson 7]
19. *quoque*, also, too; informal fallacy tū quoque, "you also"
20. *ūnā*, together, in one: see *ūnus* [Lesson 21]

3. Memorization—*Psalmus XXIII*

This lesson's lines are:

> ⁵Parāstī in conspectū meō mensam
>> *You have prepared a table in my sight*
>
> adversus eōs quī trībulant mē.
>> *against those who trouble me.*
>
> Inpinguāstī in oleō caput meum,
>> *You have anointed my head with (lit., "in") oil,*

Parāstī and *inpinguāstī* are shortened forms of *parāvistī* and *inpinguāvistī* (the -vi- syllable has dropped out). This is called the contracted or syncopated perfect, and occurs quite a bit in "real" Latin.

4. Grammar

Fourth Conjugation Verbs, Active and Passive:

Like the third conjugation, fourth conjugation verbs have some tricky vowel changes in the present system, but conjugate normally in the perfect system. The fourth conjugation is in some ways easier to learn than the third, because its philosophy is basically that wherever there can be an *-i-*, there will be an *-i-*. Although many fourth conjugation verbs do have irregular principal parts, quite a few of them end like this: *-iō, -īre, -īvī, -ītum*.

Review the present vowel chant for the third conjugation with your students: *ō, ī, i, ī, ī, u!* The vowel chant for the fourth conjugation is identical except in the third person plural, where it is *-iu-* rather than simply *-u-*.

	SINGULAR	PLURAL
1ST	-ō	-ī-
2ND	-ī-	-ī-
3RD	-i- (act.) / -ī- (pass.)	-iu-

When conjugated in the Present Active and Passive, a fourth conjugation will look something like this: *aperiō, -īre, -uī, apertum:* I open, expose

Present Active Indicative

	LATIN SINGULAR	ENGLISH SINGULAR
1ST	**aperiō**	I open
2ND	**aperīs**	you open
3RD	**aperit**	he/she/it opens

	LATIN PLURAL	ENGLISH PLURAL
1ST	**aperīmus**	we open
2ND	**aperītis**	you (pl.) open
3RD	**aperiunt**	they open

Present Passive Indicative

	LATIN SINGULAR	ENGLISH SINGULAR	LATIN PLURAL	ENGLISH PLURAL
1ST	aperior	I am (being) opened	aperīmur	we are (being) opened
2ND	aperīris	you are (being) opened	aperīminī	you (pl.) are (being) opened
3RD	aperītur	he/she/it is (being) opened	aperiuntur	they are (being) opened

Recall that, for third conjugation verbs, the second person present passive was *-eris* (rather than *-iris*); thus *dūcō* becomes *dūceris,* "you are led." However, since the fourth conjugation has a long *ī* stem vowel rather than the short *i* of the third conjugation, the long *ī* remains: *-īris,* as in *aperīris,* "you are opened."

For a third conjugation verb, the vowel for the imperfect was simply an *-ē-* for all persons, singular and plural. Since our "rule" for the fourth conjugation is that wherever an *-i-* can be found, there it shall be, the imperfect for a fourth conjugation has an *i* and an *ē* all the way down:

	SINGULAR	PLURAL
1ST	-iē-	-iē-
2ND	-iē-	-iē-
3RD	-iē-	-iē-

Our example verb will conjugate in the imperfect like this (pretty simple):

Imperfect Active Indicative

	LATIN SINGULAR	ENGLISH SINGULAR	LATIN PLURAL	ENGLISH PLURAL
1ST	aperiēbam	I was opening	aperiēbāmus	we were opening
2ND	aperiēbās	you were opening	aperiēbātis	you (pl.) were opening
3RD	aperiēbat	he/she/it were opening	aperiēbant	they were opening

Imperfect Passive Indicative

	LATIN SINGULAR	ENGLISH SINGULAR	LATIN PLURAL	ENGLISH PLURAL
1ST	aperiēbar	I was (being) opened	aperiēbāmur	we were (being) opened
2ND	aperiēbāris	you were (being) opened	aperiēbāminī	you (pl.) were (being) opened
3RD	aperiēbātur	he/she/it was (being) opened	aperiēbantur	they were (being) opened

Like the third conjugation, the fourth conjugation future tense does not use *-bō, -bis, -bit,* etc. but rather a vowel change. Whereas the future vowels for the third are *a, ē, e, ē, ē, e,* the fourth once more simply sticks an *i* in front of that pattern:

	SINGULAR	PLURAL
1ST	-ia-	-iē-
2ND	-iē-	-iē-
3RD	-ie (act.) / -iē-(pass.)	-ie-

The future active and passive will conjugate like this (and make sure you point out the fine distinction between these forms and the present tense):

Future Active Indicative

	LATIN SINGULAR	ENGLISH SINGULAR		LATIN PLURAL	ENGLISH PLURAL
1ST	aperiam	I will open		aperiēmus	we will open
2ND	aperiēs	you will open		aperiētis	you (pl.) will open
3RD	aperiet	he/she/it will open		aperient	they will open

Future Passive Indicative

	LATIN SINGULAR	ENGLISH SINGULAR		LATIN PLURAL	ENGLISH PLURAL
1ST	aperiar	I will be opened		aperiēmur	we will be opened
2ND	aperiēris	you will be opened		aperiēminī	you (pl.) will be opened
3RD	aperiētur	he/she/it will be opened		aperientur	they will be opened

As you have noticed (and hopefully the class has as well), it is now more critical than ever to know what conjugation a verb belongs to—and therefore it is important to know those principal parts. A verb could end in *-ētur* and be either present (if second conjugation) or future (if third or fourth). As you go through the vocabulary list each lesson, take a few moments to have someone identify the conjugation of each new verb.

Fourth Conjugation Imperatives

Fourth conjugation imperatives are formed just like those of the first and second conjugations: Go to the second principal part, take off the *-re,* and there you have the singular imperative: *aperīre* becomes *aperī,* open! Simply add *-te* to make it plural: *aperīte,* open!

LATIN SINGULAR	ENGLISH SINGULAR		LATIN PLURAL	ENGLISH PLURAL
aperī	open!		aperīte	open! (pl.)

Full Conjugation of *eō, īre, iī or īvī, itum,* I go

This lesson we also introduce an irregular, but highly important, fourth conjugation verb—*eō,* "I go." It's a bit tricky to learn because it is so short, but basically, most of the forms are an *i-* or an *ī-* slapped on the front of our usual endings. Unlike other fourth conjugation verbs, however, *eō* does use *-bō, -bis, -bit,* etc. in the future tense and *not* the vowel change. In the perfect system, *eō* can appear as *i-* or *īv-*. The forms with *īv-* are much less common, and therefore will appear less frequently in this book. You may simply point out that this other stem exists, so that students won't be thrown when they encounter it; however, they need not feel obligated to employ it (as in this lesson's worksheet, exercise B.3).

Present Active* Indicative

	LATIN SINGULAR	ENGLISH SINGULAR	LATIN PLURAL	ENGLISH PLURAL
1ST	eō	I go	īmus	we go
2ND	īs	you go	ītis	you (pl.) go
3RD	it	he goes	eunt	they go

Imperfect Active Indicative

	LATIN SINGULAR	ENGLISH SINGULAR	LATIN PLURAL	ENGLISH PLURAL
1ST	ībam	I was going	ībāmus	we were going
2ND	ībās	you were going	ībātis	you (pl.) were going
3RD	ībat	he was going	ībant	they go

Future Active Indicative

	LATIN SINGULAR	ENGLISH SINGULAR	LATIN PLURAL	ENGLISH PLURAL
1ST	ībō	I will go	ībimus	we will go
2ND	ībis	you will go	ībitis	you (pl.) will go
3RD	ībit	he will go	ībunt	they will go

Perfect Active Indicative (forms with alternate stem in parentheses)

	LATIN SINGULAR	ENGLISH SINGULAR	LATIN PLURAL	ENGLISH PLURAL
1ST	iī (īvī)	I went/have gone	iimus (īvimus)	we went/have gone
2ND	īstī (īvistī)	you went/have gone	īstis (īvistis)	you (pl.) went/have gone
3RD	iit (īvit)	he went/has gone	iērunt (īvērunt)	they went/have gone

Pluperfect Active Indicative

	LATIN SINGULAR	ENGLISH SINGULAR	LATIN PLURAL	ENGLISH PLURAL
1ST	ieram (īveram)	I had gone	ierāmus (īverāmus)	we had gone
2ND	ierās (īverās)	you had gone	ierātis (īverātis)	you (pl.) had gone
3RD	ierat (īverat)	he had gone	ierant (īverant)	they had gone

* Although *eō* is intransitive (doesn't take an object) and therefore doesn't have a passive (try making "I go" passive—it simply will not work), some of the compounds of *eō* are transitive and thus have passives. Only the active forms of *eō* are given here, and any passive forms of its compounds found in this book will be duly footnoted!

Future Perfect Active Indicative

	LATIN SINGULAR	ENGLISH SINGULAR
1ST	ierō (īverō)	I will have gone
2ND	ieris (īveris)	you will have gone
3RD	ierit (īverit)	he will have gone

	LATIN PLURAL	ENGLISH PLURAL
	ierimus (īverimus)	we will have gone
	ieritis (īveritis)	you (pl.) will have gone
	ierint (īverint)	they will have gone

Imperative

LATIN SINGULAR	ENGLISH SINGULAR	LATIN PLURAL	ENGLISH PLURAL
ī	go!	īte	go! (pl.)

5. Worksheet

Although this isn't a review lesson, there are quite a few exercises in this lesson's worksheet. You may want to divide up the class. Middle schoolers enjoy being divided up in interesting ways: "Everyone with blue eyes do the synopsis of *audiō* and the declension of 'wicked day'; everyone with green or brown eyes do *colō* and 'our blessed bread.'" Or you could go by color of socks, birth month, rodent-owners vs. non-rodent-owners, etc.

6. Quiz

Administer Quiz 29 when the students are ready.

Lesson 29 Worksheet

A. Vocabulary

Translate the following words from Latin to English or English to Latin as appropriate. For the verbs, also fill in the missing principal parts.

1. army: **exercitus**
2. famēlicus: **hungry**
3. dormiō, **dormīre**, **dormīvī**, **dormītum** : **I sleep**
4. aperiō, aperīre, **aperuī**, **apertum** : **I open, expose**
5. I ride: **vehō**, **vehere**, **vexī**, **vectum**
6. quoque: **also, too**
7. I go: **eō**, **īre**, **iī**, **itum**
8. audiō, **audīre**, **audīvī**, **audītum** : **I hear, listen to**
9. animus: **mind**
10. I believe: **crēdō**, **crēdere**, **crēdidī**, **crēditum**
11. impediō, **impedīre**, **impedīvī**, **impedītum** : **I hinder**
12. cōgō, **cōgere**, **coēgī**, **coactum** : **I drive together, force, compel**
13. I know: **sciō**, -īre, **sciī (scīvī)**, **scītum**
14. greatly: **magnoperē**
15. ēgregius: **outstanding, excellent**
16. clam: **secretly**
17. I come: **veniō**, **venīre**, **vēnī**, **ventum**
18. dēligō, **dēligere**, **dēlēgī**, **dēlēctum** : **I pick, choose**
19. ūnā: **together, in one**
20. bread: **pānis**
21. colō, **colere**, **coluī**, **cultum** : **I cultivate, inhabit, worship**
22. saxum: **rock**
23. inveniō, **invenīre**, **invēnī**, **inventum** : **I come upon, find**
24. improbus: **wicked**
25. resurgō, **resurgere**, **resurrēxī**, **resurrēctum** : **I rise again**

B. Grammar

1. Give a synopsis of *audiō* in the third person singular.

	ACTIVE		PASSIVE	
	LATIN	ENGLISH	LATIN	ENGLISH
PRES.	audit	he/she/it hears	audītur	he is (being) heard
IMPF.	audiēbat	he was hearing	audiēbātur	he was (being) heard
FUT.	audiet	he will hear	audiētur	he will be heard
PERF.	audīvit	he (has) heard	audītus/a/um est	he was/has been heard
PLUPF.	audīverat	he had heard	audītus/a/um erat	he had been heard
FT. PF.	audīverit	he will have heard	audītus/a/um erit	he will have been heard

2. Give a synopsis of *colō* in the second person singular.

	ACTIVE		PASSIVE	
	LATIN	ENGLISH	LATIN	ENGLISH
PRES.	colis	you worship	coleris	you are (being) worshipped
IMPF.	colēbās	you were worshipping	colēbāris	you were (being) worshipped
FUT.	colēs	you will worship	colēris	you will be worshipped
PERF.	coluistī	you (have) worshipped	cultus/a/um es	you were/have been worshipped
PLUPF.	coluerās	you had worshipped	cultus/a/um erās	you had been worshipped
FT. PF.	colueris	you will have worshipped	cultus/a/um eris	you will have been worshipped

3. Conjugate *eō* in full.

Present Active Indicative

	LATIN SINGULAR	ENGLISH SINGULAR		LATIN PLURAL	ENGLISH PLURAL
1ST	eō	I go		īmus	we go
2ND	īs	you go		ītis	you (pl.) go
3RD	it	he goes		eunt	they go

Imperfect Active Indicative

	LATIN SINGULAR	ENGLISH SINGULAR		LATIN PLURAL	ENGLISH PLURAL
1ST	ībam	I was going		ībāmus	we were going
2ND	ībās	you were going		ībātis	you (pl.) were going
3RD	ībat	he was going		ībant	they go

Future Active Indicative

	LATIN SINGULAR	ENGLISH SINGULAR		LATIN PLURAL	ENGLISH PLURAL
1ST	ībō	I will go		ībimus	we will go
2ND	ībis	you will go		ībitis	you (pl.) will go
3RD	ībit	he will go		ībunt	they will go

Perfect Active Indicative

	LATIN SINGULAR	ENGLISH SINGULAR		LATIN PLURAL	ENGLISH PLURAL
1ST	iī (īvī, etc.)	I went/have gone		iimus	we went/have gone
2ND	īstī	you went/have gone		īstis	you (pl.) went/have gone
3RD	iit	he went/has gone		iērunt	they went/have gone

Pluperfect Active Indicative

	LATIN SINGULAR	ENGLISH SINGULAR		LATIN PLURAL	ENGLISH PLURAL
1ST	ieram (īveram, etc.)	I had gone		ierāmus	we had gone
2ND	ierās	you had gone		ierātis	you (pl.) had gone
3RD	ierat	he had gone		ierant	they had gone

Future Perfect Active Indicative

	LATIN SINGULAR	ENGLISH SINGULAR
1ST	ierō (īverō, etc.)	I will have gone
2ND	ieris	you will have gone
3RD	ierit	he will have gone

	LATIN PLURAL	ENGLISH PLURAL
	ierimus	we will have gone
	ieritis	you (pl.) will have gone
	ierint	they will have gone

Imperative

LATIN SINGULAR	ENGLISH SINGULAR
ī	Go!

LATIN PLURAL	ENGLISH PLURAL
īte	Go! (pl.)

4. Decline *wicked day*.

	LATIN SINGULAR	LATIN PLURAL
NOM.	dies improbus [*or* -a]	diēs improbī [improbae]
GEN.	diēī improbī [improbae]	diērum improbōrum [improbārum]
DAT.	diēī improbō [improbae]	diēbus improbīs
ACC.	diem improbum [improbam]	diēs improbōs [improbās]
ABL.	diē improbō [improbā]	diēbus improbīs
VOC.	[Ō] diēs improbe [improba]	[Ō] diēs improbī [improbae]

5. Decline *our blessed bread*.

	LATIN SINGULAR	LATIN PLURAL
NOM.	pānis noster beātus	pānēs nostrī beātī
GEN.	pānis nostrī beātī	pānium nostrōrum beātōrum
DAT.	pānī nostrō beātō	pānibus nostrīs beātīs
ACC.	pānem nostrum beātum	pānēs nostrōs beātōs
ABL.	pāne nostrō beātō	pānibus nostrīs beātīs
VOC.	[Ō] pānis noster beāte	[Ō] pānēs nostrī beātī

C. Memorization

Fill in the blanks.

¹Psalmus Dāvīd.

 Dominus reget mē et nihil mihi dēerit.

²In locō pascuae ibī mē conlocāvit;

 super aquam refectiōnis ēducāvit mē.

³Animam meam convertit.

Dēdūxit mē super sēmitās iūstitiae

propter nōmen suum.

⁴Nam et__ sī__ ambulāverō in__ mediō__ umbrae mortis__,

nōn timēbō__ mala__ quoniam tū__ mēcum__ es;

virga__ tua et__ baculus__ tuus ipsa__ mē consōlāta__ sunt.

⁵Parāstī in conspectū__ meō mensam__

adversus__ eōs quī__ trībulant__ mē.

Inpinguāstī__ in oleō__ caput meum__,

D. English to Latin Translation

Translate each sentence from English to Latin.

1. The knight's character seemed wicked to us afterwards, and we will never listen to him again.

   Faciēs equitis improba nōbīs postea vīsa est [*or* vidēbātur], et eum numquam iterum audiēmus.

2. On the fifth day the hungry orphans went and found your mother's bread, and they will eat it secretly and speedily.

   Orbī famēlicī [*or* orbae famēlicae] quintō diē iērunt/ībant et pānem mātris tuae/vestrae invēnērunt, et [eī/eae] eum clam citōque [*or* et citō] mandūcābunt.

3. The blind man could not sleep for two nights because of the great storm and enormous thunder.

   Caecus [vir] propter tempestātem magnam et tonitrum ingentem duās noctēs dormīre nōn potuit/poterat.

4. "The sun rises again, and it is day," said the teacher, "and then the middle of the day is called noon."

   "Sōl resurgit, et diēs est," inquit/dīxit/dīcēbat magister/magistra, "et medius diēs merīdiēs deinde/tum appellātur."

5. The farmer chooses a wife, the wife chooses a son, and the son will also choose a dog.

   Agricola coniungem dēligit/legit, coniūnx fīlium dēligit/legit, et fīlius canem quoque/atque/etiam/ et tum/deinde dēliget/leget.

6. According to many, his mind is wise but his words are dry; therefore we listen to him but will soon be sleeping.

   Secundum multōs, animus eius doctus est sed verba [eius] ārida sunt; ergō/itaque [nōs] eum audīmus sed mox dormiēmus.

7. The foolish sailors knew about the great rocks near the shore, but their ship was shattered.

   Nautae stultī dē saxīs magnīs iūxta/prope/propter lītus/ōram scīvērunt/sciēbant, sed nāvis eōrum fracta est/frangēbātur.

8. The happy mother cherished the singing of the children, but we could not listen to them for a long time.

   Māter laeta/beāta/fēlix cantum līberōrum fōvit/fovēbat, sed [nōs] eōs diū audīre nōn potuimus/poterāmus.

9. The unlucky army had been exposed in the fields, and so the soldiers went and hid in the rocks and caves of the mountain.

   Exercitus infēlix in agrīs apertus erat; itaque mīlitēs iērunt/ībant et in saxīs spēluncīsque [*or* et spēluncīs] montis occultāvērunt/occultābant.

10. I love the king's daughter greatly and because of my burning love I will not be hindered by him!

    [Ego] fīliam rēgis magnopere amō, et [ego] ab eō propter amōrem meum caldum nōn impediar!

E. Latin to English Translation

1 **Dē Piscibus**

Ōlim erant duae sorōrēs, Iūlia Iūniaque. Duae pulchrae erant, et faciēs Iūliae ēgregia erat sed Iūniae improba erat. Iūnia omnēs virōs amāvit, et ab improbīs modo amāta est. Bonī autem ab eā cūcurrērunt. Iūlia virōs nōn captāvit, sed labōrāvit et amōrem vērum exspectāvit. Ūnō diē eques novus ad oppidum
5 eārum īvit. Fortis erat et pulcher, et Iūlia et Iūnia eum fōvērunt. Sī eum in oppidō vīsit, Iūlia urbāna[1] erat sed suum negōtium ēgit.[2] Iūnia autem eum ubīque[3] invēnit et semper eī dīcēbat. Ergō eques Iūniam vitāvit,[4] sed Iūliae saepe dīcēbat. Iūnia invidēbat,[5] et cōnsilium[6] in animō eius dēnique cultum est. Iūliae dīxit: "Ī mēcum[7] in nāve in lacū." Sed Iūlia āit, "Nāvis nostra vetus[8] et pertūsa[9] est." "Nōn est; refecta est,"[10] dīxit Iūnia (sed nāvis nōn refecta erat). "Venī, nōs ūnā in lacū nāvigābimus quod diēs pulcher est."
10 Ergō duae sorōrēs ad lacum iērunt et in nāve nāvigāvērunt. Eques pulcher prope piscābātur.[11] Secundum cōnsilium Iūniae nāvis vetus pertūsaque cadere incēpit.[12] Iūnia equitī ululāvit: "Iuvā! Heu! Nōs iuvā!" Iūlia timuit sed placida[13] mānsit. Ex nāve saluit[14] et Iūniae clāmāvit, "Nāre possumus, scīs!" Ecce! Lacus nōn altus est, et Iūlia stāre potuit. Rīsit. Eques omnia vīderat et quoque rīsit. Iūnia autem īrāta erat. Eques ad Iūliam per aquam ambulāvit. "Cupis[15] mēcum piscārī?" rogāvit. Ergō Iūlia vērum amōrem in
15 lacū invēnit, sed Iūnia vestēs aquōsās[16] et veterem nāvem pertūsam modo habuit.

Glossary
1. *urbānus, -a, -um*: polite
2. *suum negōtium agere*: to mind one's own business (idiom)
3. *ubīque*: everywhere
4. *vitō* (1): I avoid, shun
5. *invideō, -ēre, -vīdī, -vīsum*: I envy
6. *cōnsilium, -ī* (n): plan
7. *mēcum = cum mē*: *cum* is a coward and likes to hide behind and attach to many personal pronouns.
8. *vetus, (gen.) -teris*: old
9. *pertūsus, -a, -um*: leaky
10. *reficiō, -ere, -fēcī, -fectum*: I repair
11. *piscor, -ārī, -ātus sum*: I fish (Yes, it only has passive forms but it is translated actively—this type of verb is called a deponent and you will learn about it later.) *Piscārī* is the infinitive form, "to fish."
12. *incipiō, -ere, -cēpī, -ceptum*: I begin
13. *placidus, -a, -um*: calm, quiet
14. *saliō, -īre, -uī, saltum*: I jump, leap
15. *cupiō, -ere, cupīvī, cupītum*: I wish (for), desire
16. *aquōsus, -a, -um*: sopping wet

<u>Concerning Fish</u>

<u>Once upon a time there were two sisters, Iulia and Iunia. They were both [lit., the two were] beautiful, and Iulia's character was excellent but Iunia's was wicked. Iunia loved all men, and was loved only by the wicked ones. The good men, however, ran from her. Iulia did not hunt men, but worked and waited for true love. One day a new knight came to their town. He was strong and handsome, and both Iulia and Iunia esteemed him. If she saw him in town, Iulia was polite but minded her own business. Iunia, however, came upon him everywhere and was always talking to him. Therefore the knight avoided Iunia, but he would talk to Iulia often. Iunia was jealous, and finally a plan was cultivated in her mind. She said to Iulia, "Go with me in the boat on the lake," but Iulia said, "Our boat is old and leaky." "It isn't, it has been repaired," said Iunia (but the boat had not been repaired). "Come, we will sail together on the lake because it is a beautiful day." Therefore the two sisters went to the lake and sailed in the boat.</u>

The handsome knight was fishing nearby. The leaky old boat began to sink, according to Iunia's plan. Iunia screamed to the knight, "Help! Alas! Help us!" Iulia was afraid but remained calm. She jumped out of the boat and shouted to Iunia, "We can swim, you know!" Behold! The lake was not deep, and Iulia could stand up. She laughed. The knight had seen everything and also laughed. Iunia however was angry. The knight walked through the water to Iulia. "Do you want to fish with me?" he asked. Therefore Iulia found true love in the lake, but Iunia only had sopping wet clothes and an old leaky boat.

Lesson 29 Quiz (89 points)

A. Vocabulary (10 points)

Translate the following words.

1. clam: **secretly**
2. hungry: **famēlicus**
3. quoque: **also, too**
4. I come: **veniō**
5. colō: **I cultivate, inhabit, worship**
6. agō: **I do, act, drive**
7. audiō: **I hear, listen to**
8. magnoperē: **greatly, very much**
9. dormiō: **I sleep**
10. ūnā: **together, in one**

B. Grammar (21 points)

Give a synopsis of *inveniō* in the third person plural.

	ACTIVE			PASSIVE	
	LATIN	ENGLISH		LATIN	ENGLISH
PRES.	inveniunt	they find		inveniuntur	they are (being) found
IMPF.	inveniēbant	they were finding		inveniēbantur	they were (being) found
FUT.	invenient	they will find		invenientur	they will be found
PERF.	invēnērunt	they (have) found		inventī/ae/a sunt	they were/have been found
PLUPF.	invēnerant	they had found		inventī/ae/a erant	they had been found
FT. PF.	invēnerint	they will have found		inventī/ae/a erunt	they will have been found

C. Translation (20 points)

Translate each sentence.

1. Jesus rose again on the third day and afterwards went into heaven.

   Iēsus tertiā diē resurrēxit et in caelum posteā iit.

2. Mīles hostem videt et eum citō impediet.

   The soldier sees the enemy and will quickly hinder him.

D. Memorization (38 points)

Write Psalm 23:1–5a in Latin.

[1] Psalmus Dāvīd.

Dominus reget mē et nihil mihi dēerit.

[2] In locō pascuae ibī mē conlocāvit;

super aquam refectiōnis ēducāvit mē.

[3] Animam meam convertit.

Dēdūxit mē super sēmitās iūstitiae

propter nōmen suum.

[4] Nam et sī ambulāverō in mediō umbrae mortis,

nōn timēbō mala quoniam tū mēcum es;

virga tua et baculus tuus ipsa mē consōlāta sunt.

[5] Parāstī in conspectū meō mensam

adversus eōs quī trībulant mē.

Inpinguāstī in oleō caput meum,

LESSON 30 (Student Edition p. 289)

Demonstratives

1. Word List

10. *vetus*, old—Now at least you can distinguish between the "old" of *antiquus* (refers to ancient things, as in "olden times") and *vetus* ("old" as in aged; "old man," "old car," etc.).

17. *satis* (adv. & indecl. adj./noun): enough, sufficient(ly)—*Satis* is often followed by the partitive genitive. When saying something like "He had eaten enough cookies," the Romans preferred to say *Satis crustulōrum mandūcāverat* rather than *Satis crustula mandūcāverat*. When your students are translating from the Latin, encourage them to use good English for the Latin idiom; we don't usually say "enough of cookies" and therefore they can translate it "enough cookies."

2. Derivatives/Memorization Helps

1. *adulescens*, young man/woman: adolescent, adolescence, adult
2. *classis*, group, class, fleet (of ships): class, classic, classification
3. *cōnsilium*, plan, counsel, advice; wisdom: counsel, counselor
4. *uxor*, wife: uxorial, uxoricide
5. *hic*, this; (pl.) these
6. *ille*, that; (pl.) those; that famous: definite articles in various Romance languages (e.g., Italian, Spanish, and French) such as *il*, *el*, *le*, and *la*
7. *iste*, that (of yours); such (sometimes used with tone of contempt)
8. *dexter*, right(-handed); skilled, favorable: dexterous, ambidexterous
9. *sinister*, left(-handed); inauspicious: sinister, sinistral
10. *vetus*, old: veteran, inveterate
11. *dīmittō*, I send away, dismiss, forgive: dismiss, dismissal
12. *nesciō*, I do not know: see *sciō* [Lesson 29]
13. *occīdō*, I kill, cut down, slay: from *ob* + *caedō*, which gives us the suffix –cide, as in homocide, infanticide, and insecticide
14. *trahō*, I draw, drag: traction, tractor, contract, subtract

15. *vinciō*, I bind, tie: vinculum (a type of ligament); don't confuse with *vincō*

16. *vītō* (1), I avoid, shun: inevitable; don't confuse with *vivō*

17. *satis*, enough, sufficient(ly): satisfy, satiate, satisfactory

18. *sīve*, or

19. *tamen*, yet, nevertheless, still: memory help—"I know what people say, but *nevertheless, yet, still,* I like eating Top Ramen."

20. *undique*, on/from all sides, from every direction

3. Memorization—*Psalmus XXIII*

This lesson's lines are:

> et calix meus inēbrians quam praeclārus est.
>> *and my cup is intoxicating like splendid [wine].*
>
> ⁶Et misericordia tua subsequitur mē
>> *And Your mercy follows me*
>
> omnibus diēbus vītae meae,
>> *all the days of my life,*

Notice the nice ablative of time, *omnibus diēbus*.

4. Grammar

Demonstratives:

A demonstrative adjective or pronoun points to something (*demonstrō*, I show, point out). You have already been using a demonstrative for some time—*is, ea, id*—which also happens to function as the third person personal pronoun. Now it is time to learn some other extremely common demonstratives.

hic, haec, hoc—this; (pl.) these

Hic, haec, hoc, meaning "this" and "these" in the plural, points to things that are near to the speaker. Imagine a roomful of chairs, and the speaker points to "this chair" right next to him, versus "that chair" way across the room. Although its chant does share similarities to that of *is, ea, id*, the whole thing should be memorized (and, it is easier to chant this one horizontally rather than vertically—*hic, haec, hoc; huius, huius, huius; huic, huic, huic;* etc.) The plural is fairly regular with first and second declension adjective endings, except for the neuter plural nominative and accusative. Here is its full declension (odd forms in bold):

	SINGULAR			PLURAL		
	MASCULINE	FEMININE	NEUTER	MASCULINE	FEMININE	NEUTER
NOM.	hic	haec	hoc	hī	hae	**haec**
GEN.	huius	huius	huius	hōrum	hārum	hōrum
DAT.	huic	huic	huic	hīs	hīs	hīs
ACC.	hunc	hanc	hoc	hōs	hās	**haec**
ABL.	hōc	hāc	hōc	hīs	hīs	hīs

ille, illa, illud—that; (pl.) those; that famous

Ille, illa, illud means "that" (or "those" when plural), and as indicated above, points to something farther away from the speaker—"that chair" over there. It can also sometimes imply "that famous," (think *ille eques Oswaldus*) and so of course context would help you out with that one. It is happily a bit more regular than *hic* (unusual forms in bold):

	SINGULAR			PLURAL		
	MASCULINE	FEMININE	NEUTER	MASCULINE	FEMININE	NEUTER
NOM.	**ille**	**illa**	**illud**	illī	illae	illa
GEN.	**illīus**	**illīus**	**illīus**	illōrum	illārum	illōrum
DAT.	**illī**	**illī**	**illī**	illīs	illīs	illīs
ACC.	illum	illam	**illud**	illōs	illās	illa
ABL.	illō	illā	illō	illīs	illīs	illīs

iste, ista, istud—that (of yours); such (sometimes used with tone of contempt)

While *hic* refers to something close to the speaker and *ille* to something distant, *iste, ista, istud* points to something close to the audience: "This is my cookie, that one in your hand is yours." In certain contexts (e.g., Cicero's orations which took place in a courtroom setting), *iste* refers to the speaker's opponent and therefore can have a hostile or contemptuous tone (it is easy to hiss *iste,* but not the other demonstratives!). Translating that tone into English can be difficult, so cultivate your students' creativity in that arena.

	SINGULAR			PLURAL		
	MASCULINE	FEMININE	NEUTER	MASCULINE	FEMININE	NEUTER
NOM.	**iste**	ista	**istud**	istī	istae	ista
GEN.	**istīus**	**istīus**	**istīus**	istōrum	istārum	istōrum
DAT.	**istī**	**istī**	**istī**	istīs	istīs	istīs
ACC.	istum	istam	**istud**	istōs	istās	ista
ABL.	istō	istā	istō	istīs	istīs	istīs

N.B.: Demonstratives do not have a vocative. (This is possibly because you are already pointing at them by using a demonstrative and you don't need to use a vocative to point to them—plus, I dare you to try to use "this" vocatively—it just doesn't work.) Therefore, when your students are declining noun-adjective phrases including a demonstrative, they can omit that demonstrative in the vocative.

Usage: Demonstratives can function either as pronouns (standing alone) or as adjectives.

Pronoun: Ille dracōnem necāvit. *That (famous) man killed the dragon.*

Adjective: Ille eques dracōnem necāvit. *That (famous) knight killed the dragon.*

5. Worksheet

D9: This sentence is an allusion to the story of Gaius Mucius Scaevola, told by Livy in his history of Rome (*Ab Urbe Condita,* Book II). Rome was being besieged by the Etruscans, and Scaevola entered their camp in disguise to assassinate their king. When he killed the wrong man, he was caught and the king ordered him to be burned. Scaevola voluntarily thrust his right hand into the fire to show that he (and the Romans) did not fear death. The king thought this quite brave of him, and let him go. Thereafter Gaius Mucius was called "Scaevola" (another word for "left-handed").

The Latin to English story tells the famous myth of Theseus overcoming the Minotaur with the help of Ariadne.

Crossword Puzzle: The crossword puzzle clues have to do with vocabulary and noun and verb endings (the students should be ready for anything covered so far!), and can be an optional but enjoyable review for the quiz.

6. Quiz

Administer Quiz 30 when the students are ready.

Lesson 30 Worksheet

A. Vocabulary

Translate the following words from Latin to English or English to Latin as appropriate. For the verbs, also fill in the missing principal parts.

1. occīdō, **occīdere**, **occīdī**, **occīsum** : **I kill, cut down, slay**
2. sīve (seū): **or**
3. vetus: **old**
4. I go: **eō, īre, iī, itum**
5. vītō, **vītāre**, **vītāvī**, **vītātum** : **I avoid, shun**
6. that famous: **ille**
7. modo: **only, just, merely, but**
8. I do not know: **nesciō**, **nescīre**, **nescīvī**, **nescītum**
9. adulescens: **young man/woman**
10. hic: **this**
11. plan: **cōnsilium**
12. truth: **vēritas**
13. vinciō, **vincīre**, **vinxī**, **vinctum** : **I bind, tie**
14. from all sides: **undique**
15. uxor: **wife**
16. enough: **satis**
17. iterum: **again, a second time**
18. cāsus: **event, incident; misfortune, downfall**
19. such: **iste**
20. classis: **group, class, fleet (of ships)**
21. sinister: **left(-handed); inauspicious**
22. tamen: **yet, nevertheless, still**
23. I draw: **trahō**, **trahere**, **trāxī**, **trāctum**
24. dīmittō, **dīmittere**, **dīmīsī**, **dīmissum** : **I send away, dismiss, forgive**
25. right: **dexter**

B. Grammar

1. Decline *that (famous) left-handed young man.*

	LATIN SINGULAR	LATIN PLURAL
NOM.	ille adulescens sinister	illī adulescentēs sinistrī
GEN.	illīus adulescentis sinistrī	illōrum adulescentium sinistrōrum
DAT.	illī adulescentī sinistrō	illīs adulescentibus sinistrīs
ACC.	illum adulescentem sinistrum	illōs adulescentēs sinistrōs
ABL.	illō adulescente sinistrō	illīs adulescentibus sinistrīs
VOC.	[Ō] adulescens sinister	[Ō] adulescentēs sinistrī

2. Decline *such an old rock* (use *vetus* for "old").

	LATIN SINGULAR	LATIN PLURAL
NOM.	istud saxum vetus	ista saxa veteria
GEN.	istīus saxī veteris	istōrum saxōrum veterium
DAT.	istī saxō veterī	istīs saxīs veteribus
ACC.	istud saxum vetus	ista saxa veteria
ABL.	istō saxō veterī	istīs saxīs veteribus
VOC.	[Ō] saxum vetus	[Ō] saxa veteria

3. Decline *this ordinary hand.*

	LATIN SINGULAR	LATIN PLURAL
NOM.	haec manus mediōcris	hae manūs mediōcrēs
GEN.	huius manūs mediōcris	hārum manuum mediōcrium
DAT.	huic manuī mediocrī	hīs manibus mediōcribus
ACC.	hanc manum mediōcrem	hās manūs mediōcrēs
ABL.	hāc manū mediōocrī	hīs manibus mediōcribus
VOC.	[Ō] manus mediōcris	[Ō] manūs mediōcrēs

4. Give a synopsis of *vinciō* in the first person singular.

	ACTIVE		PASSIVE	
	LATIN	ENGLISH	LATIN	ENGLISH
PRES.	vinciō	I bind	vincior	I am (being) bound
IMPF.	vinciēbam	I was binding	vinciēbar	I was (being) bound
FUT.	vinciam	I will bind	vinciar	I will be bound
PERF.	vinxī	I (have) bound	vinctus/a/um sum	I was/have been bound
PLUPF.	vinxeram	I had bound	vinctus/a/um eram	I had been bound
FT. PF.	vinxerō	I will have bound	vinctus/a/um erō	I will have been bound

5. Give a synopsis of *trahō* in the second person singular.

	ACTIVE		PASSIVE	
	LATIN	ENGLISH	LATIN	ENGLISH
PRES.	trahis	you drag	traheris	you are (being) dragged
IMPF.	trahēbās	you were dragging	trahēbāris	you were (being) dragged
FUT.	trahēs	you will drag	trahēris	you will be dragged
PERF.	trāxistī	you (have) dragged	trāctus/a/um es	you were/have been dragged
PLUPF.	trāxerās	you had dragged	trāctus/a/um erās	you had been dragged
FT. PF.	trāxeris	you will have dragged	trāctus/a/um eris	you will have been dragged

C. Memorization

Fill in the blanks.

¹Psalmus Dāvīd.

Dominus reget mē et nihil mihi dēerit.

²In locō pascuae ibī mē conlocāvit;

super aquam refectiōnis ēducāvit mē.

³Animam meam convertit.

Dēdūxit mē super sēmitās iūstitiae

propter nōmen suum.

⁴Nam **et** **sī** ambulāverō in **mediō** umbrae **mortis**,

nōn **timēbō** **mala** quoniam tū **mēcum** es;

virga tua **et** **baculus** tuus **ipsa** mē **consōlāta** sunt.

⁵**Parāstī** in **conspectū** meō **mensam**

adversus eōs **quī** trībulant **mē**.

Inpinguāstī in **oleō** **caput** meum,

et **calix** meus **inēbrians** **quam** praeclārus **est**.

⁶Et **misericordia** tua **subsequitur** mē

omnibus diēbus vītae **meae**,

D. English to Latin Translation

Translate each sentence from English to Latin.

1. If we will believe in Jesus, our evils will be forgiven us and we will rise again in glory.

   Sī [nōs] in Iēsum crēdēmus, mala nostra nōbīs dīmittentur et in glōriā resurgēmus.

2. That famous man's wife was beautiful and she was greatly desired by many.

   Uxor illīus pulchra erat et ab multīs magnoperē cupīta est [*or* cupiēbātur].

3. That black fleet has sailed to our shores and the enemy will besiege us for ten years.

   Ista [*or* illa, *but this sentence is about an enemy, after all*] classis atra ad litora nostra [*or* orās nostrās] nāvigāvit et hostis nōs decem annōs obsidēbit.

4. Nevertheless, lead this woman into the fortifications and there she will prepare enough bread and cookies for all the soldiers.

   Tamen dūc [*or* dūcite] hanc [fēminam] in moenia et [ea] omnibus mīlitibus satis pānis crustulōrumque [*or* et crustulōrum] ibī parābit.

5. I was approaching the cave and there I saw a huge dark shape—whether man or beast, I do not know—but I did not go into the cave afterwards.

   [Ego] ad spēluncam [*or* spēluncae, *omitting* ad] appropinquābam et ibī faciem ingentem [et] ātram vīdī—seū/sīve virum/hominem seū/sīve bēstiam, nesciō—sed in spēluncam posteā nōn iī.

6. This foolish young man did not know about horses, and so he fell down from my tall horse and was dragged by it for a long time.

   Hic adulēscēns stultus dē equīs nescīvit, itaque dē meō equō altō cecidit et ab eō diū trāctus est [*or* trahēbātur].

7. Three swift lions attacked this shepherd from all directions and yet he was able to defend the animals and kill all of the lions.

   Trēs leōnēs celerēs hunc pāstōrem undique oppugnāvērunt et tamen animālia dēfendere et omnēs leōnēs occīdere/necāre potuit/poterat.

8. These men and women cherished that famous woman, because she was their queen and had governed and ruled their land well for many years.

   Hī [virī] et hae [*or* haeque] [fēminae] illam [fēminam] fōvērunt, quia/quod/quoniam rēgīna eōrum erat et patriam/terram eōrum multōs annōs bene gubernāverat et rēxerat [*or* rēxeratque].

9. The brave soldier put [his] right hand into the fire because he feared neither the king nor the army of the enemy.

   Mīles fortis dexteram manuum in ignem posuit/mīsit quod/quia/quoniam nec rēgem nec exercituum hostium timuit/timēbat.

10. That wicked man's plans were destroyed by this faithful knight, and then that man paid the penalty.

    Cōnsilia istīus/illīus improbī [virī] ab hōc equite fīdō perdita sunt [*or* perdēbantur], et iste/ille [vir] poenās tum/deinde dedit.

E. Latin to English Translation

1 **Thēseūs[1] Mīnōtaurusque[2]**

Ōlim in īnsulā Crētā[3] ille Rex Mīnos[4] habitāvit. Bellum contrā Athēniēnsēs[5] gesserat et urbem eōrum vīcerat. Ergō dēclārāvit: "Omnī annō nōnō puerōs septem et septem puellās vinciētis, et eōs ad īnsulam meam quam tribūtum[6] mittētis." Cūr prō hīs quattuordecim līberīs rogāvit? In īnsula eius Mīnōtaurus
5 mōnstrum[7] cum capite taurī et corpore virī, quoque habitāvit. Ferus foedusque erat, et carnem[8] hominum modo mandūcābat. Mīnos Daedalō[9] dīxerat: "Mihi fac[10] labyrinthum[11] multīs cum viīs. Mīnōtaurum in labyrinthō pōnam et ex eō deinde īre nōn poterit." Daedalus ergō hunc labyrinthum fēcit et Mīnōtaurus in eō positus est.

Tertiō cāsū tribūtī, Thēseūs, filius Rēgis Aegeī[12] Athēnārum, patrī dīxit: "Ō pater, ad Crētam ībō et
10 ego Mīnōtaurum occīdam." Pater eius tristis erat sed eum īre permīsit.[13] Thēseūs dīxit, "Valē, pater. Sī istam bēstiam occīdam, haec nāvis vēla[14] alba geret; sī nōn, vēla ātra manēbunt!" Ergō, nāvis vēlīs cum ātrīs ab Athēnīs ad Crētam nāvigāvit. Ibī Ariadna[15] fīlia Mīnōis Thēseūm vīdit et amōre prō eō arsit. Eum iūvit et eī pilam[16] ex fīlō[17] dedit. Fīlō viam in medium labyrinthum invēnit, Mīnōtaurum occīdit, et fīlum ex labyrinthō deinde secūtus est.[18] Ab īnsulā cum Ariadnā nāvigāvit, sed eam in parvā īnsulā
15 relīquit. Itaque ea eum maledīxit:[19] "Dē vēlīs albīs nōn cōgitābis!" Thēseūs ad Athēnās nāvigāvit, sed in nāve vēla ātra vīsa sunt. Pater eius in scopulō[20] altō stābat et haec vīdit. Cōgitāvit: "Fīlius meus Thēseūs occīsus est!" et ab scopulō saluit[21] et ergō in mare occīsus est. Itaque hoc mare Mare Aegeum appellātur.

Glossary
1. *Thēseūs, -eī* (m): Theseus, Greek hero and founder of Athens
2. *Mīnōtaurus, -ī* (m): the Minotaur
3. *Crēta, -ae* (f): Crete
4. *Mīnos, Mīnōis* (m): Minos, a notorious king of Crete
5. *Athēnae, -ārum* (f, pl.): Athens; *Athēniēnsis, -is* (m/f) an Athenian
6. *tribūtum, -ī* (n): tribute, tax
7. *mōnstrum, -ī* (n): monster
8. *caro, carnis* (f): flesh
9. *Daedalus, -ī* (m): Daedalus, a skilled inventor and craftsman
10. *faciō, -ere, fēcī, factum*: I make, do, build
11. *labyrinthus, -ī* (m): labyrinth, maze
12. *Aegeus, -eī* (m): Aegeus; *Aegeus, -a, -um*: Aegean
13. *permittō, -ere, -mīsī, -missum*: I permit, allow
14. *vēlum, -ī* (n): sail
15. *Ariadna, -ae* (f): Ariadne
16. *pila, -ae* (f): ball
17. *fīlum, -ī* (n): thread, string
18. *sequor, sequī, secūtus sum*: I follow (another deponent—passive in form, active in meaning)
19. *maledīcō, -ere, -dīxī, -dictum*: I speak ill, curse
20. *scopulus, -ī* (m): cliff
21. *saliō, -īre, -uī, saltum*: I jump, leap

<u>**Theseus and the Minotaur**</u>

<u>Once upon a time on the island of [**N.B.:** *it sounds better in English to put in the word* **of**] Crete lived that famous King Minos. He had waged war against the Athenians and conquered their city. Therefore he declared: "Every ninth year you will bind seven boys and seven girls and send them to my island as tribute." Why did he ask for these fourteen children? On his island also lived the Minotaur, a monster with the head of a bull and the body of a man. He was wild and horrible, and only ate the flesh of men. Minos had said to Daedalus: "Make me a labyrinth with many passages. I will put the Minotaur in the labyrinth and then he will not be able to go out of it." Daedalus therefore made this maze and the Minotaur was placed in it.</u>

On the third occasion of tribute, Theseus, the son of King Aegeus of Athens, said to [his] father: "O father, I will go to Crete and I will slay the Minotaur." His father was sorrowful but allowed him to go. Theseus said, "Farewell, father. If I [will] slay that beast, this ship will bear white sails; if not, the sails will remain black." Therefore, the ship with black sails sailed from Athens to Crete. There, Ariadne the daughter of Minos saw Theseus and burned with love for him. She helped him and gave him a ball of string. With the string he found the path into the middle of the labyrinth, killed the Minotaur, and then followed the string out of the maze. He sailed from the island with Ariadne, but abandoned her on a small island. She therefore cursed him: "You will forget about [lit., you will not think about] the white sails!" Theseus sailed [back] to Athens but black sails were seen on the ship. His father was standing on a high cliff and saw these things. He thought: "My son Theseus has been killed!" and jumped from the cliff and was therefore killed in the sea. Therefore this sea is called the Aegean Sea.

F. Crossword Puzzle

Fill in the correct forms of the Latin words, and as appropriate translate the italicized English words into Latin. (Don't use macrons for the Latin words in the puzzle.)

ACROSS

3. *you (pl.) will join*
7. first person plural perfect active indicative of the verb meaning *I believe*
10. *it will be placed*
11. first person singular present active indicative of the verb meaning *I touch*
12. feminine ablative singular of *grātus*
13. nominative singular of the word meaning *wife*
14. the word for *storm* in the accusative singular
16. *she is cherished*
18. *together*
22. first person plural present passive indicative of *trahō*
24. *house*
25. *he was destroying*
26. third person singular present active indicative of the verb meaning *I put*
27. neuter plural dative of *sanctus*
30. *nevertheless*
31. *in what way*
33. first person singular perfect active indicative of *eō*
36. *I will know*
37. third person plural future passive indicative of the verb meaning *I write*
38. *or*
40. *resurgō* in the third person plural future perfect active indicative
42. *you will be ruled*
43. masculine singular accusative of the adjective meaning *left*
46. the word meaning *mind* in the nominative singular
48. neuter singular ablative of *ēgregius*
51. *perhaps*
52. *the wife's*
53. *vehō* in the second person singular future passive indicative
55. *it is choosing*
56. *in the presence of*
57. *you had worshipped*

DOWN

1. *I have broken*
2. first person singular future active indicative of *mittō*
3. *again*
4. *gerō* in the first person singular present passive indicative
5. *he touched*
6. *of the holy ones*
8. *hands* (nominative)
9. ablative singular of *spēs*
14. *tonitrus* in the dative plural
15. *we had approached*
17. *versus* in the nominative plural
19. first person plural imperfect active indicative of the verb meaning *I avoid*
20. *you were hindering*
21. *of the hope*
23. the word meaning *fear* in the ablative singular
28. masculine singular genitive of *novus*
29. second person singular future passive indicative of *iungō*
32. *you (pl.) choose*
34. feminine plural accusative of *iste*
35. *they were being opened*
37. ablative plural of the word meaning *rock*
39. *you will have done*
41. *you have touched*
44. *greatly*
45. *also*
47. the word for *Jesus* in the nominative singular
49. *you will hear*
50. ablative singular of the word meaning *grace*
54. neuter accusative singular of the demonstrative *this*

UNIT FOUR \\ LESSON 30

Lesson 30 Quiz (95 points)

A. Vocabulary (10 points)

Translate the following words.

1. I avoid: **vītō**
2. trahō: **I draw, drag**
3. classis: **group, class, fleet (of ships)**
4. quam: **as, than, how**
5. that (famous): **ille**
6. vetus: **old**
7. yet: **tamen**
8. satis: **enough, sufficient(ly)**
9. nesciō: **I do not know**
10. iste: **that (of yours); such**

B. Grammar (25 points)

Decline *hic*.

	SINGULAR			PLURAL		
	MASCULINE	FEMININE	NEUTER	MASCULINE	FEMININE	NEUTER
NOM.	hic	haec	hoc	hī	hae	haec
GEN.	huius	huius	huius	hōrum	hārum	hōrum
DAT.	huic	huic	huic	hīs	hīs	hīs
ACC.	hunc	hanc	hoc	hōs	hās	haec
ABL.	hōc	hāc	hōc	hīs	hīs	hīs

C. Translation (20 points)

Translate each sentence.

1. Adulescens et vetus dracōnem ūnā occīdērunt.

   The young man and old man together killed the dragon.

2. This woman's character is excellent and she will go to the palace and stand in the presence of the king.

   Faciēs huius [fēminae] ēgregia est et [ea] ad rēgiam ībit et cōram rēge stābit.

D. Memorization (40 points)

Write Psalm 23:1–6a in Latin.

[1]Psalmus Dāvīd.

Dominus reget mē et nihil mihi dēerit.

[2]In locō pascuae ibī mē conlocāvit;

super aquam refectiōnis ēducāvit mē.

[3]Animam meam convertit.

Dēdūxit mē super sēmitās iūstitiae

propter nōmen suum.

[4]Nam et sī ambulāverō in mediō umbrae mortis,

nōn timēbō mala quoniam tū mēcum es;

virga tua et baculus tuus ipsa mē consōlāta sunt.

[5]Parāstī in conspectū meō mensam

adversus eōs quī trībulant mē.

Inpinguāstī in oleō caput meum,

et calix meus inēbrians quam praeclārus est.

[6]Et misericordia tua subsequitur mē

omnibus diēbus vītae meae,

Lesson 31 (Student Edition p. 302)

Verbs: Third -io Conjugation, Active & Passive / Irregular Verbs *faciō* & *fīō*

1. Word List

Introduce the Word List for Lesson 31.

2. Derivatives/Memorization Helps

1. *barbarus*, foreigner, barbarian: barbarian
2. *caro*, flesh, meat: carnage, carnal, carnation, incarnate, incarnation
3. *fenestra*, window: fenestra, fenestration, defenestration
4. *gēns*, clan, tribe, nation: Gentile, genteel, gentry, gentle
5. *grex*, flock, herd: egregious, gregarious
6. *hōra*, hour: hour
7. *mensa*, table: mensa, mensal, mesa; don't confuse with *mensis*, "month"
8. *porta*, door, gate: portal, portico; don't confuse with *portō* or *portus*
9. *sella*, seat, chair: memory help—"We can't *sell* all our *chairs*! What will we sit on?"
10. *barbarus*, foreign, strange, savage: barbarian
11. *gelidus*, cold, icy: gelid; gelatin and gelato from related verb *gelō*, "I freeze"
12. *accipiō*, I accept, receive, take: accept, accipiter (a type of hawk); see *capiō* below
13. *capiō*, I take, capture, seize: capture, captive; suffix –cept as in intercept, precept
14. *cupiō*, I wish (for), desire, long (for): Cupid, cupidity, covet
15. *faciō*, I make, do: faculty, fact, faction; suffix -fy as in magnify, pacify; suffix -fect as in infect, perfect; suffix -fic as in soporific, pacific
16. *fīō*, I am made, am done, become, happen: fiat
17. *fugiō*, I flee, run away: fugitive, centrifugal
18. *iaciō*, I throw, cast, hurl: trajectory, inject, reject, projectile, object
19. *incipiō*, I begin, commence: incipient, inception; see *capiō* above
20. *interficiō*, I kill, slay, destroy: memory help—Since this literally means "to make/put between," have students think of its meaning "I kill" as making a division between soul and body.
21. *rapiō*, I snatch, seize, carry (off): rapt, rapture, raptor, rape, ravine, rapid

3. Memorization—*Psalmus XXIII*

This lesson's lines are:

> et ut inhabitem in domō Dominī
>> *so that I also may dwell in the house of the Lord*
>
> in longitūdinem diērum.
>> *for the length of [my] days.*

4. Grammar

Third *-io* Conjugation Verbs:

Congratulations. You have arrived at the third *-iō* conjugation, final conjugation of Latin verbs! And it isn't even really a whole new conjugation; it's more of a hybrid between the third and fourth conjugations. Therefore, some grammar books do not consider it its own separate thing and include it in with the third (its verbs can also be referred to as third conjugation i-stems).

How is such a verb identified? By the principal parts, of course. Our example verb for this chapter is word #18, *iaciō, -ere, iēcī, iactum,* "I throw, cast, hurl." We go to the second principal part and take off the *-re,* and are left with *iace-*. Clearly, the short *e* of the stem indicates that it belongs to the third conjugation. However, we also must look at the first principal part, and there we see *iaciō,* which looks an awful lot like the first principal parts of all the fourth conjugation verbs we've learned. Thus we have a third *-iō* verb.

Like verbs of the third and fourth conjugation, third *-iō* verbs are only a bit tricky in the present system. They also use a vowel change for the future tense rather than *-bō, -bis, -bit*. Here is a review of the vowels used in the present tense in third and fourth conjugation verbs, with the new conjugation's vowels:

Present Vowels

	3RD CONJ. PRESENT ACTIVE		4TH CONJ. PRESENT ACTIVE		3RD CONJ. -IO PRESENT ACTIVE	
	SINGULAR	PLURAL	SINGULAR	PLURAL	SINGULAR	PLURAL
1ST	-ō	-i-	-iō	-ī-	-iō	-i-
2ND	-i-	-i-	-ī-	-ī-	-i-	-i-
3RD	-i-	-u-	-i-	-iu-	-i-	-iu-

	3RD CONJ. PRESENT PASSIVE		4TH CONJ. PRESENT PASSIVE		3RD CONJ. -IO PRESENT PASSIVE	
	SINGULAR	PLURAL	SINGULAR	PLURAL	SINGULAR	PLURAL
1ST	-o	-i-	-io	-ī-	-io	-i-
2ND	-e-	-i-	-ī-	-ī-	-e-	-i-
3RD	-i-	-u-	-ī-	-iu-	-i-	-iu-

As you can see, third -iō verbs follow the general ō, i, i, i, i, u pattern—they imitate the third conjugation in the second singular, third singular, first plural, and second plural. Like the fourth conjugation, however, they have an -iō/-ior in the first person singular, and an -iu- in the third person plural. Here is *iaciō* fully conjugated in the present active and passive to give you a fuller picture of its vowels in their proper context:

iaciō, -ere, iēcī, iactum—I throw, cast, hurl

Present Active Indicative

	LATIN SINGULAR	ENGLISH SINGULAR	LATIN PLURAL	ENGLISH PLURAL
1ST	iaciō	I throw	iacimus	we throw
2ND	iacis	you throw	iacitis	you (pl.) throw
3RD	iacit	he/she/it throws	iaciunt	they throw

Present Passive Indicative

	LATIN SINGULAR	ENGLISH SINGULAR	LATIN PLURAL	ENGLISH PLURAL
1ST	iacior	I am (being) thrown	iacimur	we are (being) thrown
2ND	iaceris	you are (being) thrown	iaciminī	you (pl.) are (being) thrown
3RD	iacitur	he/she/it is (being) thrown	iaciuntur	they are (being) thrown

The imperfect of third -iō verbs copies the fourth conjugation -iē- all the way down:

	3RD CONJ. IMPERF. ACT./PASS.		4TH CONJ. IMPERF. ACT./PASS.		3RD CONJ. -IO IMPERF. ACT./PASS.	
	SINGULAR	PLURAL	SINGULAR	PLURAL	SINGULAR	PLURAL
1ST	-ē-	-ē-	-iē-	-iē-	-iē-	-iē-
2ND	-ē-	-ē-	-iē-	-iē-	-iē-	-iē-
3RD	-ē-	-ē-	-iē-	-iē-	-iē-	-iē-

And here is *iaciō* conjugated in the imperfect active and passive, with English translation:

Imperfect Active Indicative

	LATIN SINGULAR	ENGLISH SINGULAR	LATIN PLURAL	ENGLISH PLURAL
1ST	iaciēbam	I was throwing	iaciēbāmus	we were throwing
2ND	iaciēbās	you were throwing	iaciēbātis	you (pl.) were throwing
3RD	iaciēbat	he/she/it was throwing	iaciēbant	they were throwing

Imperfect Passive Indicative

	LATIN SINGULAR	ENGLISH SINGULAR	LATIN PLURAL	ENGLISH PLURAL
1ST	iaciēbar	I was (being) thrown	iaciēbāmur	we were (being) thrown
2ND	iaciēbāris	you were (being) thrown	iaciēbāminī	you (pl.) were (being) thrown
3RD	iaciēbātur	he/she/it was (being) thrown	iaciēbantur	they were (being) thrown

In the future tense, third -iō verbs will generally follow the vowel change pattern of *a, ē, e, ē, ē, e* (rather than using the -bō, -bis, -bit endings). In both the active and passive, they imitate fourth conjugation verbs by inserting that extra *i* in front of the future vowel:

	3RD CONJ. FUTURE ACTIVE	
	SINGULAR	PLURAL
1ST	-a-	-ē-
2ND	-ē-	-ē-
3RD	-e-	-e-

	4TH CONJ. FUTURE ACTIVE	
	SINGULAR	PLURAL
1ST	-ia-	-iē-
2ND	-iē-	-iē-
3RD	-ie-	-ie-

	3RD CONJ. -iO FUTURE ACTIVE	
	SINGULAR	PLURAL
1ST	-ia-	-iē-
2ND	-iē-	-iē-
3RD	-ie-	-ie-

	3RD CONJ. FUTURE PASSIVE	
	SINGULAR	PLURAL
1ST	-a-	-ē-
2ND	-ē-	-ē-
3RD	-ē-	-e-

	4TH CONJ. FUTURE PASSIVE	
	SINGULAR	PLURAL
1ST	-ia-	-iē-
2ND	-iē-	-iē-
3RD	-iē-	-ie-

	3RD CONJ. -iO FUTURE PASSIVE	
	SINGULAR	PLURAL
1ST	-ia-	-iē-
2ND	-iē-	-iē-
3RD	-iē-	-ie-

And so here is our example verb fully conjugated in the future active and passive:

Future Active Indicative

	LATIN SINGULAR	ENGLISH SINGULAR	LATIN PLURAL	ENGLISH PLURAL
1ST	iaciam	I will throw	iaciēmus	we will throw
2ND	iaciēs	you will throw	iaciētis	you (pl.) will throw
3RD	iaciet	he/she/it will throw	iacient	they will throw

Future Passive Indicative

	LATIN SINGULAR	ENGLISH SINGULAR	LATIN PLURAL	ENGLISH PLURAL
1ST	iaciar	I will be thrown	iaciēmur	we will be thrown
2ND	iaciēris	you will be thrown	iaciēminī	you (pl.) will be thrown
3RD	iaciētur	he/she/it will be thrown	iacientur	they will be thrown

Although all of these minute vowel differences may seem a bit bewildering at the moment, these verbs are really quite easy to translate—in the midst of working on a sentence your mind will not have a panic attack about whether this particular verb is at this particular moment imitating a third or fourth conjugation verb!

Finally we come to our imperatives. Since third -iō verbs have that short -e once the -re is removed, we should not wonder that they will imitate third conjugation imperatives (stem ending in -e) rather than fourth (which end in -ī). Like the third conjugation, that short -e gets trimmed down to a short -i- when the plural -te ending is added:

	3RD CONJ. IMPERATIVE		4TH CONJ. IMPERATIVE		3RD CONJ. -IO IMPERATIVE	
	SINGULAR	PLURAL	SINGULAR	PLURAL	SINGULAR	PLURAL
2ND	-e	-ite	-ī	-īte	-e	-ite

Imperative

LATIN SINGULAR	ENGLISH SINGULAR	LATIN PLURAL	ENGLISH PLURAL
iace!	throw!	iacite!	throw!

Just in case you (or your students) are reeling from this new conjugation, here is *iaciō* conjugated alongside a third and a fourth conjugation verb so that you can more easily spot the differences and similarities:

Comparison of Third, Fourth, and Third *-iō* Conjugations in the Present System

regō, impediō, and *iaciō*

	ACTIVE			PASSIVE		
	THIRD	FOURTH	THIRD -IŌ	THIRD	FOURTH	THIRD -IŌ
PRES.	regō regis regit regimus regitis regunt	impediō impedīs impedit impedīmus impedītis impediunt	iaciō iacis iacit iacimus iacitis iaciunt	regor regeris regitur regimur regiminī reguntur	impedior impedīris impedītur impedīmur impedīminī impediuntur	iacior iaceris iacitur iacimur iaciminī iaciuntur
IMPF.	regēbam regēbās regēbat regēbāmus regēbātis regēbant	impediēbam impediēbās impediēbat impediēbāmus impediēbātis impediēbant	iaciēbam iaciēbās iaciēbat iaciēbāmus iaciēbātis iaciēbant	regēbar regēbāris regēbātur regēbāmur regēbāminī regēbantur	impediēbar impediēbāris impediēbātur impediēbāmur impediēbāminī impediēbantur	iaciēbar iaciēbāris iaciēbātur iaciēbāmur iaciēbāminī iaciēbantur
FUT.	regam regēs reget regēmus regētis regent	impediam impediēs impediet impediēmus impediētis impedient	iaciam iaciēs iaciet iaciēmus iaciētis iacient	regar regēris regētur regēmur regēminī regentur	impediar impediēris impediētur impediēmur impediēminī impedientur	iaciar iaciēris iaciētur iaciēmur iaciēminī iacientur
	IMPERATIVE SINGULAR			IMPERATIVE PLURAL		
	rege!	impedī!	iace!	regite!	impedīte!	iacite!

As for the perfect system of third conjugation *-iō* verbs, there is nothing new or tricky to be learned. Once you have the third and fourth principal parts (which very likely could be a bit irregular), they will conjugate in the perfect, pluperfect, and future perfect active and passive just like all the other verbs you have been using.

Irregular Verbs: *faciō* and *fīō*

The verb *faciō, -ere, fēcī, factum* means "I make, do," and is a *very* commonly used verb in Latin. And, like most commonly used words, it has some interesting aspects to it. For one thing, in the present system, the Romans did not conjugate it with regular passive endings (*facior, faceris, facitur*, etc.). Rather, they used another verb entirely to express the present, imperfect, and future passive of *faciō: fīō, fierī, factus sum. Fīō* means "I am made, am done, become, happen." Although it is **active in form, some of its meanings are passive.** *Fīō* lacks a perfect passive system, so it borrows from *faciō* just like *faciō* borrows from it in the present system.

Otherwise, *faciō* is conjugated like other "normal" third *-iō* verbs, and its full conjugation can be written out thus:

	ACTIVE		PASSIVE	
	LATIN	ENGLISH	LATIN	ENGLISH
PRES.	faciō	facimus	**fīō**	**fīmus**
	facis	facitis	**fīs**	**fītis**
	facit	faciunt	**fit**	**fīunt**
IMPF.	faciēbam	faciēbāmus	**fīēbam**	**fīēbāmus**
	faciēbās	faciēbātis	**fīēbās**	**fīēbātis**
	faciēbat	faciēbant	**fīēbat**	**fīēbant**
FUT.	faciam	faciēmus	**fīam**	**fīēmus**
	faciēs	faciētis	**fīēs**	**fīētis**
	faciet	facient	**fīet**	**fīent**
PERF.	fēcī	fēcimus	factus/a/um sum	factī/ae/a sumus
	fēcistī	fēcistis	factus/a/um es	factī/ae/a estis
	fēcit	fēcērunt	factus/a/um est	factī/ae/a sunt
PLUPF.	fēceram	fēcerāmus	factus/a/um eram	factī/ae/a erāmus
	fēcerās	fēcerātis	factus/a/um erās	factī/ae/a erātis
	fēcerat	fēcerant	factus/a/um erat	factī/ae/a erant
FT. PF.	fēcerō	fēcerimus	factus/a/um erō	factī/ae/a erimus
	fēceris	fēceritis	factus/a/um eris	factī/ae/a eritis
	fēcerit	fēcerint	factus/a/um erit	factī/ae/a erunt

A synopsis of *faciō* will be tricky (warn your students), since in the present passive system a form of *fīō* will have to be used. For example, if you had asked for a synopsis of *faciō* in the third person singular, it would look like this:

	ACTIVE			PASSIVE	
	LATIN	ENGLISH		LATIN	ENGLISH
PRES.	facit	he/she/it makes/does		**fit**	it is (being) made/done
IMPF.	faciēbat	it was doing		**fiēbat**	it was (being) done
FUT.	faciet	it will do		**fiet**	it will be done
PERF.	fēcit	it did, has done		factus/a/um est	it was/has been done
PLUPF.	fēcerat	it had done		factus/a/um erat	it had been done
FT. PF.	fēcerit	it will have done		factus/a/um erit	it will have been done

5. Worksheet

Follow the directions to complete the worksheet.

6. Quiz

Administer Quiz 31 when the students are ready.

Lesson 31 Worksheet

A. Vocabulary

Translate the following words from Latin to English or English to Latin as appropriate. For the verbs, also fill in the missing principal parts. For each preposition, include which case(s) it takes.

1. sella: **seat, chair**
2. perhaps: **fortasse**
3. interficiō, **interficere**, **-fēcī**, **-fectum**: **I kill, slay, destroy**
4. I desire: **cupiō**, **cupere**, **cupīvī**, **cupītum**
5. accipiō, **accipere**, **-cēpī**, **-ceptum**: **I accept, receive, take**
6. knee: **genū**
7. fenestra: **window**
8. I make: **faciō**, **facere**, **fēcī**, **factum**
9. porta: **door, gate**
10. capiō, **capere**, **cēpī**, **captum**: **I take, capture, seize**
11. fīō, **fierī**, **factus sum**: **I am made, am done, become, happen**
12. according to: **secundum (+acc.)**
13. fugiō, **fugere**, **fūgī**, **fugitum**: **I flee, run away**
14. flesh: **carō**
15. grex: **flock, herd**
16. I throw: **iaciō**, **iacere**, **iēcī**, **iactum**
17. foreign: **barbarus**
18. gēns: **clan, tribe, nation**
19. animus: **mind**
20. I snatch: **rapiō**, **rapere**, **rapuī**, **raptum**
21. gelidus: **cold, icy**
22. hour: **hōra**
23. I begin: **incipiō**, **incipere**, **incēpī**, **inceptum**
24. mensa: **table**
25. grātia: **grace, favor, kindness, thanks**

B. Grammar

1. Give a synopsis of *capiō* in the third person singular and give its singular and plural imperatives.

	ACTIVE		PASSIVE	
	LATIN	ENGLISH	LATIN	ENGLISH
PRES.	capit	he/she/it captures	capitur	he is (being) captured
IMPF.	capiēbat	he was capturing	capiēbātur	he was (being) captured
FUT.	capiet	he will capture	capiētur	he will be captured
PERF.	cēpit	he (has) captured	captus/a/um est	he was/has been captured
PLUPF.	cēperat	he had captured	captus/a/um erat	he had been captured
FT. PF.	cēperit	he will have captured	captus/a/um erit	he will have been captured

IMPERATIVE			
LATIN SINGULAR	ENGLISH SINGULAR	LATIN PLURAL	ENGLISH PLURAL
cape!	capture!	capite!	capture! (pl.)

2. Give a synopsis of *vinciō* in the third person singular and give its singular and plural imperatives.

	ACTIVE		PASSIVE	
	LATIN	ENGLISH	LATIN	ENGLISH
PRES.	vincit	he/she/it binds	vincitur	he is (being) bound
IMPF.	vinciēbat	he was binding	vinciēbatur	he was (being) bound
FUT.	vinciet	he will bind	vinciētur	he will be bound
PERF.	vinxit	he (has) bound	vinctus/a/um est	he was/have been bound
PLUPF.	vinxerat	he had bound	vinctus/a/um erat	he had been bound
FT. PF.	vinxerit	he will have bound	vinctus/a/um erit	he will have been bound

IMPERATIVE			
LATIN SINGULAR	ENGLISH SINGULAR	LATIN PLURAL	ENGLISH PLURAL
vincī!	bind!	vincīte!	bind! (pl.)

3. Give a synopsis of *dūcō* in the third person singular and give its singular and plural imperatives.

	ACTIVE		PASSIVE	
	LATIN	ENGLISH	LATIN	ENGLISH
PRES.	dūcit	he/she/it leads	dūcitur	he is (being) led
IMPF.	dūcēbat	he was leading	dūcēbātur	he was (being) led
FUT.	dūcet	he will lead	dūcētur	he will be led
PERF.	dūxit	he (has) led	ductus/a/um est	he was/has been led
PLUPF.	dūxerat	he had led	ductus/a/um erat	he had been led
FT. PF.	dūxerit	he will have led	ductus/a/um erit	he will have been led

IMPERATIVE			
LATIN SINGULAR	ENGLISH SINGULAR	LATIN PLURAL	ENGLISH PLURAL
dūc!	lead!	dūcite!	lead!

4. Decline *ille* in full.

	SINGULAR			PLURAL		
	MASCULINE	FEMININE	NEUTER	MASCULINE	FEMININE	NEUTER
NOM.	ille	illa	illud	illī	illae	illa
GEN.	illīus	illīus	illīus	illōrum	illārum	illōrum
DAT.	illī	illī	illī	illīs	illīs	illīs
ACC.	illum	illam	illud	illōs	illās	illa
ABL.	illō	illā	illō	illīs	illīs	illīs

C. Memorization

Fill in the blanks.

¹**Psalmus Dāvīd.**

Dominus reget mē et nihil mihi dēerit.

²**In locō pascuae ibī mē conlocāvit;**

super aquam refectiōnis ēducāvit mē.

³**Animam meam convertit.**

Dēdūxit mē super sēmitās iūstitiae

propter nōmen suum.

⁴**Nam et sī ambulāverō in mediō umbrae mortis,**

nōn timēbō mala quoniam tū mēcum es;

virga tua et baculus tuus ipsa mē consōlāta sunt.

⁵**Parāstī in conspectū meō mensam**

adversus eōs quī trībulant mē,

Inpinguāstī **in** oleō **caput** meum,

et **calix** **meus** inēbrians **quam** **praeclārus** est.

⁶Et **misericordia** **tua** subsequitur **mē**

omnibus diēbus **vītae** **meae**,

et ut **inhabitem** in **domō** Dominī

in **longitūdinem** diērum.

D. English to Latin Translation

Translate each sentence from English to Latin.

1. The daughter of the goddess of grain was going to the fields of flowers and then she was snatched suddenly by that god and carried swiftly under the earth.

    Fīlia deae frūmentī ad agrōs flōrum ībat, et [ea] ab istō/illō deō deinde/tum repentē rapta est et sub terram citō portāta est.

2. Light was made by God, and He also afterwards made the sun and moon.

    Lūx ab Deō facta est [*or* fiēbat], et quoque/atque/etiam [Is] sōlem lūnamque [*or* et lūnam] posteā fēcit.

3. These soldiers will hurl spears and rocks toward the enemy, but not all of them will be killed.

    Hī/eī mīlitēs hastās et saxa [*or* saxaque] ad hostēs iacient, sed omnēs ex eīs nōn interficientur/occīdentur/necābuntur.

4. We are hungry and greatly desire much bread and meat and wine—put them on the table now!

    [Nōs] famēlicī/famēlicae sumus, et multum pānem et carnem et vīnum magnopere cupimus—pōne/pōnite nunc ea in mēnsā! [*N.B. Usually when an adjective is referring to inanimate nouns of differing genders, the neuter is used—thus,* ea].

5. At the seventh hour that wicked knight fled through the gates of the city and was received by the foreign tribe of the enemy.

    Septimā hōrā iste [*or* ille] eques improbus per portās urbis fūgit et ab gente barbarā hostium [*or* hostis] acceptus est.

6. The night was cold and the white stars shone, but then the fiery dragon carried off their flock of sheep.

    Nox gelida erat et stellae candidae lūcēbant [*or* lūxērunt] sed dracō caldus gregem eōrum ovium tum/deinde rapuit.

7. Those leaders will throw the city's enemy from the window of the castle.

    Illī [*or* istī] ducēs hostem/hostēs urbis dē/ex fenestrā castellī iacient.

8. Many chairs have been placed next to the table; we will now begin to eat and drink.

    Multae sellae iūxtā mēnsam positae sunt; [nōs] mandūcāre pōtāreque [*or* et pōtāre] nunc incipiēmus.

9. I have sailed on the cold deep sea for many days and I greatly long for my wife and my native land.

    [Ego] in mare gelidō [et] altō multōs diēs nāvigāvī et uxōrem meam et patriam [meam] magnopere cupiō.

10. You had seen the lions, and because of fear you turned and fled into the house.

[Tū/vōs] leōnēs vīderās/vīderātis et propter metum vertistī/vertistis et in domum fūgistī/fūgistis.

E. Latin to English Translation

1 **Illud Ōrāculum**

Ōlim rex vetus septem fīliōs habēbat. Ille rēgīnaque hōs fīliōs ad illam vātem¹ in spēluncā dūxērunt quia ōrācula² dē eīs audīre cupīvērunt. Vātes nihil dē sex fīliīs maiōribus³ dīxit, sed minimum⁴ (modo īnfantem⁵) spectāvit et praedīxit:⁶ "Ūnō diē ille īnfans regnum dē perīculō magnō servābit et rex fiet."
5 Maximus⁷ frāter, adulescens, dē hōc ōrāculō īrātus erat, itaque ūnā nocte īnfantem frātrem rapuit, eum ex castellō portāvit, eum in nāviculā⁸ parvā pōsuit, et nāviculam in flūmine mīsit. Hic raptus⁹ numquam inventus est, et post multōs annōs maximus frāter rex factus est.

Uxor pastōris veteris nāviculam parvam cum īnfante interim invēnerat, et illī duo puerum cūrābant et quoque eum fovēbat quod līberōs nōn habuērunt. Nōmen *Oswaldum* eī dedērunt. Ūnō diē, draco barbarus
10 super terram volāvit et omnia cremāre incēpit. Metus super omnēs cecidit. Rex novus dē dracōnibus nescīvit et magnoperē timuit. Iste draco multa animālia ex grege Oswaldī iam perdiderat; itaque is ad castellum iit et "Ego," āit, "tuus servus pastor sum, sed ego istum dracōnem occīdam." Rex eī dīxit, "Sī eum occīdēs, ego tibī multum aurum dabō et tē equitem faciam." Ergō Oswaldus ab castellum cessit, dracōnem appropinquāvit in spēluncam ātram eius, et eum gladiō antīquō pastōris interfēcit. Omnēs
15 laetī erant, et Oswaldum rēgem facere cupīvērunt quoniam is fortior¹⁰ erat quam rex novus. Ille, "Sed quis,"¹¹ inquit, "est pater eius? Bonus rex erit? Pastor modo est." Oswaldus cōram rēge dīxit: "Ego modo pastor sum, sed meum patrem vērum nesciō. Quam īnfans ego in nāviculā parvā ab pastōre veterī et uxōre eius inventus sum." Rex magnoperē timuit, tum enim suum¹² frātrem scīvit. "Tū vērus rex es," flēvit. "Ego tuus frāter maximus sum, et ego tē in illā nāviculā parvā istā nocte posuī propter ōrāculum.
20 Mē dīmitte!" Et Oswaldus rex deinde factus est, frātrem suum dīmīsit, et multōs annōs laetōs bene rexit.

Glossary
1. *vātes, -is* (m/f): prophet/prophetess
2. *ōrāculum, -ī* (n): oracle, prophecy
3. *māior, māius* (gen. *māiōris*): greater; here, "older"
4. *minimus, -a, -um*: least; here, "youngest"
5. *īnfans, -fantis* (adj. & noun, m/f): baby, infant
6. *praedīcō, -ere, -dīxī, -dictum*: I predict, prophesy
7. *maximus, -a, -um*: greatest; here, "oldest"
8. *nāvicula, -ae* (f): boat
9. *raptus, -ūs* (m): kidnapping, abduction
10. *fortior, -tius* (gen. *fortiōris*): braver
11. *quis*: who?
12. *suus, -a, -um*: his own, her own, its own

That Famous Oracle

Once upon a time an old king had seven sons. He [lit., that man] and the queen led these sons to that famous prophetess in the cave because they desired to hear prophecies about them. The prophetess said nothing about the six older sons, but looked at the youngest (only a baby) and prophesied: "One day that baby will save the kingdom from great danger and he will become king." The oldest brother, a young man, was angry about this prophecy, and so one night he snatched [his] baby brother, carried him out of the castle, placed him in a small boat, and put the boat in the river. This kidnapping was never discovered, and after many years the oldest brother became king.

Meanwhile, an old shepherd's wife had found the little boat with the baby, and those two cared for the boy and also cherished him because they had no children [lit., they did not have children]. They gave him the name Oswald. One day, a savage dragon flew over the land and began to burn all things. Fear fell on all [the people]. The new king did not know about dragons, and he was greatly afraid. That dragon had already destroyed many animals from Oswald's herd; and so he went to the castle and said: "I am your servant a shepherd, but I will kill that dragon." The king said to him, "If you [will] kill it, I will give you much gold and make you a knight." Therefore Oswald went from the castle, approached the dragon in its dark cave, and slew it with the shepherd's ancient sword. All the people were happy, and desired to make Oswald king because he was braver than the new king. That man said, "But who is his father? Will he be a good king? He is only a shepherd." Oswald said in the presence of the king, "I am only a shepherd, but I do not know my true father. As an infant I was found in a little boat by the old shepherd and his wife." The king feared greatly, for then he knew his own brother. "You are the true king," he wept. "I am your oldest brother, and I put you in that small boat that night because of the prophecy. Forgive me!" And Oswald then became king, forgave his brother, and ruled well for many happy years.

Lesson 31 Quiz (115 points)

A. Vocabulary (10 points)

Translate the following words.

1. sella: **seat, chair**
2. undique: **on/from all sides, from every direction**
3. I desire: **cupiō**
4. caro: **flesh, meat**
5. iaciō: **I throw, cast, hurl**
6. fīō: **I am made, am done, become, happen**
7. fenestra: **window**
8. gelidus: **cold, icy**
9. mensa: **table**
10. accipiō: **I accept, receive, take**

B. Grammar (25 points)

Give a synopsis of *interficiō* in the second person singular.

	ACTIVE		PASSIVE	
	LATIN	ENGLISH	LATIN	ENGLISH
PRES.	interficis	you kill	interficeris	you are (being) killed
IMPF.	interficiēbās	you were killing	interficiēbāris	you were (being) killed
FUT.	interficiēs	you will kill	interficiēris	you will be killed
PERF.	interfēcistī	you (have) killed	interfectus/a/um es	you were/have been killed
PLUPF.	interfēcerās	you had killed	interfectus/a/um erās	you had been killed
FT. PF.	interfēceris	you will have killed	interfectus/a/um eris	you will have been killed

C. Translation (35 points)

Translate each sentence.

1. We will accept your bread and meat and will put wine on the table also.

   [Nōs] tuum pānem et [tuam] carnem [*or* carnemque] accipiēmus et vīnum quoque [*or* etiam/atque] in mensā ponēmus.

2. Illā hōrā eques fortis dracōnem barbarum gladiō veteris pastōris interfēcit.

   In that hour the brave knight killed the savage dragon with the old shepherd's sword.

D. Memorization (45 points)

Write out all of Psalm 23 in Latin from memory.

¹Psalmus Dāvīd.

Dominus reget mē et nihil mihi dēerit.

²In locō pascuae ibī mē conlocāvit;

super aquam refectiōnis ēducāvit mē.

³Animam meam convertit.

Dēdūxit mē super sēmitās iūstitiae

propter nōmen suum.

⁴Nam et sī ambulāverō in mediō umbrae mortis,

nōn timēbō mala quoniam tū mēcum es;

virga tua et baculus tuus ipsa mē consōlāta sunt.

⁵Parāstī in conspectū meō mensam

adversus eōs quī trībulant mē.

Inpinguāstī in oleō caput meum

et calix meus inēbrians quam praeclārus est.

⁶Et misericordia tua subsequitur mē

omnibus diēbus vītae meae,

et ut inhabitem in domō Dominī

in longitūdinem diērum.

LESSON 32 (Student Edition p. 316)

Review & Test

1. Word List

There is no new Word List this lesson. Sudents will be responsible for Unit 4 words in the vocabulary portion of the test, as well as words from Units 1, 2, and 3 in translation.

2. Derivatives/Memorization Helps

There won't be any derivatives on the Unit 4 Test. However, you may want to review derivatives if you feel it will assist your students in remembering their vocabulary.

3. Memorization—*Psalmus XXIII*

There is no new memorization this lesson. Review the entirety of the Psalm 23.

4. Grammar

This lesson brings you not only to the end of a unit, but the end of an entire year of Latinic study. Take time to correct any recurring grammatical errors or translational confusions. Make sure that over the summer months your students will remember what they have studied! Review the following:

- Verbs: how to conjugate first, second, third, fourth, and third *-iō* verbs in the active and passive
- Nouns: fourth and fifth declensions especially, but brush up on the first, second, and third declensions as well
- Pronouns: Demonstratives *hic, ille, iste*; review *is*
- Adjectives: Review first/second and third declension adjectives, as well as numerals

5. Worksheet

This lesson does not include any English to Latin sentences. Rather, there is a nice *long* translation about David and Goliath. I paraphrased this passage from the Vulgate, removing the more complicated grammar that the students have not encountered yet (relative clauses, participles, subjunctives, etc.). There are no macrons, because most Latin Bibles will not have any (but I did include punctuation for ease of translation, even though some texts do not have that either!). Notice how the story contains some "bad" grammar—using *dīxit ad eum* ("he said to him") instead of the dative *dīxit eī*. It's good to point out to the students that grammar books usually teach rules and guidelines for good classical Latin (i.e., of Cicero's day), and that Latin did evolve and change a bit over the years and the miles. And of course some people made grammatical errors in their writing just as English writers do!

A note on *suus, -a, -um*: It is a reflexive possessive pronoun; that is, it refers back to the speaker. *Eius* or *eōrum* are technically used to refer to someone other than the speaker (though sometimes you see them used reflexively). The difference between these is portrayed nicely by the last sentence of the translation: *David autem caput Philisthei adsumpsit et tulit illud in Hierusalem, sed arma eius* [= Goliath's] *posuit in tabernaculo suo* [= David's].

Follow the directions given to complete the worksheet.

6. Quiz

There is no quiz this lesson.

7. Test

Administer Unit Test 4 when the students are ready.

Lesson 32 Worksheet

A. Vocabulary

Translate the following words from Latin to English or English to Latin as appropriate. Include case(s) with prepositions.

1. and, and also: **ac**
2. cito: **quickly**
3. clam: **secretly**
4. cōram: **(+ abl.) in the presence of, before**
5. perhaps: **fortasse**
6. iterum: **again**
7. iūxta: **(+ acc.) near (to)**
8. magnoperē: **greatly**
9. modo: **only, just, merely**
10. afterwards: **postea**
11. propter: **(+ acc.) because of**
12. quam: **as, than, how**
13. how, in what way: **quōmodo**
14. quoniam: **because, since**
15. quoque: **also, too**
16. enough: **satis**
17. secundum: **(+ acc.) according to**
18. seū: **or**
19. super: **(+ acc.) over, above**
20. tamen: **yet, still, nevertheless**
21. together: **ūnā**
22. undique: **on/from all sides**
23. accipiō: **I accept**
24. agō: **I do, act, drive**
25. I open, expose: **aperiō**
26. appropinquō: **I approach**
27. audiō: **I hear, listen to**
28. cadō: **I fall, sink, drop**
29. capiō: **I take, capture**
30. I go, move, yield: **cēdō**
31. cōgō: **I force, compel**
32. colō: **I cultivate, inhabit, worship**
33. crēdō: **I believe**
34. cupiō: **I wish (for), desire**
35. I run: **currō**
36. dēfendō: **I defend**
37. dēligō: **I pick, choose**
38. dīcō: **I say, speak**
39. dīmittō: **I send away, dismiss, forgive**
40. I sleep: **dormiō**
41. dūcō: **I lead, guide**
42. eō: **I go**
43. faciō: **I make, do**
44. fīō: **I am made/done, become, happen**
45. I cherish, love, esteem: **foveō**
46. frangō: **I break, smash, shatter**
47. I flee, run away: **fugiō**

48. gerō: <u>I bear, carry on</u>
49. gubernō: <u>I steer, direct, govern</u>
50. I throw, cast, hurl: <u>iaciō</u>
51. impediō: <u>I hinder</u>
52. incipiō: <u>I begin, commence</u>
53. interficiō: <u>I kill, slay, destroy</u>
54. inveniō: <u>I come upon, find</u>
55. I join, unite, yoke: <u>iungō</u>
56. legō: <u>I read, choose</u>
57. lūdō: <u>I play, tease, trick</u>
58. mittō: <u>I send, let go</u>
59. nesciō: <u>I do not know</u>
60. occīdō: <u>I kill, cut down, slay</u>
61. I destroy, ruin, lose: <u>perdō</u>
62. pōnō: <u>I put, place</u>
63. rapiō: <u>I snatch, seize, carry (off)</u>
64. regō: <u>I rule</u>
65. I abandon, leave behind: <u>relinquō</u>
66. resurgō: <u>I rise again</u>
67. sciō: <u>I know</u>
68. scrībō: <u>I write</u>
69. I (a)rise: <u>surgō</u>
70. I touch, strike: <u>tangō</u>
71. trahō: <u>I draw, drag</u>
72. vehō: <u>I carry, ride, convey</u>
73. vertō: <u>I turn, change</u>
74. veniō: <u>I come</u>
75. I bind, tie: <u>vinciō</u>
76. vincō: <u>I defeat, conquer</u>
77. vītō: <u>I avoid, shun</u>
78. vīvō: <u>I live</u>
79. adulescens: <u>young man/woman</u>
80. mind: <u>animus</u>
81. bow, arch, rainbow: <u>arcus</u>
82. cantus: <u>song, singing</u>
83. caro: <u>flesh, meat</u>
84. cāsus: <u>event, incident; misfortune, downfall</u>
85. classis: <u>group, class, fleet (of ships)</u>
86. cōnsilium: <u>plan, counsel, advice; wisdom</u>
87. cornū: <u>horn</u>
88. day, period of time: <u>diēs</u>
89. domus: <u>house, home</u>
90. exercitus: <u>army</u>
91. faciēs: <u>shape, form; face; character</u>
92. fenestra: <u>window</u>
93. fidēs: <u>faith</u>
94. frūctus: <u>fruit, profit</u>
95. gēns: <u>clan, tribe, nation</u>
96. knee: <u>genū</u>
97. grātia: <u>grace, favor, kindness, thanks</u>
98. grex: <u>flock, herd</u>
99. hour: <u>hōra</u>
100. Iēsus: <u>Jesus</u>
101. lacus: <u>lake, tub, hollow</u>
102. lingua: <u>language/tongue</u>
103. littera: <u>letter</u>
104. manus: <u>hand</u>
105. table: <u>mensa</u>

106. merīdiēs: **noon**
107. metus: **fear, dread**
108. pānis: **bread**
109. poena: **penalty, punishment**
110. porta: **door, gate**
111. port, harbor: **portus**
112. rēs: **thing**
113. saxum: **rock**
114. sella: **seat, chair**
115. spēs: **hope**
116. spīritus: **spirit, breath**
117. weather, storm: **tempestās**
118. tonitrus: **thunder**
119. wife: **uxor**
120. vēritas: **truth**
121. versus: **row, line (of poetry), furrow**
122. vultus: **face, expression**
123. āridus: **dry**
124. barbarus: **foreign(er)**
125. blind: **caecus**
126. dexter: **right(-handed); skilled/favorable**
127. ēgregius: **outstanding, excellent**
128. hungry: **famēlicus**
129. gelidus: **cold, icy**
130. grātus: **grateful, pleasing**
131. hic: **this**
132. ille: **that**
133. improbus: **wicked**
134. iste: **that (of yours): such**
135. middle, midst (of): **medius**
136. new: **novus**
137. salvus: **safe, saved, well, sound**
138. sanctus: **holy, sacred, consecrated**
139. sinister: **left(-handed); inauspicious**
140. old: **vetus**

B. Grammar

1. Conjugate *vītō* in the future perfect passive indicative.

	LATIN SINGULAR	ENGLISH SINGULAR	LATIN PLURAL	ENGLISH PLURAL
1ST	vītātus/a/um erō	I will have been shunned	vītātī/ae/a erimus	we will have been shunned
2ND	vītātus/a/um eris	you will have been shunned	vītātī/ae/a eritis	you (pl.) will have been shunned
3RD	vītātus/a/um erit	he/she/it will have been shunned	vītātī/ae/a erunt	they will have been shunned

2. Conjugate *dīmittō* in the perfect passive indicative.

	LATIN SINGULAR	ENGLISH SINGULAR	LATIN PLURAL	ENGLISH PLURAL
1ST	dīmissus/a/um sum	I have been/was dismissed	dīmissī/ae/a sumus	we have been dismissed
2ND	dīmissus/a/um es	you have been dismissed	dīmissī/ae/a estis	you (pl.) have been dismissed
3RD	dīmissus/a/um est	he has been dismissed	dīmissī/ae/a sunt	they have been dismissed

3. Conjugate *dormiō* in the imperfect active indicative.

	LATIN SINGULAR	ENGLISH SINGULAR	LATIN PLURAL	ENGLISH PLURAL
1ST	dormiēbam	I was sleeping	dormiēbāmus	we were sleeping
2ND	dormiēbās	you were sleeping	dormiēbātis	you (pl.) were sleeping
3RD	dormiēbat	he was sleeping	dormiēbant	they were sleeping

4. Conjugate *gubernō* in the pluperfect passive indicative.

	LATIN SINGULAR	ENGLISH SINGULAR	LATIN PLURAL	ENGLISH PLURAL
1ST	gubernātus/a/um eram	I had been governed	gubernātī/ae/a erāmus	we had been governed
2ND	gubernātus/a/um erās	you had been governed	gubernātī/ae/a erātis	you (pl.) had been governed
3RD	gubernātus/a/um erat	he had been governed	gubernātī/ae/a erant	they had been governed

5. Conjugate *perdō* in the future active indicative.

	LATIN SINGULAR	ENGLISH SINGULAR	LATIN PLURAL	ENGLISH PLURAL
1ST	perdam	I will destroy	perdēmus	we will destroy
2ND	perdēs	you will destroy	perdētis	you (pl.) will destroy
3RD	perdet	he will destroy	perdent	they will destroy

6. Conjugate *rapiō* in the present passive indicative.

	LATIN SINGULAR	ENGLISH SINGULAR	LATIN PLURAL	ENGLISH PLURAL
1ST	rapior	I am (being) snatched	rapīmur	we are (being) snatched
2ND	raperis	you are (being) snatched	rapīminī	you (pl.) are (being) snatched
3RD	rapītur	he is (being) snatched	rapiuntur	they are (being) snatched

7. Conjugate *faciō* in the future passive indicative.

	LATIN SINGULAR	ENGLISH SINGULAR	LATIN PLURAL	ENGLISH PLURAL
1ST	fīam	I will be made	fīēmus	we will be made
2ND	fīēs	you will be made	fīētis	you (pl.) will be made
3RD	fīet	he will be made	fīent	they will be made

8. Conjugate *surgō* in the perfect active indicative.

	LATIN SINGULAR	ENGLISH SINGULAR	LATIN PLURAL	ENGLISH PLURAL
1ST	surrēxī	I arose/have arisen	surrēximus	we arose
2ND	surrēxistī	you arose	surrēxistis	you (pl.) arose
3RD	surrēxit	he arose	surrēxērunt	they arose

9. Conjugate *eō* in the present active indicative.

	LATIN SINGULAR	ENGLISH SINGULAR	LATIN PLURAL	ENGLISH PLURAL
1ST	eō	I go	īmus	we go
2ND	īs	you go	ītis	you (pl.) go
3RD	it	he goes	eunt	they go

10. Conjugate *vinciō* in the pluperfect active indicative.

	LATIN SINGULAR	ENGLISH SINGULAR	LATIN PLURAL	ENGLISH PLURAL
1ST	vinxeram	I had bound	vinxerāmus	we had bound
2ND	vinxerās	you had bound	vinxerātis	you (pl.) had bound
3RD	vinxerat	he had bound	vinxerant	they had bound

11. Conjugate *foveō* in the imperfect passive indicative.

	LATIN SINGULAR	ENGLISH SINGULAR	LATIN PLURAL	ENGLISH PLURAL
1ST	fovēbar	I was (being) cherished	fovēbāmur	we were (being) cherished
2ND	fovēbāris	you were (being) cherished	fovēbāminī	you (pl.) were (being) cherished
3RD	fovēbātur	he was (being) cherished	fovēbantur	they were (being) cherished

12. Conjugate *accipiō* in the future perfect active indicative.

	LATIN SINGULAR	ENGLISH SINGULAR	LATIN PLURAL	ENGLISH PLURAL
1ST	accēperō	I will have received	accēperimus	we will have received
2ND	accēperis	you will have received	accēperitis	you (pl.) will have received
3RD	accēperit	he will have received	accēperint	they will have received

13. Give the imperatives of the following verbs.

	VERB	LATIN SINGULAR	ENGLISH SINGULAR	LATIN PLURAL	ENGLISH PLURAL
1.	appropinquō	appropinquā!	approach!	appropinquāte!	approach! (pl.)
2.	augeō	augē!	increase!	augēte!	increase! (pl.)
3.	dūcō	dūc!	lead!	ducite!	lead! (pl.)
4.	audiō	audī!	listen!	audīte!	listen! (pl.)
5.	capiō	cape!	capture!	capite!	capture! (pl.)

14. Decline *this old animal* (use *hic* and *vetus*).

	LATIN SINGULAR	LATIN PLURAL
NOM.	hoc animal vetus	haec animālia veteria
GEN.	huius animālis veteris	hōrum animālium veterium
DAT.	huic animālī veterī	hīs animālibus veteribus
ACC.	hoc animal vetus	haec animālia veteria
ABL.	hōc animālī veterī	hīs animālibus veteribus
VOC.	Ō animal vetus	Ō animālia veteria

15. Decline *that holy fear* (use *ille*).

	LATIN SINGULAR	LATIN PLURAL
NOM.	ille metus sanctus	illī metūs sanctī
GEN.	illīus metūs sanctī	illōrum metuum sanctōrum
DAT.	illī metuī sanctō	illīs metibus sanctīs
ACC.	illum metum sanctum	illōs metūs sanctōs
ABL.	illō metū sanctō	illīs metibus sanctīs
VOC.	Ō metus sancte	Ō metūs sanctī

16. Decline *such a savage face* (use *faciēs*).

	LATIN SINGULAR	LATIN PLURAL
NOM.	ista faciēs barbara	istae faciēs barbarae
GEN.	istīus faciēī barbarae	istārum faciērum barbarārum
DAT.	istī faciēī barbarae	istīs faciēbus barbarīs
ACC.	istam faciem barbaram	istās faciēs barbarās
ABL.	istā faciē barbarā	istīs faciēbus barbarīs
VOC.	Ō faciēs barbara	Ō faciēs barbarae

C. Memorization

Below is the first word from each line of *Psalmus XXIII*. Fill in the rest. (Be prepared on the test to write out the entire psalm without any hints!)

¹Psalmus **Dāvīd.**

Dominus **reget mē et nihil mihi dēerit.**

²In **locō pascuae ibī mē conlocāvit;**

super **aquam refectiōnis ēducāvit mē.**

³Animam **meam convertit.**

Dēdūxit **mē super sēmitās iūstitiae**

propter **nōmen suum.**

⁴Nam **et sī ambulāverō in mediō umbrae mortis,**

nōn **timēbō mala quoniam tū mēcum es;**

virga **tua et baculus tuus ipsa mē consōlāta sunt.**

⁵Parāstī **in conspectū meō mensam**

adversus **eōs quī trībulant mē.**

Inpinguāstī **in oleō caput meum,**

et **calix meus inēbrians quam praeclārus est.**

⁶Et **misericordia tua subsequitur mē**

omnibus **diēbus vītae meae,**

et **ut inhabitem in domō Dominī**

in **longitūdinem diērum.**

D. Latin to English Translation

1 **David* et Goliath***

(adapted from the Vulgate, 1 Samuel 17:12–54)

David autem erat unus ex octo filiis viris Isai* Ephrathei.[1] Et abierunt[2] tres filii maiores[3] post Saul* in proelium. David autem erat minimus,[4] et abiit David et pascebat[5] gregem patris sui[6] in Bethleem.* Dixit
5 autem Isai ad David filium suum, "Accipe fratribus tuis frumentum et decem panes istos, et curre in castra ad fratres tuos."

Surrexit itaque David mane[7] et venit ad exercitum, et invenit fratres suos, et dicebat eis. Deinde vir ille spurius,[8] Goliath nomine Philistheus[9] de Geth,* ex castris Philistheorum abiit et castra Israhelitarum[10] ad proelium provocavit.[11] Omnes autem Israhelitae viderunt virum et fugerunt a facie eius quod
10 eum magnopere timuerunt. Sed ait David ad viros: "Quis[12] est enim hic Philistheus incircumcisus?[13] Exprobravit[14] enim exercitum Dei vivi." Ergo ad Saul regem ductus est et dixit: "Ego servus tuus ibo et pugnabo contra Philistheum." Et ait Saul ad David, "Non vales vincere Philistheum istum nec pugnare contra eum quia puer es; hic autem vir bellator[15] ab adulescentia[16] sua."

Dixitque David ad Saul, "Pascebat servus tuus patris sui gregem et saepe veniebat leo vel[17] ursus[18]
15 rapiebatque arietem[19] de medio grege, et currebam ad eos et occidebam rapiebamque eum de ore eorum interficiebamque eos. Nam[20] et leonem et ursum interfeci ego servus tuus. Philistheum igitur hunc incircumcisum quoque vincere potero, quia exercitum Dei vivi reprobrare audebat." Et ait David, "Dominus me rapuit de manu leonis et de manu ursi, et is liberabit me de manu Philisthei huius." Dixit autem Saul ad David, "I et Dominus tecum[21] sit."[22]

20 Et David baculum[23] suum portavit, et quinque limpidissimos[24] lapides[25] de torrente[26] delegit et misit eos in peram[27] pastoralem[28] et fundam[29] manu gessit et iit contra Philistheum. Autem Philistheus David appropinquavit et eum vidit, etiam despexit[30] eum enim adulescens rufus[31] erat et pulcher facies erat. Et dixit Philistheus ad David: "Ego canis sum, quod[32] tu venis ad me cum baculo?" et maledixit[33] Philistheus David in diis suis.[34]

25 Dixitque ad David: "Veni ad me et dabo carnes tuas avibus caeli et bestiis terrae." Dixit autem David ad Philistheum: "Tu venis ad me cum gladio et hasta et clypeo;[35] ego autem venio ad te in nomine Domini exercituum. Hodie et dabit te Dominus in manum meam et percutiam[36] te et auferam[37] caput tuum a te. Et dabo cadaver[38] castrorum Philistheorum hodie avibus caeli et bestiis terrae, et sciet omnis terra quia[39] est Deus in Israhel,* et tradet[40] vos in manus nostras."

30 Ergo surrexit Philistheus et venit et appropinquavit contra David. Festinavit David et cucurrit ad Philistheum, et misit manum suam in peram tulitque[41] unum lapidem. Et funda iecit et percussit Philistheum in fronte[42] et infixus est[43] lapis in fronte eius et cecidit in faciem suam super terram. Cucurrit et stetit super Philistheum et tulit gladium eius et interfecit eum praeciditque[44] caput eius. Viderunt autem Philisthei eum mortuum fortissimum[45] eorum, et fugerunt. Et viri Israhel surgerunt
35 et clamaverunt et Philistheos persecuti sunt[46] cecideruntque. David autem caput Philisthei adsumpsit[47] et tulit illud in Hierusalem,* sed arma[48] eius posuit in tabernaculo[49] suo.

Glossary

*The following names are indeclinable: *David, Goliath, Isai* (Jesse), *Bethleem, Saul, Geth, Israhel, Hierusalem* (Jerusalem)

1. *Ephratheus, -ī* (m): an Ephramite
2. *abeō, -īre, -iī, -itum*: I go away, depart
3. *māior, māius* (gen. *māioris*): greater; here, "older"
4. *minimus, -a, -um*: least; here, "youngest"
5. *pascō, -ere, pāvī, pastum*: I feed, pasture
6. *suus, -a, -um*: his (own), her (own), its (own). This is a reflexive possessive adjective—it refers back to the subject.
7. *māne*: in the morning, early
8. *spurius, -a, -um*: spurious, false
9. *Philistheus, -ī*: (m) Philistine
10. *Israhelita, -ae*: (m) Israelite
11. *prōvocō* (1): I challenge
12. *quis*: who?
13. *incircumcisus, -a, -um*: uncircumcised
14. *exprobrō* (1): I reproach
15. *bellātor, -tōris* (m): warrior
16. *adulescentia, -ae* (f): youth
17. *vel*: or
18. *ursus, -ī* (m): bear
19. *ariēs, -ietis* (m): ram
20. *nam*: for
21. *tēcum = cum tē*
22. *sit*: third person singular present active subjunctive of *sum*; here, translate it as "may he be"
23. *baculum, -ī* (n): staff
24. *limpidissimus, -a, -um*: very bright, very clear
25. *lapis, -idis* (m): stone
26. *torrens, -ntis* (m): a torrent, stream
27. *pēra, -ae* (f): bag, satchel
28. *pastōrālis, -e*: of/belonging to a shepherd, pastoral
29. *funda, -ae* (f): sling
30. *dēspiciō, -ere, -spexī, -spectum*: I look down on, despise
31. *rūfus, -a, -um*: red, ruddy
32. *quod*: here, translate as "that"
33. *maledīcō, -ere, -dīxī, -dictum*: I curse, speak evil
34. *in diīs suīs = in deīs suīs*; here, translate "in" as "by"
35. *clypeum, -ī* (n): shield
36. *percutiō, -ere, -cussī, -cussum*: I strike down, cut down
37. *auferō, -ferre* (3rd conj. irreg.), *abstulī, ablātum*: I carry away/off, remove
38. *cadāver, -veris* (n): dead body, carcass
39. *quia*: here, translate as "that"
40. *tradō, -ere, -didī, -ditum*: I hand over, surrender
41. *ferō, ferre* (irreg. 3rd conj.), *tulī, lātum*: I carry, bring (forth), bear
42. *frōns, -ontis*: (f) forehead
43. *infīgō, -ere, -fīxī, -fīxum*: I fix in, fasten in
44. *praecīdō, -ere, -cīdī, -cīsum*: I cut off, lop
45. *fortissimus, -a, -um*: bravest, strongest
46. *persequor, -sequī, -secūtus sum*: I pursue (with hostile intent), hunt down; this is a deponent verb—it is active in meaning but has passive forms
47. *adsūmō, -ere, -sumpsī, -sumptum*: I take for myself
48. *arma, -ōrum* (n, pl.): arms, armor, weapons
49. *tabernāculum, -ī* (n): tent

David and Goliath

Moreover David was one of eight sons of Jesse the Ephramite. And the three older sons departed after Saul into battle. However, David was the youngest, and David went away and pastured his father's flock in Bethlehem. Moreover Jesse said to David his son, "Take your brothers grain and those ten loaves, and run into the camp to your brothers."

Therefore David arose in the morning and came to the army, and found his brothers and was talking to them. Then that spurious man, Goliath by name, a Philistine from Gath, came out of the camp of the Philistines and challenged the camp of the Israelites to battle. Moreover, all the Israelites saw the man and fled from his face because they feared him greatly. But David said to the men: "Indeed, who is this uncircumcised Philistine? For he has reproached the army of the living God." Therefore he was led to Saul and said: "I your servant will go and fight against the Philistine." And Saul said to David, "You are not strong [enough] [or "You are not able"] to conquer that Philistine nor fight against him, because you are a boy; however, this man [has been] a warrior from his youth."

And David said to Saul, "Your servant pastured his father's flock and often a lion or bear would come, and snatch away a ram from the midst of the flock, and I would run toward them and I would cut [them] down and snatch it [the ram] from their mouth and I would kill them. For I your servant have killed both lion and bear. Therefore I will also be able to conquer this uncircumcised Philistine, because he dared to reproach the army of the living God." And David said, "The Lord has snatched me from the hand of the lion and from the hand of the bear, and he will deliver me from the hand of this Philistine." Moreover Saul said to David, "Go and may the Lord be with you."

And David carried his staff, and chose five very bright stones from the stream and put them into his shepherd's satchel and carried a sling in (his) hand and went against the Philistine. Moreover the Philistine approached David and saw him, and also despised him for he was a ruddy youth and his appearance/face was handsome. And the Philistine said to David: "Am I a dog, that you come to me with a staff?" and the Philistine cursed David by his gods. And he said to David: "Come to me and I will give your flesh to the birds of heaven and the beasts of the earth." Moreover David said to the Philistine: "You come to me with sword and spear and shield; but I come to you in the name of the Lord of armies [or hosts]. Today also the Lord will give you into my hand and I will strike you down and I will carry off your head from you. And I will give the carcass of the camp of the Philistines today to the birds of heaven and the beasts of the earth, and the whole earth will know that there is a God in Israel, and He will hand you over into our hands."

Therefore the Philistine arose and came and drew near against David. David hastened and ran toward the Philistine, and put his hand into his satchel and brought forth one stone. And he hurled [it] with [his] sling and struck the Philistine in [his] forehead, and the stone was fixed in his forehead and he fell on his face upon the earth. He ran and stood over the Philistine and took his sword and killed him and cut off his head. Morover, the Philistines saw him dead, their bravest [warrior], and they fled. And the men of Israel arose and shouted and pursued the Philistines and they fell. David moreover took the head of the Philistine for himself and carried it into Jerusalem, but his [i.e., Goliath's] weapons/armor he put in his own [i.e., David's] tent.

Unit 4 Test (185 points)

A. Vocabulary (25 points)

Translate the following words.

1. undique: **on/from all sides, from every direction**
2. satis: **enough, sufficient(ly)**
3. tamen: **yet, nevertheless, still**
4. ūnā: **together, in one**
5. iūxta: **(+ acc.) near (to), close to/by**
6. fortasse: **perhaps**
7. afterwards: **postea**
8. quam: **as, than, how**
9. quoque: **also, too**
10. quoniam: **because, since**
11. quōmodo: **how, in what way**
12. atque: **and, and also**
13. quickly: **cito**
14. secundum: **(+ acc.) after; according to**
15. cōram: **(+ abl.) in the presence of, before; (adv.) openly**
16. modo: **only, just, merely, but**
17. secretly: **clam**
18. seu: **or**
19. greatly: **magnoperē**
20. super: **(+ acc. / + abl.) over, above, beyond**
21. iterum: **again, a second time**
22. propter: **(+ acc.) because of, on account of, near**
23. veniō: **I come**
24. vertō: **I turn, change**
25. vincō: **I defeat, conquer**

B. Grammar (35 points)

1. Give a synopsis of *trahō* in the third person plural, then give its singular and plural imperatives.

	ACTIVE		PASSIVE	
	LATIN	ENGLISH	LATIN	ENGLISH
PRES.	trahunt	they drag	trahuntur	they are (being) dragged
IMPF.	trahēbant	they were dragging	trahēbantur	they were (being) dragged
FUT.	trahent	they will drag	trahentur	they will be dragged
PERF.	trāxērunt	they (have) dragged	trāctī/ae/a sunt	they were/have been dragged
PLUPF.	trāxerant	they had dragged	trāctī/ae/a erant	they had been dragged
FT. PF.	trāxerint	they will have dragged	trāctī/ae/a erunt	they will have been dragged

IMPERATIVE			
LATIN SINGULAR	ENGLISH SINGULAR	LATIN PLURAL	ENGLISH PLURAL
trahe!	drag!	trahite!	drag! (pl.)

2. Decline "this old song," *hic cantus vetus*.

	LATIN SINGULAR	LATIN PLURAL
NOM.	hic cantus vetus	hī cantūs veterēs
GEN.	huius cantūs veteris	hōrum cantuum veterium
DAT.	huic cantuī veterī	hīs cantibus veteribus
ACC.	hunc cantum veterem	hōs cantūs veterēs
ABL.	hōc cantū veterī	hīs cantibus veteribus
VOC.	Ō cantus vetus!	Ō cantūs veterēs

C. Translation (80 points)

1　Ūnā nocte ātrā pīrāta improbus ātrō cum corde dē malīs in nāve in mare gelidō et ātrō cōgitābat. "Montem aurī, multum cibum, et vīnum bonum magnoperē cupiō. Cōnsilia mea faciam. In portum illīus urbis parvae clam nāvigābō. Ibī ego et meī nautae sinistrī surgēmus et cito oppugnābimus quod omnēs dormient. Omnēs fēminās pulchrās rapiēmus, omnēs virōs occīdēmus, et līberōs quam servōs
5　nostrōs capiēmus. Ego rex omnium pīrātārum erō!" Iste improbus rīsit, et multum vīnum pōtāvit. Sed cōnsilia eius nōn facta sunt. Nāve ātrā ad illum portum vectus est, sed prope erat grex camēlōrum. Hī mandūcābant grāmen seū dormiēbant. Sed pīrāta improbus camēlōs sicā lūdere incēpit: "Venīte et mē pugnāte, camēlī stultī!" clāmāvit. Illī camēlī cito surrēxērunt et vēnērunt. Faciēs eōrum doctī et ferī erant, et pīrāta metū victus est. Ab tribus camēlīs nāvis eius fracta est; ab tribus camēlīs nautae eius
10　in mare iactī sunt, et ab tribus camēlīs deinde vinctus est. Camēlī omnem noctem eī cantūs barbarōs horrendōsque dē bellīs camēlōrum cantāvērunt. Posteā, pīrāta iit et cum mātre eius habitāvit, et animālia aut hominēs numquam iterum lūsit.

One dark night a wicked pirate with a black heart was thinking about evil things in [his] ship on the cold dark sea. "I greatly desire a mountain of gold, much food, and good wine. I will make my plans. I will secretly sail into the harbor of that little city. There my inauspicious sailors and I will rise and attack quickly, because everyone will be sleeping. We will seize all the beautiful women, kill all the men, and capture the children as our slaves. I will be king of all pirates!" That wicked one laughed, and drank much wine. But his plans did not happen. He was conveyed by the black ship to that harbor, but there was a herd of camels nearby. These [animals] were eating grass or sleeping. But the wicked pirate began to tease the camels with [his] dagger: "Come and fight me, stupid camels!" he shouted. Those camels arose swiftly and came. Their faces were wise and fierce, and the pirate was overcome by fear. His ship was shattered by three camels; his sailors were hurled into the sea by three camels; and by three camels he was then bound. All night the camels sang to him strange and dreadful songs about the wars of the camels. Afterwards the pirate went and lived with his mother, and never teased animals or people again.

D. Memorization (45 points)

Write out all of Psalm 23 in Latin.

¹Psalmus Dāvīd.

Dominus reget mē et nihil mihi dēerit.

²In locō pascuae ibī mē conlocāvit;

super aquam refectiōnis ēducāvit mē.

³Animam meam convertit.

Dēdūxit mē super sēmitās iūstitiae

propter nōmen suum.

⁴Nam et sī ambulāverō in mediō umbrae mortis,

nōn timēbō mala quoniam tū mēcum es;

virga tua et baculus tuus ipsa mē consōlāta sunt.

⁵Parāstī in conspectū meō mensam

adversus eōs quī trībulant mē.

Inpinguāstī in oleō caput meum,

et calix meus inēbrians quam praeclārus est.

⁶Et misericordia tua subsequitur mē

omnibus diēbus vītae meae,

et ut inhabitem in domō Dominī

in longitūdinem diērum.

Appendices

- Chant Charts
- Latin to English Glossary
- English to Latin Glossary
- Sources and Helps
- Verb Formation Chart

Chant Charts

VERBS

Present Active Indicative Verb Endings (*Lesson 1*)

	SINGULAR	PLURAL
1ST	-ō	-mus
2ND	-s	-tis
3RD	-t	-nt

	SINGULAR	PLURAL
1ST	I am *verbing*, I *verb*	we are *verbing*
2ND	you are *verbing*	you all are *verbing*
3RD	he/she/it is *verbing*	they are *verbing*

Imperfect Active Indicative Verb Endings (*Lesson 6*)

	SINGULAR	PLURAL
1ST	-bam	-bāmus
2ND	-bās	-bātis
3RD	-bat	-bant

	SINGULAR	PLURAL
1ST	I was *verbing*	we were *verbing*
2ND	you were *verbing*	you all were *verbing*
3RD	he/she/it was *verbing*	they were *verbing*

Future Active Indicative Verb Endings (*Lesson 6*)

	SINGULAR	PLURAL
1ST	-bō	-bimus
2ND	-bis	-bitis
3RD	-bit	-bunt

	SINGULAR	PLURAL
1ST	I will *verb*	we will *verb*
2ND	you will *verb*	you all will *verb*
3RD	he/she/it will *verb*	they will *verb*

Perfect Active Indicative Verb Endings (*Lesson 14*)

	LATIN SINGULAR	ENGLISH SINGULAR
1ST	-ī	I *verbed*, have *verbed*
2ND	-istī	you *verbed*, have *verbed*
3RD	-it	he/she/it *verbed*, has *verbed*

LATIN PLURAL	ENGLISH PLURAL
-imus	we *verbed*, have *verbed*
-istis	you (pl.) *verbed*, have *verbed*
-ērunt	they *verbed*, have *verbed*

Pluperfect Active Indicative Verb Endings (*Lesson 15*)

	LATIN SINGULAR	ENGLISH SINGULAR
1ST	-eram	I had *verbed*
2ND	-erās	you had *verbed*
3RD	-erat	he/she/it had *verbed*

LATIN PLURAL	ENGLISH PLURAL
-erāmus	we had *verbed*
-erātis	you (pl.) had *verbed*
-erant	they had *verbed*

Future Perfect Active Indicative Verb Endings (Lesson 15)

	LATIN SINGULAR	ENGLISH SINGULAR		LATIN PLURAL	ENGLISH PLURAL
1ST	-erō	I will have verbed		-erimus	we will have verbed
2ND	-eris	you will have verbed		-eritis	you (pl.) will have verbed
3RD	-erit	he/she/it will have verbed		-erint	they will have verbed

Present Passive Indicative Verb Endings (Lesson 20)

	LATIN SINGULAR	ENGLISH SINGULAR		LATIN PLURAL	ENGLISH PLURAL
1ST	-r	I am (being) verbed		-mur	we are (being) verbed
2ND	-ris	you are (being) verbed		-minī	you (pl.) are (being) verbed
3RD	-tur	he/she/it is (being) verbed		-ntur	they are being verbed

Imperfect Passive Indicative Verb Endings (Lesson 20)

	LATIN SINGULAR	ENGLISH SINGULAR		LATIN PLURAL	ENGLISH PLURAL
1ST	-ba**r**	I was (being) verbed		-bā**mur**	we were (being) verbed
2ND	-bā**ris**	you were (being) verbed		-bā**minī**	you (pl.) were (being) verbed
3RD	-bā**tur**	he/she/it was (being) verbed		-ban**tur**	they were (being) verbed

Future Passive Indicative Verb Endings (Lesson 20)

	LATIN SINGULAR	ENGLISH SINGULAR		LATIN PLURAL	ENGLISH PLURAL
1ST	-bo**r**	I will be verbed		-bi**mur**	we will be verbed
2ND	-be**ris**	you will be verbed		-bi**minī**	you (pl.) will be verbed
3RD	-bi**tur**	he/she/it will be verbed		-bu**ntur**	they will be verbed

Perfect Passive Indicative (Lesson 22)

	LATIN SINGULAR	ENGLISH SINGULAR		LATIN PLURAL	ENGLISH PLURAL
1ST	4th principal part (sg.) + sum	I was/have been verbed		4th p.p. (pl.)+ sumus	we were/have been verbed
2ND	4th p.p. (sg.) + es	you were/have been verbed		4th p.p. (pl.)+ estis	you (pl.) were/have been verbed
3RD	4th p.p. (sg.) + est	he/she/it was/has been verbed		4th p.p. (pl.)+ sunt	they were/have been verbed

Pluperfect Passive Indicative (Lesson 22)

	LATIN SINGULAR	ENGLISH SINGULAR		LATIN PLURAL	ENGLISH PLURAL
1ST	4th principal part (sg.) + eram	I had been verbed		4th p.p. (pl.)+ erāmus	we had been verbed
2ND	4th p.p. (sg.) + erās	you had been verbed		4th p.p. (pl.)+ erātis	you (pl.) had been verbed
3RD	4th p.p. (sg.) + erat	he/she/it had been verbed		4th p.p. (pl.)+ erant	they had been verbed

Future Perfect Passive Indicative *(Lesson 22)*

	LATIN SINGULAR	ENGLISH SINGULAR
1ST	4th principal part (sg.) + erō	I will have been *verbed*
2ND	4th p.p. (sg.) + eris	you will have been *verbed*
3RD	4th p.p. (sg.) + erit	he/she/it will have been *verbed*

	LATIN PLURAL	ENGLISH PLURAL
1ST	4th p.p. (pl.)+ erimus	we will have been *verbed*
2ND	4th p.p. (pl.)+ eritis	you (pl.) will have been *verbed*
3RD	4th p.p. (pl.)+ erunt	they will have been *verbed*

Irregular Verb: Sum, *I am*—Present Active *(Lesson 3)*

	LATIN SINGULAR	ENGLISH SINGULAR
1ST	sum	I am
2ND	es	you are
3RD	est	he/she/it is

	LATIN PLURAL	ENGLISH PLURAL
1ST	sumus	we are
2ND	estis	you all are
3RD	sunt	they are

Irregular Verb: Eram, *I was*—Imperfect Active of *Sum* *(Lesson 10)*

	LATIN SINGULAR	ENGLISH SINGULAR
1ST	eram	I was
2ND	erās	you were
3RD	erat	he/she/it was

	LATIN PLURAL	ENGLISH PLURAL
1ST	erāmus	we were
2ND	erātis	you all were
3RD	erant	they were

Irregular Verb: Erō, *I will be*—Future Active of *Sum* *(Lesson 10)*

	LATIN SINGULAR	ENGLISH SINGULAR
1ST	erō	erimus
2ND	eris	eritis
3RD	erit	erunt

	LATIN PLURAL	ENGLISH PLURAL
1ST	I will be	we will be
2ND	you will be	you all will be
3RD	he/she/it will be	they will be

Irregular Verb: Fuī, *I was, have been*—Perfect Active Indicative of *Sum* *(Lesson 14)*

	LATIN SINGULAR	ENGLISH SINGULAR
1ST	fuī	I was, have been
2ND	fuistī	you were, have been
3RD	fuit	he/she/it was, has been

	LATIN PLURAL	ENGLISH PLURAL
1ST	fuimus	we were, have been
2ND	fuistis	you (pl.) were, have been
3RD	fuērunt	they were, have been

Irregular Verb: Possum, *I am able*—Present Active Indicative *(Lesson 11)*

	LATIN SINGULAR	ENGLISH SINGULAR
1ST	possum	I am able
2ND	potes	you are able
3RD	potest	he/she/it is able

	LATIN PLURAL	ENGLISH PLURAL
1ST	possumus	we are able
2ND	potestis	you (pl.) are able
3RD	possunt	they are able

Irregular Verb: Poteram, *I was able*—Imperfect Active Indicative of *Possum* (Lesson 11)

	LATIN SINGULAR	ENGLISH SINGULAR		LATIN PLURAL	ENGLISH PLURAL
1ST	poteram	I was able		poterāmus	we were able
2ND	poterās	you were able		poterātis	you (pl.) were able
3RD	poterat	he/she/it was able		poterant	they were able

Irregular Verb: Poterō, *I will be able*—Future Active Indicative of *Possum* (Lesson 11)

	LATIN SINGULAR	ENGLISH SINGULAR		LATIN PLURAL	ENGLISH PLURAL
1ST	poterō	I will be able		poterimus	we will be able
2ND	poteris	you will be able		poteritis	you (pl.) will be able
3RD	poterit	he/she/it will be able		poterunt	they will be able

Irregular Verb: Potuī, *I was able, have been able*—Perfect Active Indicative of *Possum* (Lesson 14)

	LATIN SINGULAR	ENGLISH SINGULAR		LATIN PLURAL	ENGLISH PLURAL
1ST	potuī	I was able, have been able		potuimus	we were able, have been able
2ND	potuistī	you were able, have been able		potuistis	you (pl.) were able, have been able
3RD	potuit	he/she/it was able, has been able		potuērunt	they were able, have been able

NOUNS

First Declension Feminine Noun Endings *(Lesson 2)*

	LATIN SG.	ENGLISH SG.		LATIN PL.	ENGLISH PL.
NOM.	-a	a/the *noun* [subject]		-ae	the *nouns* [subject]
GEN.	-ae	of the *noun*, the *noun's*		-ārum	of the *nouns*, the *nouns'*
DAT.	-ae	to/for the *noun*		-īs	to/for the *nouns*
ACC.	-am	a/the *noun* [direct object]		-ās	the *nouns* [direct object]
ABL.	-ā	by/with/from the *noun*		-īs	by/with/from the *nouns*
VOC.	-a	[O] *noun*!		-ae	[O] *nouns*!

Second Declension Masculine Noun Endings *(Lesson 4)*

	LATIN SG.	ENGLISH SG.		LATIN PL.	ENGLISH PL.
NOM.	-us/ -r	a/the *noun* [subject]		-ī	the *nouns* [subject]
GEN.	-ī	of the *noun*, the *noun's*		-ōrum	of the *nouns*, the *nouns'*
DAT.	-ō	to/for the *noun*		-īs	to/for the *nouns*
ACC.	-um	a/the *noun* [direct object]		-ōs	the *nouns* [direct object]
ABL.	-ō	by/with/from the *noun*		-īs	by/with/from the *nouns*
VOC.	-e/ -r	[O] *noun*!		-ī	[O] *nouns*!

Second Declension Neuter Noun Endings (Lesson 5)

	LATIN SG.	ENGLISH SG.	LATIN PL.	ENGLISH PL.
NOM.	-um	a/the *noun* [subject]	-a	the *nouns* [subject]
GEN.	-ī	of the *noun*, the *noun's*	-ōrum	of the *nouns*, the *nouns'*
DAT.	-ō	to/for the *noun*	-īs	to/for the *nouns*
ACC.	-um	a/the *noun* [direct object]	-a	the *nouns* [direct object]
ABL.	-ō	by/with/from the *noun*	-īs	by/with/from the *nouns*
VOC.	-um	[O] *noun*!	-a	[O] *nouns*!

Third Declension Masculine/Feminine Noun Endings (Lesson 12)

	LATIN SG.	ENGLISH SG.	LATIN PL.	ENGLISH PL.
NOM.	X	a/the *noun* [subject]	-ēs	the *nouns* [subject]
GEN.	-is	of the *noun*, the *noun's*	-um	of the *nouns*, the *nouns'*
DAT.	-ī	to/for the *noun*	-ibus	to/for the *nouns*
ACC.	-em	a/the *noun* [direct object]	-ēs	the *nouns* [direct object]
ABL.	-e	by/with/from the *noun*	-ibus	by/with/from the *nouns*
VOC.	X	[O] *noun*!	-ēs	[O] *nouns*!

Third Declension Neuter Noun Endings (Lesson 13)

	LATIN SG.	ENGLISH SG.	LATIN PL.	ENGLISH PL.
NOM.	X	a/the *noun* [subject]	-a	the *nouns* [subject]
GEN.	-is	of the *noun*, the *noun's*	-um	of the *nouns*, the *nouns'*
DAT.	-ī	to/for the *noun*	-ibus	to/for the *nouns*
ACC.	X	a/the *noun* [direct object]	-a	the *nouns* [direct object]
ABL.	-e	by/with/from the *noun*	-ibus	by/with/from the *nouns*
VOC.	X	[O] *noun*!	**-a**	[O] *nouns*!

Third Declension Masculine/Feminine i-Stem Noun Endings (Lesson 18)

	LATIN SG.	ENGLISH SG.	LATIN PL.	ENGLISH PL.
NOM.	X	a/the *noun* [subject]	-ēs	the *nouns* [subject]
GEN.	-is	of the *noun*, the *noun's*	-ium	of the *nouns*, the *nouns'*
DAT.	-ī	to/for the *noun*	-ibus	to/for the *nouns*
ACC.	-em	a/the *noun* [direct object]	-ēs	the *nouns* [direct object]
ABL.	-e/ī	by/with/from the *noun*	-ibus	by/with/from the *nouns*
VOC.	X	[O] *noun*!	-ēs	[O] *nouns*!

Third Declension Neuter i-Stem Noun Endings *(Lesson 18)*

	LATIN SG.	ENGLISH SG.	LATIN PL.	ENGLISH PL.
NOM.	X	a/the *noun* [subject]	-ia	the *nouns* [subject]
GEN.	-is	of the *noun*, the *noun's*	-ium	of the *nouns*, the *nouns'*
DAT.	-ī	to/for the *noun*	-ibus	to/for the *nouns*
ACC.	X	a/the *noun* [direct object]	-ia	the *nouns* [direct object]
ABL.	-ī	by/with/from the *noun*	-ibus	by/with/from the *nouns*
VOC.	X	[O] *noun*!	-ia	[O] *nouns*!

Fourth Declension Masculine/Feminine Noun Endings *(Lesson 25)*

	LATIN SG.	ENGLISH SG.	LATIN PL.	ENGLISH PL.
NOM.	-us	a/the *noun* [subject]	-ūs	the *nouns* [subject]
GEN.	-ūs	of the *noun*, the *noun's*	-uum	of the *nouns*, the *nouns'*
DAT.	-uī	to/for the *noun*	-ibus	to/for the *nouns*
ACC.	-um	a/the *noun* [direct object]	-ūs	the *nouns* [direct object]
ABL.	-ū	by/with/from the *noun*	-ibus	by/with/from the *nouns*
VOC.	**-us**	[O] *noun*!	-ūs	[O] *nouns*!

Fourth Declension Neuter Noun Endings *(Lesson 25)*

	LATIN SG.	ENGLISH SG.	LATIN PL.	ENGLISH PL.
NOM.	-ū	a/the *noun* [subject]	-ua	the *nouns* [subject]
GEN.	-ūs	of the *noun*, the *noun's*	-uum	of the *nouns*, the *nouns'*
DAT.	-ū	to/for the *noun*	-ibus	to/for the *nouns*
ACC.	-ū	a/the *noun* [direct object]	-ua	the *nouns* [direct object]
ABL.	-ū	by/with/from the *noun*	-ibus	by/with/from the *nouns*
VOC.	**-ū**	[O] *noun*!	-ua	[O] *nouns*!

Fifth Declension Noun Endings *(Lesson 28)*

	SINGULAR	PLURAL	SINGULAR	PLURAL
NOM.	-es	a/the *noun* [subject]	-ēs	the *nouns* [subject]
GEN.	-eī/-ēī	of the *noun*, the *noun's*	-ērum	of the *nouns*, the *nouns'*
DAT.	-eī/-ēī	to/for the *noun*	-ēbus	to/for the *nouns*
ACC.	-em	a/the *noun* [direct object]	-ēs	the *nouns* [direct object]
ABL.	-ē	by/with/from the *noun*	-ēbus	by/with/from the *nouns*
VOC.	-es	[O] *noun*!	-ēs	[O] *nouns*!

ADJECTIVES

First and Second Declension Adjective Endings *(Lesson 7)*

	SINGULAR				PLURAL		
	MASC.	FEM.	NEUT.		MASC.	FEM.	NEUT.
NOM.	-us / -r	-a	-um		-ī	-ae	-a
GEN.	-ī	-ae	-ī		-ōrum	-ārum	-ōrum
DAT.	-ō	-ae	-ō		-īs	-īs	-īs
ACC.	-um	-am	-um		-ōs	-ās	-a
ABL.	-ō	-ā	-ō		-īs	-īs	-īs
VOC.	-e / -r	-a	-um		-ī	-ae	-a

Third Declension Adjectives *(Lesson 19)*

	SINGULAR		PLURAL	
	MASC./FEM.	NEUTER	MASC./FEM.	NEUTER
NOM.	X	X	-ēs	-ia
GEN.	-is	-is	-ium	-ium
DAT.	-ī	-ī	-ibus	-ibus
ACC.	-em	X	-ēs	-ia
ABL.	-ī	-ī	-ibus	-ibus
VOC.	X	X	-ēs	-ia

Numerals *(Lesson 21)*

ūnus, ūna, ūnum, *one*

	SINGULAR		
	MASCULINE	FEMININE	NEUTER
NOM.	ūnus	ūna	ūnum
GEN.	ūnīus	ūnīus	ūnīus
DAT.	ūnī	ūnī	ūnī
ACC.	ūnum	ūnam	ūnum
ABL.	ūnō	ūnā	ūnō

duo, duae, duo, *two*

	PLURAL		
	MASCULINE	FEMININE	NEUTER
NOM.	duo	duae	duo
GEN.	duōrum	duārum	duōrum
DAT.	duōbus	duābus	duōbus
ACC.	duōs	duās	duo
ABL.	duōbus	duābus	duōbus

trēs, tria, *three* mille, *one thousand*

	PLURAL	
	M/F	N
NOM.	trēs	tria
GEN.	trium	trium
DAT.	tribus	tribus
ACC.	trēs	tria
ABL.	tribus	tribus

	SINGULAR	PLURAL
	M/F/N	N
NOM.	mille	mīlia
GEN.	mille	mīlium
DAT.	mille	mīlibus
ACC.	mille	mīlia
ABL.	mille	mīlibus

PRONOUNS

First Person Personal Pronouns *(Lesson 17)*

	LATIN SINGULAR	ENGLISH SINGULAR
NOMINATIVE	ego	I [subject]
GENITIVE	meī	of me
DATIVE	mihi	to/for me
ACCUSATIVE	mē	me [direct object]
ABLATIVE	mē	by/with/from me

	LATIN PLURAL	ENGLISH PLURAL
NOMINATIVE	nōs	we [subject]
GENITIVE	nostrum	of us
DATIVE	nōbīs	to/for us
ACCUSATIVE	nōs	us [direct object]
ABLATIVE	nōbīs	by/with/from us

Second Person Personal Pronouns *(Lesson 17)*

	LATIN SINGULAR	ENGLISH SINGULAR
NOMINATIVE	tū	you [subject]
GENITIVE	tuī	of you
DATIVE	tibī	to/for you
ACCUSATIVE	tē	you [direct object]
ABLATIVE	tē	by/with/from you

	LATIN PLURAL	ENGLISH PLURAL
NOMINATIVE	vōs	you (pl.) [subject]
GENITIVE	vestrum	of you (pl.)
DATIVE	vōbīs	to/for you (pl.)
ACCUSATIVE	vōs	you (pl.) [direct object]
ABLATIVE	vōbīs	by/with/from you (pl.)

Third Person Personal Pronouns—Singular *(Lesson 17)*

	MASCULINE	FEMININE	NEUTER	
	he/his/him	she/hers/her	it/its	ENGLISH
NOM.	is	ea	id	he/she/it (this/that, etc.)
GEN.	eius	eius	eius	of him/his, of her/hers, of it/its
DAT.	eī	eī	eī	to/for him, to/for her, to/for it
ACC.	eum	eam	id	him/her/it
ABL.	eō	eā	eō	by/with/from him/her/it

Third Person Personal Pronouns—Plural *(Lesson 17)*

	MASCULINE	FEMININE	NEUTER	
	they/their/them	they/their/them	they/their/them	ENGLISH
NOM.	eī	eae	ea	they (these/those, etc.)
GEN.	eōrum	eārum	eōrum	of them, their
DAT.	eīs	eīs	eīs	to/for them
ACC.	eōs	eās	ea	them
ABL.	eīs	eīs	eīs	by/with/from them

DEMONSTRATIVES

Various Demonstrative Pronouns *(Lesson 30)*

Hic, haec, hoc—this; (pl.) these

	SINGULAR			PLURAL		
	MASCULINE	FEMININE	NEUTER	MASCULINE	FEMININE	NEUTER
NOM.	hic	haec	hoc	hī	hae	haec
GEN.	huius	huius	huius	hōrum	hārum	hōrum
DAT.	huic	huic	huic	hīs	hīs	hīs
ACC.	hunc	hanc	hoc	hōs	hās	haec
ABL.	hōc	hāc	hōc	hīs	hīs	hīs

Ille, illa, illud—that; (pl.) those; that famous

	SINGULAR			PLURAL		
	MASCULINE	FEMININE	NEUTER	MASCULINE	FEMININE	NEUTER
NOM.	ille	illa	illud	illī	illae	illa
GEN.	illīus	illīus	illīus	illōrum	illārum	illōrum
DAT.	illī	illī	illī	illīs	illīs	illīs
ACC.	illum	illam	illud	illōs	illās	illa
ABL.	illō	illā	illō	illīs	illīs	illīs

Iste, ista, istud—that (of yours); such

	SINGULAR			PLURAL		
	MASCULINE	FEMININE	NEUTER	MASCULINE	FEMININE	NEUTER
NOM.	iste	ista	istud	istī	istae	ista
GEN.	istīus	istīus	istīus	istōrum	istārum	istōrum
DAT.	istī	istī	istī	istīs	istīs	istīs
ACC.	istum	istam	istud	istōs	istās	ista
ABL.	istō	istā	istō	istīs	istīs	istīs

Verb Memorization
Chants Applied to *amō, videō, dūcō, capiō,* and *audiō*

The chants in this section follow the conjugations of amō *(1st),* videō *(2nd),* dūcō *(3rd),* capiō *(3rd -iō), and* audiō *(4th) through the present, imperfect, and future indicative tenses. Endings have been bolded.*

	1ST	2ND	3RD	3RD -iō	4TH
PRESENT ACTIVE	am**ō**	vid**eō**	dūc**ō**	capi**ō**	audi**ō**
	amā**s**	vidē**s**	dūci**s**	capi**s**	audī**s**
	ama**t**	vide**t**	dūci**t**	capi**t**	audi**t**
	amā**mus**	vidē**mus**	dūci**mus**	capi**mus**	audī**mus**
	amā**tis**	vidē**tis**	dūci**tis**	capi**tis**	audī**tis**
	ama**nt**	vide**nt**	dūcu**nt**	capiu**nt**	audiu**nt**
IMPERFECT ACTIVE	amā**bam**	vidē**bam**	dūcē**bam**	capiē**bam**	audiē**bam**
	amā**bās**	vidē**bās**	dūcē**bās**	capiē**bās**	audiē**bās**
	amā**bat**	vidē**bat**	dūcē**bat**	capiē**bat**	audiē**bat**
	amā**bāmus**	vidē**bāmus**	dūcē**bāmus**	capiē**bāmus**	audiē**bāmus**
	amā**bātis**	vidē**bātis**	dūcē**bātis**	capiē**bātis**	audiē**bātis**
	amā**bant**	vidē**bant**	dūcē**bant**	capiē**bant**	audiē**bant**
FUTURE ACTIVE	amā**bō**	vidē**bō**	dūc**am**	capi**am**	audi**am**
	amā**bis**	vidē**bis**	dūc**ēs**	capi**ēs**	audi**ēs**
	amā**bit**	vidē**bit**	dūc**et**	capi**et**	audi**et**
	amā**bimus**	vidē**bimus**	dūc**ēmus**	capi**ēmus**	audi**ēmus**
	amā**bitis**	vidē**bitis**	dūc**ētis**	capi**ētis**	audi**ētis**
	amā**bunt**	vidē**bunt**	dūc**ent**	capi**ent**	audi**ent**
PRESENT PASSIVE	am**or**	vide**or**	dūc**or**	capi**or**	audi**or**
	amā**ris**	vidē**ris**	dūce**ris**	cape**ris**	audī**ris**
	amā**tur**	vidē**tur**	dūci**tur**	capi**tur**	audī**tur**
	amā**mur**	vidē**mur**	dūci**mur**	capi**mur**	audī**mur**
	amā**minī**	vidē**minī**	dūci**minī**	capi**minī**	audī**minī**
	ama**ntur**	vide**ntur**	dūcu**ntur**	capiu**ntur**	audiu**ntur**
IMPERFECT PASSIVE	amā**bar**	vidē**bar**	dūcē**bar**	capiē**bar**	audiē**bar**
	amā**bāris**	vidē**bāris**	dūcē**bāris**	capiē**bāris**	audiē**bāris**
	amā**bātur**	vidē**bātur**	dūcē**bātur**	capiē**bātur**	audiē**bātur**
	amā**bāmur**	vidē**bāmur**	dūcē**bāmur**	capiē**bāmur**	audiē**bāmur**
	amā**bāminī**	vidē**bāminī**	dūcē**bāminī**	capiē**bāminī**	audiē**bāminī**
	amā**bantur**	vidē**bantur**	dūcē**bantur**	capiē**bantur**	audiē**bantur**

	1ST	2ND	3RD	3RD -IŌ	4TH
FUTURE PASSIVE	amā**bor**	vidē**bor**	dūca**r**	capia**r**	audia**r**
	amā**beris**	vidē**beris**	dūcē**ris**	capiē**ris**	audiē**ris**
	amā**bitur**	vidē**bitur**	dūcē**tur**	capiē**tur**	audiē**tur**
	amā**bimur**	vidē**bimur**	dūcē**mur**	capiē**mur**	audiē**mur**
	amā**biminī**	vidē**biminī**	dūcē**minī**	capiē**minī**	audiē**minī**
	amā**buntur**	vidē**buntur**	dūce**ntur**	capie**ntur**	audie**ntur**

The chants in this section follow the conjugations of amō (1st), videō (2nd), dūcō (3rd), capiō (3rd -iō), and audiō (4th) through the perfect, pluperfect, and future perfect indicative tenses. Endings have been bolded.

	1ST	2ND	3RD	3RD -IŌ	4TH
PERFECT ACTIVE	amāv**ī**	vīd**ī**	dūx**ī**	cēp**ī**	audīv**ī**
	amāv**istī**	vīd**istī**	dūx**istī**	cēp**istī**	audīv**istī**
	amāv**it**	vīd**it**	dūx**it**	cēp**it**	audīv**it**
	amāv**imus**	vīd**imus**	dūx**imus**	cēp**imus**	audīv**imus**
	amāv**istis**	vīd**istis**	dūx**istis**	cēp**istis**	audīv**istis**
	amāv**ērunt**	vīd**ērunt**	dūx**ērunt**	cēp**ērunt**	audīv**ērunt**
PLUPERFECT ACTIVE	amāv**eram**	vīd**eram**	dūx**eram**	cēp**eram**	audīv**eram**
	amāv**erās**	vīd**erās**	dūx**erās**	cēp**erās**	audīv**erās**
	amāv**erat**	vīd**erat**	dūx**erat**	cēp**erat**	audīv**erat**
	amāv**erāmus**	vīd**erāmus**	dūx**erāmus**	cēp**erāmus**	audīv**erāmus**
	amāv**erātis**	vīd**erātis**	dūx**erātis**	cēp**erātis**	audīv**erātis**
	amāv**erant**	vīd**erant**	dūx**erant**	cēp**erant**	audīv**erant**
FUTURE PERFECT ACTIVE	amāv**erō**	vīd**erō**	dūx**erō**	cēp**erō**	audīv**erō**
	amāv**eris**	vīd**eris**	dūx**eris**	cēp**eris**	audīv**eris**
	amāv**erit**	vīd**erit**	dūx**erit**	cēp**erit**	audīv**erit**
	amāv**erimus**	vīd**erimus**	dūx**erimus**	cēp**erimus**	audīv**erimus**
	amāv**eritis**	vīd**eritis**	dūx**eritis**	cēp**eritis**	audīv**eritis**
	amāv**erint**	vīd**erint**	dūx**erint**	cēp**erint**	audīv**erint**
PERFECT PASSIVE	amāt**us sum**	vīs**us sum**	duct**us sum**	capt**us sum**	audīt**us sum**
	amāt**us es**	vīs**us es**	duct**us es**	capt**us es**	audīt**us es**
	amāt**us est**	vīs**us est**	duct**us est**	capt**us est**	audīt**us est**
	amāt**ī sumus**	vīs**ī sumus**	duct**ī sumus**	capt**ī sumus**	audīt**ī sumus**
	amāt**ī estis**	vīs**ī estis**	duct**ī estis**	capt**ī estis**	audīt**ī sumus**
	amāt**ī sunt**	vīs**ī sunt**	duct**ī sunt**	capt**ī sunt**	audīt**ī sunt**

APPENDICES \\ CHANT CHARTS

PLUPERFECT PASSIVE	amātus eram	vīsus eram	ductus eram	captus eram	audītus eram
	amātus erās	vīsus erās	ductus erās	captus erās	audītus erās
	amātus erat	vīsus erat	ductus erat	captus erat	audītus erat
	amātī erāmus	vīsī erāmus	ductī erāmus	captī erāmus	audītī erāmus
	amātī erātis	vīsī erātis	ductī erātis	captī erātis	audītī erātis
	amātī erant	vīsī erant	ductī erant	captī erant	audītī erant
FUTURE PERFECT PASSIVE	amātus erō	vīsus erō	ductus erō	captus erō	audītus erō
	amātus eris	vīsus eris	ductus eris	captus eris	audītus eris
	amātus erit	vīsus erit	ductus erit	captus erit	audītus erit
	amātī erimus	vīsī erimus	ductī erimus	captī erimus	audītī erimus
	amātī eritis	vīsī eritis	ductī eritis	captī eritis	audītī eritis
	amātī erunt	vīsī erunt	ductī erunt	captī erunt	audītī erunt

English–Latin Glossary

Here you will find the words for the English-Latin sections of your worksheets. When using any glossary, always keep in mind that two languages don't always mesh perfectly. For example, if you look up "land" you will find *patria*, *tellūs*, and *terra*. They all can mean "land," but you'll have to use good judgment to decide which is correct in a given context! In brackets you will find the number of the lesson (L), worksheet (W) or story (S) where each word is introduced.

A

abandon *relinquō, -ere, -līquī, -lictum* [L28]

abduction *raptus, -ūs (m)* [W31]

able (am able) *possum, posse, potuī, ——* [L11]

above *super (+ acc. & + abl.)* [L6]; *suprā (adv. & prep. + acc.)* [L14]

abundance *cōpia, -ae (f)* [L15]

accept *accipiō, -ere, -cēpī, -ceptum* [L31]

according to *secundum (adv. & prep. + acc.)* [L28]

accordingly *ergo (adv.)* [L18]

across *trans (+ acc.)* [L11]

act *agō, -ere, ēgi, actum* [L26]

advice *cōnsilium, -iī (n)* [L30]

Aegean *Aegeus, -a, -um* [W30]

Aegeus *Aegeus, -ei (m)* [W30]

affirm *āiō* [L14]

after (prep.) *post (+ acc.)* [L17]; *secundum (adv./prep. + acc.)* [L28]; *postquam (conj.)* [W15]

afterwards *postea* [L28]

again *iterum* [L25]

against *contrā (+ acc.)* [L11]; *in (+ acc.)* [L3]

aid *auxilium, -ī (n)* [L5]

alas! *heu (ēheu)* [L22]

alchemy *alchemia, -ae (f)* [W27]

alder *alnus, -ī (f)* [L4]

all *omnis, -e* [L19]

allow *permittō, -ere, -mīsī, -missum* [W30]

allowed (it is allowed) *licet* [W26]

almost *paene (adv.)* [L19]

already *iam* [L15]

also *et* [L1]; *etiam* [L22]; *quoque* [L29]

always *semper* [L5]

am (I am) *sum, esse, fuī, futūrum* [L3]

amazement *stupor, -ōris (m)* [W28]

among *inter (+ acc.)* [L19]

ancestor *avus, -ī (m)* [L22]

ancient *antīquus, -a, -um* [L7]

and *ac (atque)* [L27]; *et* [L1]; *-que (enclitic)* [L10]

and also *ac (atque)* [L27]

and not *nec (neque)* [L14]

and so *itaque* [L2]

anger *īra, -ae (f)* [L2]

angry *īrātus, -a, -um* [L15]

animal *animal, -ālis (n)* [L18]

announce *nuntiō (1)* [L14]

annoy *vexō (1)* [L19]

another *alius, alia, aliud* [W21]

answer *respondeō, -ēre, -spondī, -spōnsum* [L9]

anyone *ūllus, -a, -um* [W27]

anything *ūllus, -a, -um* [W27]

Apollo *Apollō, -inis (m)* [W20]

apostle *apostolus, -ī (m)* [L11]

apprentice *discipulus, -ī (m)* [L5]

approach *appropinquō (1)* [L25]

arch *arcus, -ūs (m)* [L27]

Argus *Argus, -ī (m)* [W21]

Ariadne *Ariadna, -ae (f)* [W30]

arise *surgō, -ere, surrēxī, surrēctum* [L28]

arm *bracchium, -ī (n)* [W13]

armor *arma, -ōrum (n, pl)* [W32]

arms *arma, -ōrum (n, pl)* [W32]

army *exercitus, -ūs (m)* [L25]

arrange *collocō (1)* [W21]

arrow *sagitta, -ae (f)* [L3]

as *quam* [L28]; *sīcut* [L20]

ask *rogō (1)* [L6]

assert *āiō* [L14]

astonishment *stupor, -ōris (m)* [W28]

at *ad (+ acc.)* [L3]

at that place *ibī* [L5]

at that time *tum* [L15]

at the foot of *sub (+ abl.)* [L14]

Athenian *Athēniensis, -is (m/f)* [W30]

Athens *Athēnae, -ārum (f, pl)* [W30]

attack *oppugnō (1)* [L4]

attempt *temptō (1)* [W27]

aunt *amita, -ae (f)* [L22]

avoid *vītō (1)* [L30]

away from *ā, ab (+ abl.)* [L3]

awful *horrendus, -a, -um* [L13]

B

baby *infāns, -fantis (adj./noun, m/f)* [W31]

Bacchus *Bacchus, -ī (m)* [W27]

back(ward) *retrō* [W23]

bad *malus, -a, -um* [L7]

badly *male* [L1]

bag *pēra, -ae (f)* [W32]

ball *pila, -ae (f)* [W30]

barbarian *barbarus, -ī (m)* [L31]

barber *tonsor, -ōris (m)* [W28]

barrier *spīna, -ae (f)* [W23]

battle *proelium, -ī (n)* [L15]

be *sum, esse, fuī, futūrum* [L3]

behind *retrō* [W23]

be silent *taceō, ēre, -uī, -itum* [W26]

be strong *valeō, -ēre, -uī, valitūrum* [L9]

be well *salveō, -ēre, —, —* [L9]; *valeō, -ēre, -uī, valitūrum* [L9]

beach *harēna, -ae (f)* [L3]

bear (noun) *ursus, -ī (m)* [W32]

bear (verb) *gerō, -ere, gessī, gestum* [L28]; *ferō, ferre, tulī, lātum (irreg. 3rd conj.)* [W32]

beast *bēstia, -ae (f)* [L2]

beautiful *pulcher, -chra, -chrum* [L7]

because *quandō* [L12]; *quia (conj.)* [L18]; *quod* [L10]; *quoniam* [L26]

because of *propter (+ acc.)* [L25]

become *fīō, fierī, —, factus sum* [L31]

before *ante (+ acc.)* [L17]; *cōram (+ abl.)* [L27]; *pro (+ abl.)* [L18]

begin *incipiō, -ere, -cēpī, -ceptum* [L31]

behind *post (+ acc.)* [L17]

behold! *ecce* [L17]

believe *crēdō, -ere, -didī, -ditum* [L26]

beloved *cārus, -a, -um* [L13]

below *sub (+ abl.)* [L14]

bereft *orbus, -a, -um* [L22]

beseige *obsideō, -ēre, -sēdī, -sessum* [L10]

besides *etiam* [L22]

Bethlehem *Bethleem (indecl.)* [W32]

better *melior, -ius* [W28]

between *inter (+ acc.)* [L19]

beware (of) *caveō, -ēre, cāvī, cautum* [L12]

beyond *super (+ acc./+ abl.)* [L26]

Bible (Holy Bible) *Biblia Sacra, Bibliae Sacrae (f)* [L11]

big *magnus, -a, -um* [L7]

billy goat *caper, -prī (m)* [L4]

bind *vinciō, -īre, vīnxī, vīnctum* [L30]

bird *avis, avis (f)* [L18]

bit by bit *minūtātim* [L20]

bite *mordeō, -ēre, momordī, morsum* [L9]

black (dead black) *āter, -tra, -trum* [L17]; **(shining black)** *niger, -gra, grum* [L17]

blaze *ardeō, ardēre, arsī, —* [L20]

blessed *beātus, -a, -um* [L7]

blind *caecus, -a, -um* [L27]

blue *caeruleus, -a, -um* [L17]; *hyacinthinus, -a, -um* [L17]

boat *nāvicula, -ae (f)* [W31]

body *corpus, corporis (n)* [L13]; **(dead body)** *cadaver, -veris (n)* [W32]

bold *magnanimus, -a, -um* [W9]

book *liber, librī (m)* [L11]

both…and *et…et* [L1]

boundary *fīnis, -is (m)* [W4]

bow *arcus, -ūs (m)* [L27]

boy *puer, puerī (m)* [L5]

brave *fortis, -e* [L19]; *magnanimus, -a, -um* [W9]

braver *fortior, -tius (gen. fortiōris)* [W31]

bravest *fortissimus, -a, -um* [W32]

bread *pānis, -is (m)* [L29]

break *frangō, -ere, frēgī, fractum* [L27]

breath *spīritus, -ūs (m)* [L25]

bridge *pōns, pontis (m)* [W19]

brief *brevis, -e* [L19]

bright (verb; am bright) *lūceō, lūcēre, lūxī, —* [L11]

bright (adj.; very bright) *limpidissimus, -a, -um* [W32]

bring (forth) *ferō, ferre, tulī, lātum (irreg. 3rd conj.)* [W32]

broad *lātus, -a, -um* [L20]

brother *frāter, frātris (m)* [L12]; *germānus, -ī (m)* [L4]

brown (dark-brown) *purpureus, -a, -um* [L17]

bull *bōs, bovis (m)* [L19]

burden *onus, oneris (n)* [L13]

burn (intransit.) *ardeō, ardēre, arsī, —* [L20]; *torreō, -ēre, torruī, tostum* [L17]

burn (transit.) *cremō (1)* [L2]

business (mind one's own business) *suum negōtium agere* [W29]

but *modo* [L27]; *sed* [L1]

by *iūxta (adv. & prep. + acc.)* [L28]

C

cabin (of a ship) *diaeta, -ae (f)* [W18]

call *appellō (1)* [L15]; *vocō (1)* [L1]

calm *placidus, -a, -um* [W29]

camel *camēlus, -ī (m/f)* [L4]

camp *castra, -ōrum (n, pl)* [L15]

can *possum, posse, potuī, —* [L11]

capture *capiō, -ere, cēpī, captum* [L31]

carcass *cadaver, -veris (n)* [W32]

care for *cūrō (1)* [L15]

carry (off) *rapiō, -ere, rapuī, raptum* [L31]

carry away/off *auferō, -ferre, abstulī, ablatum (3rd conj. irreg.)* [W32]

carry *ferō, ferre, tulī, lātum (irreg. 3rd conj.)* [W32]; *portō (1)*; *vehō, -ere, vexī, vectum* [L27]

carry on *gerō, -ere, gessī, gestum* [L28]

cast *iaciō, -ere, iēcī, iactum* [L31]

cast down *dēiciō, -icere, -iēcī, iectum* [W23]

castle *castellum, -ī (n)* [L5]

cattle *plural of bōs, bovis (m/f)* [L19]

cavalryman *eques, -quitis (m)* [L20]

cave *spēlunca, -ae (f)* [L3]

centaur *centaurus, -ī (m)* [L10]

certainly *enim (postpositive conj.)* [L17]

chair *sella, -ae (f)* [L31]

challenge *provocō (1)*

change *mūtō (1)* [L20]; *vertō, -ere, vertī, versum* [L28]

chant *carmen, -inis (n)* [L13]

character *faciēs, -ēī (f)* [L28]

chariot (four-horse chariot) *quadrīgae, -ārum (f)* [W23]

charioteer *aurīga, -ae (m/f)* [W23]

cherish *foveō, -ēre, fōvī, fōtum* [L25]

chew *mandūcō (1)* [L6]

children *līberī, ōrum (m, pl)* [L10]

choice *optio, optiōnis (f)* [W12]

choose *dēligō, -ere, lēgī, -lēctum* [L28]; *legō, -ere, lēgī, lēctum* [L28]

Christ *Christus, -ī (m)* [L4]

church *ecclēsia, -ae (f)* [L11]

Circus Maximus *Circus Maximus, Circī Maximī (m)* [W23]

city *urbs, urbis (f)* [L18]

city walls *moenia, -ium (n, pl)* [L18]

clan *gens, -ntis (f)* [L31]

class *classis, -is (f)* [L30]

clear (very clear) *limpidissimus, -a, -um* [W32]

clemency *clēmentia, -ae (f)* [W21]

cliff *scopulus, -ī (m)* [W30]

close *iūxta (adv. & prep. + acc.)* [L28]

close to *sub (+ acc.)* [L14]

clothing *vestis, vestis (f)* [L18]

cloud *nūbēs, nūbis (f)* [L18]

coin *nummus, -ī (m)* [W22]

cold *gelidus, -a, -um* [L31]

come upon *inveniō, -īre, -vēnī, -ventum* [L29]

come *veniō, -īre, vēnī, ventum* [L29]

commence *incipiō, -ere, -cēpī, -ceptum* [L31]

compel *cōgō, -ere, -ēgī, -āctum* [L28]

complete *perficiō, -ere, -fēcī, -fectum* [W23]

conceal *occultō (1)* [L22]

concerning *dē (+ abl.)* [L4]

conquer *superō (1)* [L2]; *vincō, -ere, vīcī, victum* [L26]

consecrated *sanctus, -a, -um* [L25]

consequently *ergo (adv.)* [L18]

consume by fire *cremō (1)* [L2]

contest *certāmen, -minis (n)* [W23]

convey *vehō, -ere, vexī, vectum* [L27]

cookie *crustulum, -ī (n)* [L5]

counsel *cōnsilium, -iī (n)* [L30]

country house *villa, -ae (f)* [L2]

courage *virtūs, virtūtis (f)* [L12]

course *curriculum, -ī (n)* [W23]

cousin (on the father's side) *patruēlis, -is (m/f)* [L22]; **(on the mother's side)** *consōbrīna, -ae (f) & consōbrīnus, -ī (m)* [L22]

cow *bōs, bovis (m/f)* [L19]

crash *naufragium, -ī (n)* [W23]

crawl *reptō (1)* [L14]

create *creō (1)* [L6]

creep *reptō (1)* [L14]

Crete *Crēta, -ae (f)* [W30]

crops *plural of frūmentum, -ī (n)* [L15]

cross *crux, crucis (f)* [L15]

crowd *turba, -ae (f)* [L2]

crown *corōna, -ae (f)* [L2]

cry (noun) *clāmor, -oris (m)* [W20]

cultivate *colō, -ere, coluī, cultum* [L29]

Cupid *Cupīdo, -dinis (m)* [W20]

curse *maledīcō, -ere, -dīxī, -dictum* [W30]

cut down *occīdō, -ere, -cīdī, -cīsum* [L30]; *percutiō, -ere, -cussī, -cussum* [W32]

cut off *praecīdō, -ere, -cīdī, -cīsum* [W32]

D

Daedalus *Daedalus, -ī (m)* [W30]

dagger *sīca, -ae (f)* [L3]

danger *perīculum, -ī (n)* [L5]

Daphne *Daphne, -ēs (f)* [W20]

dare *audeō, -ēre, ——, ausus sum* [L11]

dark *āter, -tra, -trum* [L17]

dark-colored *niger, -gra, -grum* [L17]

darkness *tenēbrae, -ārum (f, pl)* [L11]

daughter *fīlia, -ae (f)* [L6]

David *David (indecl.)* [W32]

day *diēs, diēī (m/f)* [L28]

dead body *cadaver, -veris (n)* [W32]

dear *cārus, -a, -um* [L13]

death *mors, mortis (f)* [L18]

declare *dēclārō (1)* [L10]; *nuntiō (1)* [L14]

deep *altus, -a, -um* [L19]

deer *cervus, -ī (m)* [L10]

defeat *superō (1)* [L2]; *vincō, -ere, vīcī, victum* [L26]

defend *dēfendō, -ere, -fendī, -fēnsum* [L28]

depart *abeō, īre, -iī, -itum* [W32]

deprive of *viduō (1)* [W19]

deprived of parents/children *orbus, -a, -um* [L22]

deserve *mereō, -ēre, -uī, -itum* [L15]

desire *cupiō, -ere, cupīvī, cupītum* [L31]

despise *despiciō, -ere, -spexī, -spectum* [W32]

destroy *dēleō, -ēre, -lēvī, -lētum* [L9]; *interficiō, -ere, -fēcī, -fectum* [L31]; *perdō, -ere, perdidī, perditum* [L27]

devastate *vastō (1)* [L14]

Diana *Diāna, -ae (f)* [W20]

difficult *difficilis, -e* [L20]

dig *fodiō, -ere, fōdī, fossum* [L28]

dinner *cēna, -ae (f)* [L20]

direct *gubernō (1)* [L25]

disciple *discipula, -ae (f); discipulus, -ī (m)* [L5]

dismal *trīstis, -e* [L20]

dismiss *dīmittō, -ere, -mīsī, -missum* [L30]

distant *longinquus, -a, -um* [L7]
do *agō, -ere, ēgī, actum* [L26]; *faciō, -ere, fēcī, factum* [L31]
dog *canis, canis (m/f)* [L18]
done (be done) *fīō, fierī, ——, factus sum* [L31]
donkey *asinus, -ī (m)* [L27]
door *porta, -ae (f)* [L31]
down from *dē (+ abl.)* [L4]
downfall *cāsus, -ūs (m)* [L28]
drag *trahō, -ere, trāxī, trāctum* [L30]
dragon *dracō, dracōnis (m)* [L12]
draw near *appropinquō (1)* [L25]
draw *trahō, -ere, trāxī, trāctum* [L30]
dread *metus, -ūs (m)* [L26]
dreadful *horrendus, -a, -um* [L13]
dream (verb) *somniō (1)* [W18]
drink (heavily), *pōtō, -āre, -āvī, pōtātum or pōtum* [L6]
drive *agō, -ere, ēgī, actum* [L26]
drive together *cōgō, -ere, -ēgī, -āctum* [L28]
driver *aurīga, -ae (m/f)* [W23]
drop *cadō, -ere, cecidī, casurum* [L27]
drunk *ēbrius, -a, -um* [W13]
dry *āridus, -a, -um* [L27]
dry up *torreō, -ēre, torruī, tostum* [L17]
dwell *habitō (1)* [L3]

E

eager *ācer, ācris, ācre* [L20]
eagerly *certātim* [L20]
ear *auris, -is (f)* [W28]
early *māne* [W19]
earn *mereō, -ēre, -uī, -itum* [L15]
earth *tellūs, tellūris (f)* [L14]; *terra, -ae (f)* [L4]
easy *facilis, -e* [L20]
eat *mandūcō (1)* [L6]
eight *octō* [L21]

eighteen *duodēvīgintī* [L21]
eighteenth *duodēvīcēsimus, -a, -um* [L23]
eighth *octāvus, -a, -um* [L23]
elephant *elephantus, -ī (m)* [L19]
eleven *ūndecim* [L21]
eleventh *ūndecimus, -a, -um* [L23]
end *fīnis, -is (m)* [W4]
enemy (of the state) *hostis, -is (m)* [L18]; **(personal enemy)** *inimīcus, -ī (m)* [L10]
enormous *ingēns, (gen.) -entis* [L19]
enough *satis (adv./indecl. adj./noun)* [L30]
enter *intrō (1)* [L9]
envy *invideō, -ēre, -vīdī, -vīsum* [W29]
Ephramite *Ephratheus, -ī (m)* [W32]
epistle *plural of littera, -ae (f)* [L26]
err *errō (1)* [L14]
escape *effugiō, -ere, -fūgī, -fugitum* [W10]
esteem *foveō, -ēre, fōvī, fōtum* [L25]
eternal *aeternus, -a, -um* [L15]
even *et* [L1]; *etiam* [L22]
evening star *vesper, vesperis (m)* [L14]
evening *vesper, vesperis (m)* [L14]
event *cāsus, -ūs (m)* [L28]
ever *quandō* [L12]
every *omnis, -e* [L19]
everywhere *ubīque* [W29]
evil *malus, -a, -um* [L7]
excellent *ēgregius, -a, -um* [L29]
exercise *exerceō, ēre, -uī, -itum* [L14]
expect *exspectō (1)* [L3]
explain *dēclārō (1)* [L10]
expose *aperiō, -īre, aperuī, apertum* [L29]
expression *vultus, -ūs (m)* [L25]
extend *extendō, -ere, -tendī, -tensum* [W26]

F

Fabius *Fabius, -iī (m)* [W19]
face *faciēs, -ēī (f)* [L28]; *vultus, -ūs (m)* [L25]

fair *iūstus, -a, -um* [L7]
faith *fidēs, -eī (f)* [L28]
faithful *fīdus, -a, -um* [L7]
fall *cadō, -ere, cecidī, cāsūrum* [L27]
fame *glōria, -ae* [L15], *fāma, -ae* [W23]
family *familia, -ae* [L22]
famous (that famous) *ille, illa, illud* [L30]
far away *longinquus, -a, -um* [L7]
farmer *agricola, -ae (m)* [L3]
farmhouse *villa, -ae (f)* [L2]
fast *cito* [L27]
fasten in *infīgō, -ere, -fīxī, -fīxum* [W32]
fat *pinguis, -e* [W25]
fate *fātum, -ī (n)* [L5]
father *pater, patris (m)* [L12]
favor *grātia, -ae (f)* [L27]
favorable *dexter, -tra, -trum (or -tera, -terum)* [L30]
fear (noun) *metus, -ūs (m)* [L26]
fear (verb) *timeō, -ēre, -uī, ——* [L9]
fearful *horrendus, -a, -um* [L13]
feast *epulae, -ārum (f, pl)* [L20]
feed *pasco, -ere, pāvī, pastum* [W32]
few *paucī, -ae, -a* [L7]
field *ager, agrī (m)* [L4]
fierce *ācer, ācris, ācre* [L20]; *ferus, -a, -um* [L7]
fiery *caldus, -a, -um* [L7]
fifteen *quīndecim* [L21]
fifteenth *quīntus, -a, -um decimus, -a, -um* [L23]
fifth *quīntus, -a, -um* [L23]
fiftieth *quīnquāgēsimus, -a, -um* [L23]
fifty *quīnquāgintā* [L21]
fight *pugnō (1)* [L1]
finally *dēnique* [L10]
find *inveniō, -īre, -vēnī, -ventum* [L29]
finish *perficiō, -ere, -fēcī, -fectum* [W23]
fire *ignis, ignis* [L18]

first prīmus, -a, -um [L23]

fish (noun) piscis, -is (m) [L19]

fish (verb) piscor, -ārī, ——, -ātus sum (deponent) [W29]

five hundred quīngentī [L21]

five hundredth quīngentēsimus, -a, -um [L23]

five quīnque [L21]

fix in infīgo, -ere, -fīxī, -fīxum [W32]

flag (starting flag) mappa, -ae (f) [W23]

flee fugiō, -ere, fūgī, fugitum [L31]

fleet (of ships) classis, -is (f) [L30]

flesh carō, carnis (f) [L31]

flock grex, gregis (m) [L31]

flourish flōreō, -ēre, -uī, — [L17]

flower flōs, flōris (m) [L15]

fly volō (1) [L10]

follow sequor, sequī, ——, secūtus sum (deponent) [W30]

folly stultitia, -ae (f) [W27]

food cibus, -ī (m) [L4]

foolish stultus, -a, -um [L7]

foolishness stultitia, -ae (f) [W27]

foot (at the foot of) sub (+ abl.) [L14]

for (the sake of) pro (+ abl.) [L18]

for a long time diū [L13]

for enim (postpositive conj.) [L17]; nam [W32]

force cōgō, -ere, -ēgī, -āctum [L28]

forehead frōns, -ntis (f) [W32]

foreign barbarus, -a, -um [L31]

foreigner barbarus, -ī (m) [L31]

forest silva, -ae (f) [L3]

forgive dīmittō, -ere, -mīsī, -missum [L30]

form faciēs, -ēī (f) [L28]

formerly ōlim [L6]

fortifications moenia, -ium (n, pl) [L18]

fortunate fēlix, (gen.) -līcis [L19]

four quattuor [L21]

four-horse chariot quadrīgae, -ārum (f) [W23]

fourteen quattuordecim [L21]

fourteenth quārtus, -a, -um decimus, -a, -um [L23]

fourth quārtus, -a, -um [L23]

free līberō (1) [L1]

fresh viridis, -e [L17]

friend amīca, -ae (f) [L15]; amīcus, -ī (m) [L15]

frighten terreō, -ēre, -uī, -itum [L9]

from ā, ab (+ abl.) [L3]; dē (+ abl.) [L4]; ē, ex (+ abl.) [L3]

from all sides undique [L30]

from every direction undique [L30]

from that place deinde [L24]

fruit frūctus, -ūs (m) [L25]

funeral pyre pyra, -ae (f) [W8]

furrow versus, -ūs (m) [L27]

G

garment vestis, vestis (f) [L18]

gate porta, -ae (f) [L31]

gates (starting gates of a horse race) plural of carcer, -eris (m) [W23]

general dux, ducis (m) [L14]

generation saeculum, -ī (n) [L6]

giant gigās, gigantis (m) [L15]

gift dōnum, -ī (n) [L5]

girl puella, -ae (f) [L3]

give dō, dare, dedī, datum [L1]

give thanks grātiās agō (+ dat.) [L27]

glad laetus, -a, -um [L7]

gloom nūbēs, nūbis (f) [L18]

gloomy place tenēbrae, -ārum (f, pl) [L11]

gloomy trīstis, -e [L20]

glory glōria, -ae [L15]

go away abeō, īre, -iī, -itum [W32]

go cēdō, -ere, cessī, cessum [L28]; eō, īre, iī (īvī), itum [L29]

goal mēta, -ae (f) [W23]

goat caper, -prī (m) [L4]

goblet calix, calicis (m) [W13]

god deus, -i (m) [L4]

God Deus, -ī (m) [L4]

goddess dea, -ae (f) [L6]

gold (noun) aurum, -ī (n) [L5]

gold(en) aureus, -a, -um [L17]

good bonus, -a, -um [L7]

Good day! salvē(te) [L9]

good news ēvangelium, -ī [L5]

Goodbye! valē(te) [L9]

gospel ēvangelium, -ī [L5]

govern gubernō (1) [L25]; regnō (1) [L6]

grace grātia, -ae (f) [L27]

gradually minūtātim [L20]

grain frūmentum, -ī (n) [L15]

grandfather avus, -ī (m) [L22]

grandmother avia, -ae (f) [L22]

grass grāmen, grāminis (n) [L13]

grateful grātus, -a, -um [L27]

greater māior, māius (gen. māioris) [W31]

greatest māximus, -a, -um [W31]

greatly magnopere [L29]

greedy avārus, -a, -um [L7]

green vīridis, -e [L17]

greenery grāmen, grāminis (n) [L13]

ground tellūs, tellūris (f) [L14]

group classis, -is (f) [L30]

guard against caveō, -ēre, cāvī, cautum [L12]

guide (verb) dūcō, -ere, duxī, ductum [L26]

guide (noun) dux, ducis (m) [L14]

H

hall aula, -ae (f) [W13]

hand manus, -ūs (f) [L25]; palma, -ae (f) [W13]

hand over trādō, -ere, -didī, -ditum [W13]

handsome pulcher, -chra, -chrum [L7]

happen *fīō, fierī, ——, factus sum* [L31]
happily ever after *felīciter in aeternum* [W6]
happiness *gaudium, -ī (n)* [L5]
happy *beātus, -a, -um* [L7]; *fēlix, (gen.) -līcis* [L19]; *laetus, -a, -um* [L7]
harbor *portus, -ūs (m)* [L25]
hardship *labor, labōris (m)* [L12]
hasten *festīnō (1)* [L9]
haughty *superbus, -a, -um* [W18]
have *habeō, -ēre, -uī, -itum* [L9]
he *is, ea, id* [L17]
head *caput, -itis (n)* [L13]
hear *audiō, -īre, -īvī, -ītum* [L29]
heart *cor, cordis (n)* [L13]
heaven *caelum, -ī (n)* [L5]
Hello! *salvē(te)* [L9]
help (noun) *auxilium, -ī (n)* [L5]
help (verb) *iuvō, -āre, iūvī, iūtum* [L22]
her (own) *suus, -a, -um (reflexive possessive adj.)* [W31]
herd *grex, gregis (m)* [L31]
herself *sē (acc. reflexive pronoun)* [W8]
hide *occultō (1)* [L22]; *celō* [W28]
high *altus, -a, -um* [L19]
himself *sē (acc. reflexive pronoun)* [W8]
hinder *impediō, -īre, -īvī, -ītum* [L29]
his (own) *suus, -a, -um (reflexive possessive adj.)* [W31]
hold *habeō, -ēre, -uī, -itum* [L9]; *teneō, -ēre, tenuī, tentum* [L9]
hollow *lacus, -ūs (m)* [L27]
Holy Bible *Biblia Sacra, Bibliae Sacrae (f)* [L11]
holy *sanctus, -a, -um* [L25]
home *domus, -ūs (f)* [L25]
hope *spēs, speī (f)* [L28]
horn *cornū, -ūs (n)* [L25]
horrible *foedus, -a, -um* [L7]
horse *equus, -ī (m)* [L4]

horseman *eques, -quitis (m)* [L20]
hot *caldus, -a, -um* [L7]
hour *hōra, -ae (f)* [L31]
house *domus, -ūs (f)* [L25]; *(country house) villa, -ae (f)* [L2]
household *familia, -ae* [L22]
how (?) *quam* [L28]; *quōmodo* [L25]
however *autem (postposit. conj.)* [L12]
howl *ululō (1)* [L6]
huge *ingēns, (gen.) -entis* [L19]
human being *homō, hominis (m)* [L12]
hungry *famēlicus, -a, -um* [L29]
hunt *captō (1)* [L10]
hunt down *persequor, -sequī, ——, -secūtus sum (deponent)* [W32]
hurl down *dēicio, -icere, -iēcī, -iectum* [W23]
hurl *iaciō, -ere, iēcī, iactum* [L31]
hurry *festīnō (1)* [L9]; *properō (1)* [L20]
husband *coniunx, -iugis (m)* [L22]

I

I *ego (sg)* [L17]
icy *gelidus, -a, -um* [L31]
if *sī (conj.)* [L16]
ill *male* [L1]
immediately *statim* [L13]
impartial *iūstus, -a, -um* [L7]
in *in (+ abl.)* [L3]
in front of *pro (+ abl.)* [L18]
in one *ūnā* [L29]
in the presence of *cōram (+ abl.)* [L27]
in what way *quōmodo* [L25]
Inachus *Īnachus, -ī (m)* [W21]
inauspicious *sinister, -stra, -strum* [L30]
incident *cāsus, -ūs (m)* [L28]
increase *augeō -ēre, auxī, auctum* [L19]
indeed *enim (postpositive conj.)* [L17]
infant *īnfāns, -fantis (adj. & noun, m/f)* [W31]

inhabit *colō, -ere, coluī, cultum* [L29]; *habitō (1)* [L3]
inner court *aula, -ae (f)* [W13]
instead of *prō (+ abl.)* [L18]
into *in (+ acc.)* [L3]
intoxicated *ēbrius, -a, -um* [W13]
invite *vocō (1)* [L1]
Io *Īō, -ōnis (f)* [W21]
island *īnsula, -ae (f)* [L3]
Israel *Israhel (indecl.)* [W32]
Israelite *Israhelita, -ae (m)* [W32]
it *is, ea, id* [L17]
Italy *Ītalia, -ae (f)* [W8]
its (own) *suus, -a, -um (reflexive possessive adj.)* [W31]
itself *sē (acc. reflexive pronoun)* [W8]
Iulia *Iūlia, -ae (f)* [W11]
Iulius *Iūlius, -iī (m)* [W19]
Iunia *Iūnia, -ae (f)* [W11]

J

Jerusalem *Hierusalem (indecl.)* [W32]
Jesse *Isai (indecl.)* [W32]
Jesus *Iēsus, -ūs (m)* [L25]
join *iungō, -ere, iūnxī, iūnctum* [L27]
journey *iter, itineris (n)* [L13]
Jove *Iuppiter, Iovis (m)* [W21]
joy *gaudium, -ī (n)* [L5]
joyful *laetus, -a, -um* [L7]
judge *iūdex, -dicis (m)* [W28]
Julia *Iūlia, -ae (f)* [W11]
Julius *Iūlius, -iī (m)* [W19]
jump *saliō, -īre, saluī, saltum* [W29]
Junia *Iūnia, -ae (f)* [W11]
Juno *Iūno, -ōnis (f)* [W21]
Jupiter *Iuppiter, Iovis (m)* [W21]
just as *sīcut* [L20]
just (adj.) *iūstus, -a, -um* [L7]
just (adv.) *modo* [L27]

K

kidnapping *raptus, -ūs (m)* [W31]
kill *interficiō, -ere, -fēcī, -fectum* [L31]; *necō (1)* [L1]; *occīdō, -ere, -cīdī, -cīsum* [L30]
kindness *grātia, -ae (f)*
king *rēx, rēgis (m)* [L12]
kingdom *regnum, -ī (n)* [L5]
knee *genū, -ūs (n)* [L25]
knight *eques, -quitis (m)* [L20]
know *sciō, -īre, sciī (scīvī), scītum* [L29]
kraken *cētus, -ī (m)* [L10]

L

labor (noun) *labor, labōris (m)* [L12]
labyrinth *labyrinthus, -ī (m)* [W30]
lake *lacus, -ūs (m)* [L27]
land *tellūs, tellūris (f)* [L14]; *terra, -ae (f)* [L4]; **(native land)** *patria, -ae (f)* [L3]
language *lingua, -ae* [L26]
lap (of a race) *curriculum, -ī (n)* [W23]
large *magnus, -a, -um* [L7]
laugh *rīdeō, -ēre, rīsī, rīsum* [L9]
laurel (tree) *laurus, -ī (f)* [W20]
lay waste *vastō (1)* [L14]
lead (of lead) *plumbeus, -a, -um* [W20]
lead (verb) *dūcō, -ere, duxī, ductum* [L26]
leaden *plumbeus, -a, -um* [W20]
leader *dux, ducis (m)* [L14]
leaf *folium, -ī (n)* [W20]
leaky *pertūsus, -a, -um* [W29]
leap *saliō, -īre, -uī, saltum* [W29]
learned *doctus, -a, -um* [L13]
least *minimus, -a, -um* [W31]
leave behind *relinquō, -ere, -līquī, -lictum* [L28]
left(-handed) *sinister, -stra, -strum* [L30]
leg *crūs, crūris (n)* [W19]
legend *fābula, -ae (f)* [L2]
let go *mittō, -ere, mīsī, missum* [L26]
letter (of the alphabet) *littera, -ae (f)* [L26]
letter *plural of littera, -ae (f)* [L26]
lie *iaceō, -ēre, -uī, ——* [L9]
lie down *iaceō, -ēre, -uī, ——* [L9]
lie flat *iaceō, -ēre, -uī, ——* [L9]
life *vīta, -ae* [L11]
lift up *tollō, -ere, sustulī, sublātum* [W25]
light *lux, lūcis (f)* [L12]
lightning *fulgur, -uris (n)* [W25]
like *sīcut* [L20]
limit *fīnis, -is (m)* [W4]
line (of poetry) *versus, -ūs (m)* [L27]
lion *leō, leōnis (m)* [L12]
listen to *audiō, -īre, -īvī, -ītum* [L29]
little *parvus, -a, -um* [L7]
live *habitō (1)* [L3]; *vīvō, -ere, vīxī, victum* [L27]
living *vīvus, -a, -um* [L20]
load *onus, oneris (n)* [L13]
lofty *altus, -a, -um* [L19]
long (for) (verb) *cupiō, -ere, cupīvī, cupītum* [L31]
long (adj.) *longus, -a, -um* [L20]
look at *spectō (1)* [L1]
look down on *dēspiciō, -ere, -spexī, -spectum* [W32]
lop *praecīdō, -ere, -cīdī, -cīsum* [W32]
lord *dominus, -ī (m)* [L4]
lose *perdō, -ere, perdidī, perditum* [L27]
love (noun) *amor, amōris (m)* [L14]
love (verb) *amō (1)* [L1]; *foveō, -ēre, fōvī, fōtum* [L25]
lucky *fēlix, (gen.) -līcis* [L19]
lyre *lyra, -ae (f)* [W28]

M

made (am made) *fīō, fierī, ——, factus sum* [L31]
maiden *virgō, virginis (f)* [L12]
make clear *dēclārō (1)* [L10]
make *faciō, -ere, fēcī, factum* [L31]
man (as opposed to animal) *homō, hominis (m)* [L12]; **(as opposed to woman)** *vir, virī (m)* [L4]
manliness *virtūs, virtūtis (f)* [L12]
many *multus, -a, -um* [L7]
marriage *mātrimōnium, -ī (n)* [L20]
master *dominus, -ī (m)* [L4]
maze *labyrinthus, -ī (m)* [W30]
meal *cēna, -ae (f)* [L20]
meantime (in the meantime) *interim* [L9]
meanwhile *interim* [L9]
meat *caro, carnis (f)* [L31]
Mercury *Mercurius, -ī (m)* [W21]
mercy *clēmentia, -ae (f)* [W21]
merely *modo* [L27]
Midas *Midās, -ae (m)* [W27]
middle (of) *medius, -a, -um* [L26]
midst (of) *medius, -a, -um* [L26]
milk *lac, lactis (n)* [L13]
mind *animus, -ī (m)* [L29]
mind one's own business *suum negōtium agere* [W29]
mine *meus, -a, -um* [L11]
Minos *Mīnōs, -ōnis (m)* [W30]
Minotaur *Mīnōtaurus, -ī (m)* [W30]
miserable *infēlix, (gen.) -līcis* [L19]; *miser, -era, -erum* [L7]
misfortune *cāsus, -ūs (m)* [L28]
mistaken (am mistaken) *errō (1)* [L14]
mob *turba, -ae (f)* [L2]
money *argentum, -ī (n)* [L5]; *peccnia, -ae (f)* [L3]
monster *mōnstrum* [W30]
moon *lūna, -ae* [L2]
moreover *autem (postposit. conj.)* [L12]
morning (in the morning) *māne* [W19]
mother *māter, mātris (f)* [L12]
mountain *mōns, montis* [L18]
mouth *ōs, ōris (n)* [L13]

move (intransit.) *cēdō, -ere, cessī, cessum* [L28]

move (transit.) *moveō, -ēre, mōvī, mōtum* [L14]

much *multus, -a, -um* [L7]

musician *musicus, -ī (m)* [W28]

my *meus, -a, -um* [L11]

N

name (verb) *appellō (1)* [L15]

name (noun) *nōmen, nōminis (n)* [L13]

napkin *mappa, -ae (f)* [W23]

nation *gens, -ntis (f)* [L31]; *populus, -ī (m)* [L11]

native land *patria, -ae (f)* [L3]

near (to) *iūxta (adv. & prep. + acc.)* [L28]

near *ad (+ acc.)* [L3]; *prope (adv. & prep. + acc.)* [L19]; *propter (+ acc.)* [L25]

neither...nor *nec...nec* [L14]

never *numquam* [L5]

nevertheless *tamen* [L30]

new *novus, -a, -um* [L26]

next *deinde* [L22]; *tum* [L15]

next to *prope (adv. & prep. + acc.)* [L19]

night *nox, noctis (f)* [L18]

nine *novem* [L21]

nineteen *ūndēvigintī* [L21]

nineteenth *ūndēvīcēsimus, -a, -um* [L23]

ninth *nōnus, -a, -um* [L23]

no longer *nōn iam* [L15]

noble *magnanimus, -a, -um* [W9]

noon *merīdiēs, -ēī (m)* [L28]

nor *nec (neque)* [L14]

not at all *nihil (n. indecl.)* [L6]

not know *nesciō, -īre, -īvī, -ītum* [L30]

not *nōn* [L1]; *nec (neque)* [L14]

nothing *nihil (n, indecl.)* [L6]

now *iam* [L15]; *nunc* [L1]

nymph *nympha, -ae (f)* [W20]

O

ocean *ōceanus, -ī (m)* [L4]

of/belonging to a shepherd *pastoralis, -e* [W32]

often *saepe* [L6]

oh! *heu (ēheu)* [L22]

old man *senex, senis (m)* [L14]

old *vetus, -teris* [L30]

older *māior, māius (gen. māioris)* [W31]

oldest (son) *postnatus, -ī (m)* [W19]

oldest *māximus, -a, -um* [W31]

on *in (+ abl.)* [L3]

on account of *propter (+ acc.)* [L25]

on all sides *undique* [L30]

once upon a time *ōlim* [L6]

one (in one) *ūnā* [L29]

one another *invicem* [W26]

one hundred *centum* [L21]

one hundredth *centēsimus* [L23]

one *ūnicus, -a, -um* [W22]; *ūnus, -a, -um* [L21]

only (adv.) *modo* [L27]

only (adj.) *sōlus, -a, -um* [W12]; *ūnicus, -a, -um* [W22]

open *aperiō, -īre, -uī, apertum* [L29]

openly *cōram* [L27]

or *aut* [L1]; *sīve (seū)* [L30]

oracle *ōrāculum, -ī (n)* [W31]

ordinary *mediōcris, -e* [L19]

orphan *orba, -ae (f)/orbus, -ī (m)* [L22]

Oswald *Oswaldus, -ī (m)* [W19]

other *alius, alia, aliud* [W21]

ought *dēbeō, -ēre, -uī, -itum* [L11]

our(W) *noster, -stra, -strum* [L11]

out of *ē, ex (+ abl.)* [L3]

outstanding *ēgregius, -a, -um* [L29]

over *super (+ acc./+ abl.)* [L26]; *suprā (adv./prep. + acc.)* [L14]

owe *dēbeō, -ēre, -uī, -itum* [L11]

ox *bōs, bovis (m/f)* [L19]

P

Pactolus *Pactōlus, -ī (m)* [W27]

palace *rēgia, -ae (f)* [L2]

Pan *Pān, Pānos (acc. Pāna) (m)* [W28]

pan pipe *avēna, -ae (f)* [W21]

parch *torreō, -ēre, torruī, tostum* [L17]

parent *parens, -ntis (m/f)* [W11]

pastoral *pastoralis, -e* [W32]

pasture *pasco, -ere, pāvī, pastum* [W32]

pay the penalty *poenās dō* [L27]

peace *pāx, pācis (f)* [L15]

peacock *pāvo, -ōnis (m)* [W21]

penalty *poena, -ae (f)* [L27]

people *populus, -ī (m)* [L11]

perhaps *fortasse* [L26]

period of time *diēs, diēī (m/f)* [L28]

permit *permittō, -ere, -mīsī, -missum* [W30]

permitted (it is permitted) *licet* [W26]

personally *cōram* [L27]

persuade *persuādeō, -ere, -suāsī, -suāsum (+ dat.)* [W15]

Philistine *Philistheus, -ī (m)*

Phrygia *Phrygia, -ae (f)* [W27]

pick *dēligō, -ere, lēgī, -lēctum* [L28]

pig *porcus, -ī (m)* [L10]

pig-sty *hara, -ae (f)* [W25]

pipe (reed-pipe) *calamus, -ī (m)* [W28]

pirate *pīrāta, -ae (m)* [L2]

place (verb) *collocō (1)* [W21]; *pōnō, -ere, posuī, positum* [L26]

plan *cōnsilium, -iī (n)* [L30]

play (music) *cantō (1)* [L1]

play *lūdō, lūdere, lūsī, lūsum* [L26]

pleasing *grātus, -a, -um* [L27]

plenty *cōpia, -ae (f)* [L15]

poem *carmen, -inis (n)* [L13]

poet *poēta, -ae* [L2]

poison *venēnum, -ī (n)* [L10]

polite *urbānus, -a, -um* [W29]
port *portus, -ūs (m)* [L25]
possess *teneō, -ēre, tenuī, tentum* [L9]
powerful *potēns, (gen.) -entis* [L19]
praise (noun) *laus, laudis (f)* [L15]
praise (verb) *laudō (1)* [L1]
pray *ōrō (1) (takes double acc.)* [L6]
predict *cantō (1)* [L1]; *praedīcō, -ere, -dīxī, -dictum* [W31]
prepare *parō (1)* [L14]
presence (in the presence of) *cōram (+ abl.)* [L27]
prison *carcer, -eris (m)* [W23]
profit *frūctus, -ūs (m)* [L25]
prophecy *carmen, -inis (n)* [L13]; *ōrāculum, -ī (n)*
prophesy *praedīcō, -ere, -dīxī, -dictum* [W31]
prophet *vātēs, -is (m)* [W31]
prophetess *vātēs, -is (f)* [W31]
proud *superbus, -a, -um* [W18]
punishment *poena, -ae (f)* [L27]
purple *purpureus, -a, -um* [L17]
purplish-blue *hyacinthinus, -a, -um* [L17]
pursue (with hostile intent) *persequor, -sequī, ——, -secutus sum (deponent)* [W32]
put *pōnō, -ere, posuī, positum* [L26]
pyre *pyra, -ae (f)* [W8]

Q

quake *tremō, -ere, -uī, ——* [W25]
queen *rēgīna, -ae (f)* [L2]
quick *celer, celeris, celere* [L19]
quickly *cito* [L27]
quiet *placidus, -a, -um* [W29]

R

race *certāmen, -minis (n)* [W23]
rainbow *arcus, -ūs (m)* [L27]
raise *tollō, -ere, sustulī, sublātum* [W25]

ram *ariēs, -ietis (m)* [W32]
ravage *vexō (1)* [L19]
read *legō, -ere, lēgī, lēctum* [L28]
receive *accipiō, -ere, -cēpī, ceptum* [L31]
reciprocally *invicem* [W26]
recount *narrō (1)* [L2]
red *ruber, -bra, -brum* [L17]; *rūfus, -a, -um* [W32]; **(dark-red)** *purpureus, -a, -um* [L17]
reed *calamus, -ī (m)* [W28]
reign *regnō (1)* [L6]
rejoice *gaudeō, -ēre, ——, gāvīsus sum* [L22]
relate *narrō (1)* [L2]
remain *maneō, -ēre, mansī, mansum* [L10]
remain near *obsideō, -ēre, -sēdī, -sessum* [L10]
remove *auferō, -ferre, abstulī, ablātum (3rd conj. irreg.)* [W32]; *removeō, -ēre, -mōvī, -mōtum* [L14]
repair *reficiō, -ere, -fēcī, -fectum* [W29]
report *fāma, -ae (f)* [W23]
reproach *exprobrō (1)* [W32]
reputation *fāma, -ae (f)* [W23]
respond *respondeō, -ēre, -spondī, -spōnsum* [L9]
reward *praemium, -ī (n)* [W27]
riches *dīvitiae, -ārum (f, pl)* [L2]
riddle *enigma, -matis (n)* [W19]
ride *vehō, -ere, vexī, vectum* [L27]
right *iūstus, -a, -um* [L7]
right(-handed) *dexter, -tra, -trum (or -tera, -terum)* [L30]
righteous *iūstus, -a, -um* [L7]
rise again *resurgō, -ere, -surrēxī, -surrēctum* [L29]
rise *surgō, -ere, surrēxī, surrēctum* [L28]
river *flūmen, flūminis (n)* [L13]
road *iter, itineris (n)* [L13]; *via, -ae (f)* [L11]
rock *saxum, -ī (n)* [L29]

route *iter, itineris (n)* [L13]
row *versus, -ūs (m)* [L27]
royal court *aula, -ae (f)* [W13]
ruddy *ruber, -bra, -brum* [L17]; *rūfus, -a, -um* [W32]
ruin *perdō, -ere, perdidī, perditum* [L27]
rule *regnō (1)* [L6]; *regō, -ere, rēxī, rectum* [L26]
run away *fugiō, -ere, fūgī, fugitum* [L31]
run *currō, -ere, cūcurrī, cursum* [L26]
rush *properō (1)* [L20]

S

Sabbath *sabbata, -ōrum (n, pl)* [W26]
sacred *sanctus, -a, -um* [L25]
sad *trīstis, -e* [L20]
safe *salvus, -a, -um* [L25]
sail (noun) *vēlum, -ī (n)* [W30]
sail (verb) *nāvigō (1)* [L4]
sailor *nauta, -ae (m)* [L3]
sand *harēna, -ae (f)* [L3]
satchel *pēra, -ae (f)* [W32]
Saul *Saul (indecl.)* [W32]
savage *barbarus, -a, -um* [L31]
save *servō (1)* [L6]
saved *salvus, -a, -um* [L25]
say *āiō* [L14]; *dīcō, -ere, dīxī, dictum* [L26]
scream *ululō (1)* [L6]
sea *mare, maris (n)* [L18]
sea serpent *hydrus, -ī (m)*
seat *sella, -ae (f)* [L31]
second (adv.; a second time) *iterum* [L25]
second (adj.) *secundus, -a, -um* [L23]
secret *sēcrētum, -ī (n)* [W28]
secretly *clam* [L29]
see *videō, -ēre, vīdī, vīsum* [L9]
seize *capiō, -ere, cēpī, captum* [L31]; *occupō (1)* [L6]; *rapiō, -ere, rapuī, raptum* [L31]

send away *dīmittō, -ere, -mīsī, -missum* [L30]

send *mittō, -ere, mīsī, missum* [L26]

servant *serva, -ae (f)* [L4]; *servus, -ī (m)* [L4]

set *collocō (1)* [W21]

set free *līberō (1)* [L1]

seven *septem* [L21]

seventeen *septendecim* [L21]

seventeenth *septimus, -a, -um decimus, -a, -um* [L23]

seventh *septimus, -a, -um* [L23]

shadows *tenēbrae, -ārum (f, pl)* [L11]

shape *faciēs, -ēī (f)* [L28]

sharp *ācer, ācris, ācre* [L20]

shatter *frangō, -ere, frēgī, fractum* [L27]

she *is, ea, id* [L17]

shepherd (of/belonging to a shepherd) *pastorālis, -e* [W32]

shepherd *pastor, pastōris (m)* [L20]

shepherd's pipe *avēna, -ae (f)* [W21]

shield *clypeum, -ī (n)* [W32]; *scūtum, -ī (m)* [L10]

shine *lūceō, lūcēre, lūxī, ——* [L11]

ship *nāvis, -is (f)* [L18]; *alnus, -ī (f)* [L4]

shipwreck *naufragium, -ī (n)* [W23]

shoot *petō, -ere, -īvī, -ītum* [W20]

shore *lītus, lītoris (n)* [L13]; *ōra, -ae (f)* [L13]

shoreline *lītus, lītoris (n)* [L13]

short *brevis, -e* [L19]

shout (noun) *clāmor, -ōris (m)* [W20]

shout (verb) *clāmō (1)* [L1]

shrine *templum, -ī (n)* [W25]

shun *vītō (1)* [L30]

silent (be silent) *taceō, ēre, -uī, -itum* [W26]

Silenus *Silēnus, -ī (m)* [W27]

silver (adj.) *argenteus, -a, -um* [L17]

silver (noun) *argentum, -ī (n)* [L5]

since *quandō* [L12]; *quia* [L18]; *quoniam* [L26]

sing *cantō (1)* [L1]

singing *cantus, -ūs (m)* [L25]

single *sōlus, -a, -um* [W12]

sink *cadō, -ere, cecidī, cāsūrum* [L27]

sister *germāna, -ae (f)* [L4]; *soror, sorōris (f)* [L12]

sit *sedeō, -ēre, sēdī, sessum* [L9]

six *sex* [L21]

sixteen *sēdecim* [L21]

sixteenth *sextus, -a, -um decimus, -a, -um* [L23]

sixth *sextus, -a, -um* [L23]

skilled *dexter, -tra, -trum (or -tera, -terum)* [L30]; *doctus, -a, -um* [L13]

sky *caelum, -ī (n)* [L5]

slave *serva, -ae (f)* [L4]; *servus, -ī (m)* [L4]

slay *interficiō, -ere, -fēcī, -fectum* [L31]; *necō (1)* [L1]; *occīdō, -ere, -cīdī, -cīsum* [L30]

sleep *dormiō, -īre, -īvī, -ītum* [L29]

sling *funda, -ae (f)* [W32]

small *brevis, -e* [L19]; *parvus, -a, -um* [L7]

small cake *crustulum, -ī (n)* [L5]

smash *frangō, -ere, frēgī, fractum* [L27]

smile *rīdeō, -ēre, rīsī, rīsum* [L9]

snatch *rapiō, -ere, rapuī, raptum* [L31]

soldier *mīles, mīlitis (m)* [L12]

sole *ūnicus, -a, -um* [W22]

son *fīlius, -ī (m)* [L4]

song *cantus, -ūs (m)* [L25]; *carmen, -inis (n)* [L13]

soon *mox* [L15]

sound (adj.) *salvus, -a, -um* [L25]

speak *dīcō, -ere, dīxī, dictum* [L26]; *ōrō (1) (takes double acc.)* [L6]

speak ill *maledīcō, -ere, -dīxī, -dictum* [W30]

spear *hasta, -ae (f)* [L3]

speedily *citō* [L27]

spine *spīna, -ae (f)* [W23]

spirit of the age *saeculum, -ī (n)* [L6]

spirit *spīritus, -ūs (m)* [L25]

spurious *spurius, -a, -um* [W32]

staff *baculum, -ī (n)* [W32]

stag *cervus, -ī (m)* [L10]

stand *stō, stāre, stetī, statum* [L1]

star *stella, -ae* [L11]

starting gates (of a horse race) plural of *carcer, -eris (m)* [W23]

statue *simulacrum, -ī (n)* [W25]

steer *gubernō (1)* [L25]

step-mother *noverca, -ae (f)* [W22]

still *etiam* [L22]; *tamen* [L30]

sting *mordeō, -ēre, momordī, morsum* [L9]

stone *lapis, -idis (m)* [W27]

storm *tempestās, -tātis (f)* [L26]

story *fābula, -ae (f)* [L2]

strange *barbarus, -a, -um* [L31]; *mīrus, -a, -um* [L7]

stream *torrens, -ntis (m)* [W32]

strength *virtūs, virtūtis (f)* [L12]

stretch out *extendō, -ere, -tendī, -tensum* [W26]

strike down *percutiō, -ere, -cussī, -cussum* [W32]

strike *tangō, -ere, tetigī, tactum* [L27]

string *fīlum, -ī (n)* [W30]

strong *fortis, -e* [L19]

strongest *fortissimus, -a, -um* [W32]

student (female) *discipula, -ae (f)* & **(male)** *discipulus, -ī (m)* [L5]

subdue *domō, -āre, domuī, domitum* [L12]

such *iste, ista, istud* [L30]

suddenly *repentē* [L10]

sufficient(ly) *satis (adv. & indecl. adj./noun)* [L30]

summon *vocō (1)* [L1]

sun *sōl, sōlis (m)* [L12]

supply *cōpia, -ae (f)* [L15]

surrender *trādō, -ere, -didī, -ditum* [W13]

suspicious *suspīciōsus, -a, -um* [W21]

swamp *palus, palūdis (f)* [W13]

sweet *dulcis, -e* [L19]

swift *celer, celeris, celere* [L19]

swim *nō (1)* [L14]

sword *gladius, -ī (m)* [L4]

synagogue *synagōga, -ae (f)* [W26]

T

table *mensa, -ae (f)* [L31]

tail *cauda, -ae (f)* [W21]

take *accipiō, -ere, -cēpī, ceptum* [L31]; *capiō, -ere, cēpī, captum* [L31]

take away *removeō, -ēre, -mōvī, -mōtum* [L14]

take for myself *adsūmō, -ere, -sumpsī, -sumptum* [W32]

tale *fābula, -ae (f)* [L2]

tame *domō, -āre, domuī, domitum* [L12]

tax *tribūtum, -ī (n)* [W30]

teach *doceō, -ēre, docuī, doctum* [L9]

teacher (female) *magistra, -ae (f)*/**(male)** *magister, -strī (m)* [L6]

tease *lūdō, lūdere, lūsī, lūsum* [L26]

tell *narrō (1)* [L2]

temple *templum, -ī (n)* [W25]

ten *decem* [L21]

tent *tabernāculum, -ī (n)* [W32]

tenth *decimus, -a, -um* [L23]

terrify *terreō, -ēre, -uī, -itum* [L9]

than *quam* [L28]

thank *grātiās agō (+ dat.)* [L27]

thanks *grātia, -ae (f)* [L27]

that (of yours) *iste, ista, istud* [L30]

that (adj./pron.) *ille, illa, illud* [L30]; *is, ea, id* [L17]

that (conj.) *quia* [L18]; *quod* [L10]

then (therefore) *deinde* [L22]; *ergo (adv.)* [L18]; **(of time)** *ibī* [L5]; *ōlim* [L6]; *tum* [L15]

there *ibī* [L5]

therefore *ergo (adv.)* [L18]; *itaque* [L2]

thereupon *deinde* [L22]; *tum* [L15]

these *plural of hic, haec, hoc* [L30]

Theseus *Thēseūs, -eī (m)* [W30]

they *is, ea, id* [L9]

thing *rēs, reī (f)* [L28]

think *cōgitō (1)* [L6]

third *tertius, -a, -um* [L23]

thirteen *tredecim* [L21]

thirteenth *tertius, -a, -um decimus, -a, -um* [L23]

this *hic, haec, hoc* [L30]; *is, ea, id* [L17]

those *plural of ille, illa, illud* [L30]

thousand *mīlle* [L21]

thousandth (one thousandth) *mīllēsimus, -a, -um* [L23]

thread *fīlum, -ī (n)* [W30]

three *trēs, tria* [L21]

throng *turba, -ae (f)* [L2]

through *per (+ acc.)* [L3]

throw down *dēiciō, -icere, -iēcī, -iectum* [W23]

throw *iaciō, -ere, iēcī, iactum* [L31]

thunder *tonitrus, -ūs (m)* [L25]

tie *vinciō, -īre, vīnxī, vīnctum* [L30]

tiger *tigris, tigridis (m/f)* [L12]

time *tempus, temporis (n)* [L13]

times (the times) *saeculum, -ī (n)* [L6]

tired *fessus, -a, -um* [L20]

Tmolus *Tmōlus, -ī (m)* [W28]

to *ad (+ acc.)* [L3]

today *hodiē* [L2]

together *ūnā* [L29]

toil (noun) *labor, labōris (m)* [L28]

tomorrow *crās* [L6]

tongue *lingua, -ae (f)* [L26]

too *quoque* [L29]

torrent *torrens, -ntis (m)* [W32]

touch (noun) *tactus, -ūs (m)* [W28]

touch (verb) *tangō, -ere, tetigī, tactum* [L27]

toward *ad (+ acc.)* [L3]

tower *turris, turris (f)* [L18]

town *oppidum, -ī (n)* [L5]

tragedy *tragoedia, -ae (f)* [W4]

train *exerceō, -ēre, -uī, -itum* [L14]

tree *arbor, arboris (f)* [L20]

trek *iter, itineris (n)* [L13]

tremble *tremō, -ere, -uī, ——* [W25]

tribe *gens, -ntis (f)* [L31]

tribute *tribūtum, -ī (n)* [W30]

trick *lūdō, lūdere, lūsī, lūsum* [L26]

troops *plural of cōpia, -ae (f)* [L15]

true *vērus, -a, -um* [L22]

truly *enim (postpositive conj.)* [L17]

trustworthy *fīdus, -a, -um* [L7]

truth *veritas, -tatis (f)* [L27]

tub *lacus, -ūs (m)* [L27]

turban *mītra, -ae (f)* [W28]

turn *vertō, -ere, vertī, versum* [L28]

turning-post *mēta, -ae (f)* [W23]

turret *turris, turris (f)* [L18]

twelfth *duodecimus, -a, -um* [L23]

twelve *duodecim* [L21]

twentieth *vīcēsimus, -a, -um* [L23]

twenty *vīgintī* [L21]

twenty-first *vīcēsimus, -a, -um prīmus, -a, -um* [L23]

twenty-one *vīgintī ūnus, -a, -um (ūnus et vīgintī)* [L21]

twin *geminus, -ī (m)* [L10]

two *duo, duae, duo* [L21]

U

ugly *foedus, -a, -um* [L7]

uncircumcised *incircumcisus, -a, -um* [W32]

uncle (father's brother) *patruus, -ī (m)* [L22]; **(mother's brother)** *avunculus, -ī (m)* [L22]

under *sub (+ acc.)* [L24]

under(neath) *sub (+ abl.)* [L14]

unfortunate *infēlix, (gen.) -līcis* [L19]

unhappy *miser, -era, -erum* [L7]

unimportant *parvus, -a, -um* [L7]

unite *iungō, -ere, iūnxī, iunctum* [L27]

universe *mundus, -ī (m)* [L6]

unlucky *infēlix, (gen.) -līcis* [L19]

up under *sub (+ acc.)* [L14]

V

vale *vallēs, vallis (f)* [L18]

valley *vallēs, vallis (f)* [L18]

vast *ingēns, (gen.) -entis* [L19]

very much *magnoperē* [L29]

vex *vexō (1)* [L19]

victory *victōria, -ae (f)* [L11]

vigorous *viridis, -e* [L17]

violet *hyacinthinus, -a, -um* [L17]; **(dark-violet)** *purpureus, -a, -um* [L17]

voice *vōx, vōcis (f)* [L14]

W

wage war *bellum gerō* [L28]

wait for *exspectō (1)* [L3]

walk *ambulō (1)* [L1]

walls (city walls) *moenia, -ium (n, pl)* [L18]

wander *errō (1)* [L14]

war *bellum, -ī (n)* [L15]

warm *caldus, -a, -um* [L7]

warn *moneō, -ēre, -uī, -itum* [L9]

warrior *bellator, -toris (m)* [W32]

wash *lavō, -āre, lāvī, lōtum/lavātum* [W27]

watch *spectō (1)* [L1]

water *aqua, -ae (f)* [L2]

wave *unda, -ae (f)* [L10]

way *via, -ae (f)* [L11]

we *nōs (pl.)* [L17]

wealth *dīvitiae, -ārum (f, pl)* [L2]

weapons *arma, -ōrum (n, pl)* [W32]

weary *fessus, -a, -um* [L20]

weather *tempestās, -tātis (f)* [L26]

weep *fleō, -ēre, flēvī, flētum* [L14]

weight *onus, oneris (n)* [L13]

well (adj.) *salvus, -a, -um* [L25]

well (verb; be well) *salveō, -ēre, —, —* [L9]; *valeō, -ēre, valuī, valitūrum* [L9]

well (adv.) *bene* [L1]

wet (sopping) *aquōsus, -a, -um* [W29]

what? *quid* [W19]

when (?) *quandō* [L12]; *ubi* [L12]

where (?) *ubi* [L12]

whether...or *sīve/seū... sīve/seū* [L30]

whisper *susurrō (1)* [W28]

white (dead) *albus, -a, -um* [L17]; **(glittering)** *candidus, -a, -um* [L17]

who (?) *quis* [W31]

why *cūr* [L2]

wicked *improbus, -a, -um* [L29]

wide *lātus, -a, -um* [L20]

widow *vidua, -ae (f)* [L22]

widowed *viduāta, -ae* [W19]

wife *coniūnx, -iugis (f)* [L22]; *uxor, -ōris (f)* [L30]

wild *ferus, -a, -um* [L7]

wind *ventus, -ī (m)* [W28]

window *fenestra, ae (f)* [L31]

wine *vīnum, -ī (n)* [L5]

wing *āla, -ae (f)* [L10]

wisdom *cōnsilium, -iī (n)* [L30]

wise *doctus, -a, -um* [L13]

wish (for) *cupiō, -ere, cupīvī, cupītum* [L31]

with *cum (+ abl.)* [L9]

withered *āridus, -a, -um* [L27]

without *sine (+ abl.)* [L9]

woman *fēmina, -ae (f)* [L2]; *mulier, mulieris (f)* [L22]; **(young woman)** *virgō, virginis (f)* [L12]

wonderful *mīrus, -a, -um* [L7]

word *verbum, -ī* [L5]

work (noun) *labor, labōris (m)* [L12]

work (verb) *labōrō (1)* [L22]

world *mundus, -ī (m)* [L6]

worship *colō, -ere, coluī, cultum* [L29]

worthy (am worthy of) *mereō, -ēre, -uī, -itum* [L23]

wound (noun) *vulnus, vulneris (n)* [L13]

wound (verb) *vulnerō (1)* [L1]

wrathful *īrātus, -a, -um* [L15]

wreck *naufragium, -ī (n)* [W23]

wretched *miser, -era, -erum* [L7]

write *scrībō, -ere, scrīpsī, scriptum* [L26]

wrongly *male* [L1]

Y

yesterday *herī* [L6]

yet *tamen* [L30]

yield *cēdō, -ere, cessī, cessum* [L28]

yoke *iungō, -ere, iūnxī, iunctum* [L27]

you (sg.) *tū* [L17]; **(pl.)** *vōs* [L17]

young man *adulescens, -entis (m)* [L30]

young *viridis, -e* [L17]

young woman *adulescens, -entis (f)* [L30]; *virgō, virginis (f)* [L12]

younger *minimus, -a, -um* [W31]

youngest *iuvenissimus, -a, -um* [W19]

your (sg.) *tuus, -a, -um* [L11]; **(pl.)** *vester, -stra, -strum* [L11]

yours (sg.) *tuus, -a, -um* [L11]; **(pl.)** *vester, -stra, -strum* [L11]

youth *adulescentia, -ae (f)* [W32]

Latin-English Glossary

A

ā, ab, (+ abl.) *from, away from* [L3]

abeō, -īre, -iī, -itum *I go away, depart* [W32]

ac (atque) *and, and also* [L27]

accipiō, -ere, -cēpī, -ceptum *I accept, receive, take* [L31]

ācer, ācris, ācre *sharp, eager; fierce* [L20]

ad (+ acc.) *to, toward, at, near* [L3]

adsūmō, -ere, -sumpsī, -sumptum *I take for myself* [W32]

adulescens, -entis (m/f) *young man/woman* [L30]

adulescentia, -ae (f) *youth* [W32]

Aegeus, -a, -um *Aegean* [W30]

Aegeus, -eī (m) *Aegeus* [W30]

aeternus, -a, -um *eternal* [L15]

ager, agrī (m) *field* [L4]

agō, -ere, ēgī, actum *I do, act, drive* [L26]

agricola, -ae (m) *farmer* [L3]

āiō (defective) *I say, assert, affirm* [L14]

āla, -ae (f) *wing* [L10]

albus, -a, -um *(dead) white* [L17]

alchemia, -ae (f) *alchemy* [W27]

alius, alia, aliud *another, other* [W21]

alnus, -ī (f) *ship, alder (wood)* [L4]

altus, -a, -um *high, lofty, deep* [L19]

ambulō (1) *I walk* [L1]

amīca, -ae (f) *(female) friend* [L15]

amīcus, -ī (m) *(male) friend* [L15]

amita, -ae (f) *aunt* [L22]

amō (1) *I love* [L1]

amor, amōris (m) *love* [L14]

animal, -ālis (n) *animal* [L18]

animus, -ī (m) *mind* [L29]

ante (+ acc.) *before* [L17]

antīquus, -a, -um *ancient* [L7]

aperiō, -īre, -uī, apertum *I open, expose* [L29]

Apollo, -inis (m) *Apollo (god of prophesy, music, archery, the sun, etc.)* [W20]

apostolus, -ī (m) *apostle* [L11]

appellō (1) *I name, call* [L15]

appropinquō (1) *I approach, draw near* [L25]

aqua, -ae (f) *water* [L2]

aquōsus, -a, -um *sopping wet* [W29]

arbor, arboris (f) *tree* [L20]

arcus, -ūs (m) *bow, arch, rainbow* [L27]

ardeō, ardēre, arsī, —— *I burn, blaze* [L20]

argenteus, -a, -um *silver(y)* [L17]

argentum, -ī (n) *silver, money* [L5]

Argus, -ī (m) *Argus, a hundred-eyed giant* [W21]

Ariadna, -ae (f) *Ariadne* [W30]

āridus, -a, -um *dry, withered* [L27]

ariēs, -ietis (m) *ram* [W32]

arma, -ōrum (n, pl) *arms, armor, weapons* [W32]

asinus, -ī (m) *donkey* [L19]

āter, -tra, -trum *(dead) black, dark* [L17]

Athēnae, -ārum (f, pl) *Athens* [W30]

Athēniensis, -is (m/f) *an Athenian* [W30]

atque (ac) *and, and also* [L27]

audeō, -ēre, ——, ausus sum *I dare* [L11]

audiō, -īre, -īvī, -ītum *I hear, listen to* [L29]

auferō, -ferre, abstulī, ablatum (3rd conj. irreg.) *I carry away/off, remove* [W32]

augeō, -ēre, auxī, auctum *I increase* [L19]

aula, -ae (f) *hall, inner/royal court* [W13]

aureus, -a, -um *golden, gold* [L17]

aurīga, -ae (m/f) *charioteer, driver* [W23]

auris, -is (f) *ear* [W28]

aurum, -ī (n) *gold* [L5]

aut *or* [L1]

autem (postpositive conj.) *however, moreover* [L12]

auxilium, -ī (n) *help, aid* [L5]

avārus, -a, -um *greedy* [L7]

avēna, -ae (f) *pan pipe, shepherd's pipe* [W21]

avia, -ae (f) *grandmother* [L22]

avis, avis (f) *bird* [L18]

avunculus, -ī (m) *uncle (mother's brother)* [L22]

avus, -ī (m) *grandfather, ancestor* [L22]

B

Bacchus, -ī (m) *Bacchus, the god of wine* [W27]

baculum, -ī (n) *staff* [W32]

barbarus, -a, -um *foreign, strange, savage* [L31]

barbarus, -ī (m) *foreigner, barbarian* [L31]

beātus, -a, -um *happy, blessed* [L7]

bellator, -toris (m) *warrior* [W32]

bellum, -ī (n) *war* [L15]; **bellum gerō** *I wage war* [L28]

bene *well* [L1]

bēstia, -ae (f) *beast* [L2]

Bethleem (indecl.) *Bethlehem* [W32]

Biblia Sacra, Bibliae Sacrae (f) *Holy Bible* [L11]

bonus, -a, -um *good* [L7]

bōs, bovis (m/f) *cow, bull, ox (pl.) cattle* [L19]

bracchium, -ī (n) *arm* [W13]

brevis, -e *short, small, brief* [L19]

C

cadaver, -veris (n) *dead body, carcass* [W32]

cadō, -ere, cecidī, cāsum *I fall, sink, drop* [L27]

caecus, -a, -um *blind* [L27]

caelum, -ī (n) *sky, heaven* [L5]

caeruleus, -a, -um *blue* [L17]

calamus, -ī (m) *reed, reed-pipe* [W28]

caldus, -a, -um *warm, hot, fiery* [L7]

calix, calicis (m) *goblet* [W13]

camēlus, -ī (m/f) *camel* [L4]

candidus, -a, -um *(glittering) white* [L17]

canis, canis (m/f) *dog* [L18]

cantō (1) *I sing, play (music), predict* [L1]

cantus, -ūs (m) *song, singing* [L25]

caper, -prī (m) *(billy) goat* [L4]

capiō, -ere, cēpī, captum *I take, capture, seize* [L31]

captō (1) *I hunt* [L10]

caput, -itis (n) *head* [L13]

carcer, -eris (m) *prison; (generally in pl.) starting gates (of a horse race)* [W23]

carmen, -inis (n) *song, chant, poem, prophecy* [L13]

caro, carnis (f) *flesh, meat* [L31]

cārus, -a, -um *dear, beloved* [L13]

castellum, -ī (n) *castle* [L5]

castra, -ōrum (n, pl) *camp* [L15]

cāsus, -ūs (m) *event, incident; misfortune, downfall* [L28]

cauda, -ae (f) *tail* [W21]

caveō, -ēre, cāvī, cautum *I guard against, beware (of)* [L12]

cēdō, -ere, cessī, cessum *I go, move, yield* [L28]

celer, celeris, celere *swift, quick* [L19]

celō (1) *I hide* [W28]

cēna, -ae (f) *dinner, meal* [L20]

centaurus, -ī (m) *centaur* [L10]

centēsimus, -a, -um *one hundredth* [L23]

centum *one hundred* [L21]

certāmen, -minis (n) *contest, race* [W23]

certātim *eagerly* [L20]

cervus, -ī (m) *stag, deer* [L10]

cētus, -ī (m) *sea monster, kraken, whale* [L10]

Christus, -ī (m) *Christ* [L4]

cibus, -ī (m) *food* [L4]

Circus Maximus, Circī Maximī (m) *the Circus Maximus, a famous racetrack at the foot of the Palatine Hill in Rome* [W23]

cito *quickly, fast, speedily* [L27]

clam *secretly* [L29]

clāmō (1) *I shout* [L1]

clāmor, -oris (m) *shout, cry* [W20]

classis, -is (f) *group, class, fleet (of ships)* [L30]

clēmentia, -ae (f) *mercy, clemency* [W21]

clypeum, -ī (n) *shield* [W32]

cōgitō (1) *I think* [L6]

cōgō, -ere, -ēgī, -āctum *I drive together, force, compel* [L28]

collocō (1) *I place, set, arrange* [W21]

colō, -ere, coluī, cultum *I cultivate, inhabit, worship* [L29]

coniunx, -iugis (m/f) *husband or wife* [L22]

cōnsilium, -iī (n) *plan, counsel, advice; wisdom* [L30]

cōnsōbrīna, -ae (f) *cousin (female, mother's side)* [L22]

cōnsōbrīnus, -ī (m) *cousin (male, mother's side)* [L22]

contrā (+ acc.) *against* [L11]

cōpia, -ae (f) *supply, plenty, abundance; (pl.) troops* [L15]

cor, cordis (n) *heart* [L13]

cōram (+ abl.) *in the presence of, before;* **(adv.)** *personally, openly* [L27]

cornū, -ūs (n) *horn* [L25]

corōna, -ae (f) *crown* [L2]

corpus, corporis (n) *body* [L13]

crās *tomorrow* [L6]

crēdō, -ere, -didī, -ditum *I believe* [L26]

cremō (1) *I burn, consume by fire* [L2]

creō (1) *I create* [L6]

Crēta, -ae (f) *Crete* [W30]

crūs, crūris (n) *leg* [W19]

crustulum, -ī (n) *cookie, small cake* [L5]

crux, crucis (f) *cross* [L15]

cum (+ abl.) *with* [L9]

Cupīdō, -dinis (m) *Cupid (son of Venus and god of love)* [W20]

cupiō, -ere, cupīvī, cupītum *I wish (for), desire, long (for)* [L31]

cūr *why?* [L2]

cūrō (1) *I care for* [L15]

curriculum, -ī (n) *lap (of a race), course* [W23]

currō, -ere, cūcurrī, cursum *I run* [L26]

D

Daedalus, -ī (m) *Daedalus (a skilled inventor and craftsman)* [W30]

Daphne, -ēs (f) *Daphne* [W20]

David (indecl.) *David* [W32]

dē (+ abl.) *from, down from, concerning* [L4]

dea, -ae (f) *goddess; dat. and abl. pl. usually* **deābus** [L6]

dēbeō, -ēre, -uī, -itum *I owe, ought* [L11]

decem *ten* [L21]

decimus, -a, -um *tenth* [L23]

dēclārō (1) *I declare, make clear, explain* [L10]

dēfendō, -ere, -fendī, -fēnsum *I defend* [L28]

dēiciō, -icere, -iēcī, -iectum *I throw down, cast down, hurl down* [W23]

deinde *from that place, then, thereupon, next* [L24]

dēleō, -ēre, -lēvī, -lētum *I destroy* [L9]

dēligō, -ere, lēgī, -lēctum *I pick, choose* [L28]

dēnique *finally* [L10]

dēspiciō, -ere, -spexī, -spectum *I look down on, despise* [W32]

Deus, -ī (m) *God;* **deus, -ī (m)** *a god* [L4]

dexter, -tra, -trum (or –tera, -terum) *right(-handed); skilled, favorable* [L30]

diaeta, -ae (f) *cabin (of a ship)* [W18]

Diāna, -ae (f) *Diana (virgin goddess of the moon and hunting)* [W20]

dīcō, -ere, dīxī, dictum *I say, speak* [L26]

diēs, diēī (m/f) *day, period of time* [L28]

difficilis, -e *difficult* [L20]

dīmittō, -ere, -mīsī, -missum *I send away, dismiss, forgive* [L30]

discipula, -ae (f) *student (female), disciple* [L5]

discipulus, -ī (m) *student (male), apprentice, disciple* [L5]

diū *for a long time* [L13]

dīvitiae, -ārum (f, pl) *riches, wealth* [L2]

dō, dare, dedī, datum *I give* [L1]

doceō, -ēre, docuī, doctum *I teach* [L9]

doctus, -a, -um *learned, wise, skilled* [L13]

dominus, -ī (m) *lord, master* [L4]

domō, -āre, domuī, domitum *I tame, subdue* [L12]

domus, -ūs (f) *house, home* [L25]

dōnum, -ī (n) *gift* [L5]

dormiō, -īre, -īvī, -ītum *I sleep* [L29]

draco, dracōnis (m) *dragon* [L12]

dūcō, -ere, duxī, ductum *I lead, guide* [L26]

dulcis, -e *sweet* [L19]

duo, duae, duo *two* [L21]

duodecim *twelve* [L21]

duodecimus, -a, -um *twelfth* [L23]

duodēvīcēsimus, -a, -um *eighteenth* [L23]

duodēvīgintī *eighteen* [L21]

dux, ducis (m) *leader, guide, general* [L14]

E

ē *see* **ex**

ēbrius, -a, -um *drunk, intoxicated* [W13]

ecce *behold!* [L17]

ecclēsia, -ae (f) *church* [L11]

effugiō, -ere, -fūgī, -fugitum *I escape* [W10]

ego (sg.) *I* [L17]

ēgregius, -a, -um *outstanding, excellent* [L29]

ēheu (heu) *alas! oh! (expressing grief or pain)* [L22]

elephantus, -ī (m) *elephant* [L19]

enigma, -matis (n) *riddle* [W19]

enim (postpositive conj.) *indeed, truly, certainly; for* [L17]

eō, -īre, iī (īvī), itum *I go* [L29]

Ephratheus, -ī (m) *an Ephramite* [W32]

epulae, -ārum (f, pl) *feast* [L20]

eques, -quitis (m) *knight, horseman, cavalryman* [L20]

equus, -ī (m) *horse* [L4]

ergō *therefore, then, consequently, accordingly* [L18]

errō (1) *I wander, err, am mistaken* [L14]

et *and, even, also;* **et…et** *both…and* [L1]

etiam *even, also, besides, still* [L22]

ēvangelium, -ī (n) *good news, gospel* [L5]

ex, ē (+ abl.) *out of, from* [L3]

exerceō, -ēre, -uī, -itum *I train, exercise* [L14]

exercitus, -ūs (m) *army* [L25]

exprobrō (1) *I reproach* [W32]

exspectō (1) *I wait for, expect* [L3]

extendō, -ere, -tendī, -tensum *I stretch out, extend* [W26]

F

Fabius, -ī (m) *Fabius* [W19]

fābula, -ae (f) *story, legend, tale* [L2]

faciēs, -ēī (f) *shape, form; face; character* [L28]

facilis, -e *easy* [L20]

faciō, -ere, fēcī, factum *I make, do (for present passive system, use* **fīō***)* [L31]

fāma, -ae *report, reputation, fame* [W23]

famēlicus, -a, -um *hungry* [L29]

familia, -ae *household, family* [L22]

fātum, -ī (n) *fate* [L5]

fēliciter in aeternum *happily ever after* [W6]

fēlix, (gen.) -līcis *lucky, fortunate, happy* [L19]

fēmina, -ae (f) *woman* [L2]

fenestra, -ae (f) *window* [L31]

ferō, ferre, tulī, lātum (irreg. 3rd conj.) *I carry, bring (forth), bear* [W32]

ferus, -a, -um *fierce, wild* [L7]

fessus, -a, -um *tired, weary* [L20]

festīnō (1) *I hasten, hurry* [L9]

fidēs, -eī (f) *faith* [L28]

fīdus, -a, -um *faithful, trustworthy* [L7]

fīlia, -ae (f) *daughter (dat. and abl. pl. often* **fīliābus***)* [L6]

fīlius, -ī (m) *son* [L4]

fīlum, -ī (n) *thread, string* [W30]

fīnis, -is (m) *end, boundary, limit* [W4]

fīō, fierī, ——, factus sum *I am made, am done, become, happen [used as present passive system of* **faciō***]* [L31]

fleō, -ēre, flēvī, flētum *I weep* [L14]

flōreō, -ēre, -uī, —— *I flourish* [L17]

flōs, flōris (m) *flower* [L15]

flūmen, flūminis (n) *river* [L13]

fodiō, -ere, fōdī, fossum *I dig* [W28]

foedus, -a, -um *horrible, ugly* [L7]

folium *leaf* [W20]

fortasse *perhaps* [L26]

fortior, -tius (gen. fortioris) *braver* [W31]

fortis, -e *strong, brave* [L19]

fortissimus, -a, -um *bravest, strongest* [W32]

foveō, -ēre, fōvī, fōtum *I cherish, love, esteem* [L25]

frangō, -ere, frēgī, fractum *I break, smash, shatter* [L27]

frāter, frātris (m) *brother* [L12]

frōns, -ontis (f) *forehead* [W32]

frūctus, -ūs (m) *fruit, profit* [L25]

frūmentum, -ī (n) *grain; (pl.) crops* [L15]

fugiō, -ere, fūgī, fugitum *I flee, run away* [L31]

fulgur, -uris (n) *lightning* [W25]

funda, -ae (f) *sling* [W32]

G

gaudeō, -ēre, ——, gāvīsus sum *I rejoice* [L22]

gaudium, -ī (n) *joy, happiness* [L5]

gelidus, -a, -um *cold, icy* [L31]

geminus, -ī (m) *twin* [L10]

gens, -ntis (f) *clan, tribe, nation* [L31]

genu, -ūs (n) *knee* [L25]

germāna, -ae (f) *sister* [L4]

germānus, -ī (m) *brother* [L4]

gerō, -ere, gessī, gestum *I bear, carry on;* **bellum gerō** *I wage war* [L28]

gigās, gigantis (m) *giant* [L15]

gladius, -ī (m) *sword* [L4]

glōria, -ae (f) *fame, glory* [L15]

grāmen, grāminis (n) *grass, greenery* [L13]

grātia, -ae (f) *grace, favor, kindness, thanks;* **grātiās agō (+ dat.)** *I give thanks, I thank* [L27]

grātus, -a, -um *grateful, pleasing* [L27]

grex, gregis (m) *flock, herd* [L31]

gubernō (1) *I steer, direct, govern* [L25]

H

habeō, -ēre, -uī, -itum *I have, hold* [L9]

habitō (1) *I live, dwell, inhabit* [L3]

hara, -ae (f) *pig-sty* [W25]

harēna, -ae (f) *sand, beach* [L3]

hasta, -ae (f) *spear* [L3]

herī *yesterday* [L6]

heu (ēheu) *alas! oh! (expresses grief or pain)* [L22]

hic, haec, hoc *this, (pl.) these* [L30]

Hierusalem (indecl.) *Jerusalem*

hodiē *today* [L2]

homō, hominis (m) *man, human being* [L12]

hōra, -ae (f) *hour* [L31]

horrendus, -a, -um *dreadful, awful, fearful* [L13]

hostis, -is (m) *enemy (of the state)* [L18]

hyacinthinus, -a, -um *blue, purplish-blue, violet* [L17]

hydrus, -ī (m) *sea serpent* [W12]

I

iaceō, -ēre, -uī, —— *I lie (flat), lie down* [L9]

iaciō, -ere, iēcī, iactum *I throw, cast, hurl* [L31]

iam *now, already;* **nōn iam** *no longer* [L15]

ibī *there, at that place; then* [L5]

Iēsus, -ūs (m) *Jesus* [L25]

ignis, ignis (m) *fire* [L18]

ille, illa, illud *that, (pl.) those; that famous* [L30]

impediō, -īre, -īvī, -ītum *I hinder* [L29]

improbus, -a, -um *wicked* [L29]

in (+ acc.) *into, against;* **(+ abl.)** *in, on* [L3]

Īnachus, -ī (m) *Inachus (god of the Inachus River in Argos)* [W21]

incipiō, -ere, -cēpī, -ceptum *I begin, commence* [L31]

incircumcisus, -a, -um *uncircumcised* [W32]

īnfāns, -fantis (adj. & noun, m/f) *baby, infant* [W31]

īnfēlix, (gen.) -līcis *unlucky, unfortunate, miserable* [L19]

īnfīgō, -ere, -fīxī, -fixum *I fix in, fasten in* [W32]

ingēns, (gen.) -entis *huge, vast, enormous* [L19]

inimīcus, -ī (m) *(personal) enemy* [L10]

īnsula, -ae (f) *island* [L3]

inter (+ acc.) *between, among* [L19]

interficiō, -ere, -fēcī, -fectum *I kill, slay, destroy* [L31]

interim *meanwhile, in the meantime* [L9]

intrō (1) *I enter* [L9]

inveniō, -īre, -vēnī, -ventum *I come upon, find* [L29]

invicem *reciprocally (i.e., "[to] one another")* [W26]

invideō, -ēre, -vīdī, -vīsum *I envy* [W29]

Īō, -ōnis (f) *Io (a beautiful nymph and daughter of Inachus)* [W21]

īra, -ae (f) *anger* [L2]

īrātus, -a, -um *angry, wrathful* [L15]

is, ea, id *he, she, it, they; this, that* [L17]

Isai (indecl.) *Jesse* [W32]

Israhel (indecl.) *Israel* [W32]

Israhelita, -ae (m) *Israelite* [W32]

iste, ista, istud *that (of yours); such (sometimes used with tone of contempt)* [L30]

Ītalia, -ae (f) *Italy* [W8]

itaque *and ēo, therefore* [L2]

iter, itineris (n) *journey, road, route, trek* [L13]

iterum *again, a second time* [L25]

iūdex, -dicis (m) *judge* [W28]

Iūlia, -ae (f) *Iulia or Julia* [W11]

Iūlius, -iī (m) *Iulius or Julius* [W19]

iungō, -ere, iūnxī, iunctum *I join, unite, yoke* [L27]

Iūnia, -ae (f) *Iunia or Junia* [W11]

Iūno, -ōnis (f) *Juno (queen of the gods and wife of Jupiter)* [W21]

Iuppiter, Iovis (m) *Jupiter/Jove (king of the gods)* [W21]

iūstus, -a, -um *just, right, fair, righteous* [L7]

iuvenissimus, -a, -um *youngest* [W19]

iuvō, -āre, iūvī, iūtum *I help* [L22]

iūxta, (adv. & prep. + acc.) *near (to), close to/by* [L28]

L

labor, labōris (m) *work, toil, labor, hardship* [L12]

labōrō (1) *I work* [L22]

labyrinthus, -ī (m) *labyrinth, maze* [W30]

lac, lactis (n) *milk* [L13]

lacus, -ūs (m) *lake, tub, hollow* [L27]

laetus, -a, -um *happy, joyful, glad* [L7]

lapis, -idis (m) *stone* [W27]

lātus, -a, -um *wide, broad* [L20]

laudō (1) *I praise* [L1]

laurus, -ī *laurel-tree* [W20]

laus, laudis (f) *praise* [L15]

lavō, -āre, lāvī, lōtum/lavātum *I wash* [W27]

legō, -ere, lēgī, lectum *I read, choose* [L28]

leō, leōnis (m) *lion* [L12]

liber, librī (m) *book* [L11]

līberī, -ōrum (m, pl) *children* [L10]

līberō (1) *I set free* [L1]

licet *it is permitted/allowed* [W26]

limpidissimus, -a, -um *very bright, very clear* [W32]

lingua, -ae (f) *language, tongue* [L26]

littera, -ae (f) *letter of the alphabet; (pl) letter, epistle* [L26]

lītus, lītoris (n) *shore, shoreline* [L13]

longinquus, -a, -um *distant, far away* [L7]

longus, -a, -um *long* [L20]

lūceō, lūcēre, lūxī, —— *I shine, am bright* [L11]

lūdō, lūdere, lūsī, lūsum *I play, tease, trick* [L26]

lūna, -ae (f) *moon* [L2]

lux, lūcis (f) *light* [L12]

lyra, -ae (f) *lyre* [W28]

M

magister, -strī (m) *teacher (male)* [L6]

magistra, -ae (f) *teacher (female)* [L6]

magnanimus, -a, -um *brave, bold, noble* [W9]

magnoperē *greatly, very much* [L29]

magnus, -a, -um *large, big, great* [L7]

māior, māius (gen. māioris) *greater, older* [W31]

male *badly, ill, wrongly* [L1]

maledīcō, -ere, -dīxī, -dictum *I speak ill, curse* [W30]

malus, -a, -um *bad, evil* [L7]

mandūcō (1) *I chew, eat* [L6]

māne *in the morning, early* [W19]

maneō, -ēre, mansī, mansum *I remain* [L10]

manus, -ūs (f) *hand* [L25]

mappa, -ae (f) *starting flag (lit., "napkin")* [W23]

mare, maris (n) *sea* [L18]

māter, mātris (f) *mother* [L12]

mātrimōnium -ī (n) *marriage* [L20]

maximus, -a, -um *greatest, oldest* [W31]

mediōcris, -e *ordinary* [L19]

medius, -a, -um *middle (of), midst (of)* [L26]

melior, -ius *better* [W28]

mensa, -ae (f) *table* [L31]

Mercurius, -ī (m) *Mercury (the messenger god)* [W21]

mereō, -ēre, -uī, -itum *I deserve, earn, am worthy of* [L15]

merīdiēs, -ēī (m) *noon* [L28]

mēta, -ae (f) *turning-post, goal* [W23]

metus, -ūs (m) *fear, dread* [L26]

meus, -a, -um *my, mine* [L11]

Midās, -ae (m) *Midas (king of Phrygia)* [W27]

mīles, mīlitis (m) *soldier* [L12]

mille *one thousand* [L21]

mīllēsimus, -a, -um *one thousandth* [L23]

minimus, -a, -um *least, younger* [W31]

Mīnōs, -ōnis (m) *Minos* [W30]

Mīnōtaurus, -ī (m) *the Minotaur* [W30]

minūtātim *gradually, bit by bit* [L20]

mīrus, -a, -um *strange, wonderful* [L7]

miser, -era, -erum *unhappy, wretched, miserable* [L7]

mītra, -ae (f) *turban* [W28]

mittō, -ere, mīsī, missum *I send, let go* [L26]

modo *only, just, merely, but* [L27]

moenia, -ium (n, pl) *fortifications, city walls* [L18]

moneō, -ēre, -uī, -itum *I warn* [L9]

mōns, montis *mountain* [L18]

mōnstrum *monster* [W30]

mordeō, -ēre, momordī, morsum *I bite, sting* [L9]

mors, mortis (f) *death* [L18]

moveō, -ēre, mōvī, mōtum *I move* [L14]

mox *soon* [L15]

mulier, mulieris (f) *woman* [L22]

multus, -a, -um *much, many* [L7]

mundus, -ī (m) *world, universe* [L6]
musicus, -ī (m) *musician* [W28]
mūtō (1) *I change* [L20]

N

nam *for* [W32]
narrō (1) *I tell, relate, recount* [L2]
naufragium, -ī (n) *wreck, crash (lit., shipwreck)* [W23]
nauta, -ae (m) *sailor* [L3]
nāvicula, -ae (f) *boat* [W31]
nāvigō (1) *I sail* [L4]
nāvis, -is (f) *ship* [L18]
nec (neque) *and not, nor*; **nec…nec** *neither….nor* [L14]
necō (1) *I kill, slay* [L1]
neque (nec) *and not, nor*; **nec…nec** *neither….nor* [L14]
nesciō, -īre, -īvī, -ītum *I do not know* [L30]
niger, -gra, -grum *(shining) black, dark-colored* [L17]
nihil, (n. indecl.) *nothing*; **(adv.)** *not at all* [L6]
nō (1) *I swim* [L14]
nōmen, nōminis (n) *name* [L13]
nōn *not* [L1]
nōnus, -a, -um *ninth* [L23]
nōs (pl.) *we* [L17]
noster, -stra, -strum *our, ours* [L11]
novem *nine* [L21]
noverca, -ae (f) *step-mother* [W22]
novus, -a, -um *new* [L26]
nox, noctis (f) *night* [L18]
nūbes, nūbis (f) *cloud, gloom* [L18]
nummus, -ī (m) *coin* [W22]
numquam *never* [L5]
nunc *now* [L1]
nuntiō (1) *I announce, declare* [L14]
nympha, -ae (f) *nymph* [W20]

O

obsideō, -ēre, -sēdī, -sessum *I besiege, remain near* [L10]
occīdō, -ere, -cīdī, -cīsum *I kill, cut down, slay* [L30]
occultō (1) *I hide, conceal* [L22]
occupō (1) *I seize* [L6]
ōceanus, -ī (m) *ocean* [L4]
octāvus, -a, -um *eighth* [L23]
octō *eight* [L21]
ōlim *once upon a time, formerly, then* [L6]
omnis, -e *every, all* [L19]
onus, oneris (n) *burden, load, weight* [L13]
oppidum, -ī (n) *town* [L5]
oppugnō (1) *I attack* [L4]
optio, optiōnis (f) *choice* [W12]
ōra, -ae (f) *shore* [L13]
ōrāculum, -ī (n) *oracle, prophecy* [W31]
orba, -ae (f) *orphan (female)* [L22]
orbus, -a, -um *deprived of parents or children, bereft* [L22]
orbus, -ī (m) *orphan (male)* [L22]
ōrō (1) *I pray, speak (takes double acc.)* [L6]
ōs, ōris (n) *mouth* [L13]
Oswaldus, -ī (m) *Oswald* [W19]

P

Pactōlus, -ī (m) *Pactolus (a river in Lydia in Asia Minor)* [W27]
paene (adv.) *almost* [L19]
palma, -ae (f) *hand* [W14]
palus, palūdis (f) *swamp* [W13]
Pān, Pānos (acc. Pāna) (m) *Pan (god of woods, shepherds, and flocks)* [W28]
pānis, -is (m) *bread* [L29]
parens, -ntis (m/f) *parent* [W11]
parō (1) *I prepare* [L14]
parvus, -a, -um *little, small, unimportant* [L7]
pascō, -ere, pāvī, pastum *I feed, pasture* [W32]
pastor, pastōris (m) *shepherd* [L20]
pastorālis, -e *of/belonging to a shepherd, pastoral* [W32]
pater, patris (m) *father* [L12]
patria, -ae (f) *native land* [L3]
patruēlis, -is (m/f) *cousin (on the father's side)* [L22]
patruus, -ī (m) *uncle (father's brother)* [L22]
paucī, -ae, -a (pl) *few* [L7]
pāvo, -ōnis (m) *peacock* [W21]
pāx, pācis (f) *peace* [L15]
pecūnia, -ae (f) *money* [L3]
per (+ acc.) *through* [L3]
pēra, -ae (f) *bag, satchel* [W32]
percutiō, -ere, -cussī, -cussum *I strike down, cut down* [W32]
perdō, -ere, perdidī, perditum *I destroy, ruin, lose* [L27]
perficiō, -ere, -fēci, -fectum *I complete, finish* [W23]
perīculum, -ī (n) *danger* [L5]
permittō, -ere, -mīsī, -missum *I permit, allow* [W30]
persequor, -sequī, ——, -secutus sum (deponent) *I pursue (with hostile intent), hunt down* [W32]
persuādeō, -ere, -suāsī, -suāsum (+dat.) *I persuade* [W15]
pertūsus, -a, -um *leaky* [W29]
petō, -ere, -īvī, -ītum *I shoot* [W20]
Philistheus, -ī (m) *Philistine*
Phrygia, -ae (f) *Phrygia (a land in Asia Minor)* [W27]
pila, -ae (f) *ball* [W30]
pinguis, -e *fat* [W25]
pīrāta, -ae (m) *pirate* [L2]
piscis, -is (m) *fish* [L19]

piscor, -ārī, ——, -ātus sum (deponent) *I fish* [W29]

placidus, -a, -um *calm, quiet* [W29]

plumbeus, -a, -um *leaden, of lead* [W20]

poena, -ae (f) *penalty, punishment;* **poenās dō** *I pay the penalty* [L27]

poēta, -ae (m) *poet* [L2]

pōnō, -ere, posuī, positum *I put, place* [L26]

pōns, pontis (m) *bridge* [W19]

populus, -ī (m) *people, nation* [L11]

porcus, -ī (m) *pig* [L10]

porta, -ae (f) *door, gate* [L31]

portō (1) *I carry* [L4]

portus, -ūs (m) *harbor, port* [L25]

possum, posse, potuī, —— *I am able, can* [L11]

post (+ acc.) *after, behind* [L17]

postea *afterwards* [L28]

postnatus, -ī (m) *oldest [Won]* [W19]

postquam (conj.) *after* [W15]

potēns, (gen.) -entis *powerful* [L19]

pōtō, -āre, -āvī, pōtātum or pōtum *I drink, drink heavily* [L6]

praecīdō, -ere, -cīdī, -cīsum *I cut off, lop* [W32]

praedīcō, -ere, -dīxī, -dictum *I predict, prophesy* [W31]

praemium, -ī (n) *reward* [W27]

prīmus, -a, -um *first* [L23]

prō (+ abl.) *before, in front of; for (the sake of), instead of* [L18]

proelium, -ī (n) *battle* [L15]

prope (adv./prep. + acc.) *near, next to* [L19]

properō (1) *I hurry, rush* [L20]

propter (+ acc.) *because of, on account of, near* [L25]

provocō (1) *to challenge* [W32]

puella, -ae (f) *girl* [L3]

puer, puerī (m) *boy* [L5]

pugnō (1) *I fight* [L1]

pulcher, -chra, -chrum *beautiful, handsome* [L7]

purpureus, -a, -um *purple; dark-red, dark-violet, dark-brown* [L17]

pyra, -ae (f) *funeral pyre* [W8]

Q

quadrīgae, -ārum (f, pl) *four-horse chariot* [W23]

quam *as, than, how* [L28]

quandō *when (?), ever; since, because* [L12]

quārtus, -a, -um decimus, -a, -um *fourteenth* [L23]

quārtus, -a, -um *fourth* [L23]

quattuor *four* [L21]

quattuordecim *fourteen* [L21]

-que, (enclitic) *and* [L10]

quia (conj.) *because, since, that* [L18]

quid *what?* [W19]

quīndecim *fifteen* [L21]

quīngentēsimus, -a, -um *five hundredth* [L23]

quīngentī *five hundred* [L21]

quīnquāgēsimus, -a, -um *fiftieth* [L23]

quīnquāgintā *fifty* [L21]

quīnque *five* [L21]

quīntus, -a, -um decimus, -a, -um *fifteenth* [L23]

quīntus, -a, -um *fifth* [L23]

quis *who?* [W31]

quod *because, that* [L10]

quōmodo *how, in what way* [L25]

quoniam *because, since* [L26]

quoque *also, too* [L29]

R

rapiō, -ere, rapuī, raptum *I snatch, seize, carry (off)* [L31]

raptus, -ūs (m) *kidnapping, abduction* [W31]

reficiō, -ere, -fēcī, -fectum *I repair* [W29]

rēgia, -ae (f) *palace* [L2]

rēgīna, -ae (f) *queen* [L2]

regnō (1) *I rule, govern, reign* [L6]

regnum, -ī (n) *kingdom* [L5]

regō, -ere, rexī, rectum *I rule* [L26]

relinquō, -ere, -līquī, -lictum *I abandon, leave behind* [L28]

removeō, -ēre, -mōvī, -mōtum *I remove, take away* [L14]

repentē *suddenly* [L10]

reptō (1) *I crawl, creep* [L14]

rēs, reī (f) *thing* [L28]

respondeō, -ēre, -spondī, -sponsum *I answer, respond* [L9]

resurgō, -ere, -surrēxī, -surrēctum *I rise again* [L29]

retrō *back(ward), behind* [W23]

rēx, rēgis (m) *king* [L12]

rīdeō, -ēre, rīsī, rīsum *I laugh, smile* [L9]

rogō (1) *I ask (takes double acc. or phrase with dē)* [L6]

ruber, -bra, -brum *red, ruddy* [L17]

rūfus, -a, -um *red, ruddy* [W32]

S

sabbata, -ōrum (n, pl) *Sabbath* [W26]

saeculum, -ī (n) *generation; the spirit of the age, times* [L6]

saepe *often* [L6]

sagitta, -ae (f) *arrow* [L3]

saliō, -īre, -uī, saltum *I jump, leap* [W29]

salveō, -ēre, ——, —— *I am well;* **salvē(te),** *Good day! Be well!* [L9]

salvus, -a, -um *safe, saved, well, sound* [L25]

sanctus, -a, -um *holy, sacred, consecrated* [L25]

satis (adv. & indecl. adj./noun) *enough, sufficient(ly)* [L30]

Saul (indecl.) *Saul* [W32]

saxum, -ī (n) *rock* [L29]

sciō, -īre, sciī (scīvī), scītum *I know* [L29]

scopulus, -ī (m) *cliff* [W30]

scrībō, -ere, scripsī, scriptum *I write* [L26]

scūtum, -ī (m) *shield* [L10]

sē (acc. reflexive pronoun) *himself, herself, itself* [W8]

sēcrētum, -ī (n) *secret* [W28]

secundum (adv. & prep. + acc.) *after; according to* [L28]

secundus, -a, -um *second* [L23]

sed *but* [L1]

sēdecim *sixteen* [L21]

sedeō, -ēre, sēdī, sessum *I sit* [L9]

sella, -ae (f) *seat, chair* [L31]

semper *always* [L5]

senex, senis (m) *old man* [L14]

septem *seven* [L21]

septendecim *seventeen* [L21]

septimus, -a, -um decimus, -a, -um *seventeenth* [L23]

septimus, -a, -um *seventh* [L23]

sequor, sequī, ——, secūtus sum (deponent) *I follow* [W30]

serva, -ae (f) *female slave, servant* [L4]

servō (1) *I save* [L6]

servus, -ī (m) *male slave, servant* [L4]

seū (sīve) *or*; **seū…seū** *whether…or* [L30]

sex *six* [L21]

sextus, -a, -um decimus, -a, -um *sixteenth* [L23]

sextus, -a, -um *sixth* [L23]

sī (conj.) *if* [L18]

sīca, -ae (f) *dagger* [L3]

sīcut *as, just as, like* [L20]

Sīlēnus, -ī (m) *Silenus (pudgy old fellow [usually drunk], former tutor and longtime companion of Bacchus)* [W27]

silva, -ae (f) *forest* [L3]

simulacrum, -ī (n) *statue* [W25]

sine (+ abl.) *without* [L9]

sinister, -stra, -strum *left(-handed); inauspicious* [L30]

sīve (seū) *or*; **sīve… sīve** *whether…or* [L30]

sōl, sōlis (m) *sun* [L12]

sōlus, -a, -um *only, single* [W12]

somniō (1) *I dream* [W18]

soror, sorōris (f) *sister* [L12]

spectō (1) *I look at, watch* [L1]

spēlunca, -ae (f) *cave* [L3]

spēs, speī (f) *hope* [L28]

spīna, -ae (f) *barrier (lit., "spine," the wall dividing a race course in half lengthwise)* [W23]

spīritus, -ūs (m) *spirit, breath* [L25]

spurius, -a, -um *spurious* [W32]

statim *immediately* [L13]

stella, -ae (f) *star* [L11]

stō, stāre, stetī, statum *I stand* [L1]

stultitia, -ae (f) *foolishness, folly* [W27]

stultus, -a, -um *foolish* [L7]

stupor, -ōris (m) *amazement, astonishment* [W28]

sub (+ acc.) *under, up under, close to*; (+ abl.) *below, under(neath), at the foot of* [L14]

sum, esse, fuī, futūrum *I am* [L3]

super (+ acc. /+ abl.) *over, above, beyond* [L26]

superbus, -a, -um *proud, haughty* [W18]

superō (1) *I conquer, defeat* [L2]

suprā (adv. & prep. + acc.) *above, over* [L14]

surgō, -ere, surrēxī, surrēctum *I (a)rise* [L28]

suspīciōsus, -a, -um *suspicious* [W21]

susurrō (1) *I whisper* [W28]

suum negōtium agō *(idiom) I mind my own business* [W29]

suus, -a, -um (reflexive possessive adj.) *his (own), her (own), its (own)* [W31]

synagōga, -ae (f) *synagogue* [W26]

T

tabernāculum, -ī (n) *tent* [W32]

taceō, -ēre, -uī, -itum *I am silent* [W26]

tactus, -ūs (m) *touch* [W28]

tamen *yet, nevertheless, still* [L30]

tangō, -ere, tetigī, tactum *I touch, strike* [L27]

tellūs, tellūris (f) *the earth, ground, land* [L14]

tempestās, -tātis (f) *weather, storm* [L26]

templum, -ī (n) *temple, shrine* [W25]

temptō (1) *I attempt* [W27]

tempus, temporis (n) *time* [L13]

tenēbrae, -ārum (f, pl) *darkness, gloomy place, shadows* [L11]

teneō, -ēre, tenuī, tentum *I hold, possess* [L9]

terra, -ae (f) *earth, land* [L4]

terreō, -ēre, -uī, -itum *I frighten, terrify* [L9]

tertius, -a, -um decimus, -a, -um *thirteenth* [L23]

tertius, -a, -um *third* [L23]

Thēseūs, -eī (m) *Theseus* [W30]

tigris, tigridis (m/f) *tiger* [L12]

timeō, -ēre, -uī, —— *I fear* [L9]

Tmōlus, -ī (m) *Tmolus (a god and a mountain in Lydia)* [W28]

tollō, -ere, sustulī, sublātum *I lift up, raise* [W25]

tonitrus, -ūs (m) *thunder* [L25]

tonsor, -ōris (m) *barber* [W28]

torrens, -ntis (m) *a torrent, stream* [W32]

torreō, -ēre, torruī, tostum *I burn, parch, dry up* [L17]

trādō, -ere, -didī, -ditum *I hand over, surrender* [W13]

tragoedia, -ae (f) *tragedy* [W4]

trahō, -ere, trāxī, trāctum *I draw, drag* [L30]

trans (+ acc.) *across* [L11]

tredecim *thirteen* [L21]

tremō, -ere, -uī, —— *I tremble, quake* [W25]

trēs, tria *three* [L21]

tribūtum, -ī (n) *tribute, tax* [W30]

trīstis, -e *sad, gloomy, dismal* [L20]

tū (sg.) *you* [L17]

tum *then, at that time; next, thereupon* [L15]

turba, -ae (f) *crowd, mob, throng* [L2]

turris, turris (f) *tower, turret* [L18]

tuus, -a, -um *your (sg), yours* [L11]

U

ubi *where (?), when* [L12]

ubīque *everywhere* [W29]

ūllus, -a, -um *any; anyone, anything* [W27]

ululō (1) *I howl, scream* [L6]

ūnā *together, in one* [L29]

unda, -ae (f) *wave* [L10]

ūndecim *eleven* [L21]

ūndecimus, -a, -um *eleventh* [L23]

ūndēvīcēsimus, -a, -um *nineteenth* [L23]

ūndēvīgintī *nineteen* [L21]

undique *on/from all sides, from every direction* [L30]

ūnicus, -a, -um *one, only, sole* [W22]

ūnus, -a, -um *one* [L21]

urbānus, -a, -um *polite* [W29]

urbs, urbis (f) *city* [L18]

ursus, -ī (m) *bear* [W32]

uxor, -ōris (f) *wife* [L30]

V

valeō, -ēre, -uī, -itum *I am well/strong;* **valē(te)** *Goodbye! Be well!* [L9]

valles, vallis (f) *valley, vale* [L18]

vastō (1) *I devastate, lay waste* [L14]

vātēs, -is (m/f) *prophet/prophetess* [W31]

vehō, -ere, vexī, vectum *I carry, ride, convey* [L27]

vēlum, -ī (n) *sail* [W30]

venēnum, -ī (n) *poison* [L10]

veniō, -īre, vēnī, ventum *I come* [L29]

ventus, -ī (m) *wind* [W28]

verbum, -ī (n) *word* [L5]

vēritas, -tātis (f) *truth* [L27]

versus, -ūs (m) *row, line (of poetry), furrow* [L27]

vertō, -ere, vertī, versum *I turn, change* [L28]

vērus, -a, -um *true* [L22]

vesper, vesperis (m) *evening, evening star* [L14]

vester, -stra, -strum *your (pl), yours (pl)* [L11]

vestis, vestis (f) *clothing, garment* [L18]

vetus, (gen.) -teris *old* [L30]

vexō (1) *I vex, ravage, annoy* [L19]

via, -ae (f) *road, way* [L11]

vīcēsimus, -a, -um prīmus, -a, -um *twenty-first* [L23]

vīcēsimus, -a, -um *twentieth* [L23]

victōria, -ae (f) *victory* [L11]

videō, -ēre, vīdī, visum *I see* [L9]

vidua, -ae (f) *widow* [L22]

viduō (1) *I deprive of* (**viduāta, -ae** *widowed*) [W19]

vīgintī *twenty* [L21]

vīgintī ūnus, -a, -um (ūnus et vīgintī) *twenty-one* [L21]

villa, -ae (f) *farmhouse, country house* [L2]

vinciō, -īre, vinxī, vinctum *I bind, tie* [L30]

vincō, -ere, vīcī, victum *I defeat, conquer* [L26]

vīnum, -ī (n) *wine* [L5]

vir, virī (m) *man* [L4]

virgō, virginis (f) *maiden, young woman* [L12]

viridis, -e *green; fresh, young, vigorous* [L17]

virtūs, virtūtis (f) *manliness, courage, strength* [L12]

vīta, -ae *life* [L11]

vītō (1) *I avoid, shun* [L30]

vīvō, -ere, vīxī, victum *I live* [L27]

vīvus, -a, -um *living* [L20]

vocō (1) *I call, summon, invite* [L1]

volō (1) *I fly* [L10]

vōs (pl.) *you* [L17]

vox, vōcis (f) *voice* [L14]

vulnerō (1) *I wound* [L1]

vulnus, vulneris (n) *wound* [L13]

vultus, -ūs (m) *face, expression* [L25]

Grammatical Concepts

This index will help you find where each grammatical concept is introduced in the text. The lesson numbers are indicated.

1st Conjugation Verbs: L1
1st Declension Adjectives: L7
1st Declension: L2
1st Person Personal Pronoun: L17
2nd Conjugation: L9
2nd Declension Adjectives: L7
2nd Declension: Masculine, L4; Neuter, L5
2nd Person Personal Pronoun: L17
3rd Conjugation –iō: L31
3rd Conjugation: Active, L26; Passive, L27
3rd Declension Adjectives: L19
3rd Declension: Masculine/Feminine, L12; Neuter, L13; i-stems, L18
3rd Person Personal Pronoun: L17
4th Conjugation: Active and Passive, L29
4th Declension: L25
5th Declension: L28
Ablative Case: L3; **Ablative of Time When,** L28; Ablative of Time Within Which, L28
Accusative Case: L2
Accusative of Duration of Time: L28
Active: Present Indicative, L1; Imperfect Indicative, L6; Future Indicative, L6; Perfect Indicative, L14; Pluperfect Indicative, L15; Future Perfect Indicative, L15
Adjective Agreement: L7
Adjectives: 1st/2nd Declension, L7; 3rd Declension, L19; Demonstrative, L30; Agreement, L7; Predicate, L7; Substantive, L9

āiō: L14
Cardinal Numerals: L21
Case: Ablative, L3; Accusative, L2; Dative, L2; Genitive, L3; Nominative, L2; Vocative, L11
Complementary Infinitives: L11
Conjugation: 1st, L1; 2nd, L9; 3rd Active, L26; 3rd Passive, L27; 4th, L29; 3rd –iō, L31
Dative Case: L2
Declension: 1st, L2; 2nd Masculine, L4; 2nd Neuter, L5; 3rd Masculine/Feminine, L12; 3rd Neuter, L13; 3rd i-stem, L18; 4th, L25; 5th, L28
Demonstratives: L30
Enclitic: definition, L10
eō: L29
faciō: L31
Fifth Declension: L28
fīō: L31
First Conjugation Verbs: L1
First Declension Adjectives: L7
First Declension: L2
First Person Personal Pronoun: L17
Fourth Conjugation: Active and Passive, L29
Fourth Declension: L25
Future Active Indicative: L6
Future Perfect Tense: Active Indicative, L15; Passive Indicative, L22
Future Tense: Active Indicative, L6; Passive Indicative, L20
Genitive Case: L3
Imperatives: L11

Imperfect Active Indicative: L6
Imperfect Tense: Active Indicative, L6
Indicative: Present Active, L1; Present Passive, L20; Imperfect Active, L6; Imperfect Passive, L20; Future Active, L6; Future Passive, L20; Perfect Active, L14; Pluperfect Active, L15; Future Perfect Active, L15
Infinitives: Complementary, L11
Magnificat: L9
Nicene Creed: L17
Nominative Case: L2
Numbers: Cardinal, L21; Ordinal, L23
Numerals: Cardinal, L21; Ordinal, L23
Ordinal Numerals: L23
Passive: Present Indicative, L20; Imperfect Indicative, L20; Future Indicative, L20; Perfect Indicative, L22; Pluperfect Indicative, L22; Future Perfect Indicative, L22
Pater Noster: L1
Perfect Tense: Active Indicative, L24
Passive Indicative: L22
Personal Pronouns: L17
Pluperfect Tense: Active Indicative, L15; Passive Indicative, L22
possum: **Present,** Imperfect, and Future Tenses, L11
Postpositive: definition, L12
Predicate Adjectives: L7
Prepositions: L3
Present Active Indicative: L1
Present Tense: Active Indicative, L1
Pronouns: Personal, L17; Demonstrative, L30

***Psalmus 23*:** L25

Second Conjugation: L9

Second Declension Adjectives: L7

Second Declension: Masculine: L4; Neuter, L5

Second Person Personal Pronoun: L17

Substantive Adjectives: L9

sum: **Present Tense,** L3; Imperfect Tense, L10; Future Tense, L10

***Symbolum Nicaenum*:** L17

Third Conjugation –iō: L31

Third Conjugation: Active, L26; Passive, L27

Third Declension Adjectives: L19

Third Declension: Masculine/Feminine, L12; Neuter, L13; i-stems, L18

Third Person Personal Pronoun: L17

Time Constructions: L28

Vocative Case: L11

Sources & Helps

Bennett, Charles E. *New Latin Grammar.* Wauconda, IL: Bolchazy-Carducci Publishers, Inc. 1998. A good resource for your grammar questions.

Biblia Sacra Vulgata. Stuttgart, Germany: Deutsche Bibelgesellschaft, 1994. I adapted a few selections from this for the Latin to English translations, as well as using Psalm 23 for the Unit 4 memorization. If you have extra time, read a bit from the Vulgate every day to improve your Latin skills.

Glare, P. G. W. *The Oxford Latin Dictionary.* Oxford: Oxford University Press, 1983. The *OLD* is of course "the" standard for all Latin dictionaries, although occasionally I have found nuggets in Lewis and Short's *A Latin Dictionary* that were not in the *OLD*.

Greenough, J. B., et al., ed. *Allen and Greenough's New Latin Grammar.* Newburyport, MA: Focus Publishing, R. Pullins & Company, Inc., 2001. A fantastic resource; I referred to it frequently regarding grammar concepts of all kinds.

Jenney, Charles Jr., et al. *Jenney's First Year Latin.* Newton, MA: Allyn and Bacon, Inc., 1987. I consulted this text for the order of teaching various grammatical concepts. I studied Latin from it back in my junior high days, and have always been fond of it (although it is a little too fond of Caesar for my liking). Although short on explanations, it contains plenty of exercises and translations to practice each concept.

LaFleur, Richard A. *Love and Transformation: An Ovid Reader.* Glenview, IL: Scott Foresman-Addison Wesley, 1999. I referred to this Latin text (in addition to online texts) for some of the myths in the Latin to English translations.

The Latin Library. http://www.thelatinlibrary.com. This website has numerous Latin texts from all time periods, and I used it for some of the passages I adapted from the Vulgate.

Latin Vulgate. http://www.latinvulgate.com. This website is helpful because it has side-by-side translations from the Vulgate. Although most of us are familiar with Biblical texts and stories, sometimes the Vulgate has completely different wording than what we are used to (see the discussion of Psalm 23 in Lesson 25 as an example).

Lee, A. G., ed. *Ovid: Metamorphoses, Book I.* Wauconda, IL: Bolchazy-Carducci Publishers, Inc., 1988. I also referred to this book (in addition to online texts) for some of the myths in the Latin to English translations.

Lewis, Charlton T., and Charles Short. *A Latin Dictionary.* Oxford: Oxford University Press, 1958. Lewis and Short's dictionary is a standard resource and has helpful examples and commentary on many entries.

Martin, Charles, trans. *Ovid: Metamorphoses.* New York: W. W. Norton & Company, 2004. I consulted this English translation as well as the Latin texts for some of the myths found in the Latin to English translations.

Simpson, D. P. *Cassell's New Latin Dictionary.* New York: Funk & Wagnall's, 1959. I picked this up at a used bookstore (always check out the language section for Latin books!), and it has an especially helpful English to Latin section.

Stelten, Leo F. *Dictionary of Ecclesiastical Latin.* Peabody, MA: Hendrickson Publishers, Inc., 1995. I consulted this dictionary for the translations adapted from the Vulgate, since some dictionaries don't include ecclesiastical words.

Wheelock, Frederic M.; revised by Richard A. LaFleur. *Wheelock's Latin,* 6th ed. rev. New York: HarperCollins Publishers, 2005. I have taught out of this book for several years and referred to it for some grammar matters as well as researching in what order grammatical concepts were presented. It is a good standard text and resource, but not the best for someone trying to teach himself Latin.

Whitaker, William. "Words." http://www.archives.nd.edu/cgi-bin/words.exe. This website (from which you can also download a program) has Latin to English and English to Latin search engines. You can type in any form of a Latin word and it will parse it for you and give you the meaning—pretty handy! All students seem to know about this, so it's best to face it head on. I told my students they were welcome to use it, but that they not become dependent upon it (and of course they shouldn't use it to "cheat" on parsing exercises). It's best to use it when you are stumped by a particular form and need to look it up. The English to Latin search can be very helpful when writing stories or sentences.

Vulgate Frequency. http://www.intratext.com/IXT/LAT0001/_FF1.HTM. This website tells you which words appear the most often in the Vulgate or various other Latin texts. Since I'm especially fond of the Vulgate and Vergil, I consulted this site to see which words needed to be incorporated into the vocabulary lists.

Verb Formation Chart

Which principal part is used for which tense, voice, and mood? Keep this handout all year, and fill it in as you learn the various verb forms. The principal parts of *necō* (I kill) are provided as an example.

	FIRST	SECOND	THIRD	FOURTH
	necō	necāre	necāvī	necātum
DEFINITION/ FUNCTION	1st Sg. Present Active Indicative—I kill Helps identify conjugations and shows if present stem vowel has contracted	Present Active Infinitive—to kill; Present Stem: necā-	1st. Sg. Perfect Active Indicative—I killed, have killed Perfect Active Stem: necāv-	Neuter Sg. Nom. Perfect Passive Participle—killed, having been killed Forms Perfect Passives, so in that sense may be considered Perfect Passive "stem"
INDICATIVE		Present Active Present Passive Imperfect Active Imperfect Passive Future Active Future Passive	Perfect Active Pluperfect Active Future Perfect Active	Perfect Passive Pluperfect Passive Future Perfect Passive
IMPERATIVE		Present Active Present Passive Future Active Future Passive		
INFINITIVE		Present Active Present Passive	Perfect Active	Perfect Passive Future Active Future Passive
SUBJUNCTIVE		Present Active Present Passive Imperfect Active Imperfect Passive	Perfect Active Pluperfect Active	Perfect Passive Pluperfect Passive
PARTICIPLE		Present Active Future Passive		Perfect Passive Future Active